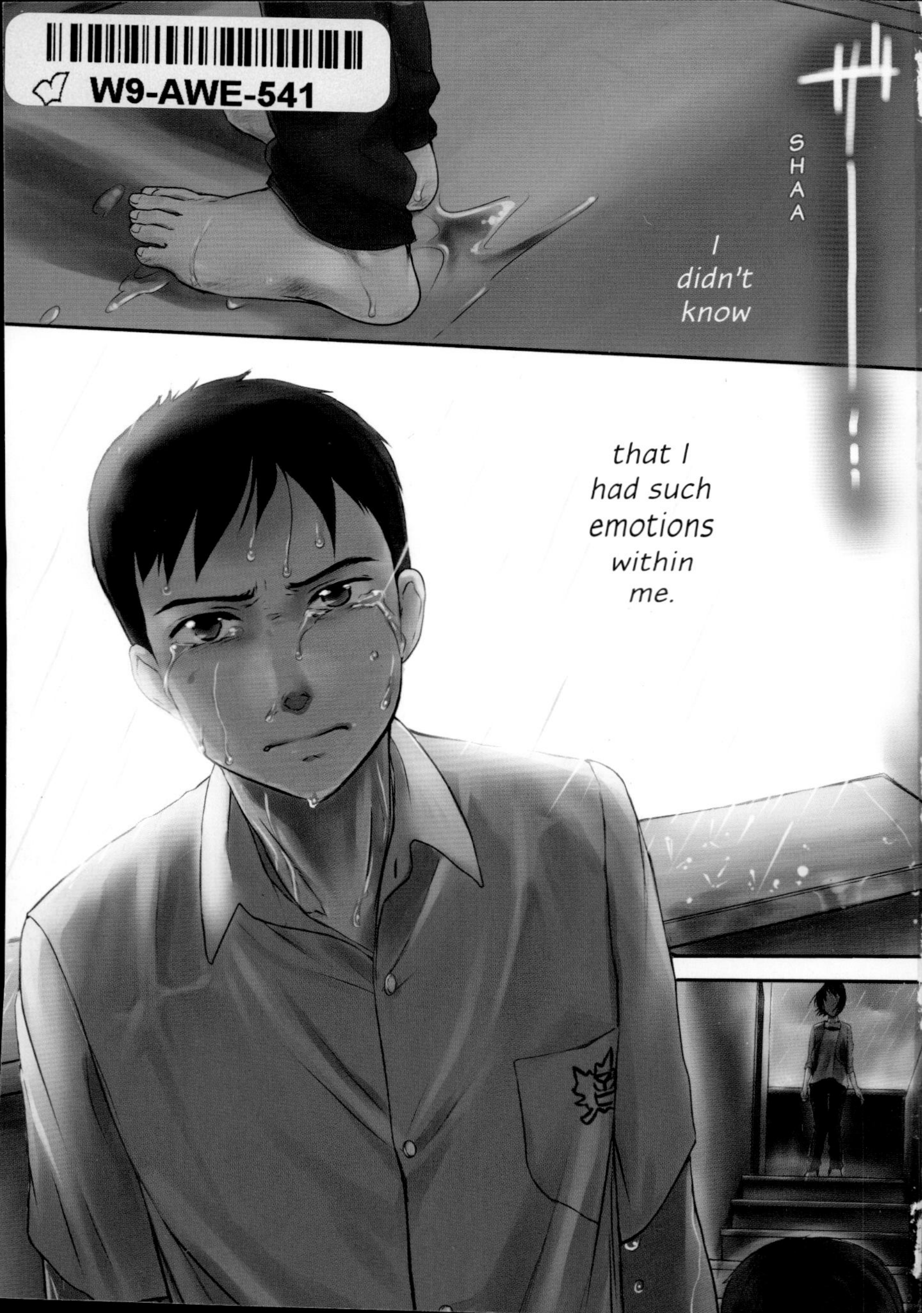
SHAA
I didn't know
that I had such emotions within me.

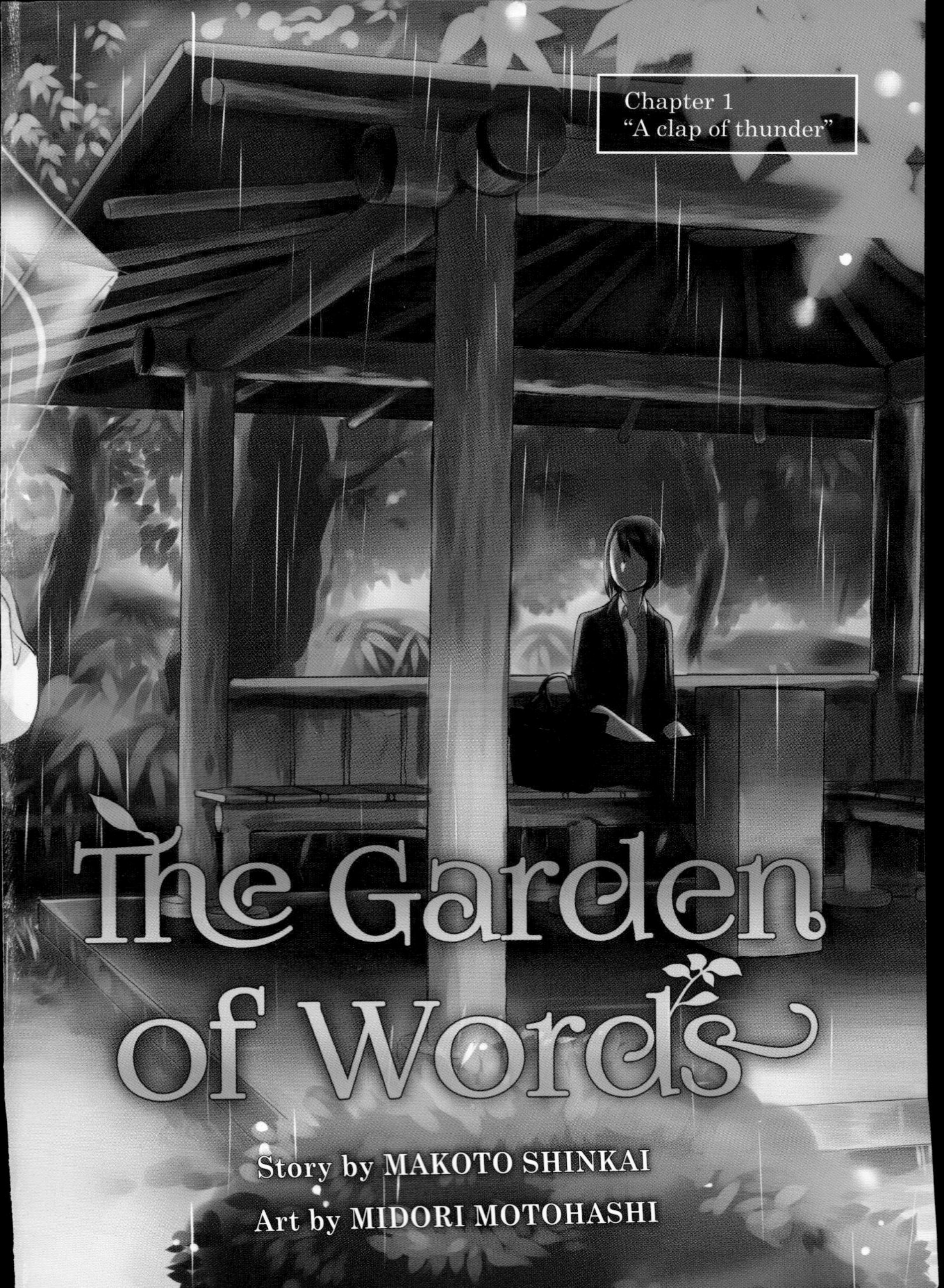

Chapter 1
"A clap of thunder"
The Garden of Words
Story by MAKOTO SHINKAI
Art by MIDORI MOTOHASHI

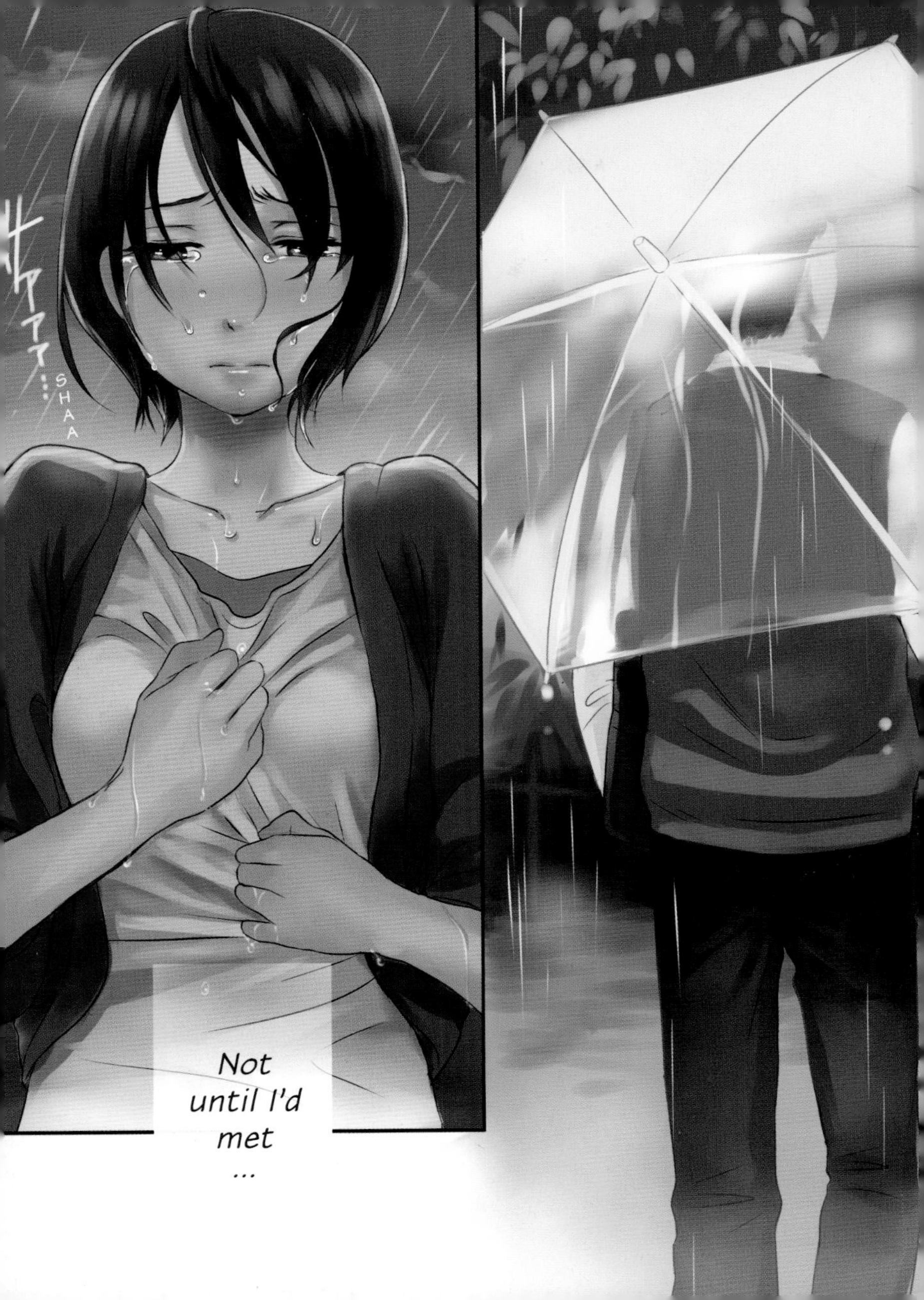
ザァァァ…
SHAA
Not until I'd met
...

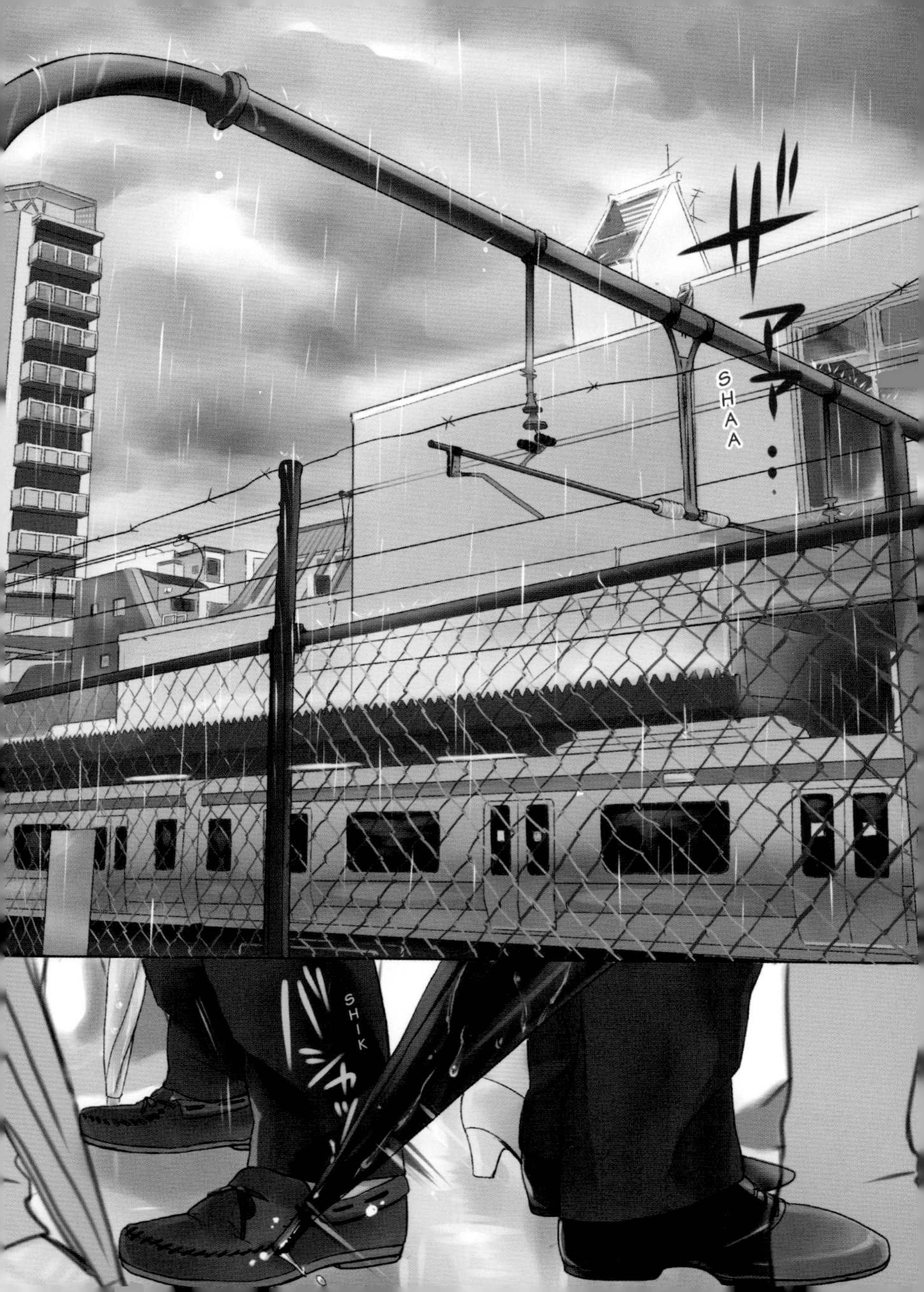
ザァァ…
SHAA
SHIK

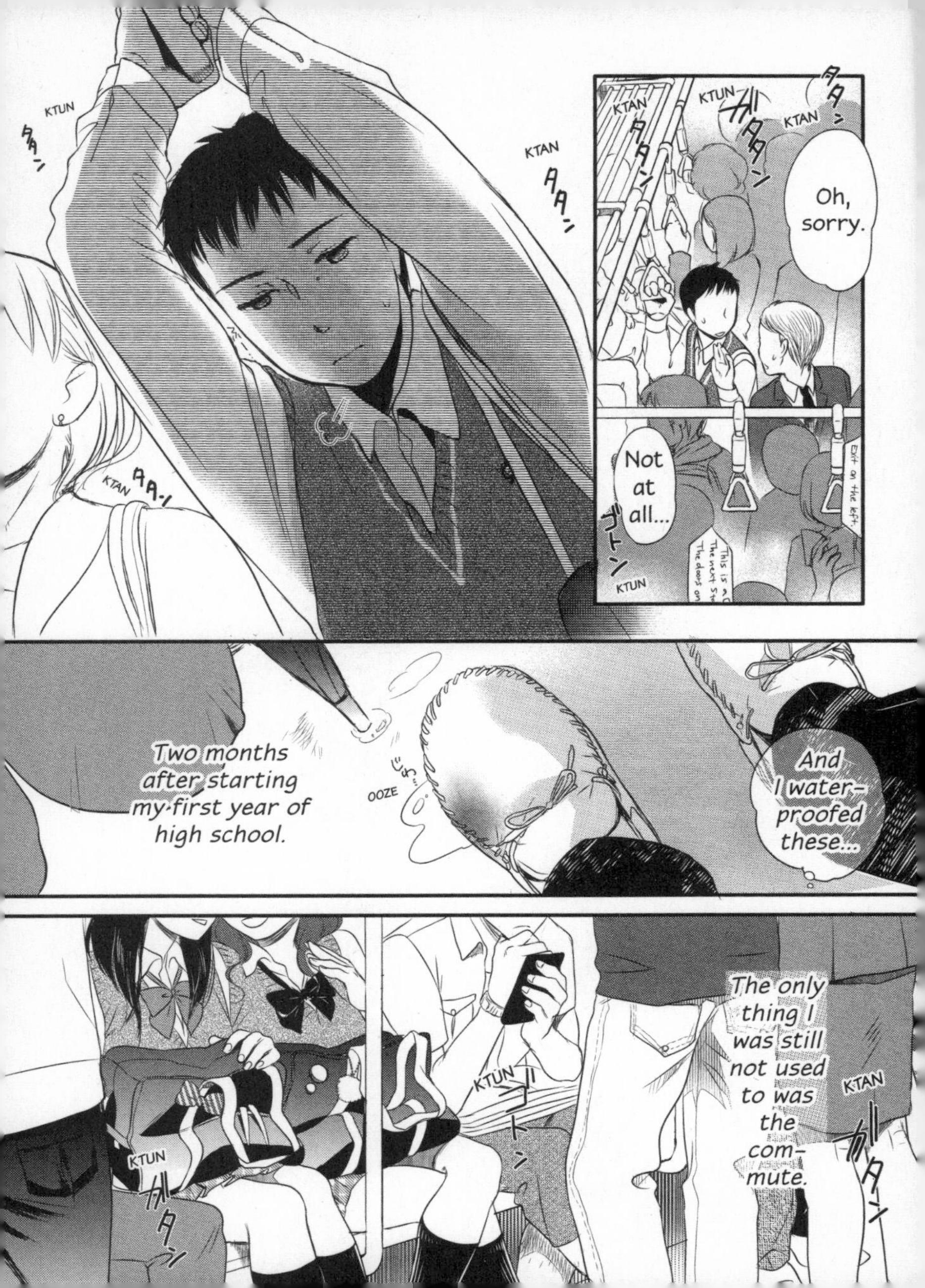
KTUN
KTAN
KTAN
Oh, sorry.
Exit on the left.
Not at all...
KTUN
KTUN
KTAN
KTAN
KTAN
And I waterproofed these...
OOZE
Two months after starting my first year of high school.
KTAN
The only thing I was still not used to was the commute.
KTUN
KTUN

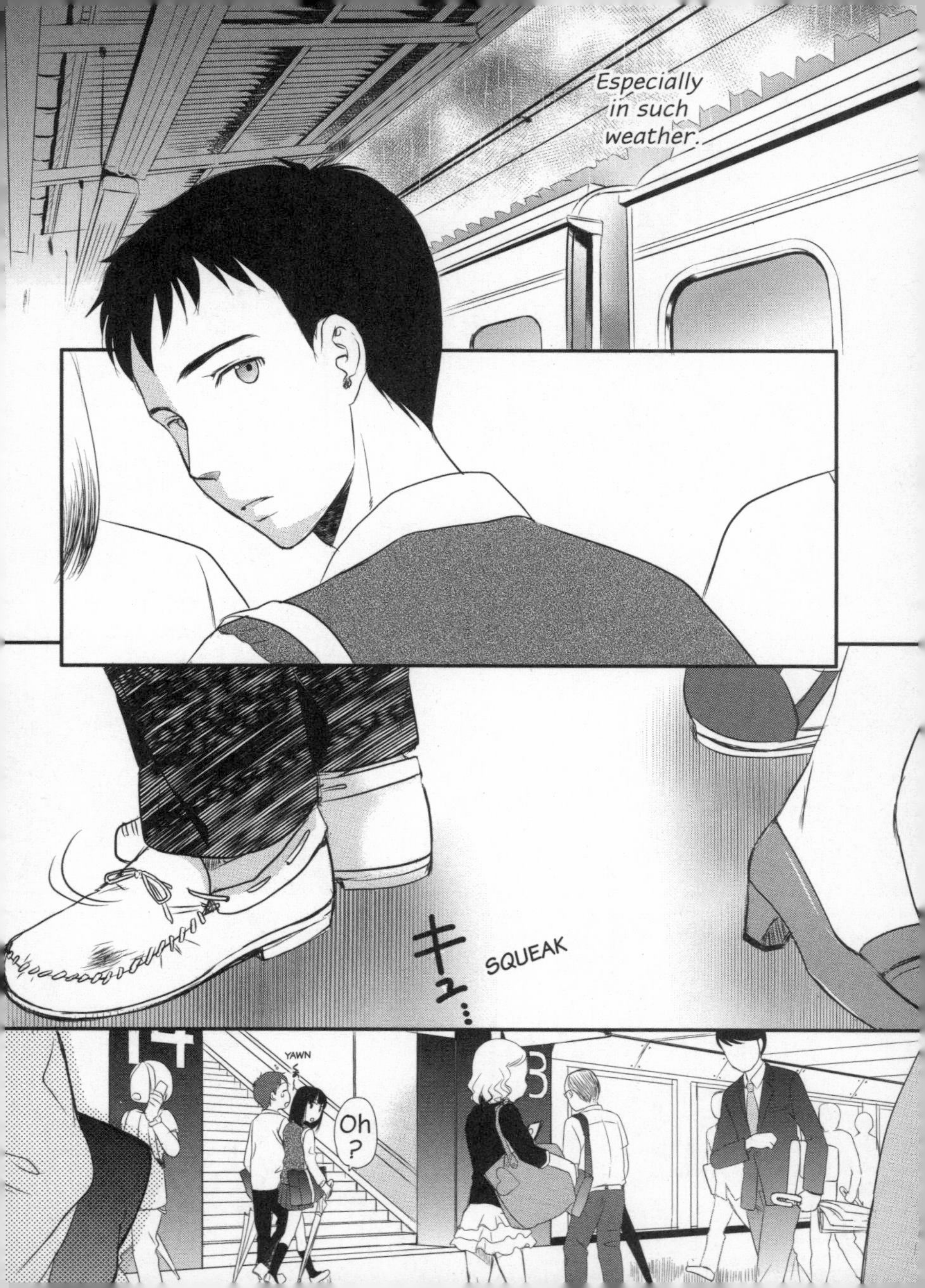
Especially in such weather.
キュ…
SQUEAK
Oh?
YAWN

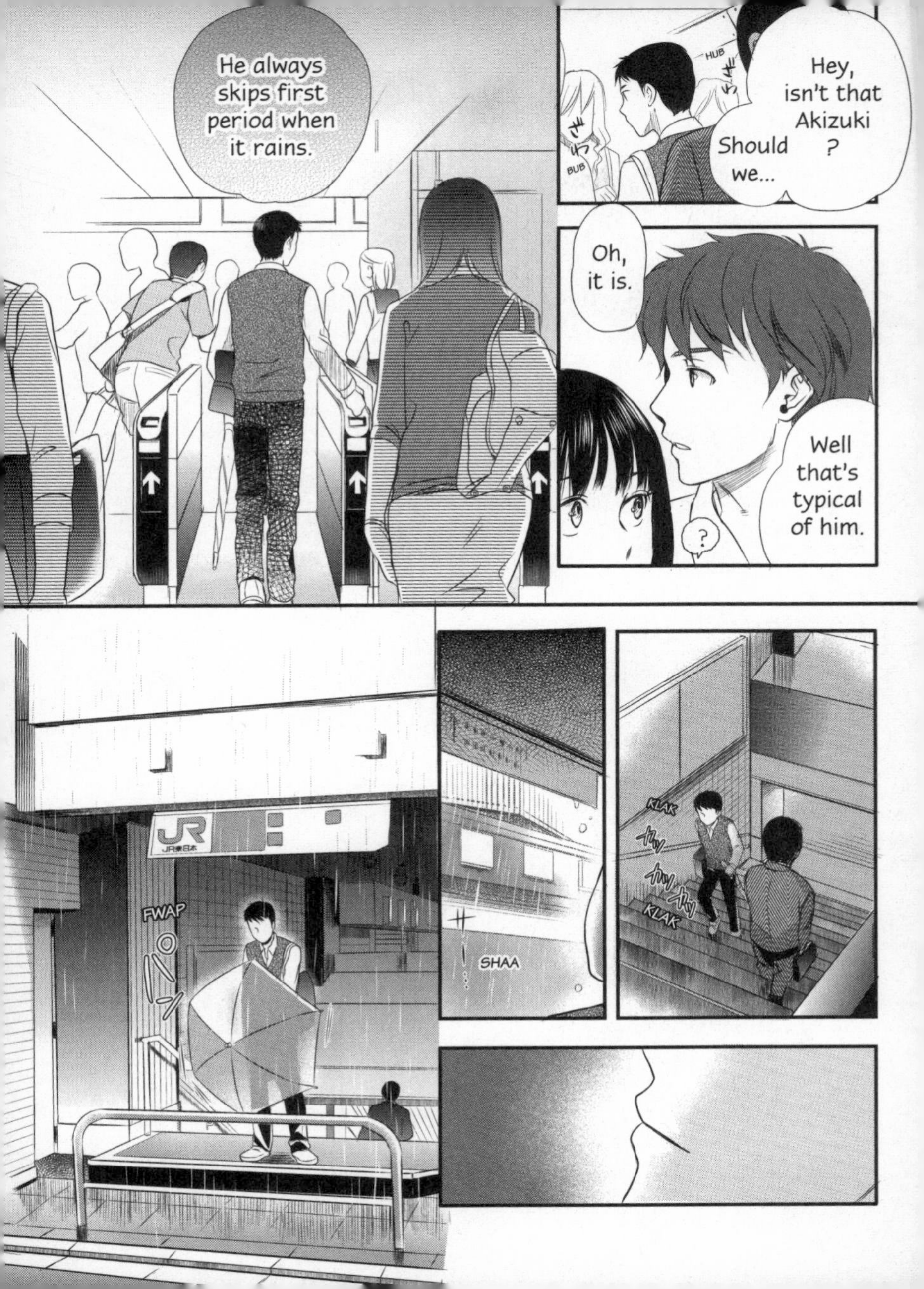

HUB
BUB
Hey, isn't that Akizuki?
Should we...
Oh, it is.
Well that's typical of him.
?
He always skips first period when it rains.
KLAK
KLAK
SHAA
FWAP

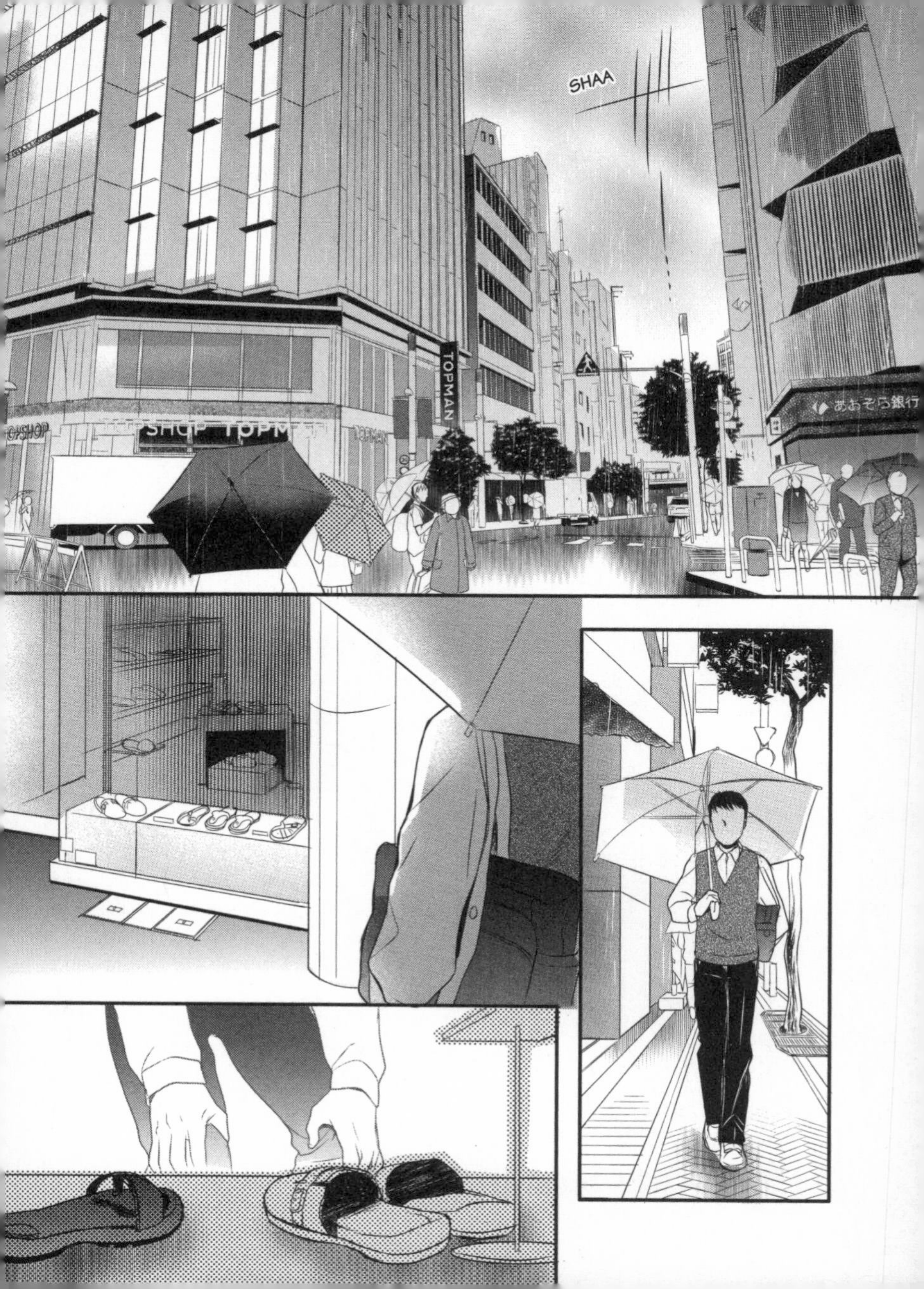
SHAA
TOPMAN
あおぞら銀行

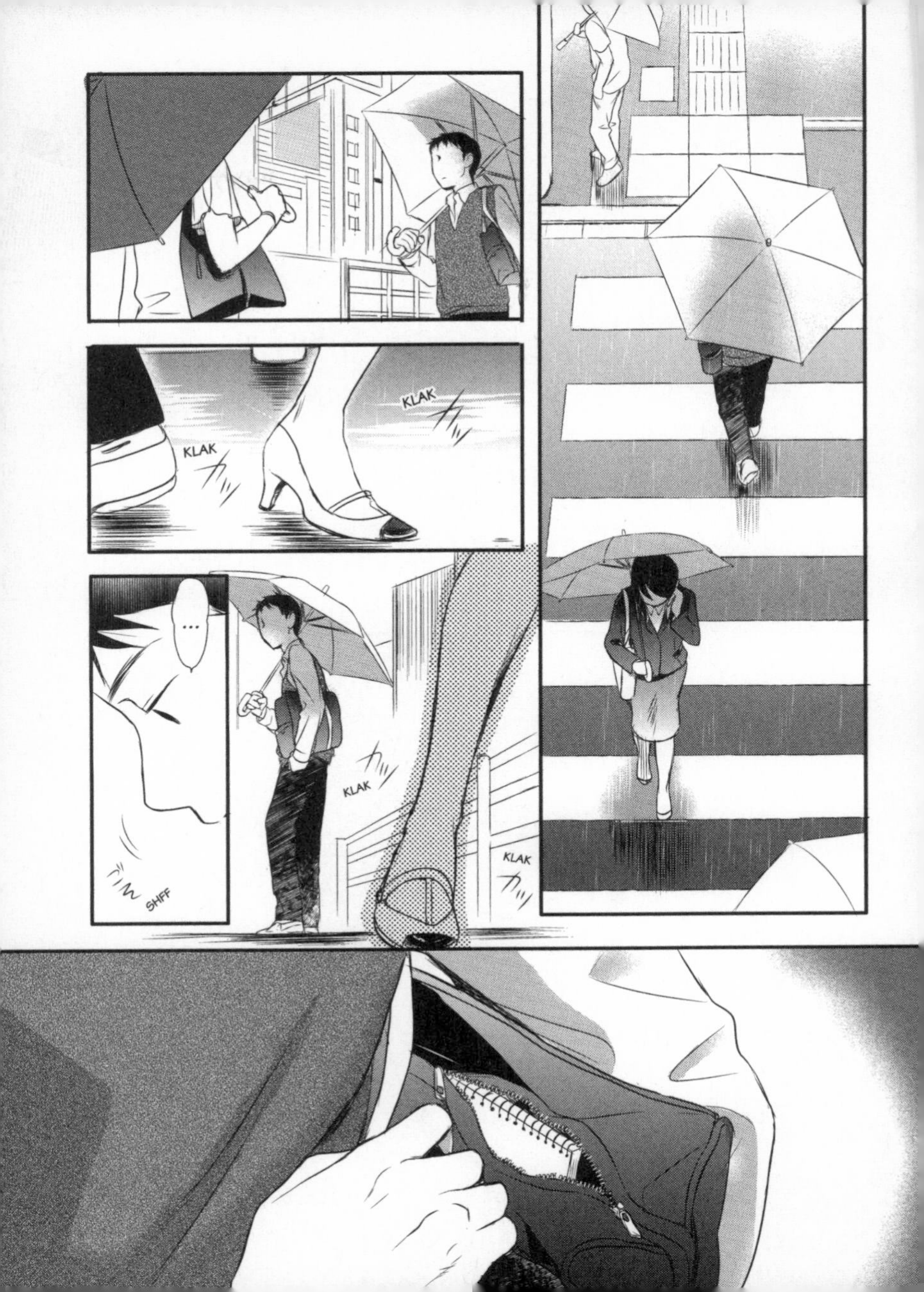
KLAK
KLAK
KLAK
KLAK
...
SHFF

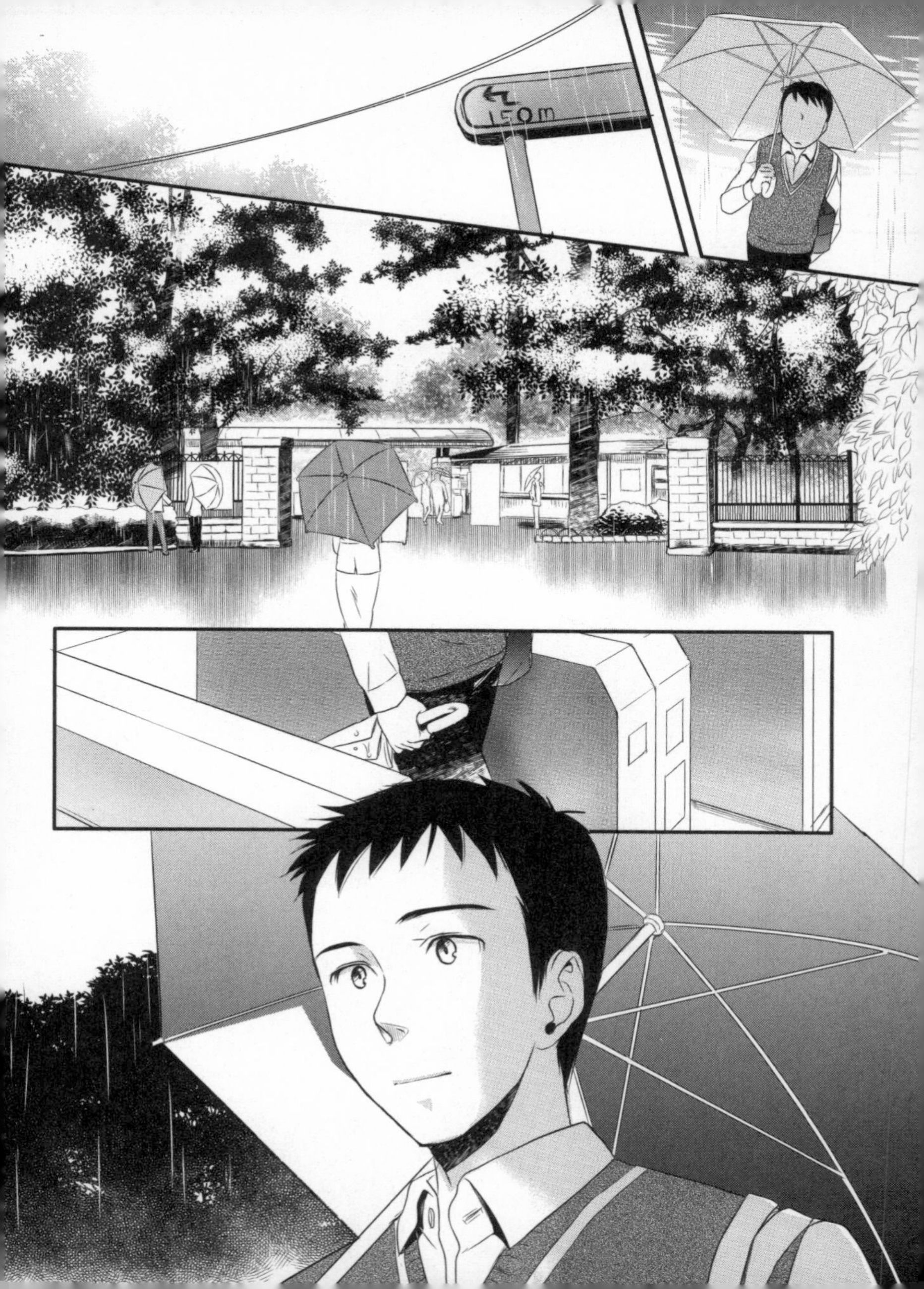
150m

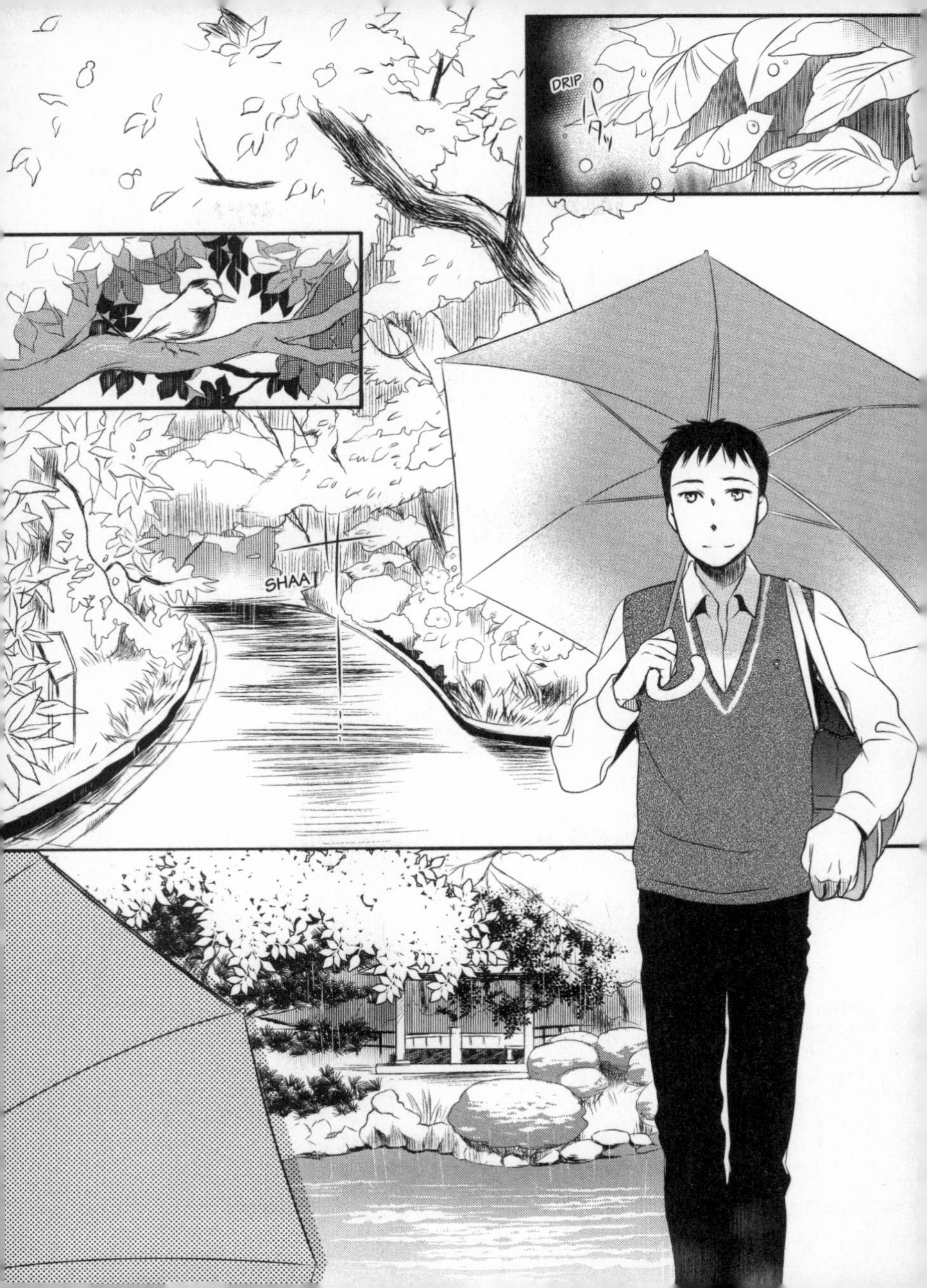
DRIP
SHAA

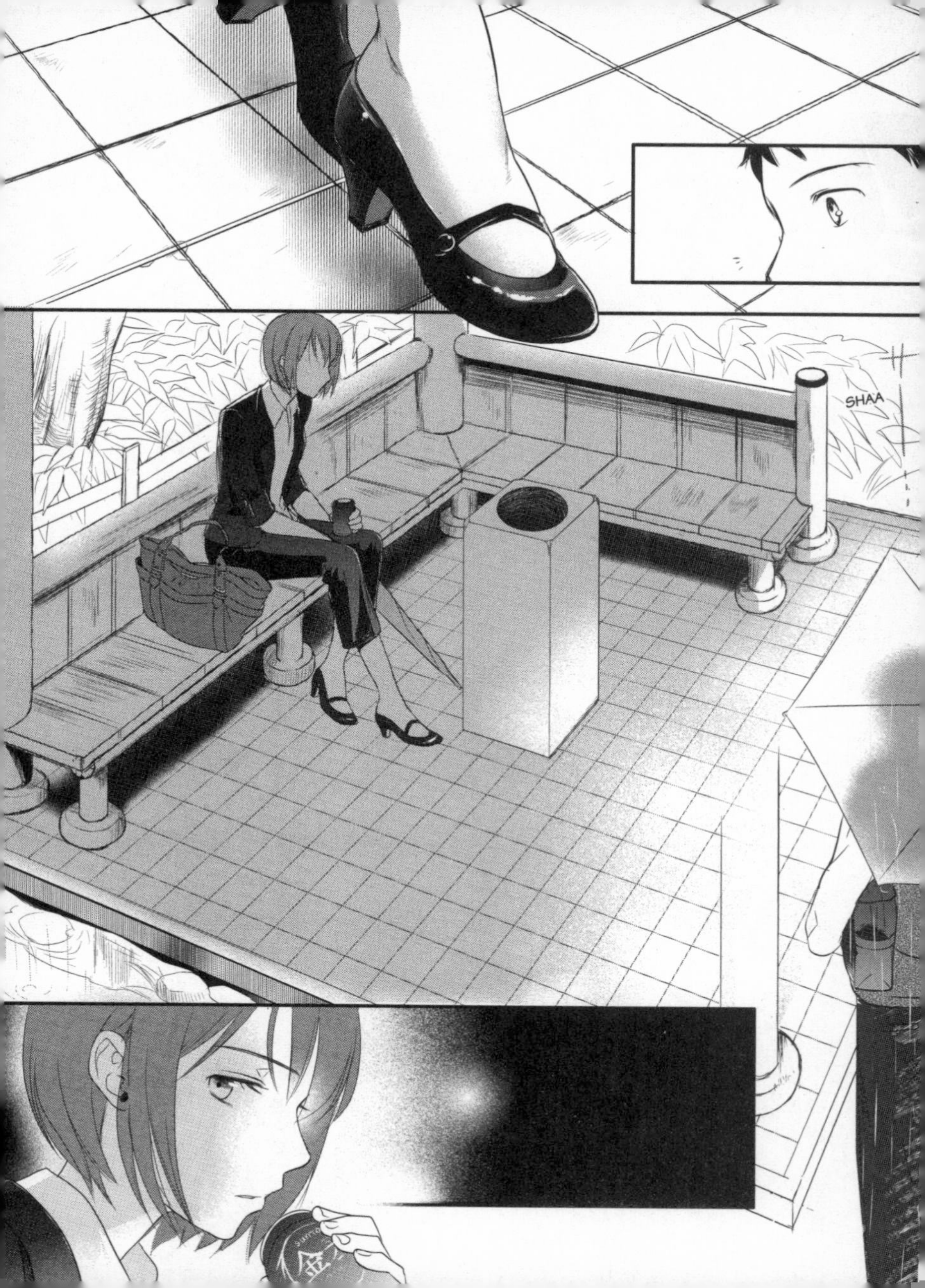
SHAA

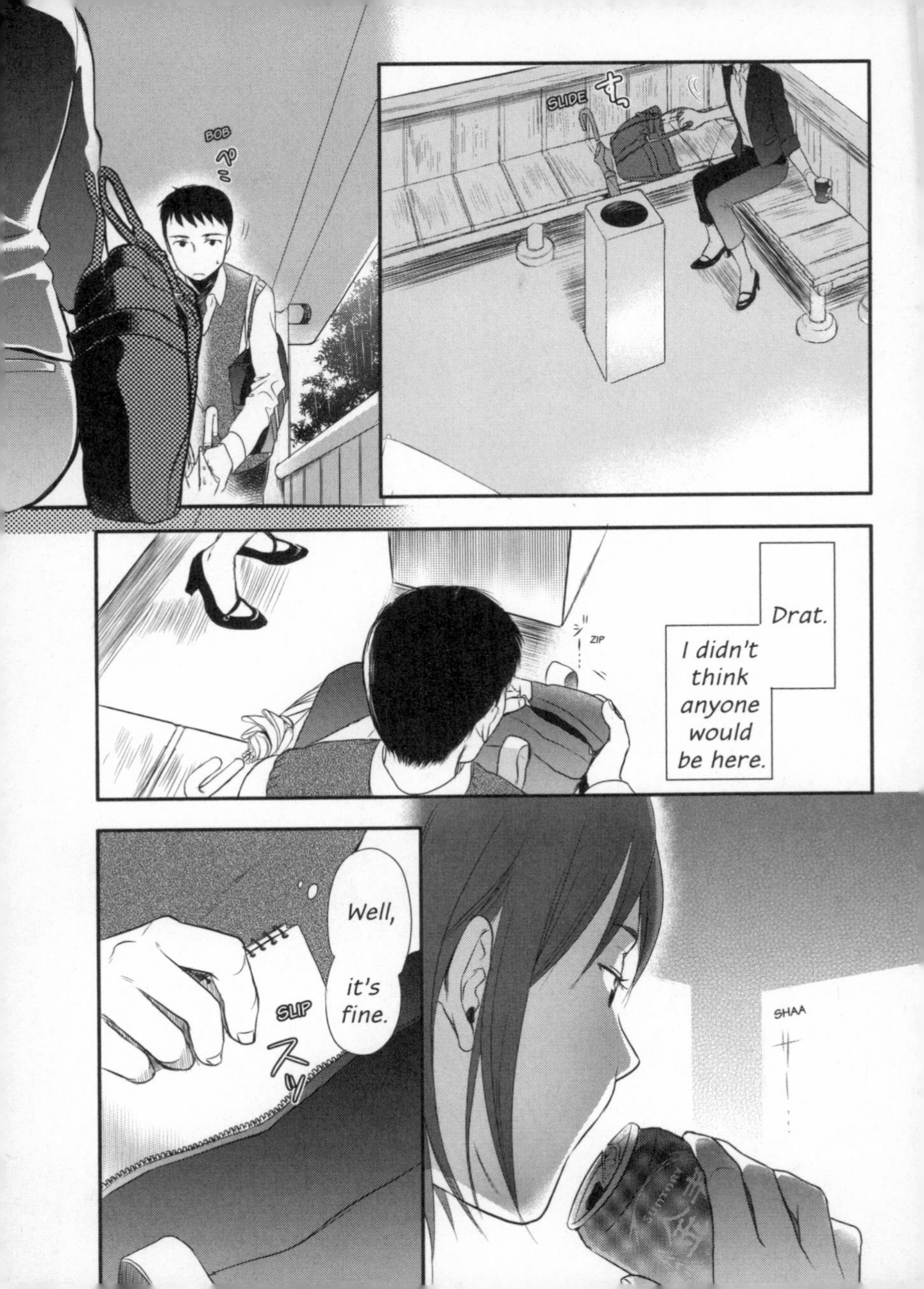
SLIDE
すっ
BOB
ぺこ
Drat.
I didn't think anyone would be here.
ZIP
SHAA
Well, it's fine.
SLIP
スッ

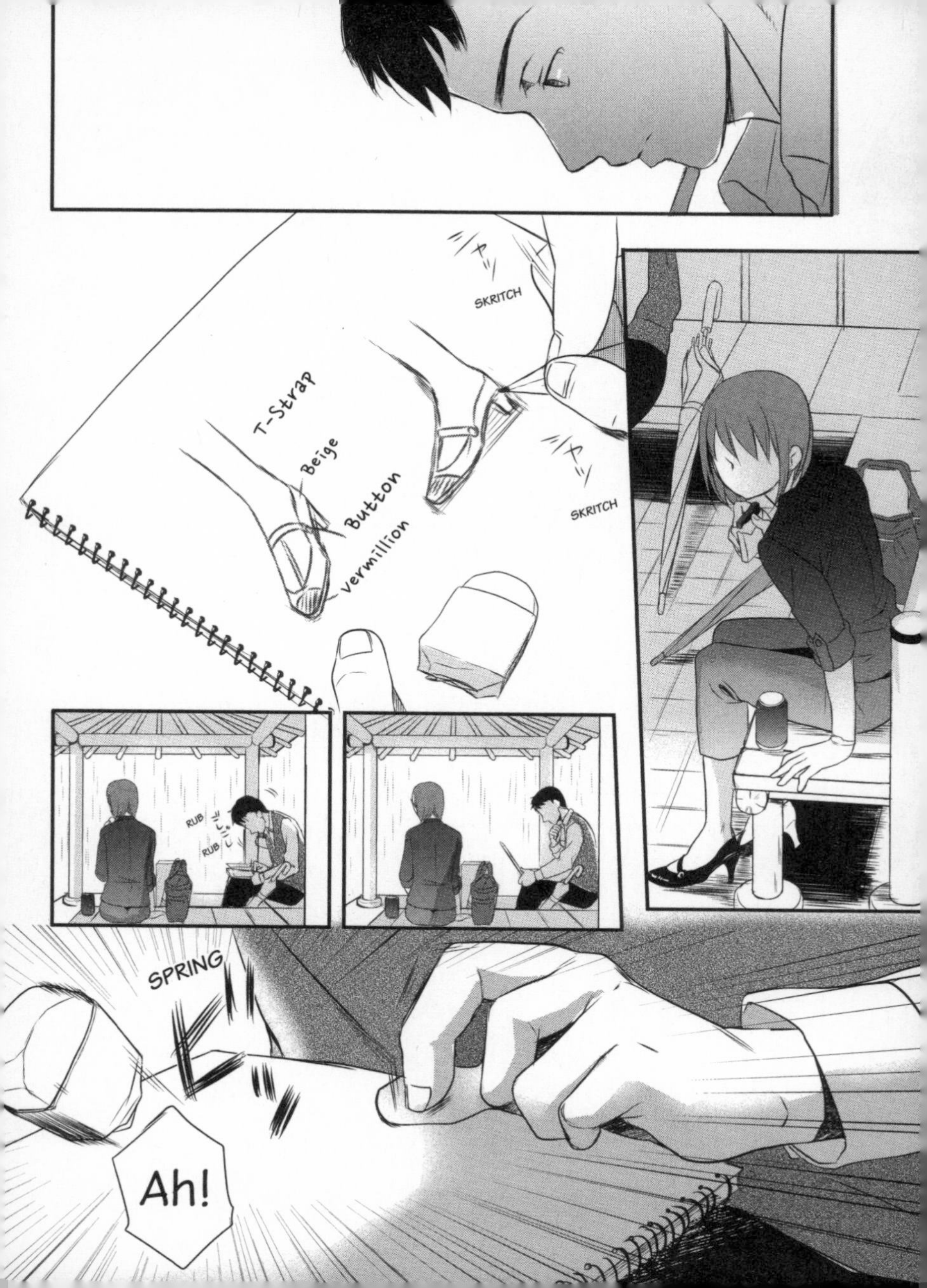
SKRITCH
SKRITCH
T-Strap
Beige
Button
vermillion
RUB
RUB
SPRING
Ah!

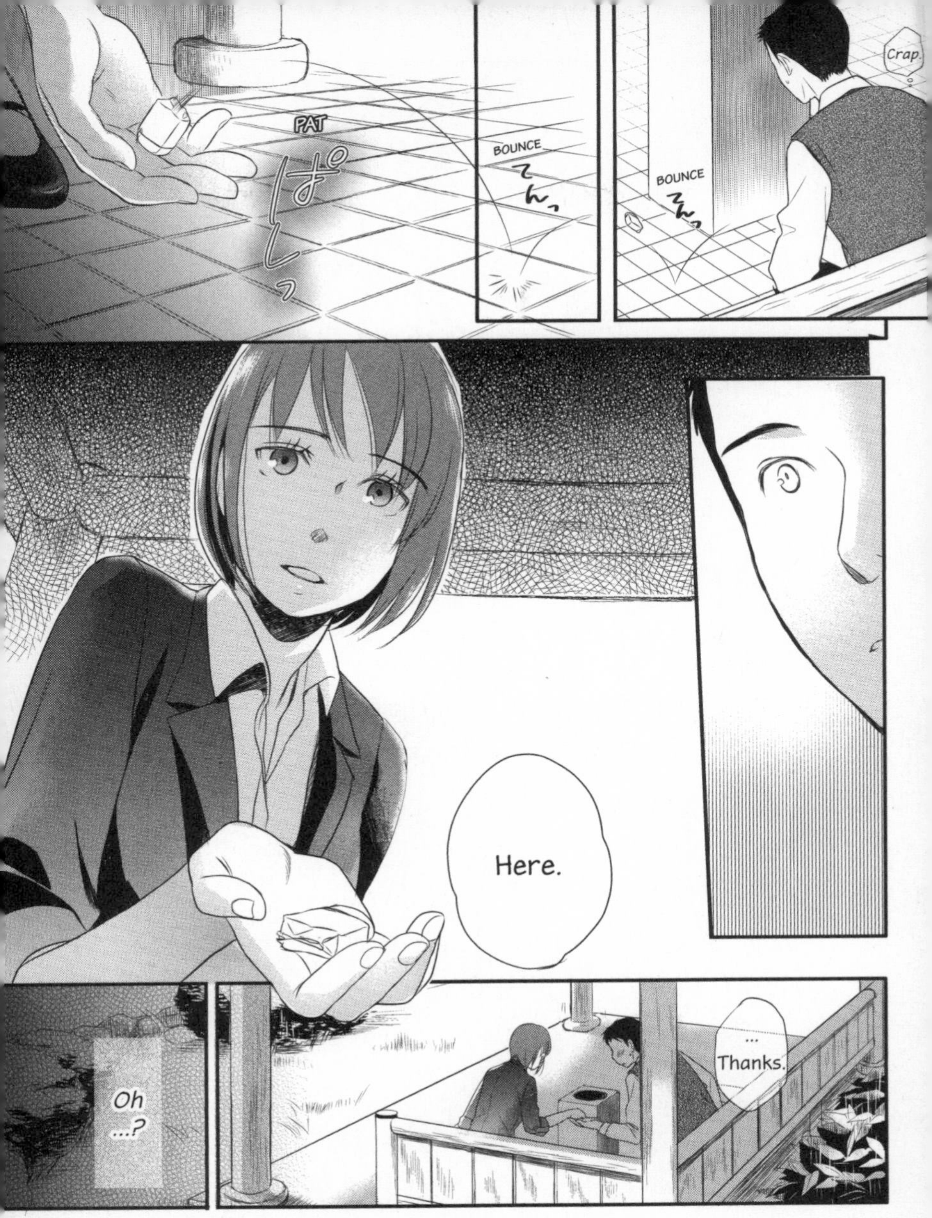
Crap.
BOUNCE
てんっ
BOUNCE
てんっ
PAT
ぱしっ
Here.
... Thanks.
Oh ...?

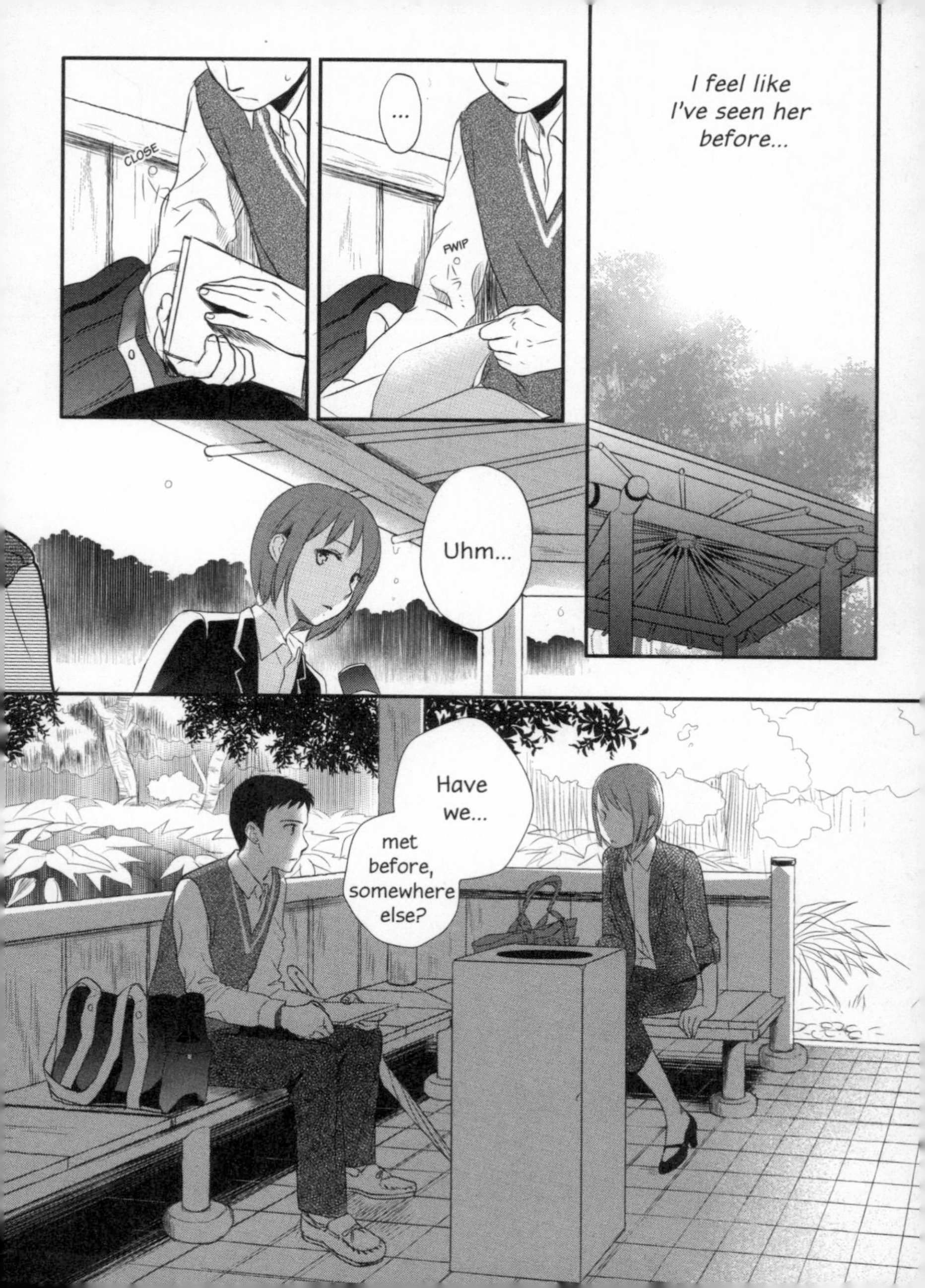
I feel like I've seen her before...
...
FWIP
CLOSE
Uhm...
Have we...
met before, somewhere else?

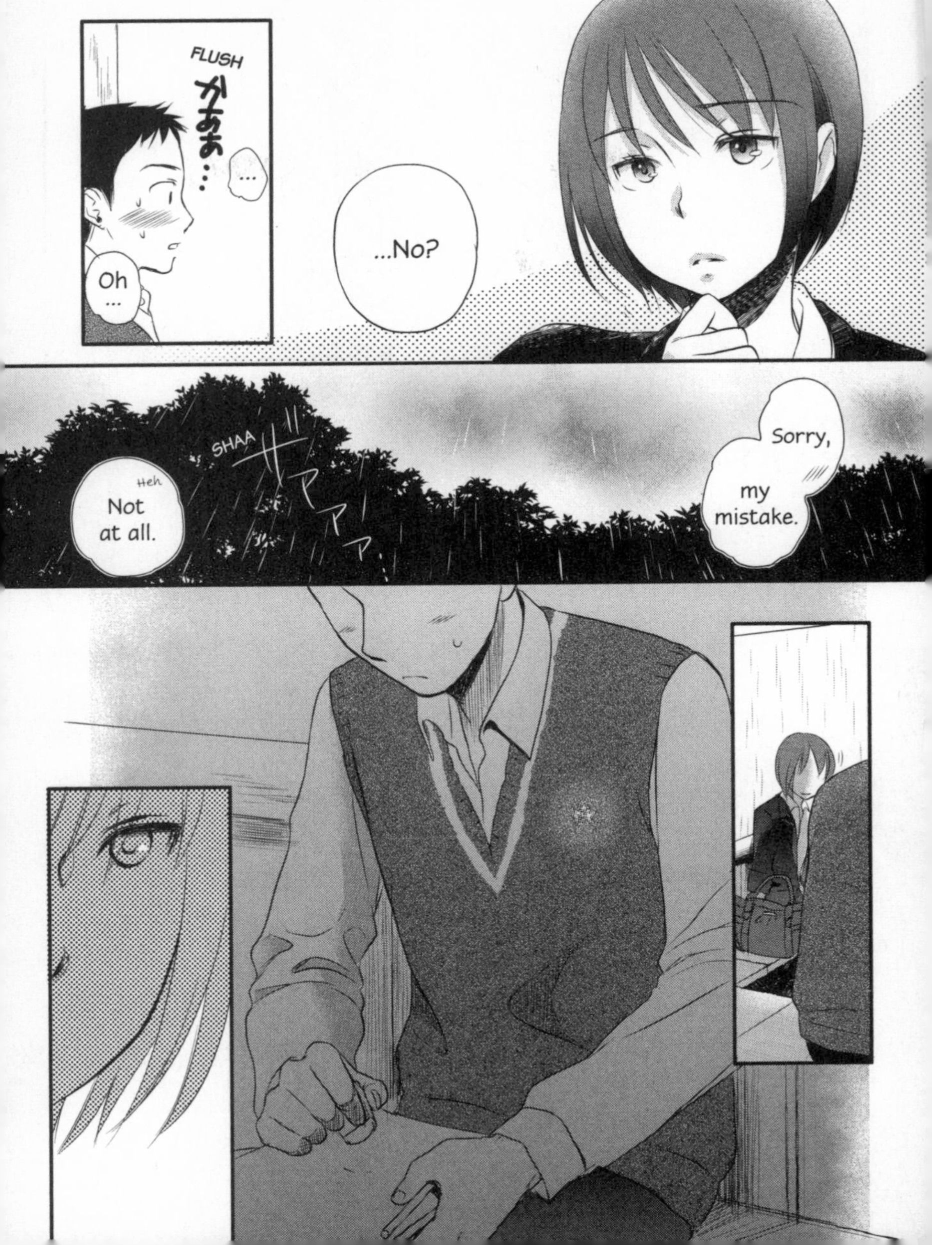
...No?
FLUSH
かあぁ…
...
Oh ...
Sorry, my mistake.
SHAA
ザアアア
Heh
Not at all.

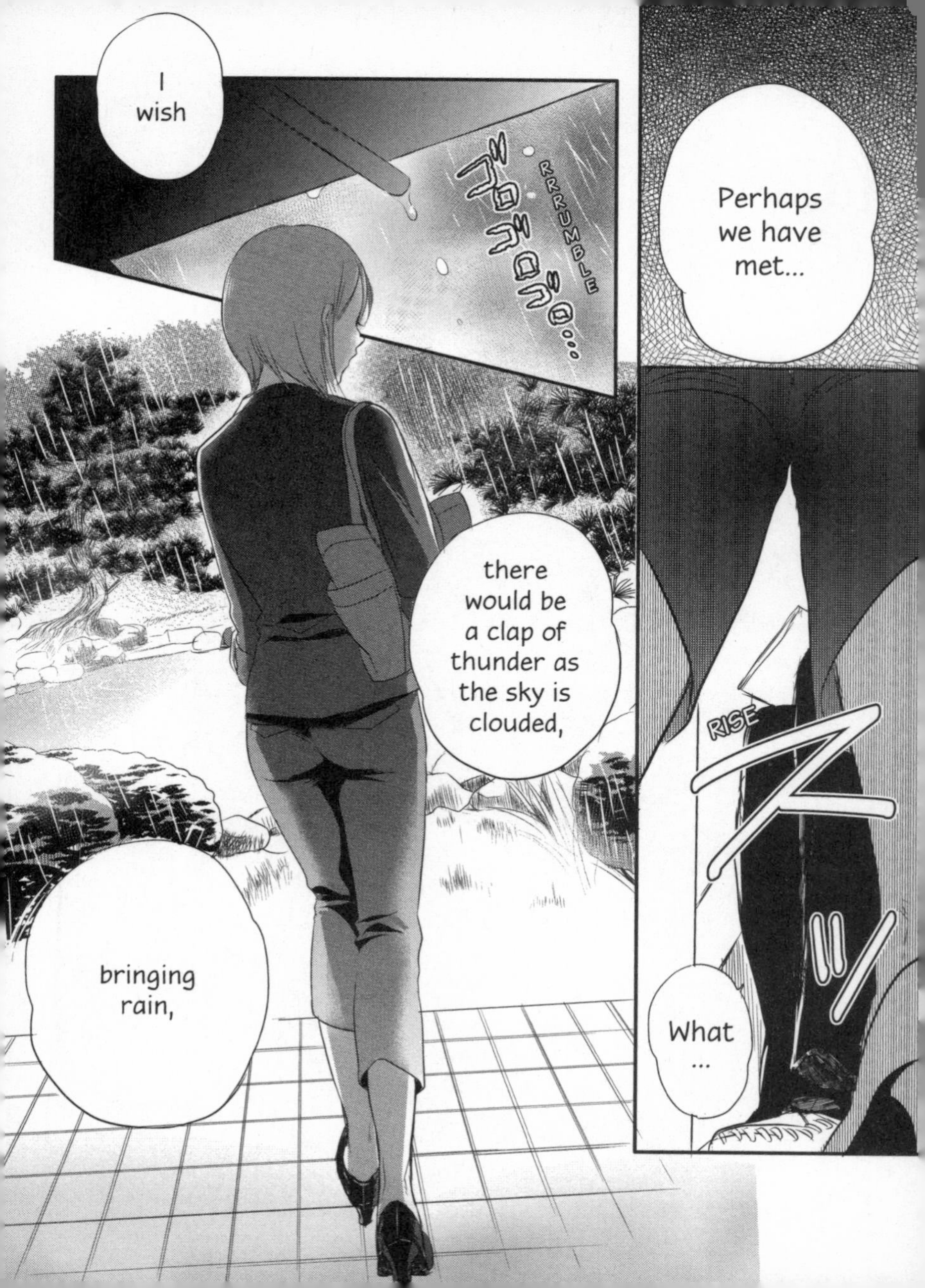
Perhaps we have met...
RISE
What ...
I wish
ゴロゴロゴロ…
RRRUMBLE
there would be a clap of thunder as the sky is clouded,
bringing rain,

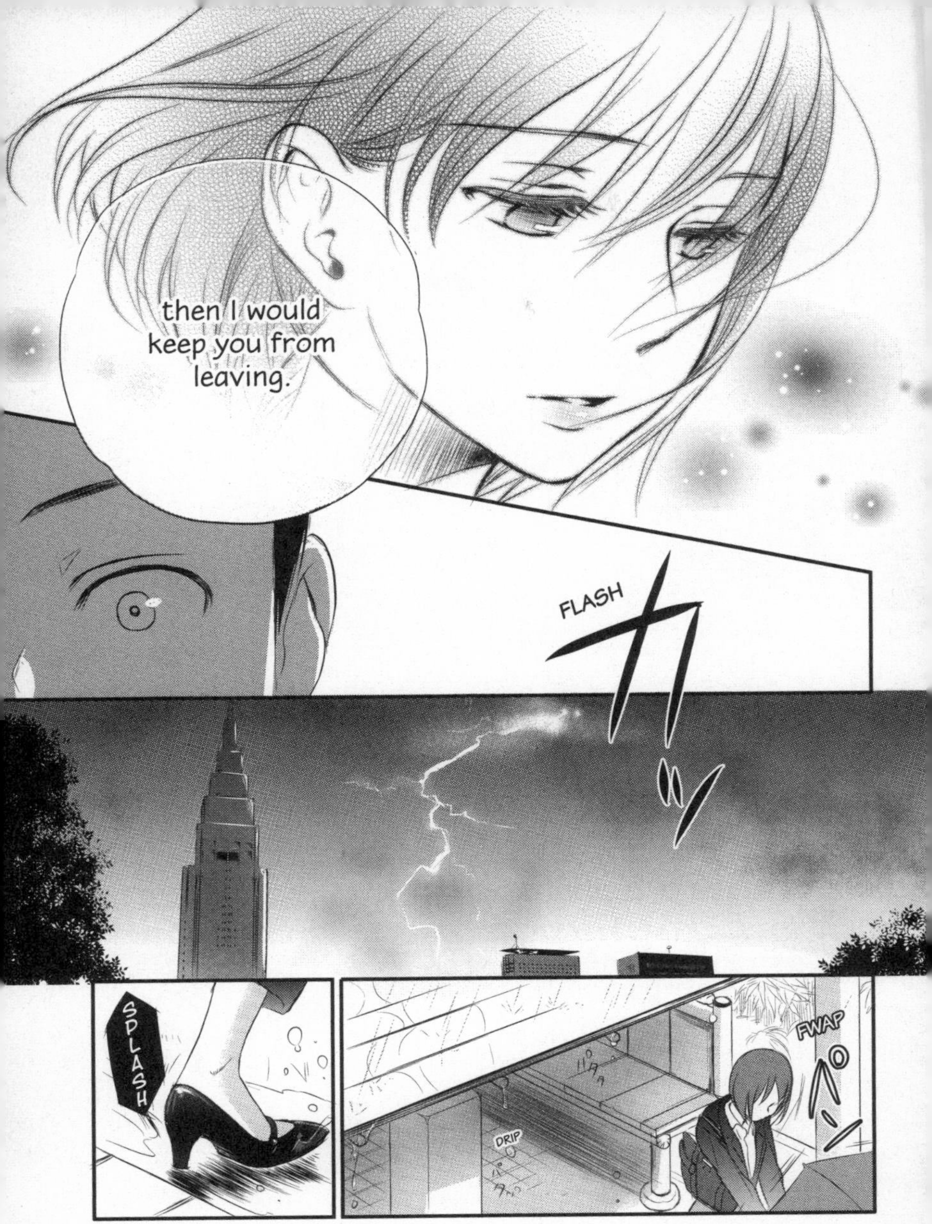
then I would keep you from leaving.
FLASH
SPLASH
FWAP
DRIP

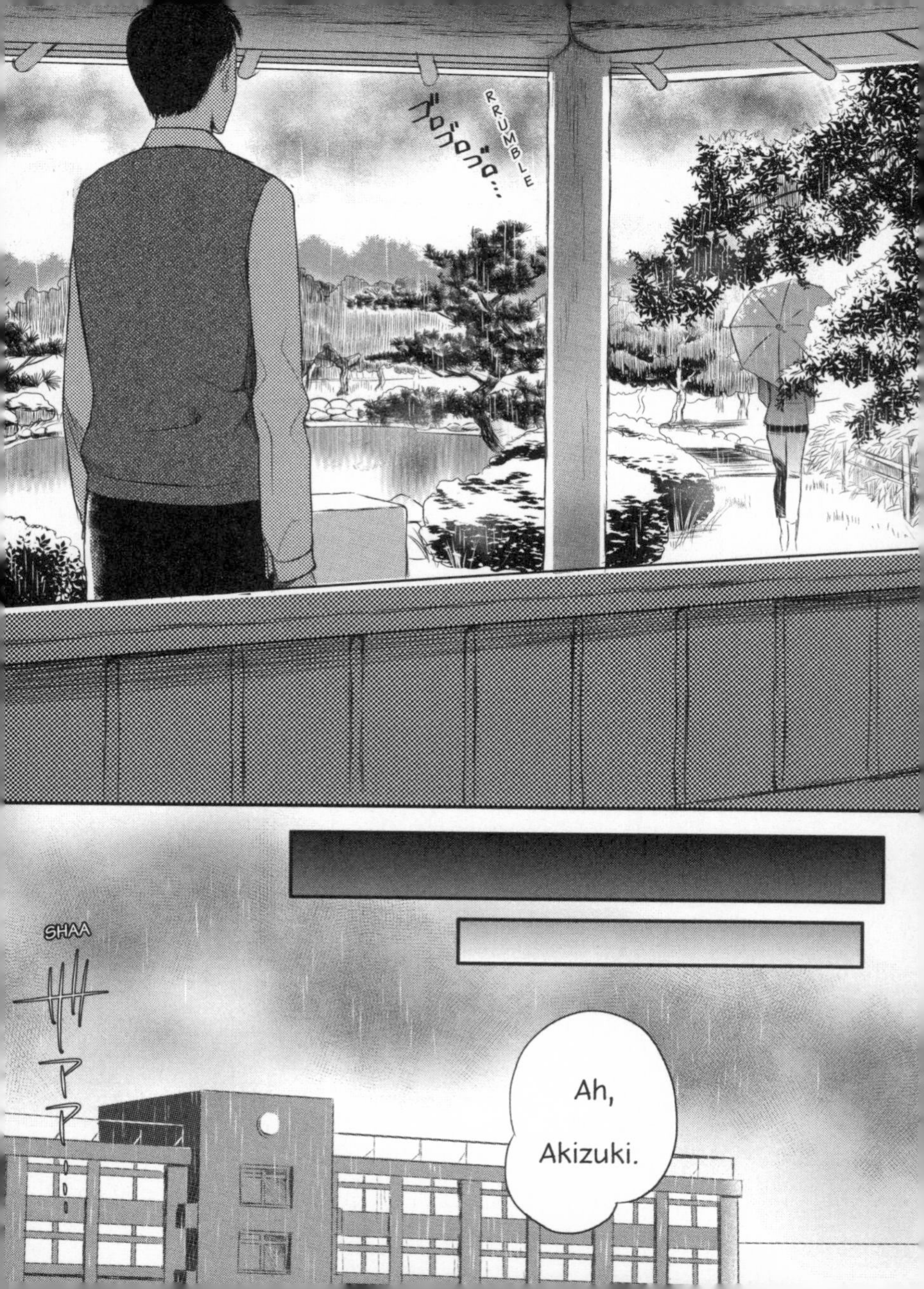
ゴロゴロゴロ…
RRUMBLE
SHAA
ザァァ…
Ah, Akizuki.

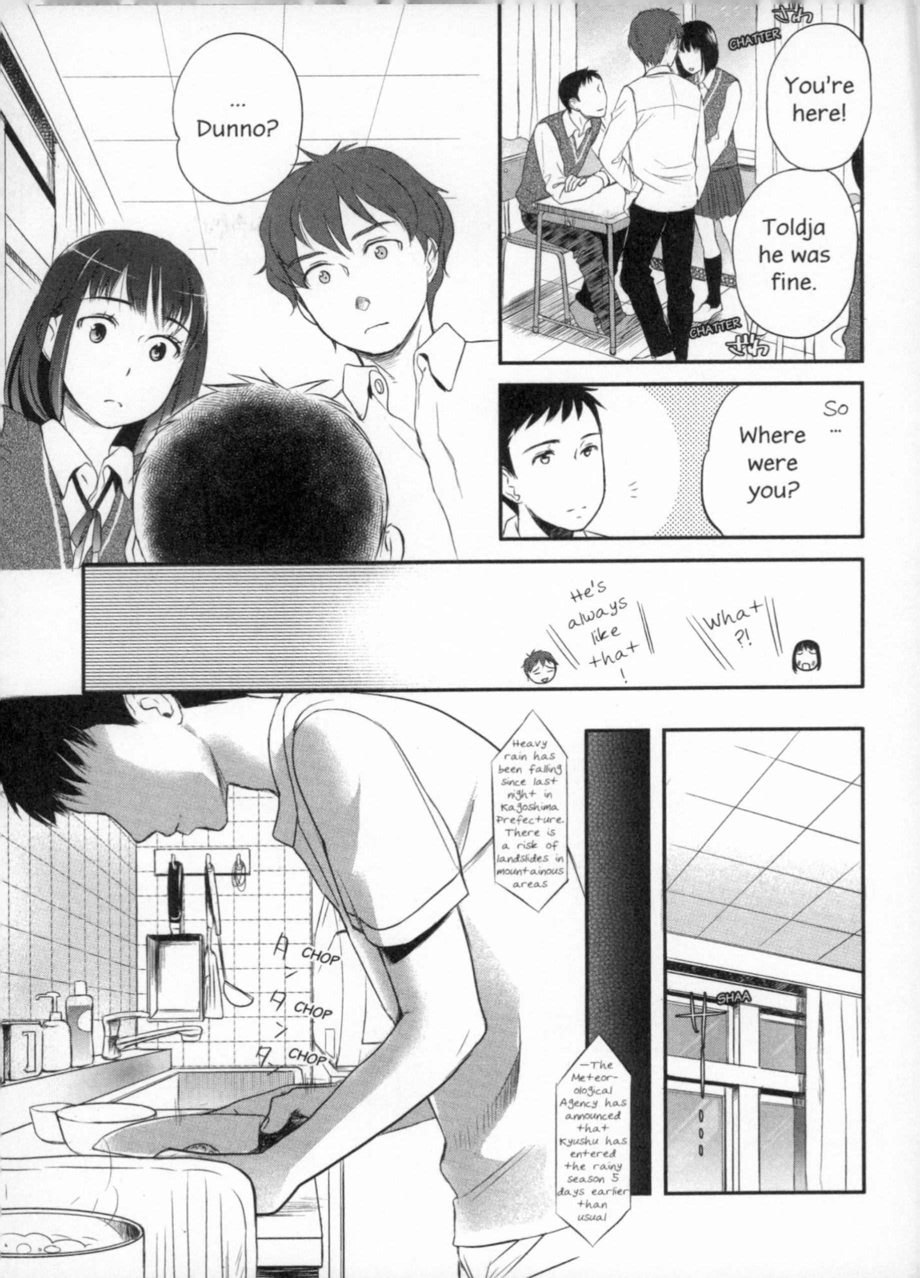
CHATTER
You're here!
Toldja he was fine.
CHATTER
So ...
Where were you?
... Dunno?
What?!
He's always like that!
SHAA
Heavy rain has been falling since last night in Kagoshima Prefecture. There is a risk of landslides in mountainous areas
—The Meteorological Agency has announced that Kyushu has entered the rainy season 5 days earlier than usual
CHOP
CHOP
CHOP

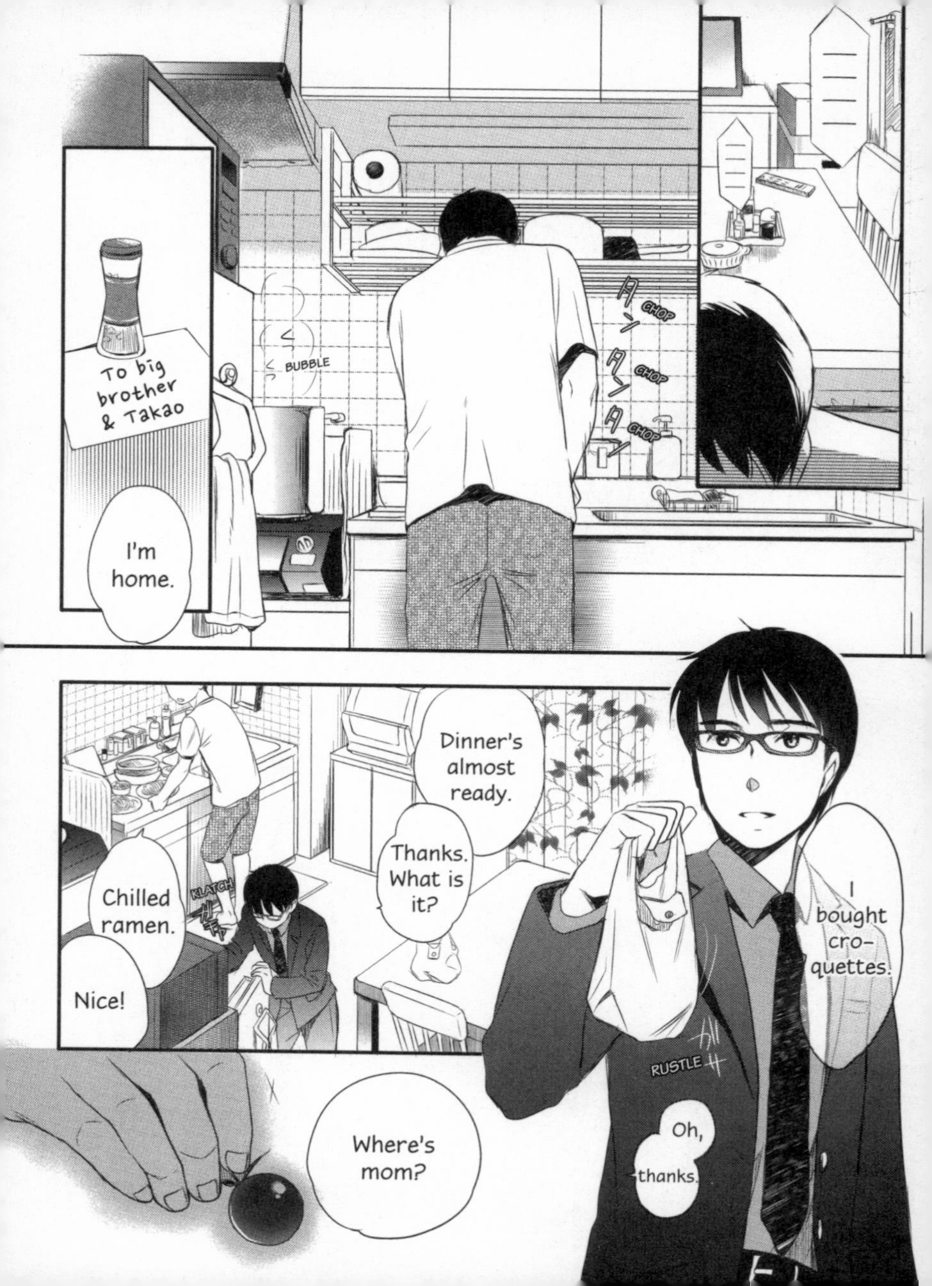
CHOP
CHOP
CHOP
BUBBLE
To big brother & Takao
I'm home.
Dinner's almost ready.
Thanks. What is it?
Chilled ramen.
KLATCH
Nice!
I bought cro-quettes.
RUSTLE
Oh, thanks.
Where's mom?

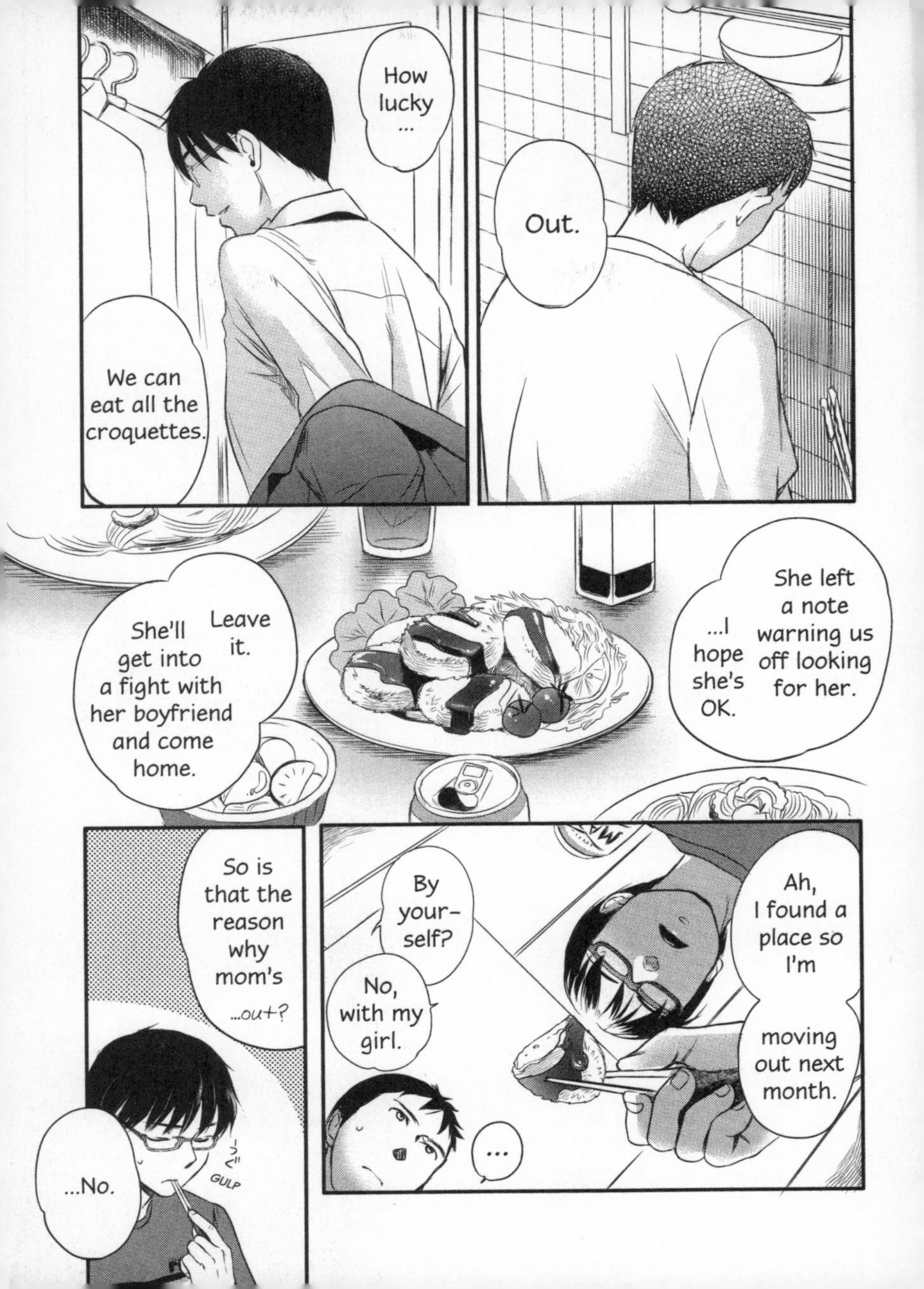
Out.
How lucky ...
We can eat all the croquettes.
She left a note warning us off looking for her.
...I hope she's OK.
Leave it.
She'll get into a fight with her boyfriend and come home.
Ah, I found a place so I'm
moving out next month.
By your-self?
No, with my girl.
...
So is that the reason why mom's ...out?
GULP
...No.

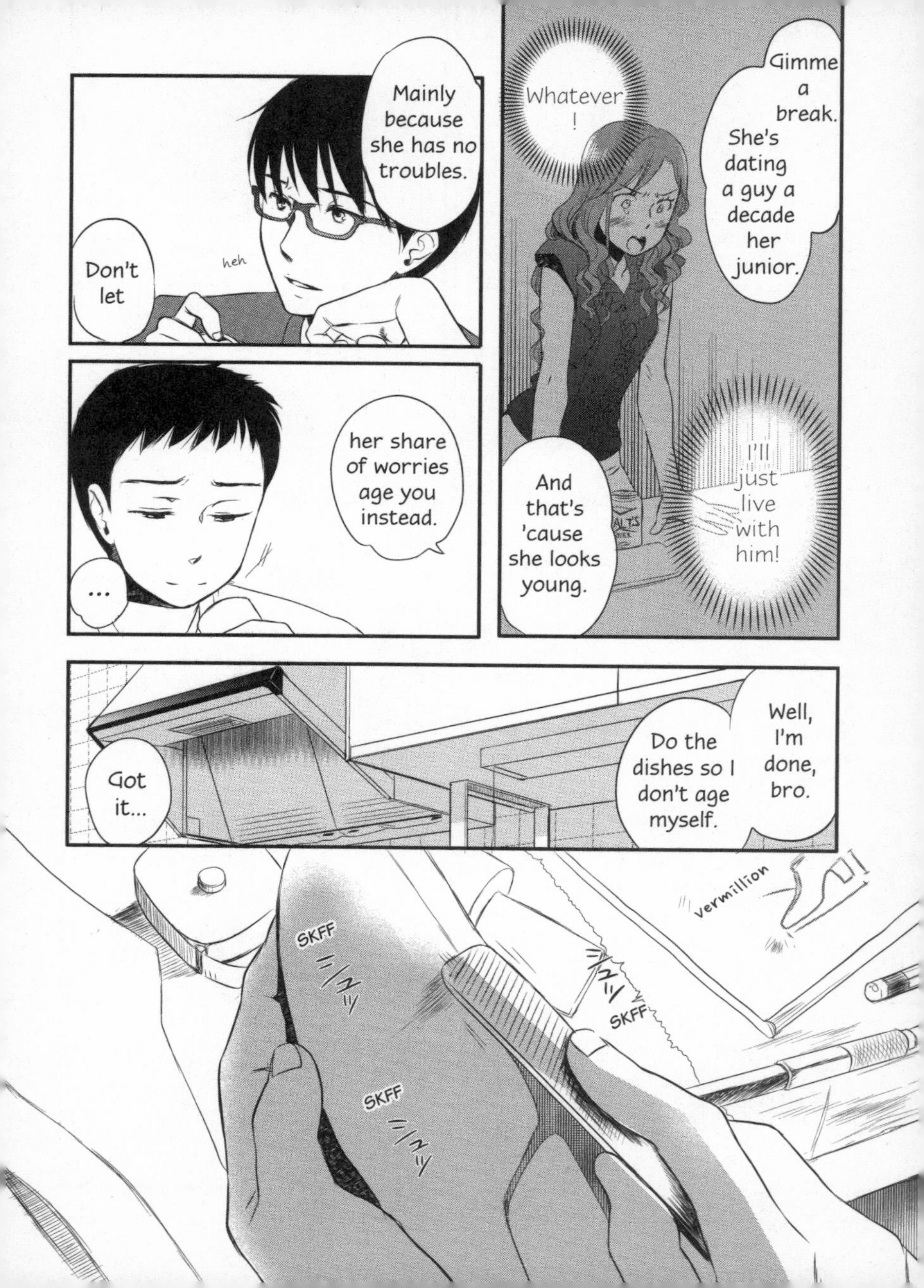

Gimme a break. She's dating a guy a decade her junior.
Whatever!
I'll just live with him!
And that's 'cause she looks young.
Mainly because she has no troubles.
heh
Don't let
her share of worries age you instead.
...
Well, I'm done, bro.
Do the dishes so I don't age myself.
Got it...
vermillion
SKFF
SKFF
SKFF

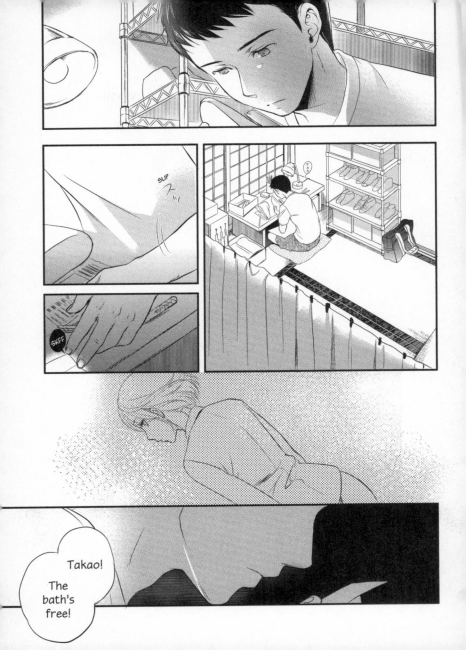

SLIP

SKFF

Takao!

The bath's free!

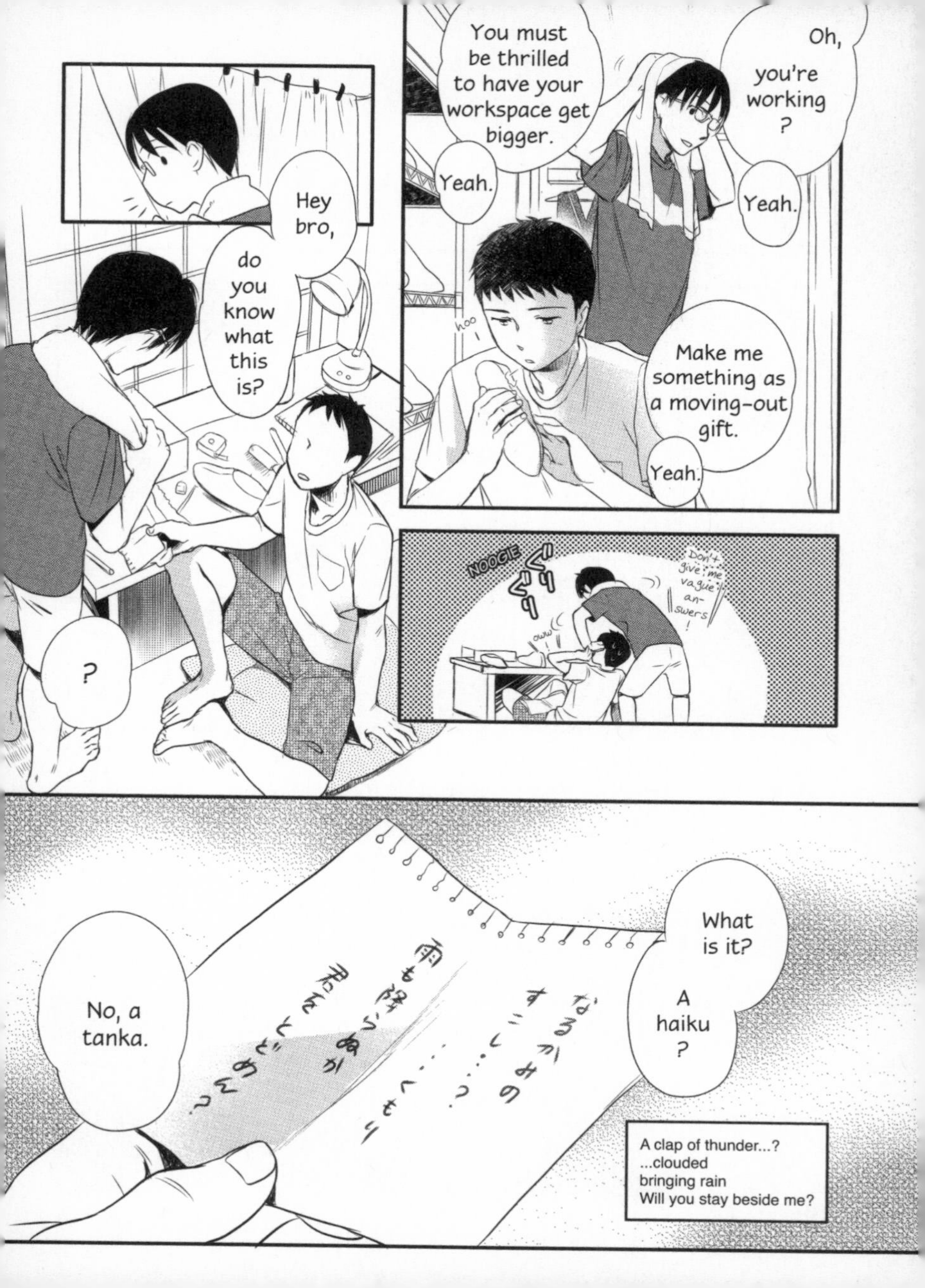
Oh, you're working?
Yeah.
You must be thrilled to have your workspace get bigger.
Yeah.
hoo
Make me something as a moving-out gift.
Yeah.
NOOGIE
Don't give me vague answers!
oww
Hey bro,
do you know what this is?
?
What is it?
A haiku?
No, a tanka.
なるかみの
すこし…?…くもり
雨も降らぬか
君をとどめむ?
A clap of thunder...?
...clouded
bringing rain
Will you stay beside me?

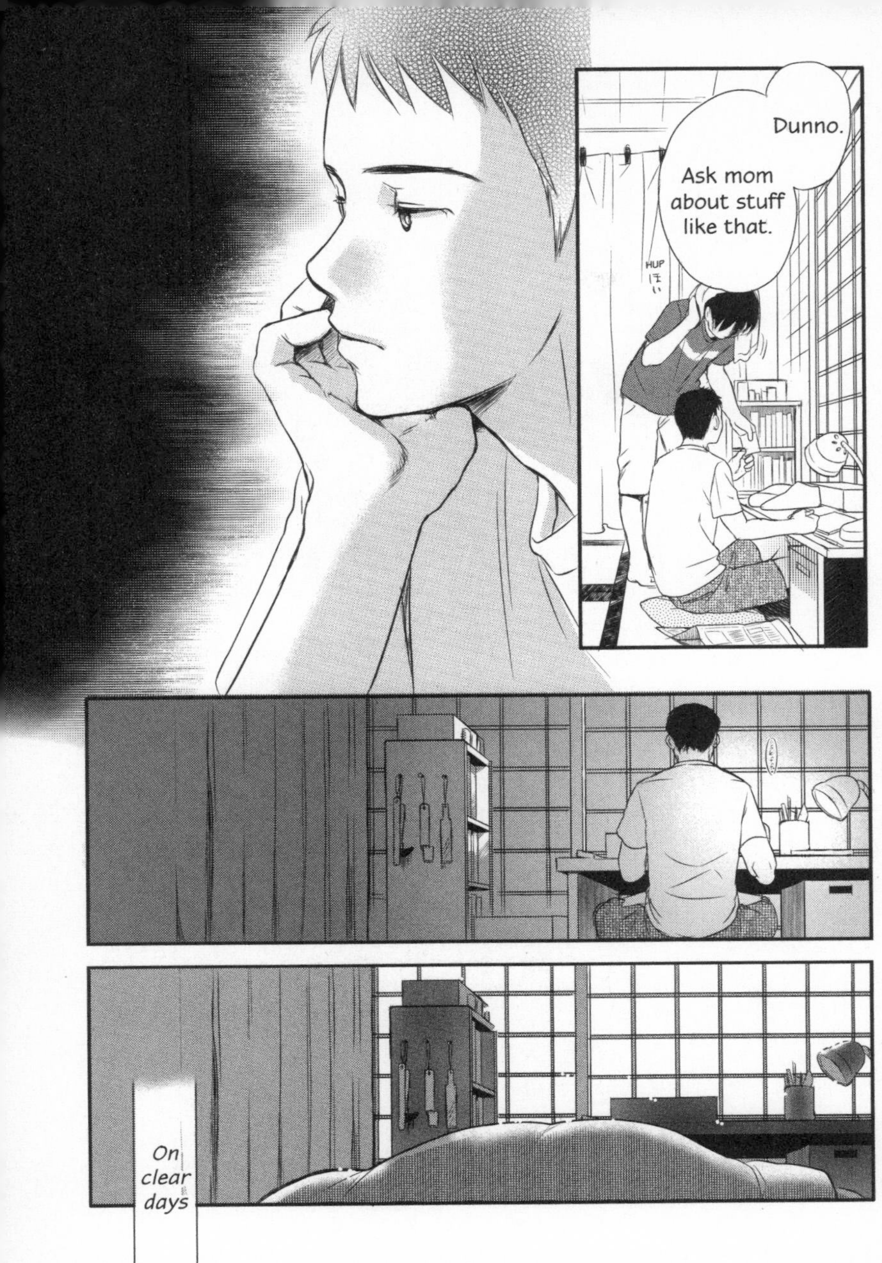
Dunno.
Ask mom about stuff like that.
HUP
ほい
On clear days

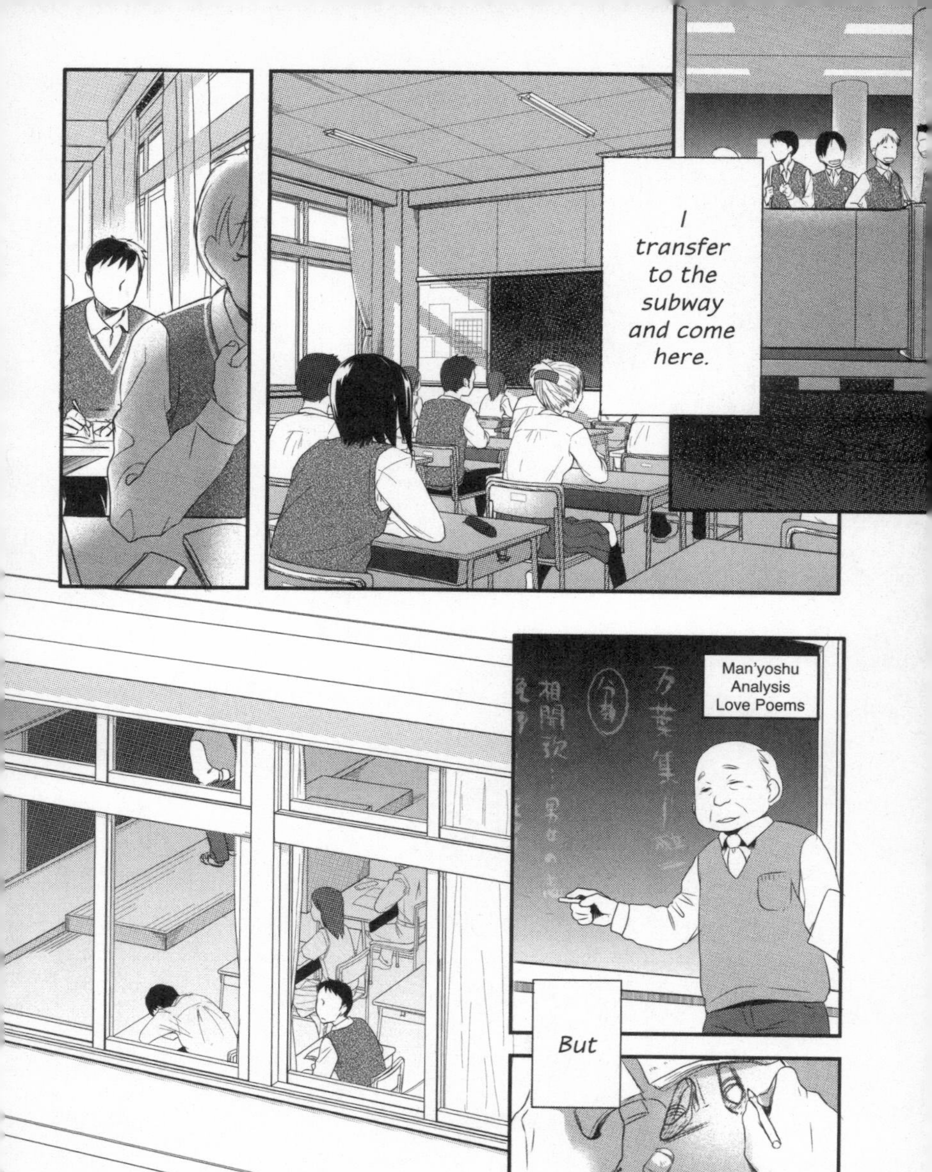
I transfer to the subway and come here.
Man'yoshu Analysis Love Poems
But

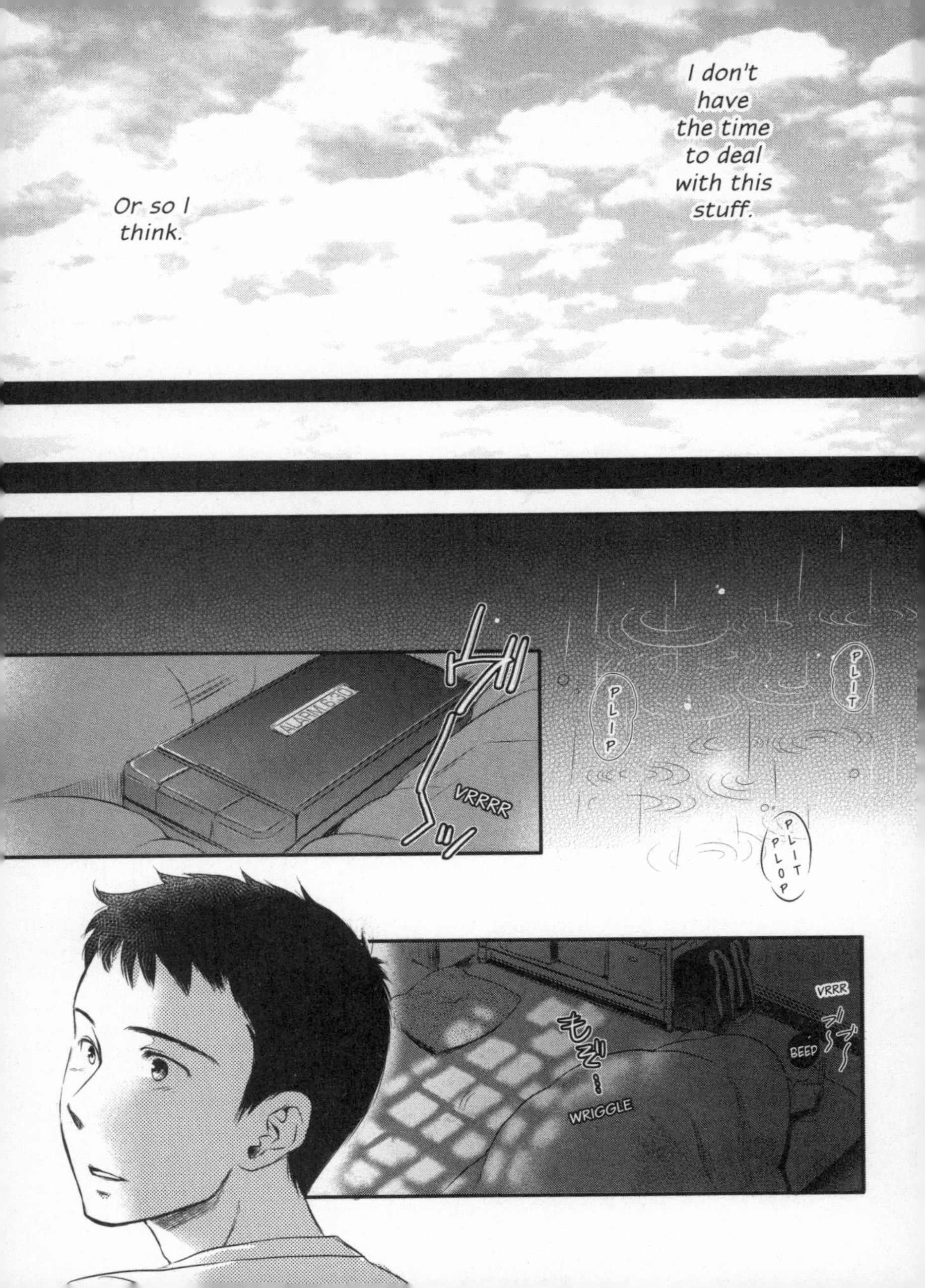

I don't have the time to deal with this stuff.
Or so I think.
PLIT
PLIP
PLIT
PLOP
ALARM 6:30
VRRRR
VRRR
BEEP
WRIGGLE

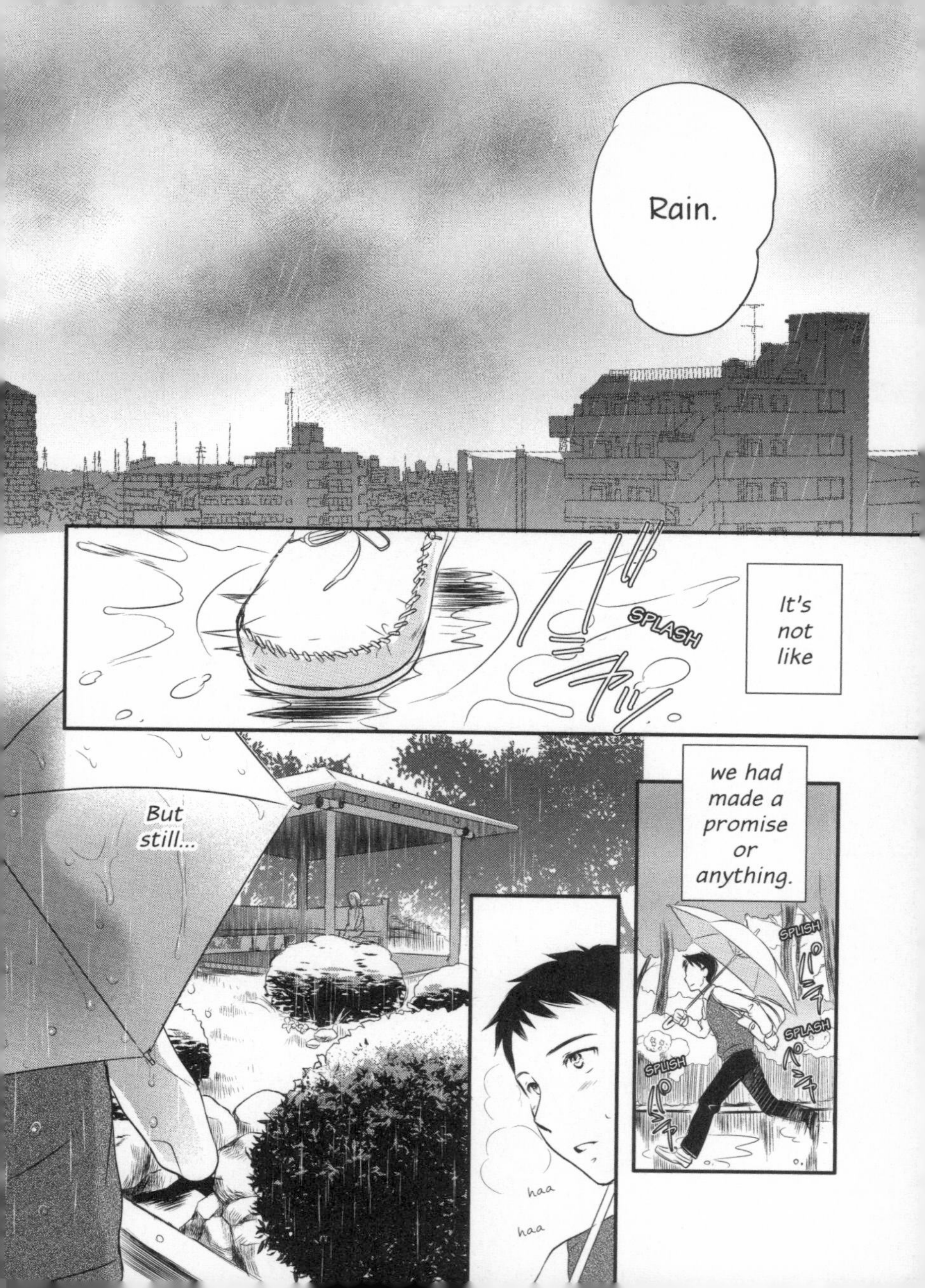
Rain.
It's not like
SPLASH
we had made a promise or anything.
SPLASH
SPLASH
SPLISH
haa
haa
But still...

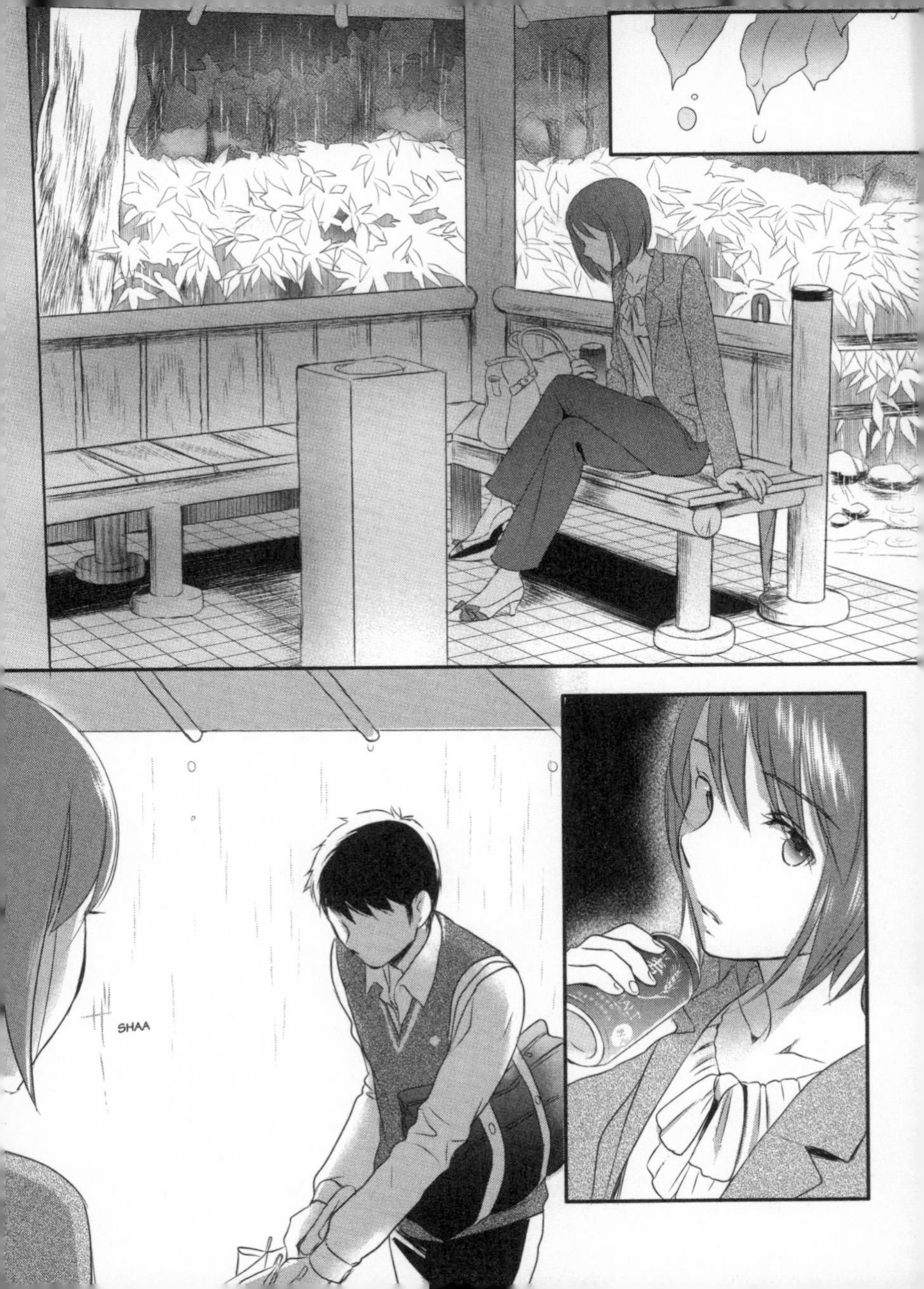
SHAA

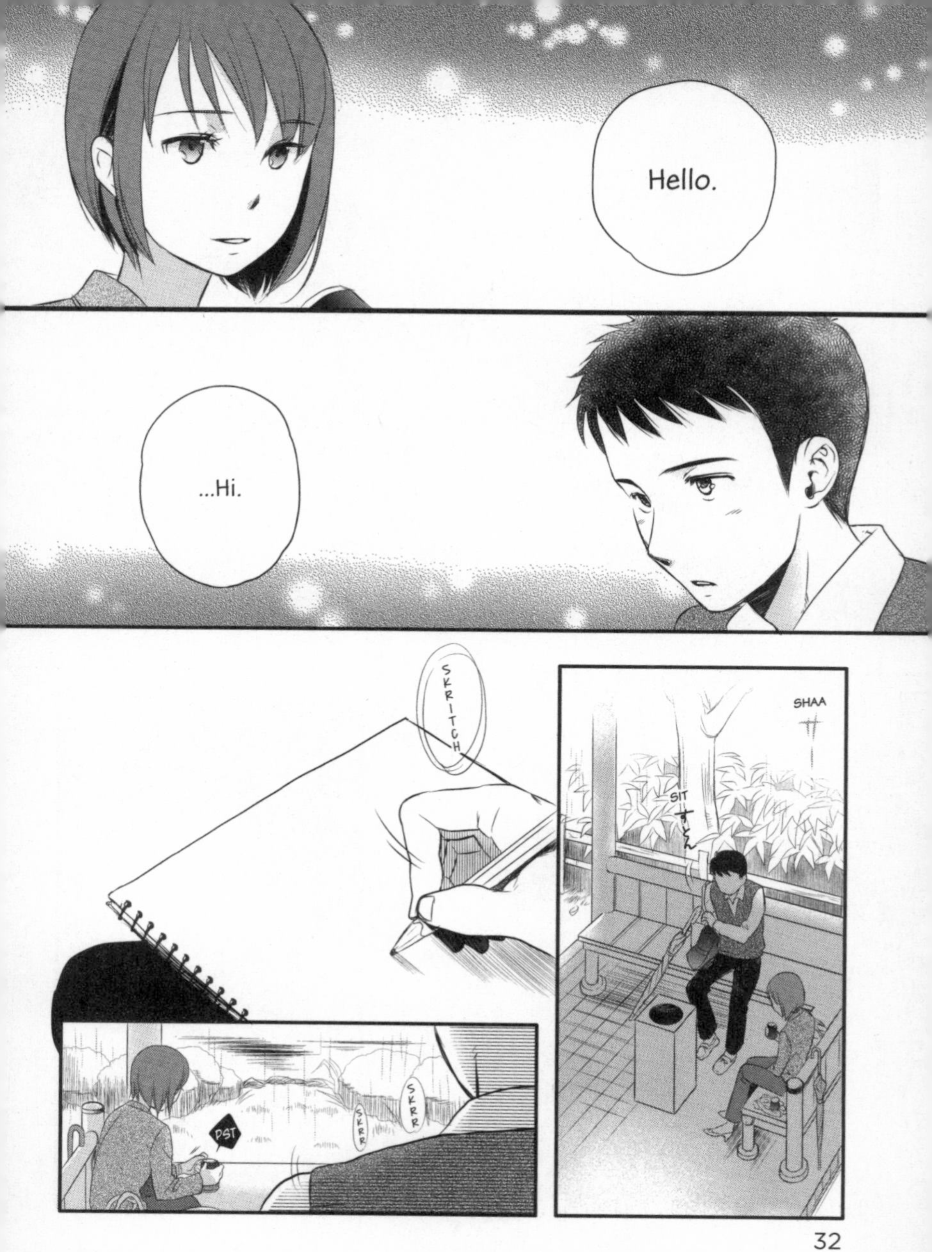
Hello.
...Hi.
SHAA
SIT
すとん
SKRITCH
SKRR
SKRR
PST

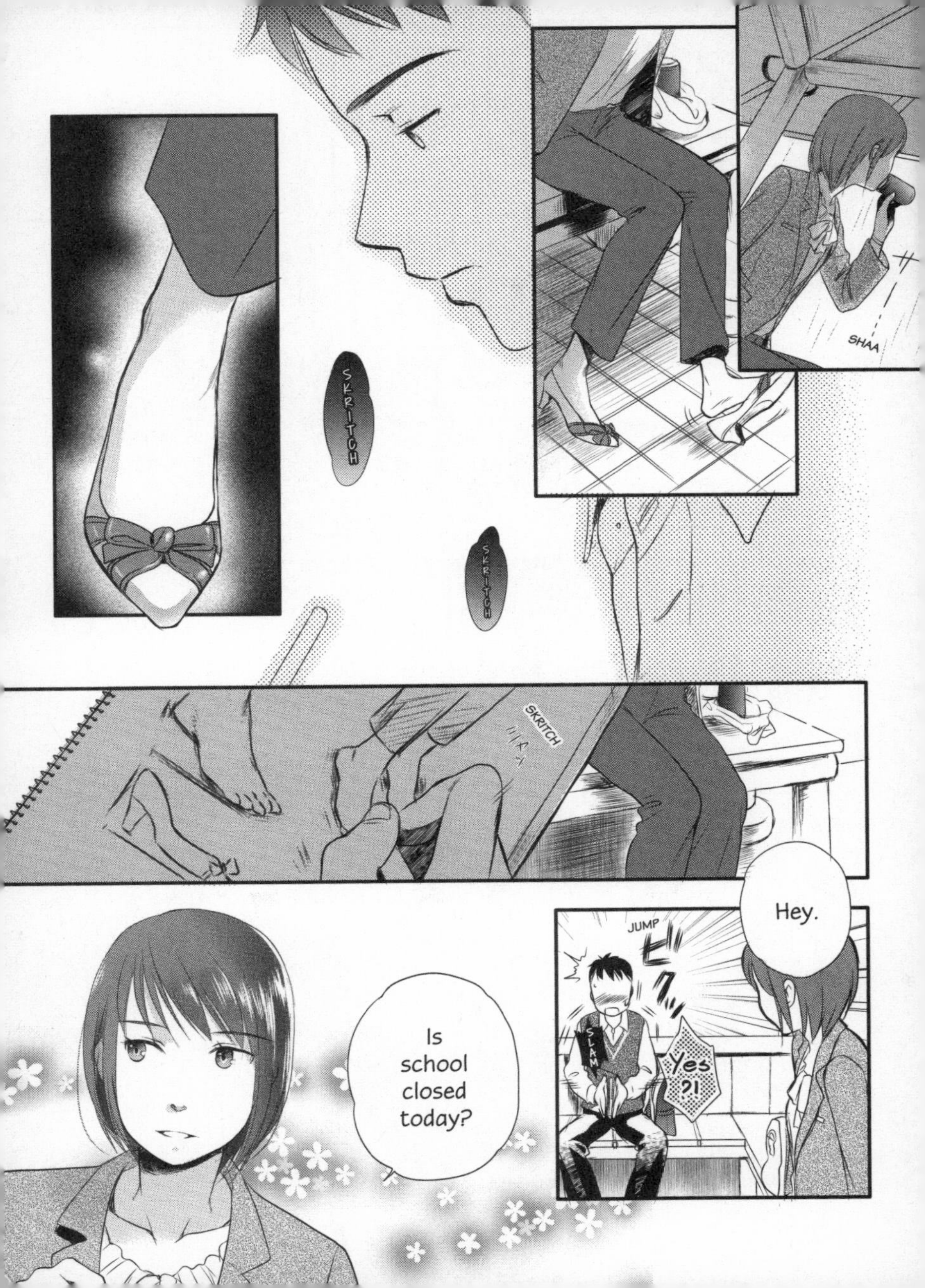
SHAA
SKRITCH
SKRITCH
SKRITCH
Hey.
JUMP
SLAM
Yes ?!
Is school closed today?

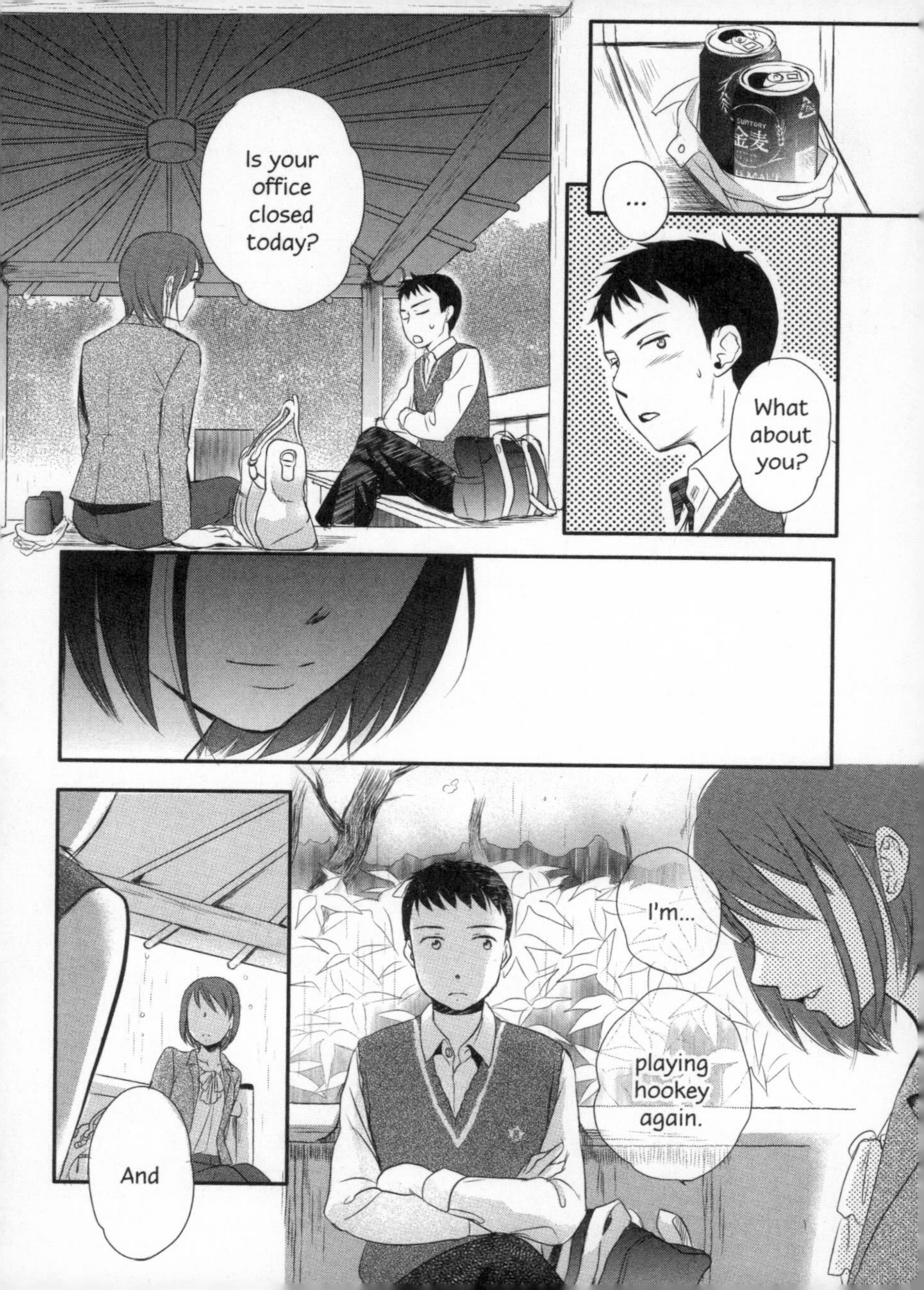
SUNTORY
金麦
...
What about you?
Is your office closed today?
I'm...
playing hookey again.
And

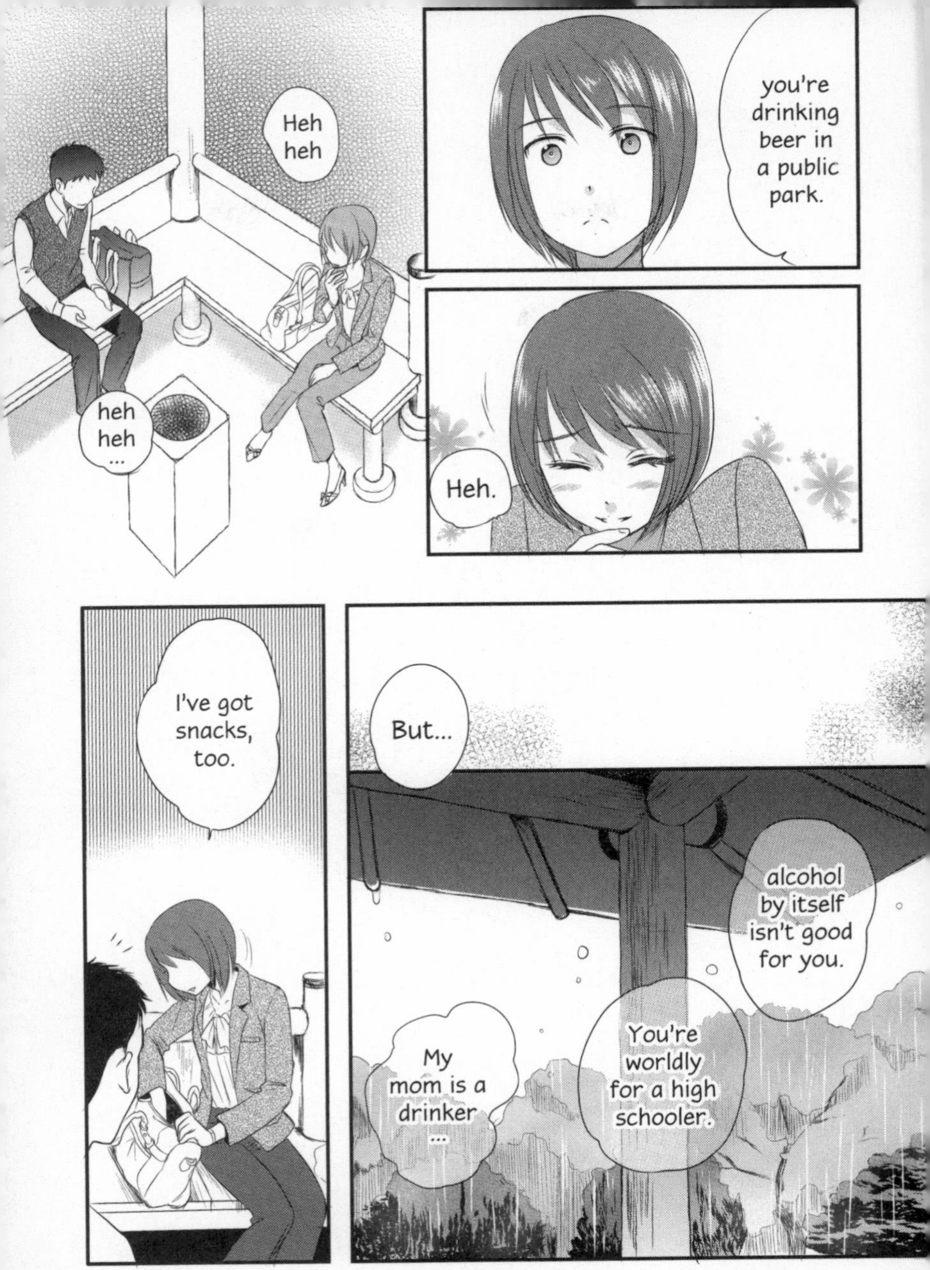
you're drinking beer in a public park.
Heh.
Heh heh
heh heh ...
But...
alcohol by itself isn't good for you.
You're worldly for a high schooler.
My mom is a drinker ...
I've got snacks, too.

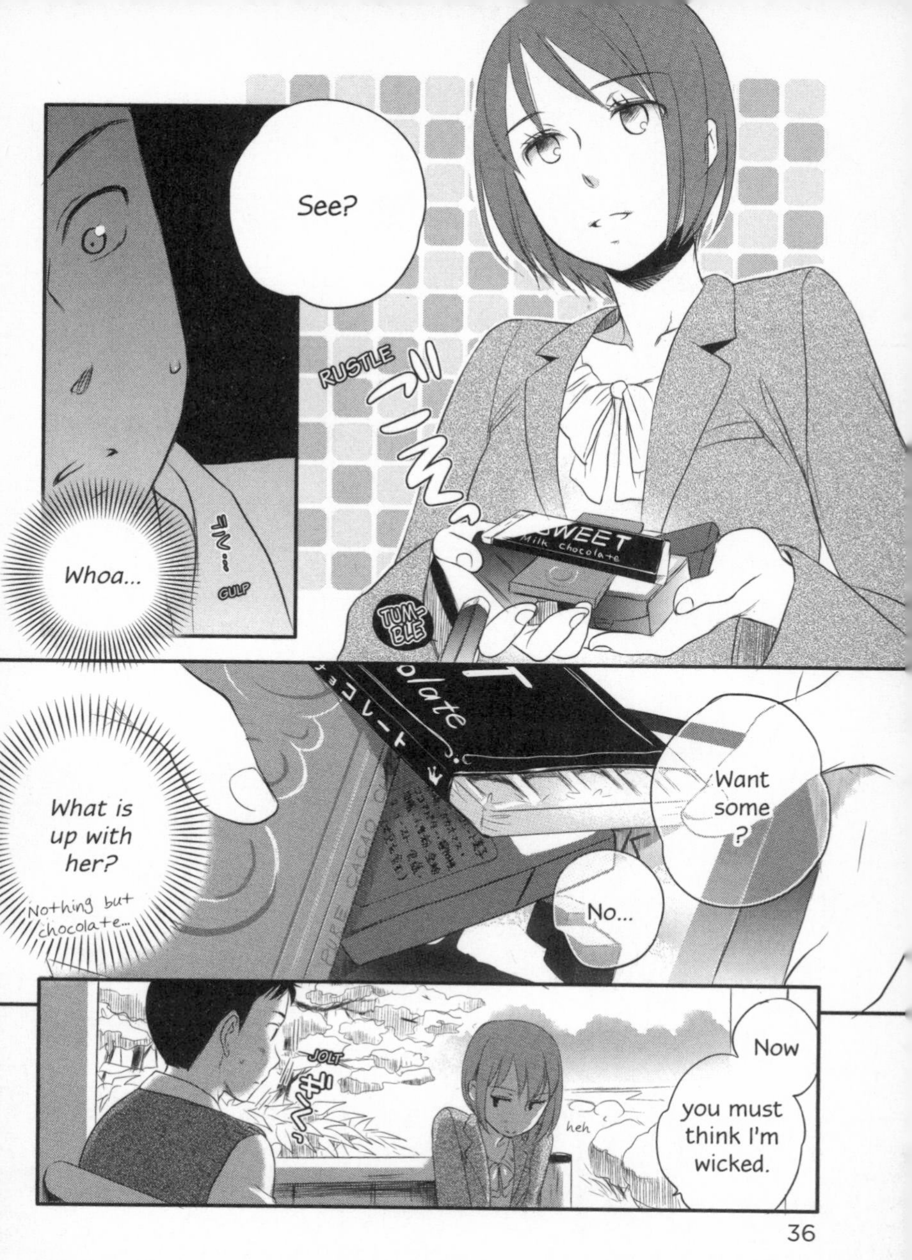
See?
RUSTLE
Milk chocolate
TUM-BLE
Whoa...
GULP
Want some?
No...
What is up with her?
Nothing but chocolate...
Now
you must think I'm wicked.
heh
JOLT

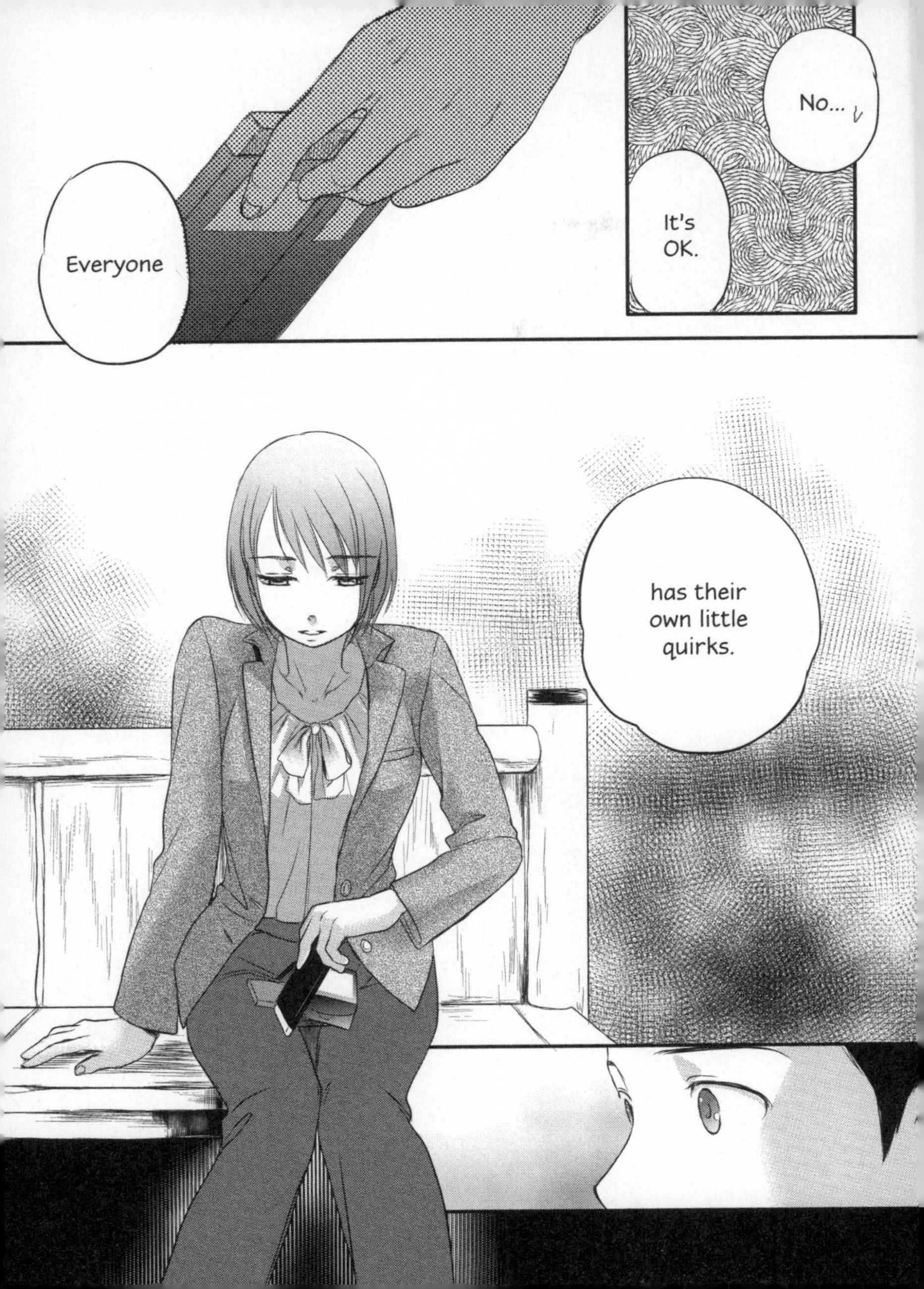
No...
It's OK.
Everyone
has their own little quirks.

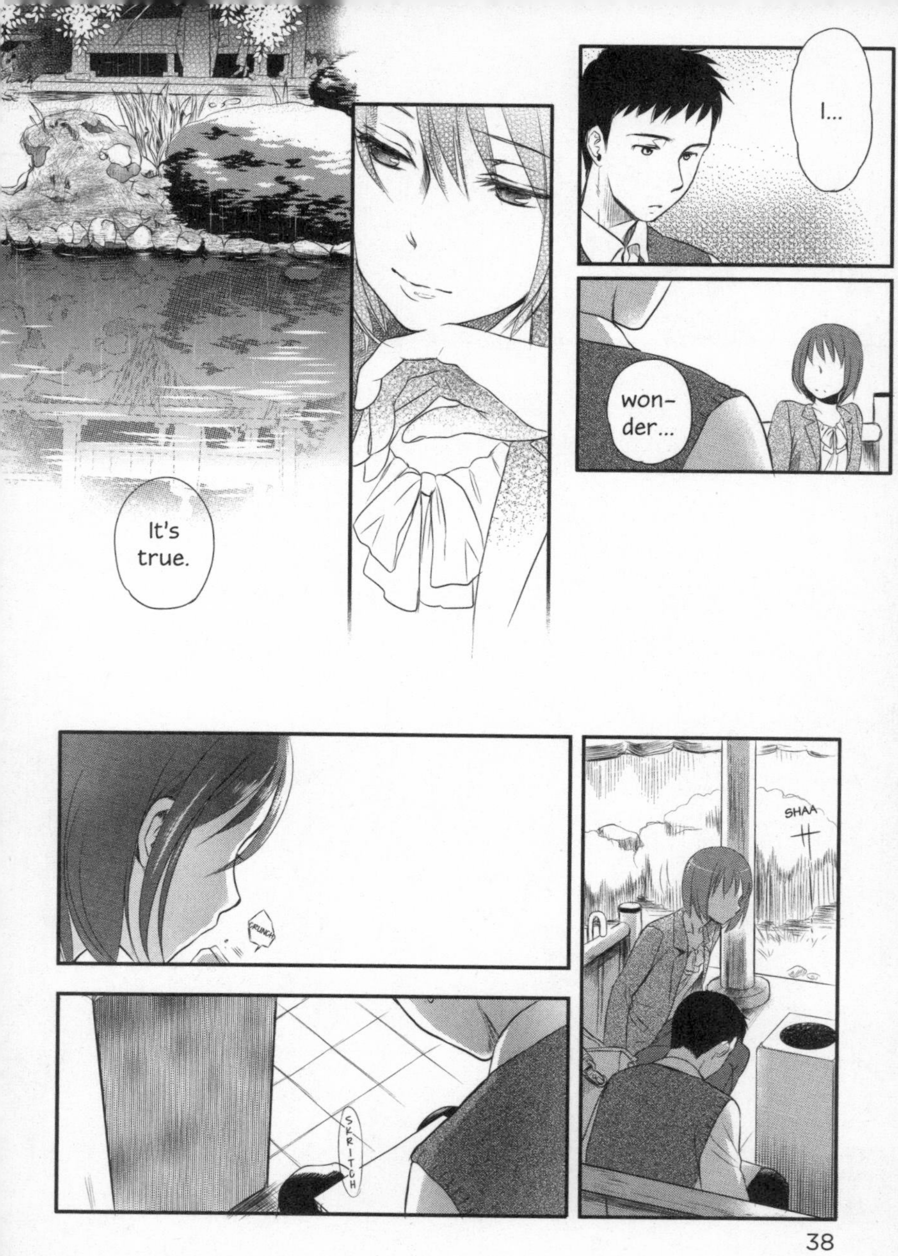
I...
won-der...
It's true.
SHAA
GRUNCH
SKRITCH

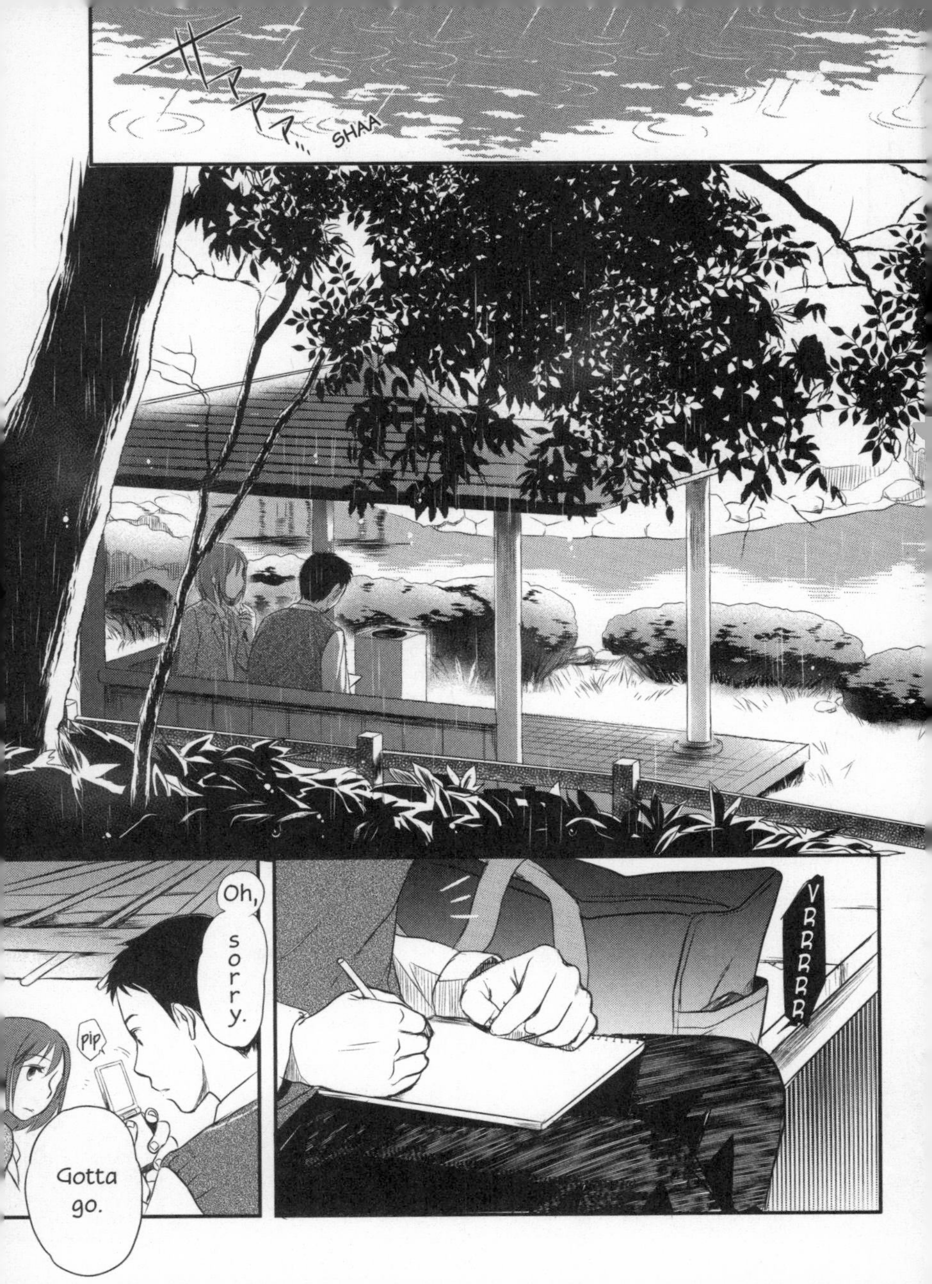
SHAA
VRRRRR
Oh, sorry.
pip
Gotta go.

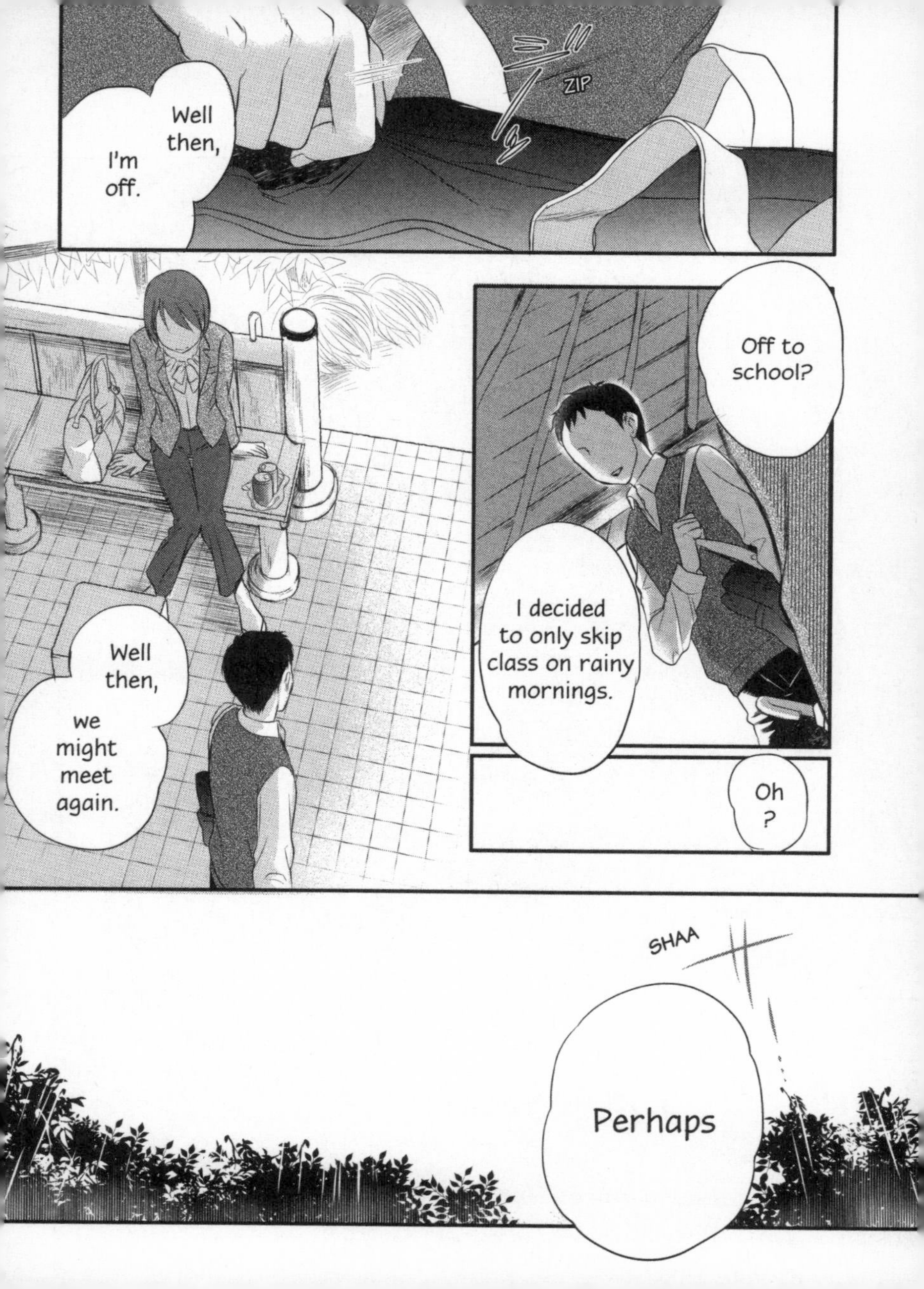
ZIP
Well then, I'm off.
Off to school?
I decided to only skip class on rainy mornings.
Oh?
Well then, we might meet again.
SHAA
Perhaps

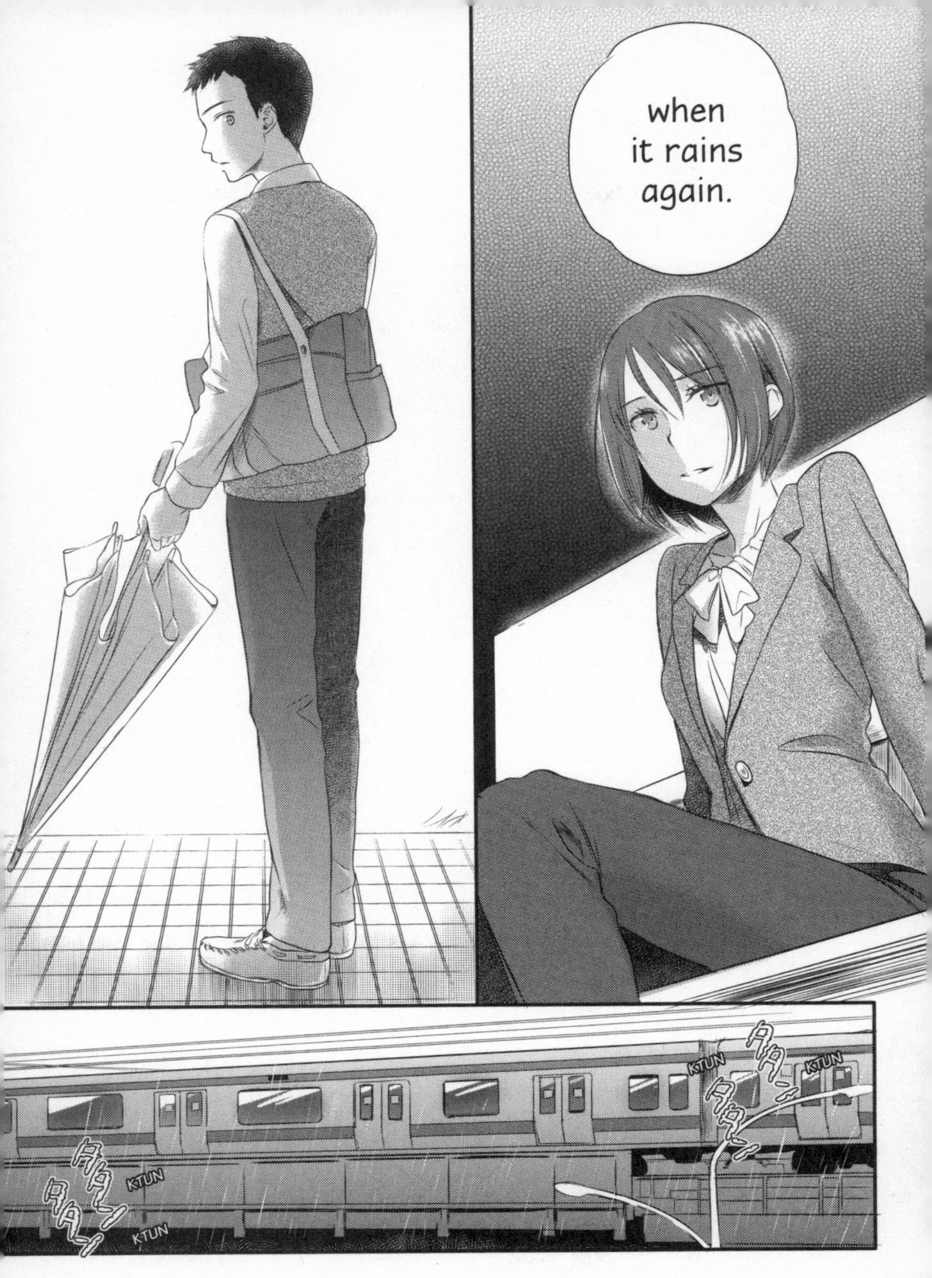
when it rains again.
KTUN
KTUN
KTUN
KTUN

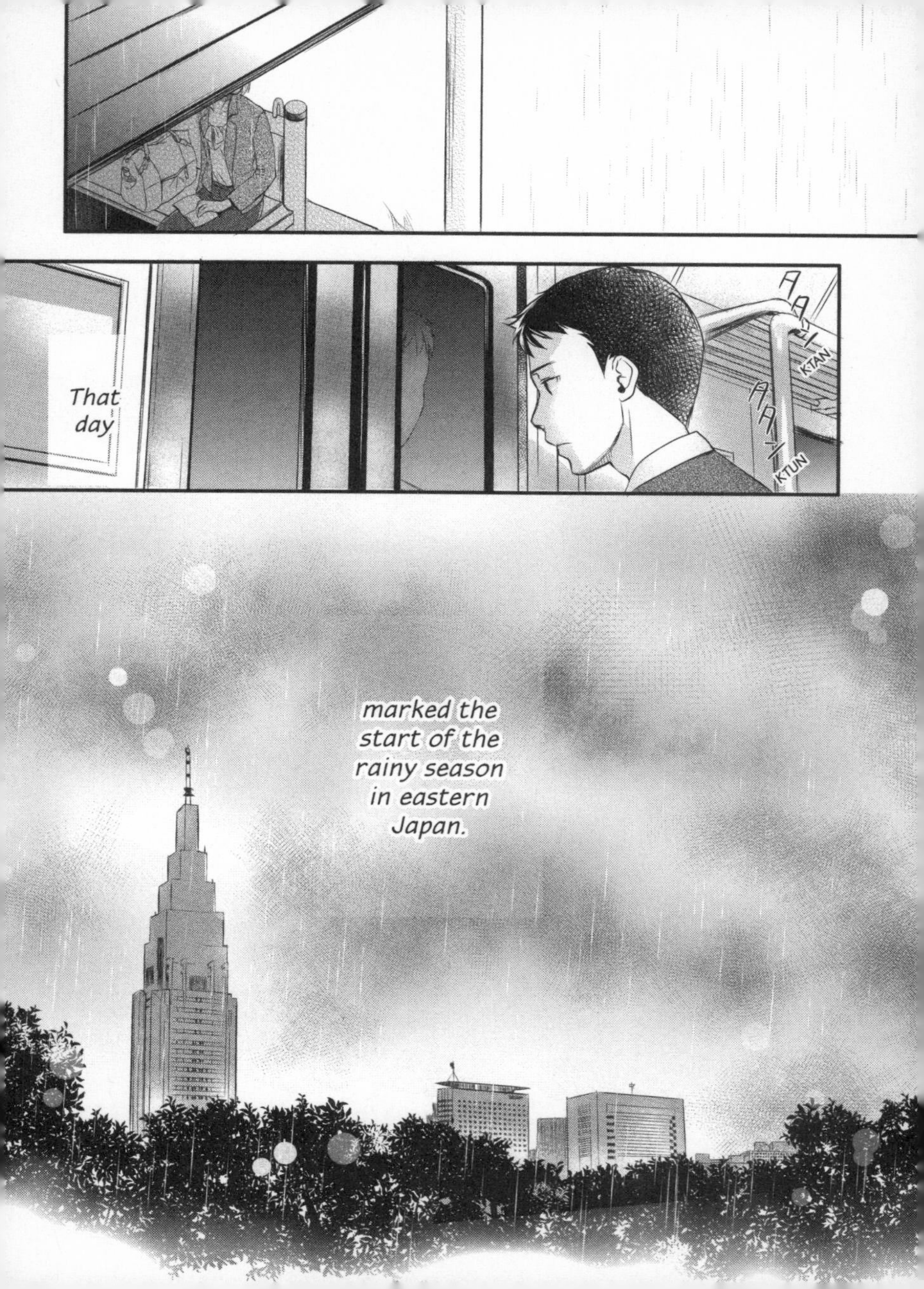
K-TAN
K-TUN
That day
marked the start of the rainy season in eastern Japan.

The Garden
of Words

Chapter 2
“When the evistal rains fall”

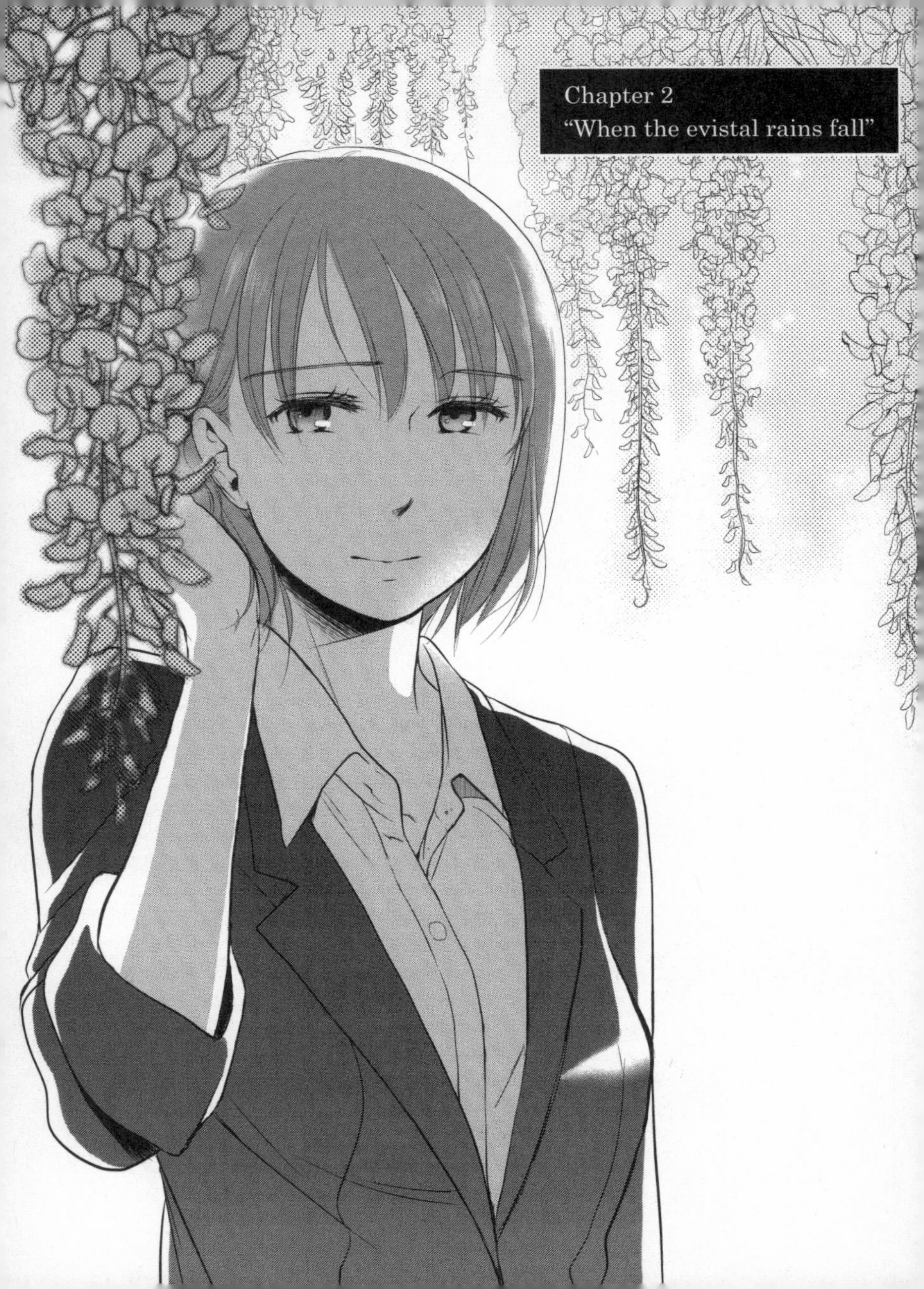

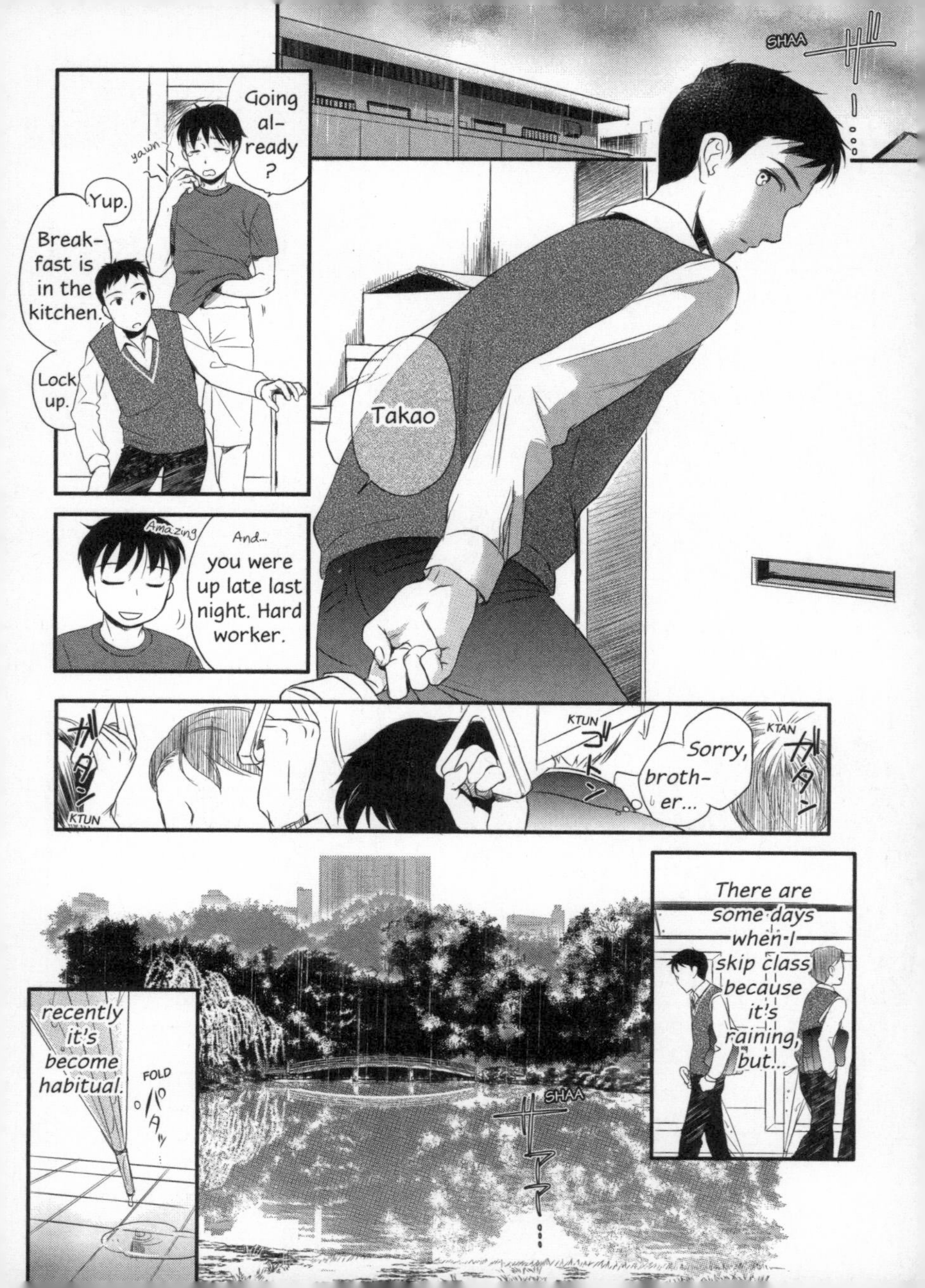
SHAA
Takao
Going al-ready?
yawn
Yup.
Break-fast is in the kitchen.
Lock up.
Amazing
And... you were up late last night. Hard worker.
KTAN
Sorry, broth-er...
KTUN
KTUN
There are some days when I skip class because it's raining, but...
SHAA
recently it's become habitual.
FOLD

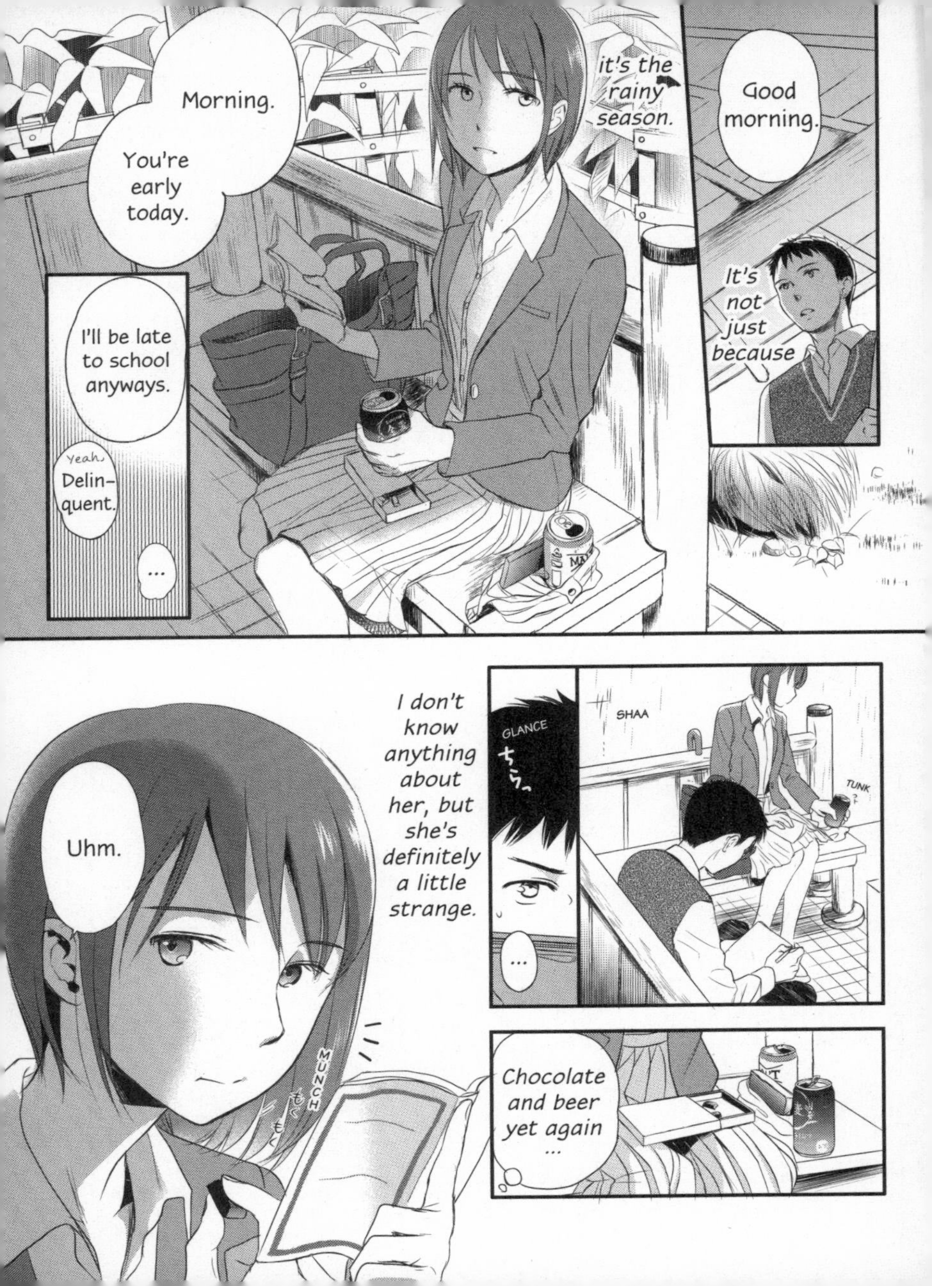
Good morning.
It's not just because
it's the rainy season.
Morning.
You're early today.
I'll be late to school anyways.
Yeah, Delinquent.
...
SHAA
TUNK
GLANCE
ちらっ
...
I don't know anything about her, but she's definitely a little strange.
Chocolate and beer yet again ...
Uhm.
MUNCH
もぐ もぐ

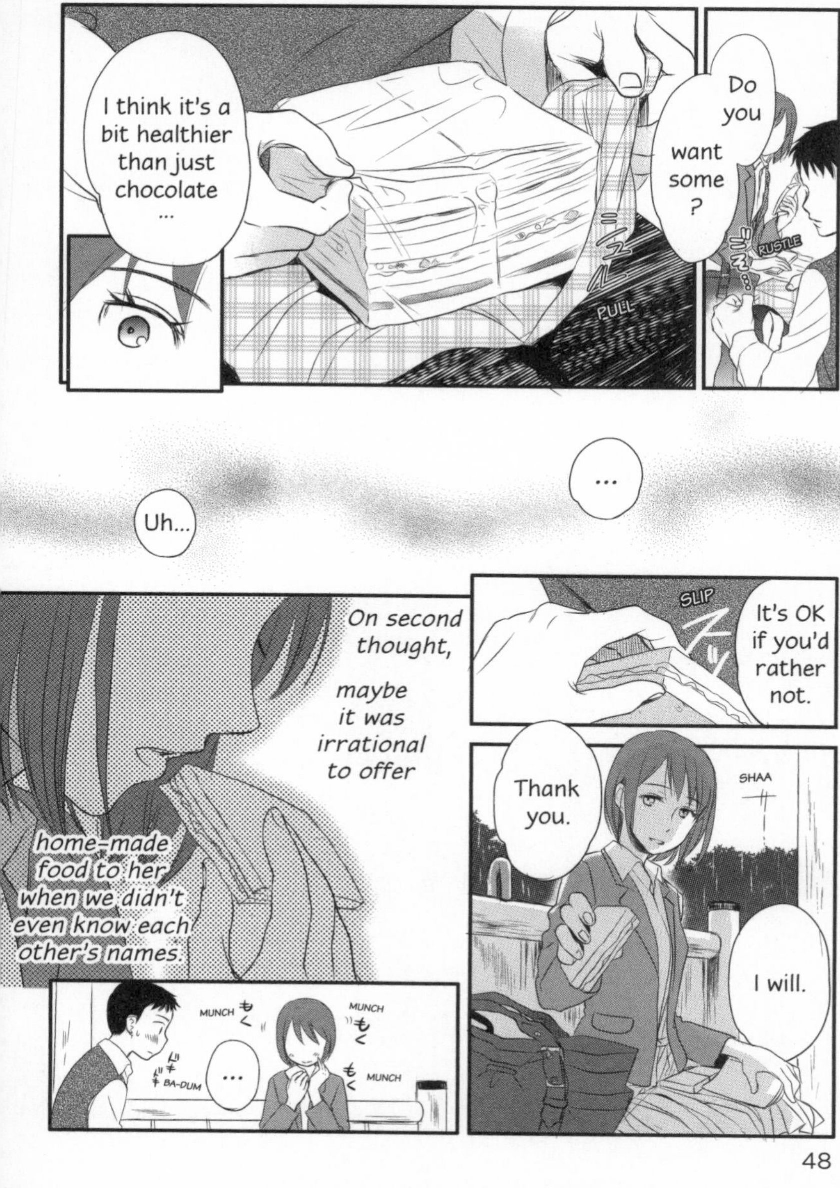
Do you want some ?
RUSTLE
PULL
I think it's a bit healthier than just chocolate ...
...
Uh...
SLIP
It's OK if you'd rather not.
Thank you.
SHAA
I will.
On second thought, maybe it was irrational to offer
home-made food to her when we didn't even know each other's names.
MUNCH
MUNCH
MUNCH
BA-DUM
...

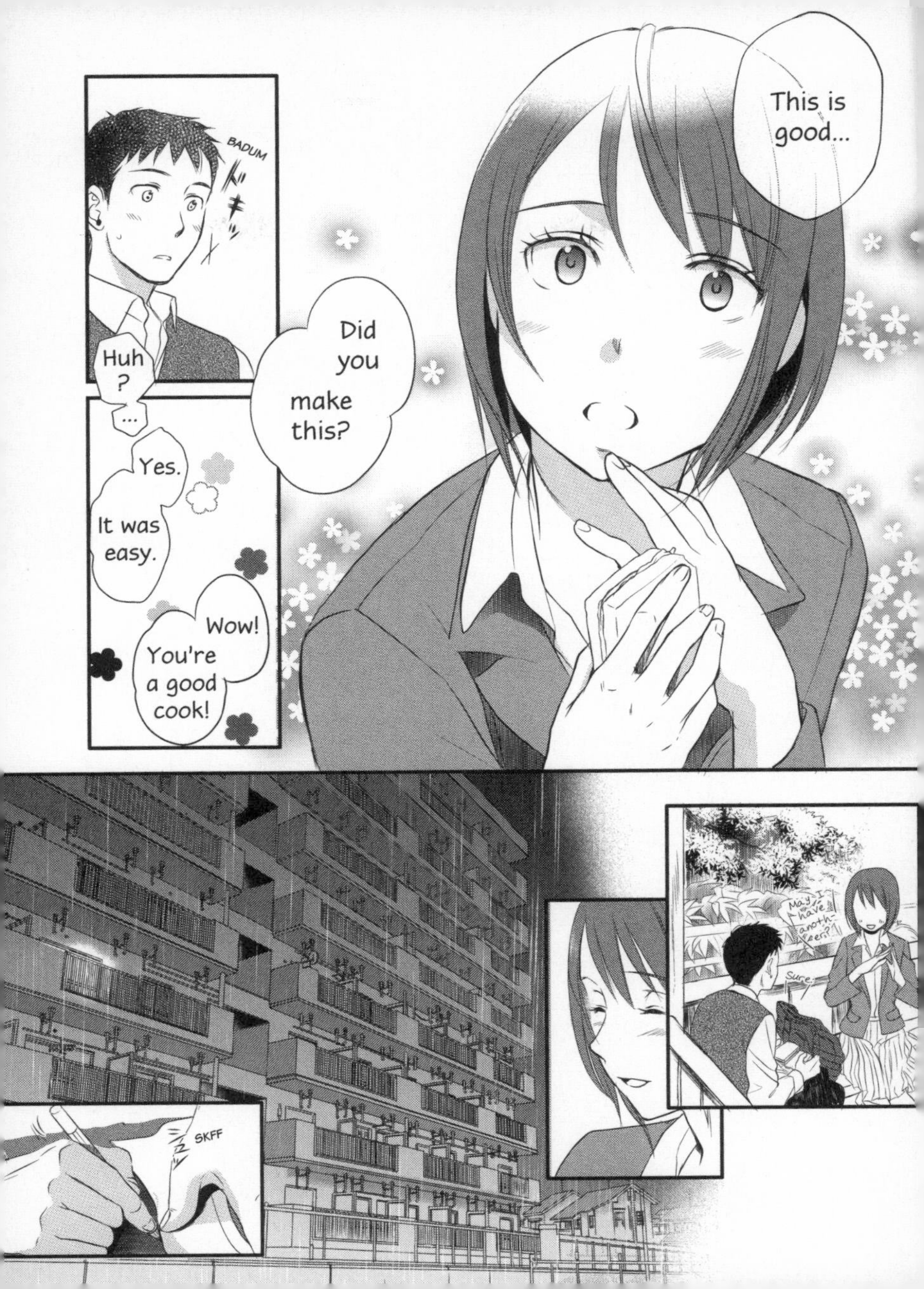
This is good...
Did you make this?
BADUM
Huh? ...
Yes. It was easy.
Wow! You're a good cook!
May I have another-?!
Sure.
SKFF

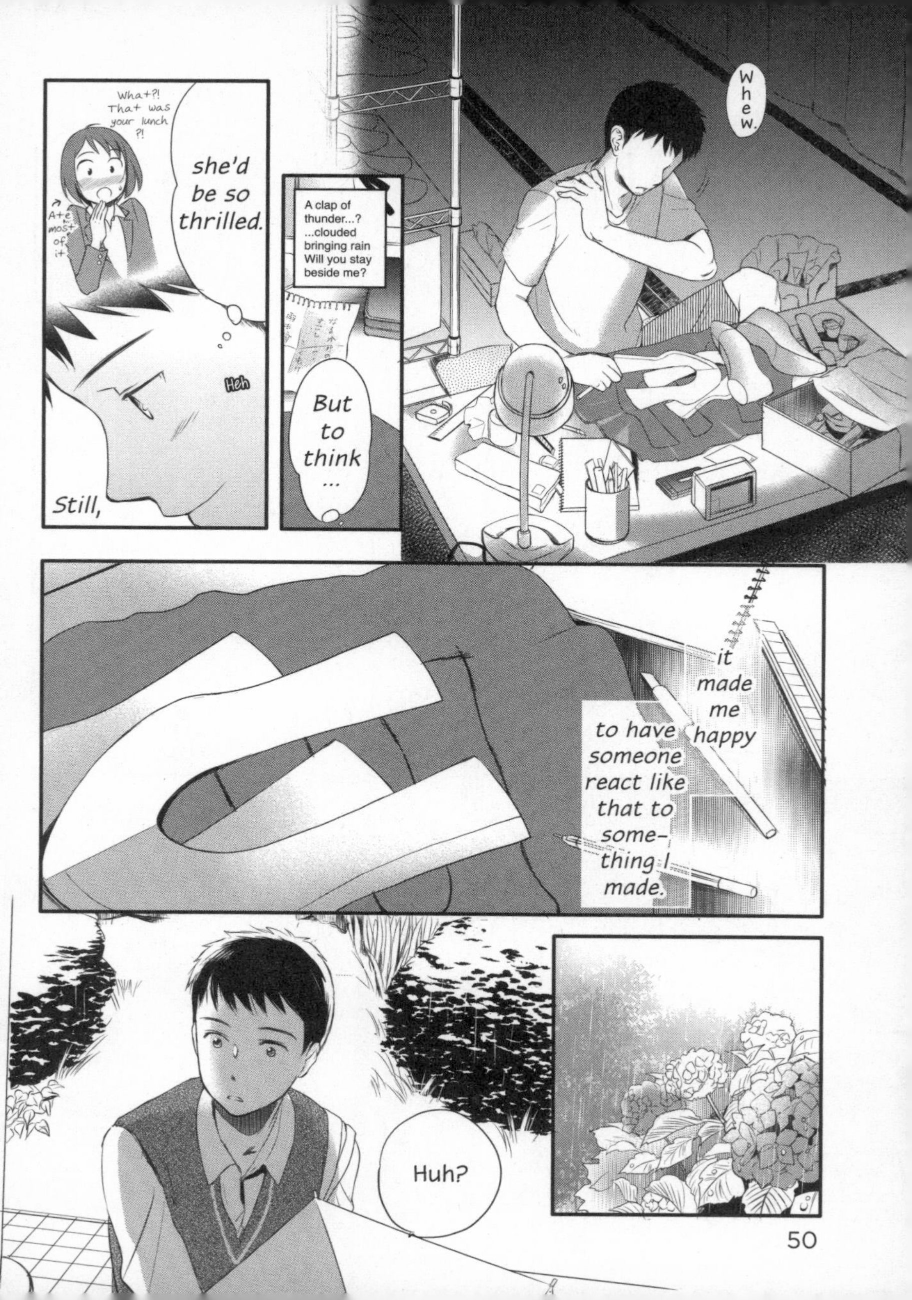
Whew.
A clap of thunder...? ...clouded bringing rain Will you stay beside me?
But to think...
What?! That was your lunch?!
Ate most of it
she'd be so thrilled.
Heh
Still,
it made me happy
to have someone react like that to some-thing I made.
Huh?

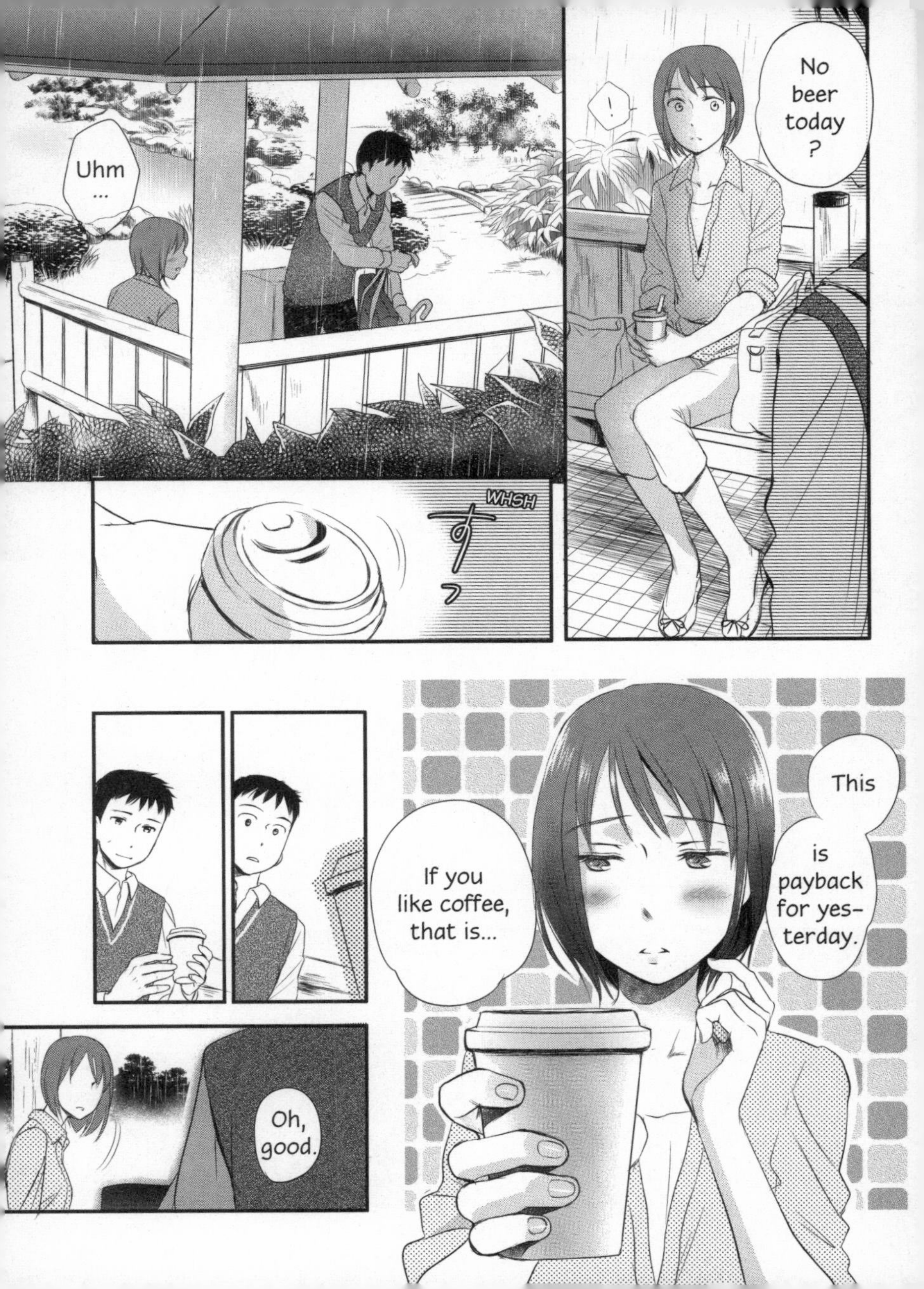
No beer today?
!
Uhm ...
WHSH
すっ
This is payback for yes-terday.
If you like coffee, that is...
Oh, good.

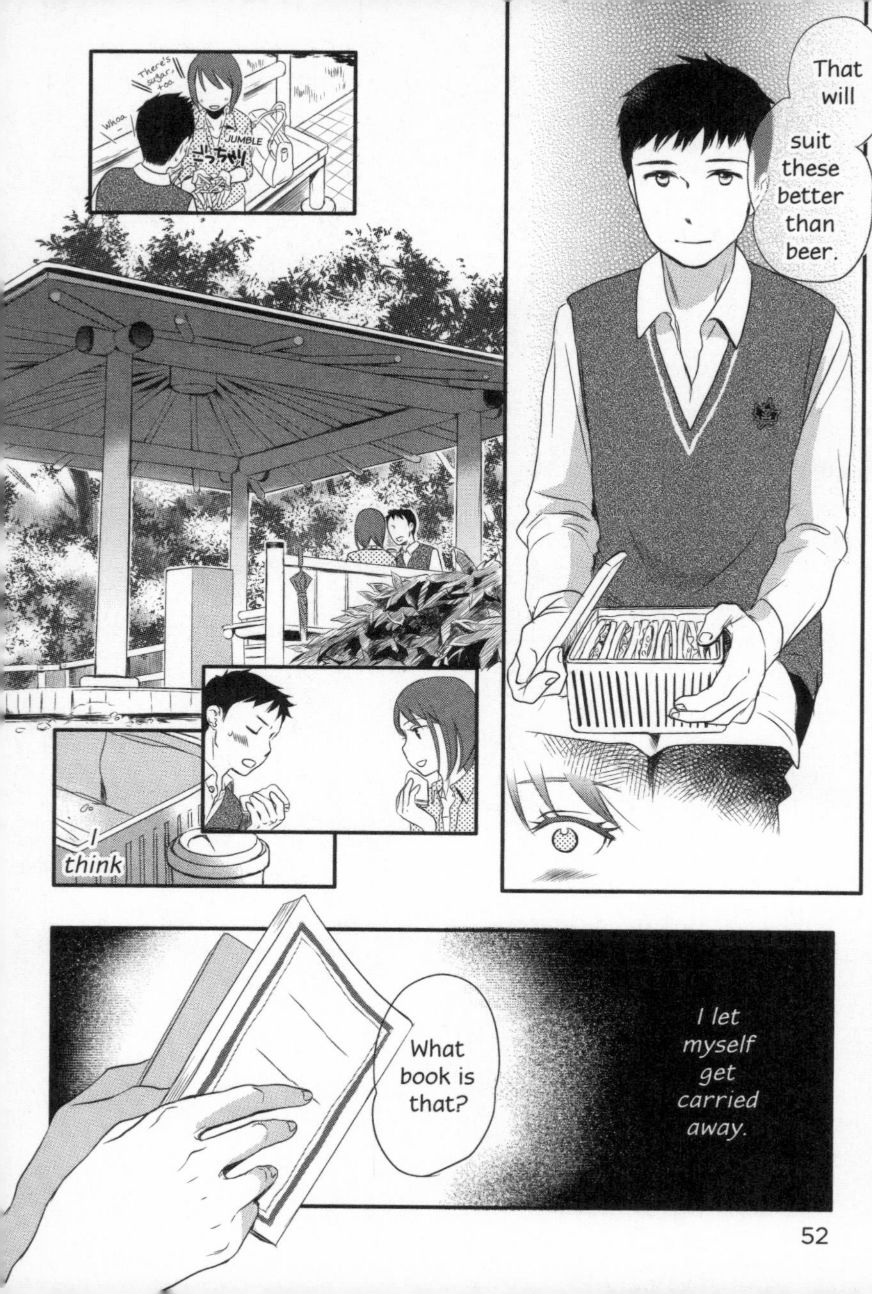
That will suit these better than beer.
There's sugar, too.
Whoa–
JUMBLE
ごっちゃり
I think
I let myself get carried away.
What book is that?

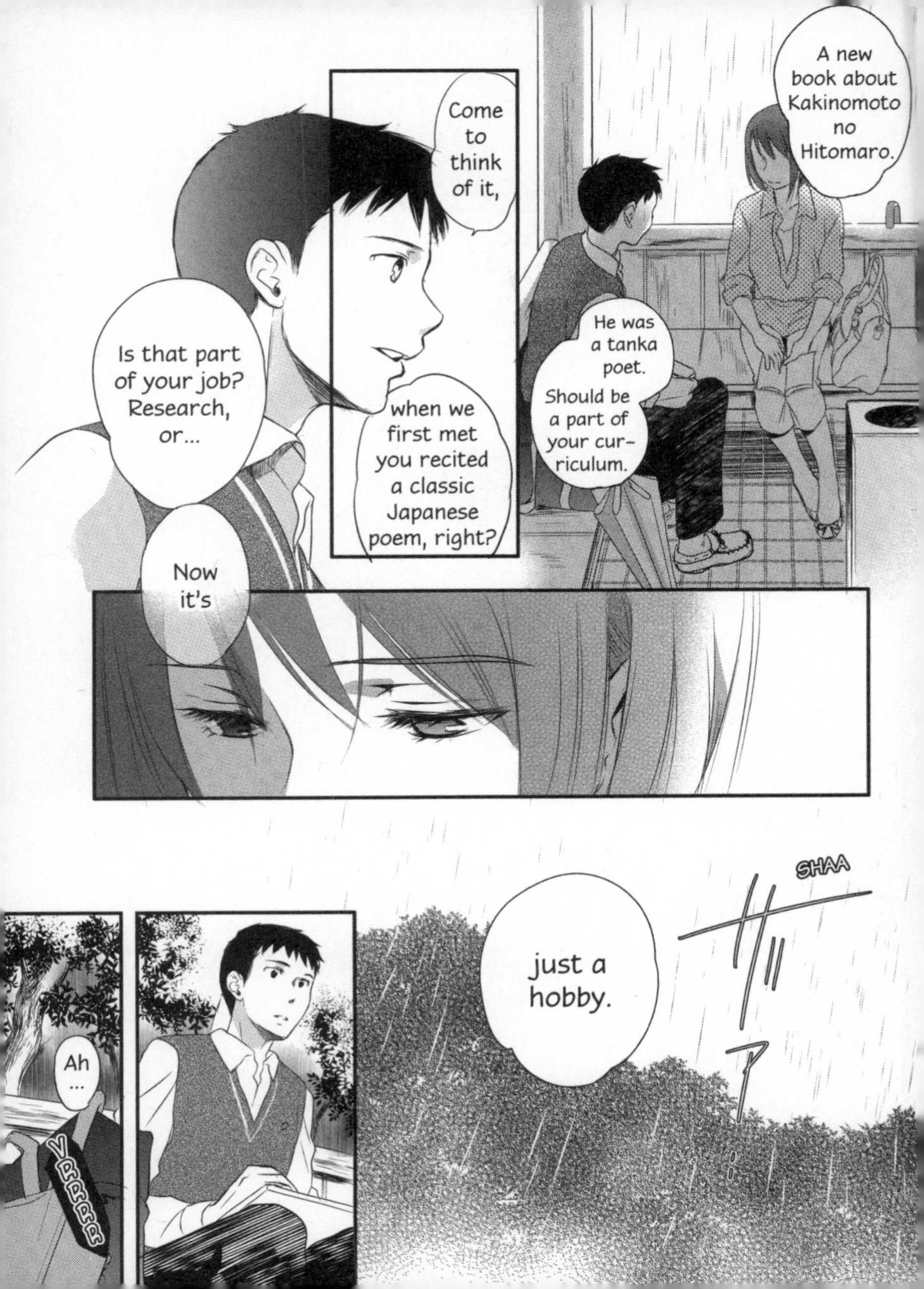
A new book about Kakinomoto no Hitomaro.
He was a tanka poet.
Should be a part of your curriculum.
Come to think of it,
when we first met you recited a classic Japanese poem, right?
Is that part of your job? Research, or...
Now it's
SHAA
just a hobby.
Ah ...
VRRRRR

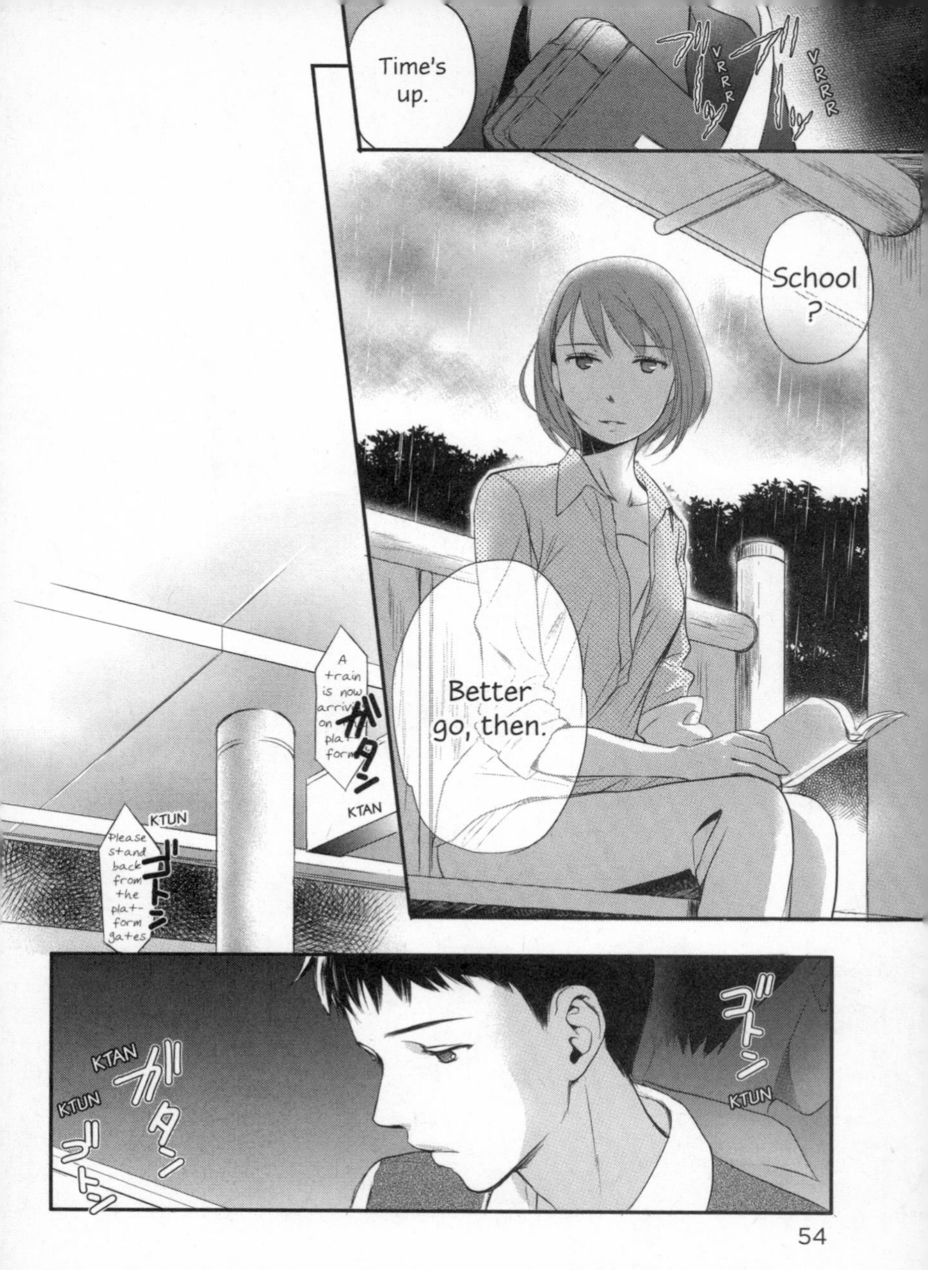
VRRR
VRRR
Time's up.
School ?
Better go, then.
A train is now arrivi on plat form
KTAN
KTUN
Please stand back from the plat-form gates
KTUN
KTAN
KTUN

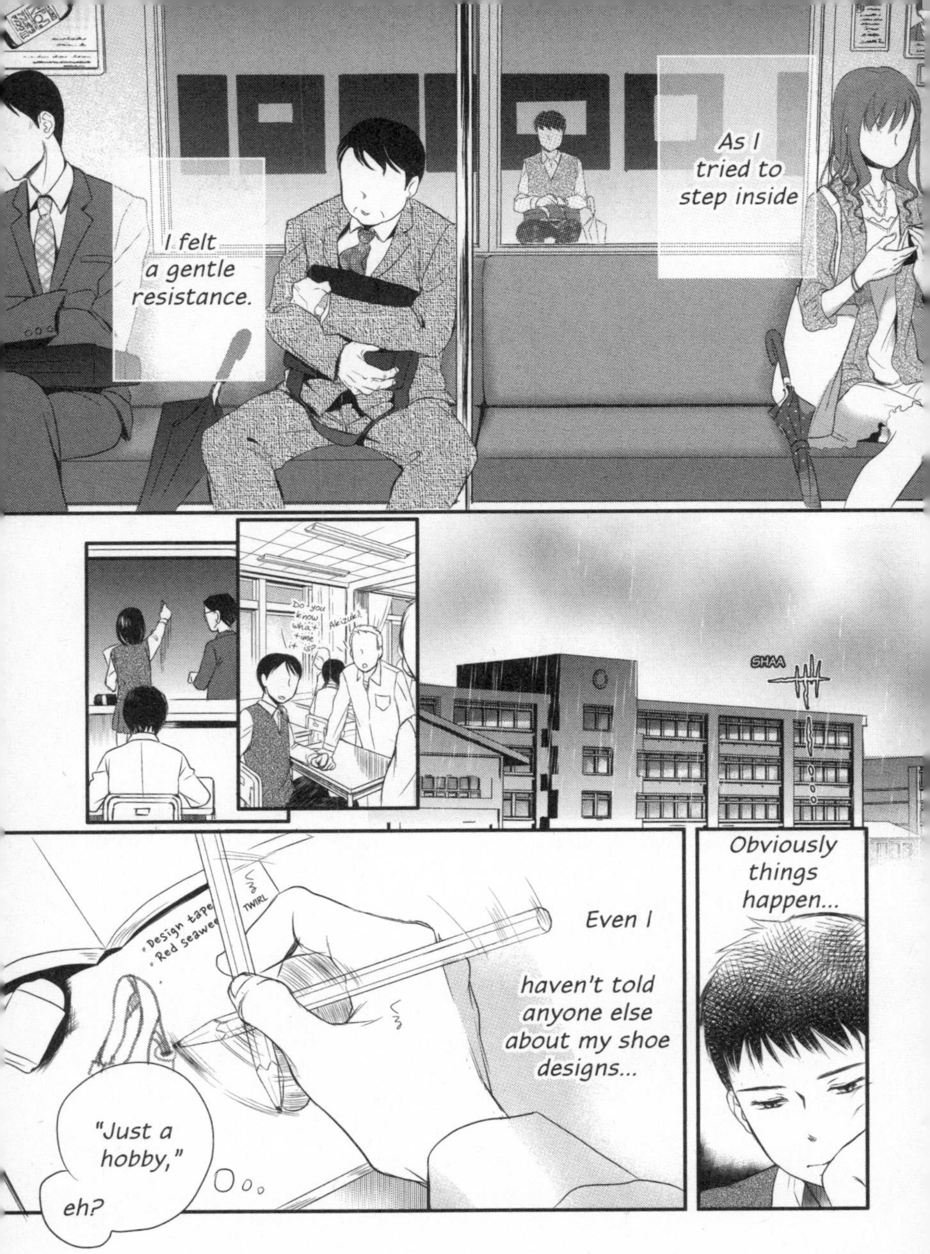
As I tried to step inside
I felt a gentle resistance.
SHAA
Akizuki!
Do you know what time it is?
Obviously things happen...
Even I
haven't told anyone else about my shoe designs...
TWIRL
• Design tape
• Red seawee
"Just a hobby," eh?

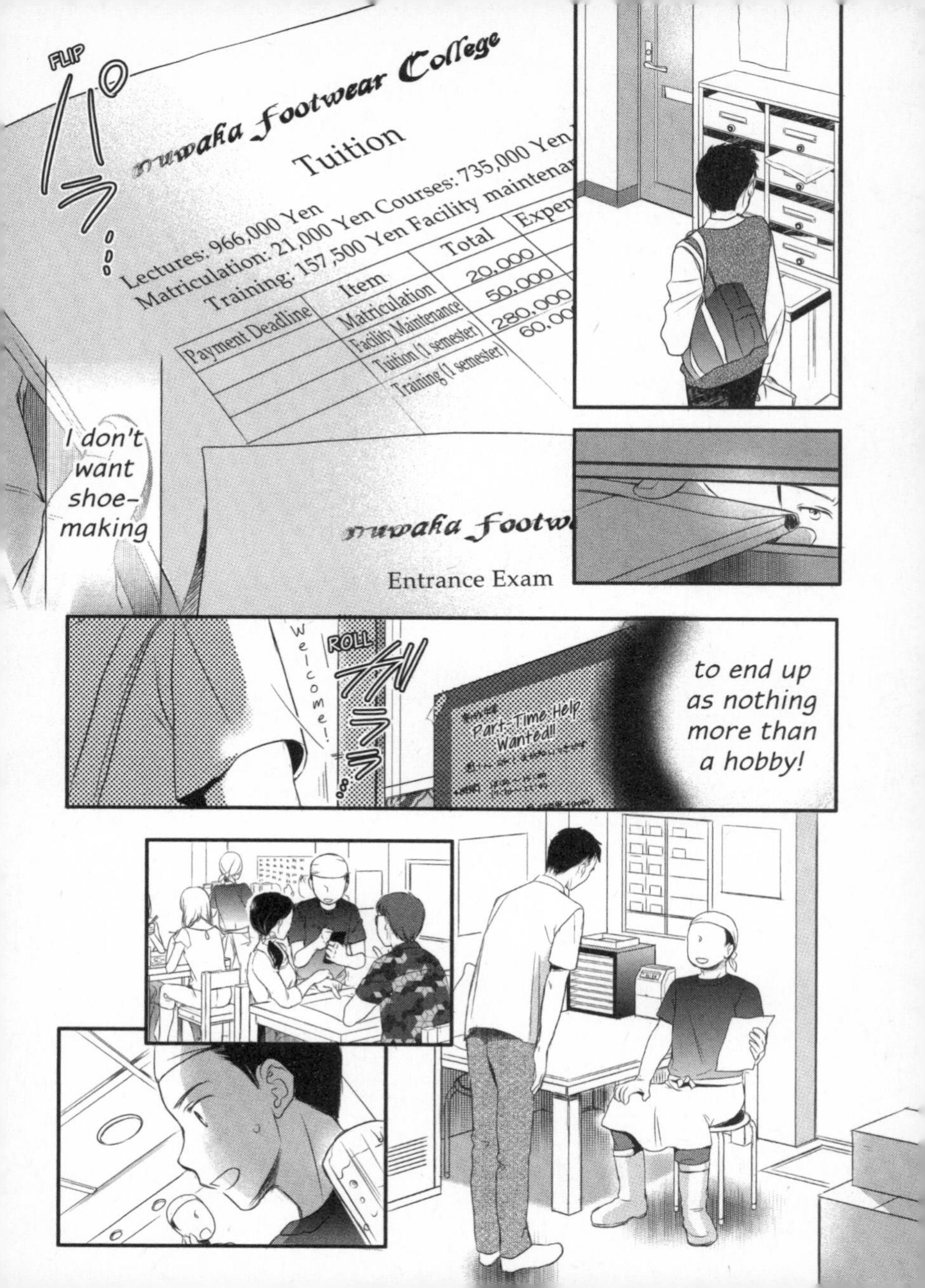
FLIP
uwaka Footwear College
Tuition
Lectures: 966,000 Yen
Matriculation: 21,000 Yen Courses: 735,000 Yen
Training: 157,500 Yen Facility maintenan
Payment Deadline
Item
Total
Expen
Matriculation 20,000
Facility Maintenance 50,000
Tuition (1 semester) 280,000
Training (1 semester) 60,00
I don't want shoe-making
uwaka Footw
Entrance Exam
to end up as nothing more than a hobby!
Part Time Help Wanted!!
ROLL
Welcome!

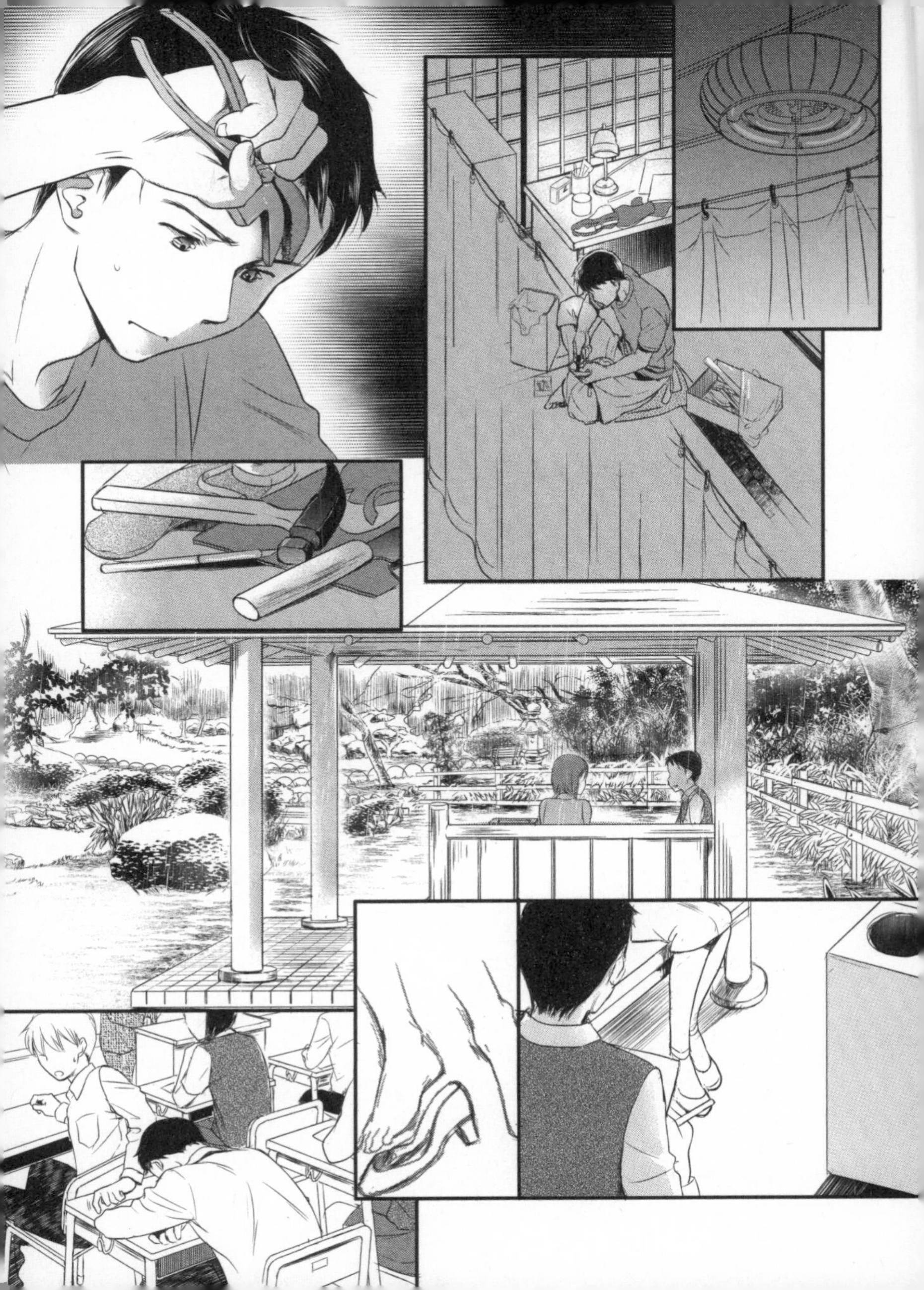

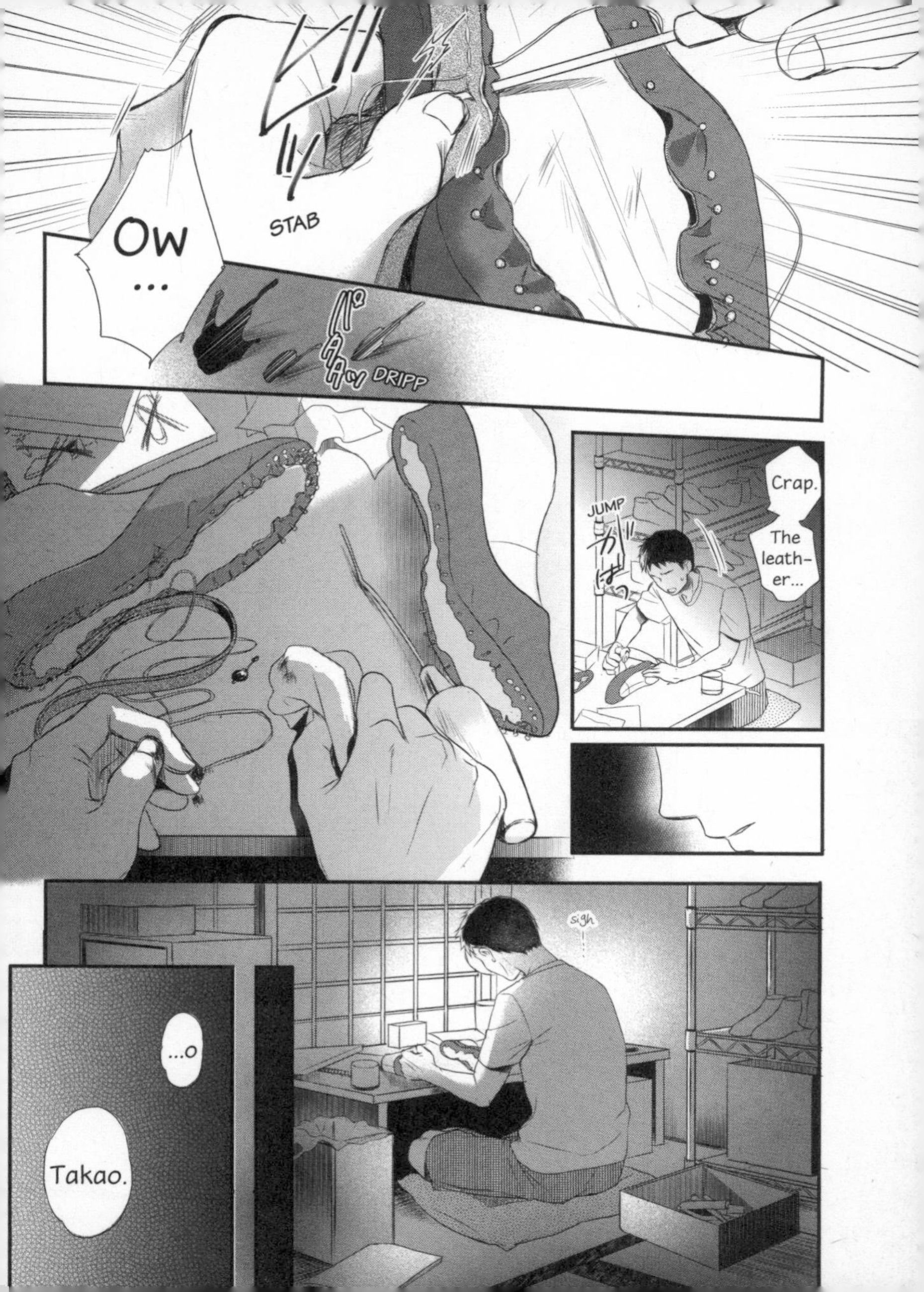
STAB
Ow
...
DRIPP
JUMP
Crap.
The leath-
er...
sigh
...o
Takao.

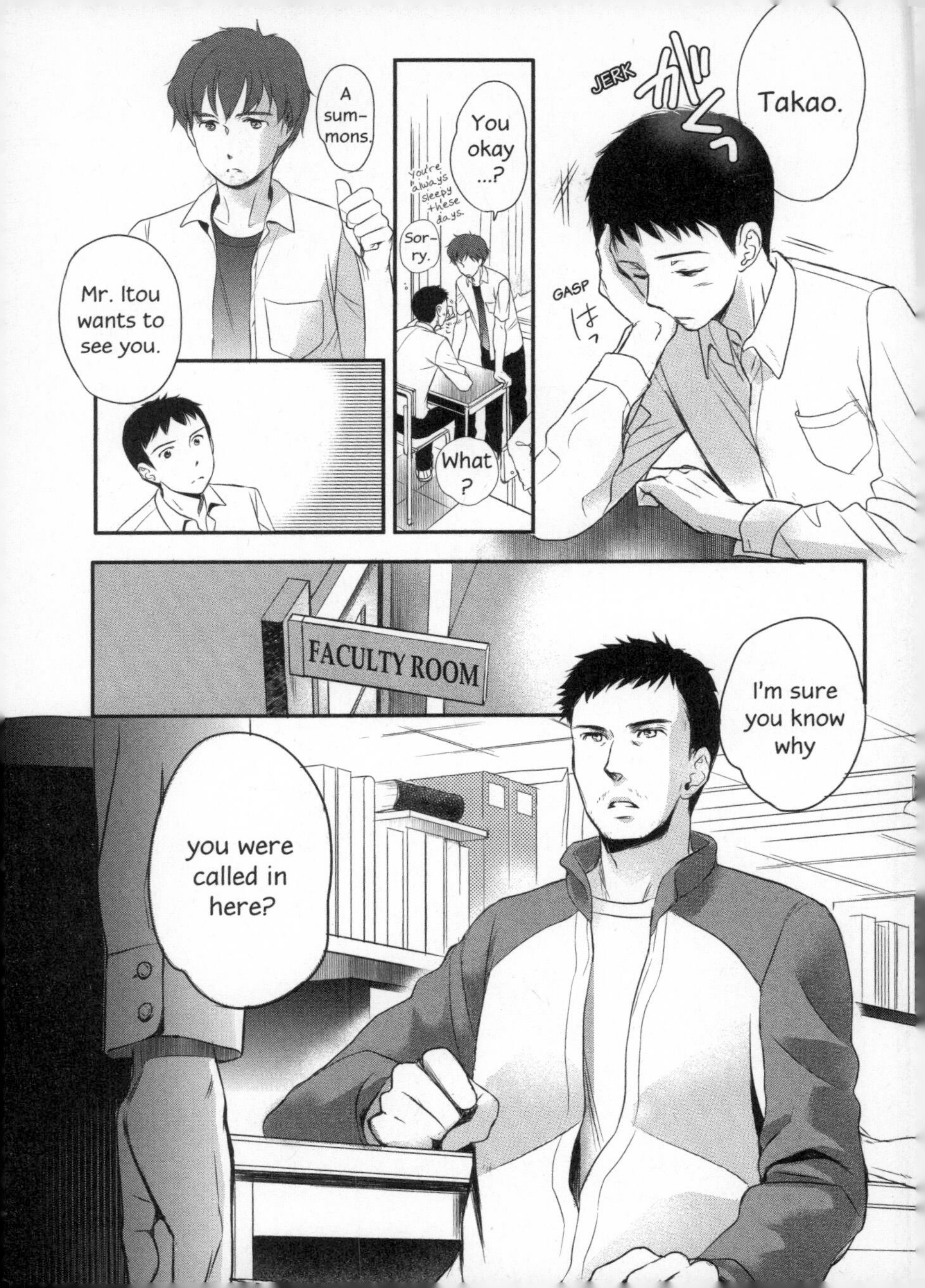

Takao.
JERK
がくっ
GASP
はっ
You okay...?
you're always sleepy these days.
Sorry.
What?
A summons.
Mr. Itou wants to see you.
FACULTY ROOM
I'm sure you know why
you were called in here?

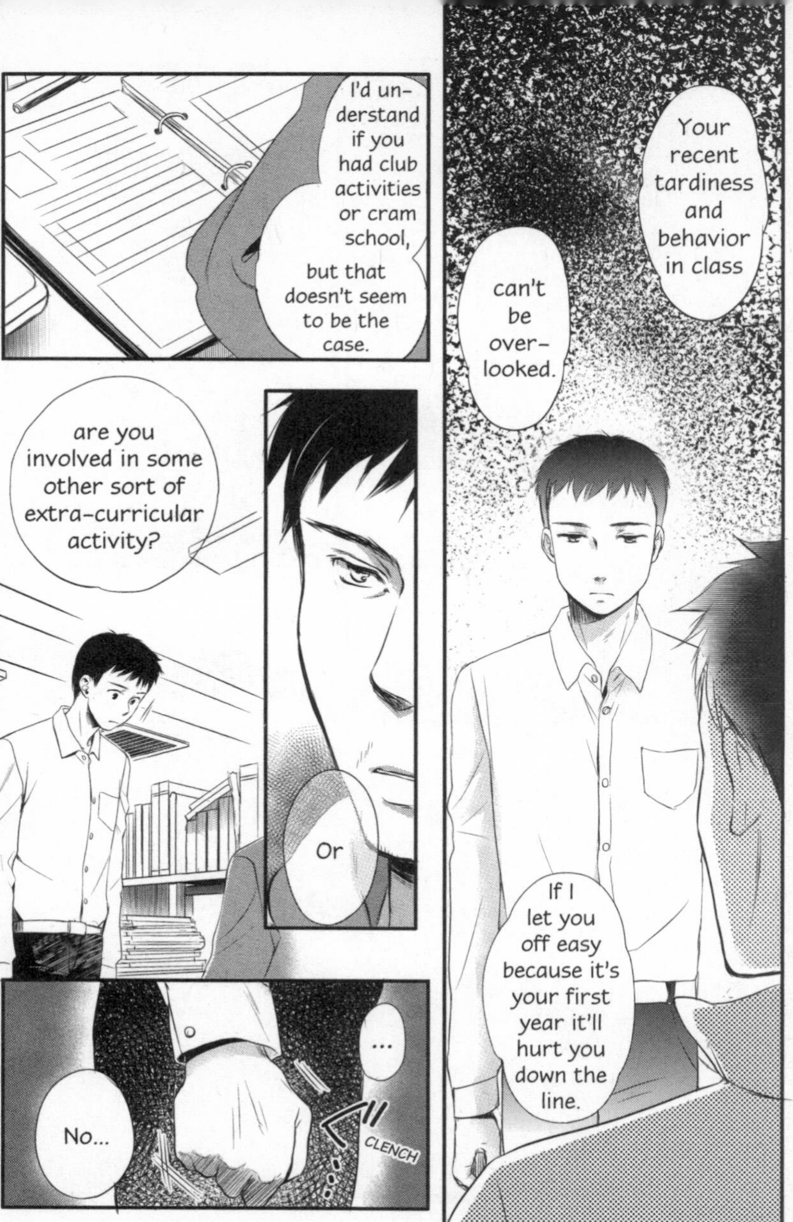
Your recent tardiness and behavior in class
can't be over-looked.
If I let you off easy because it's your first year it'll hurt you down the line.
I'd un-derstand if you had club activities or cram school,
but that doesn't seem to be the case.
Or
are you involved in some other sort of extra-curricular activity?
...
CLENCH
No...

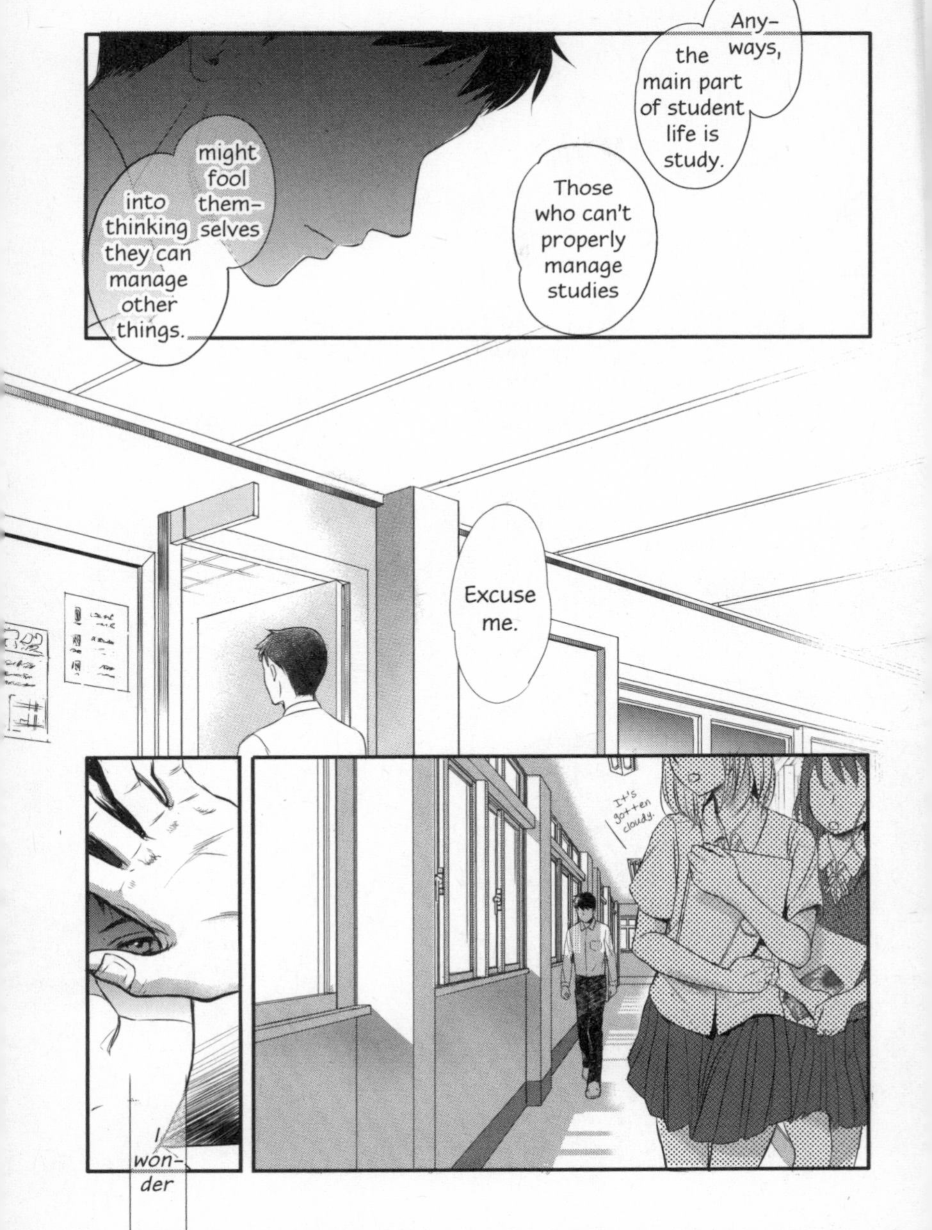
Any-ways, the main part of student life is study.
Those who can't properly manage studies
might fool them-selves into thinking they can manage other things.
Excuse me.
It's gotten cloudy.
I won-der

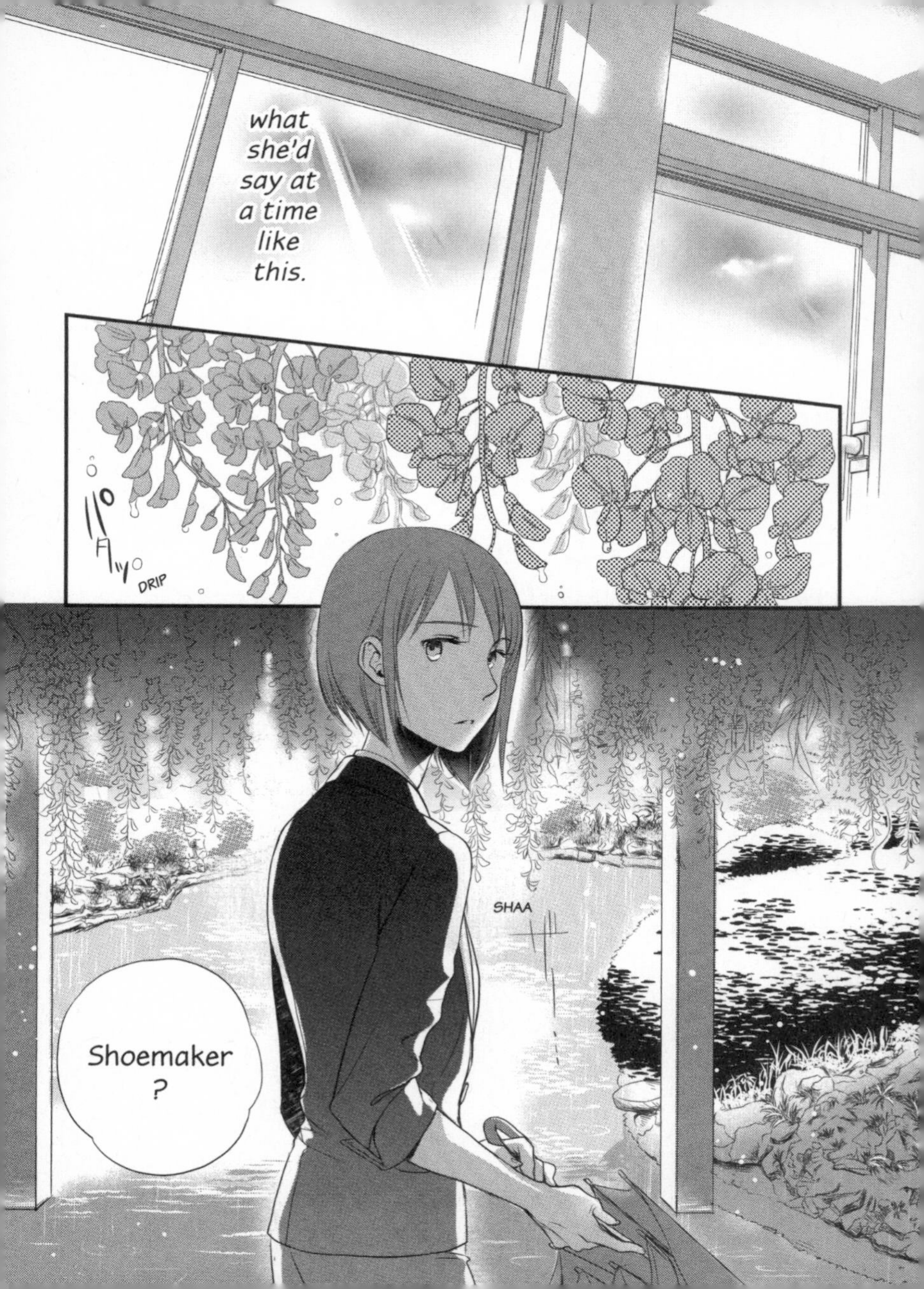
what she'd say at a time like this.
DRIP
SHAA
Shoemaker ?

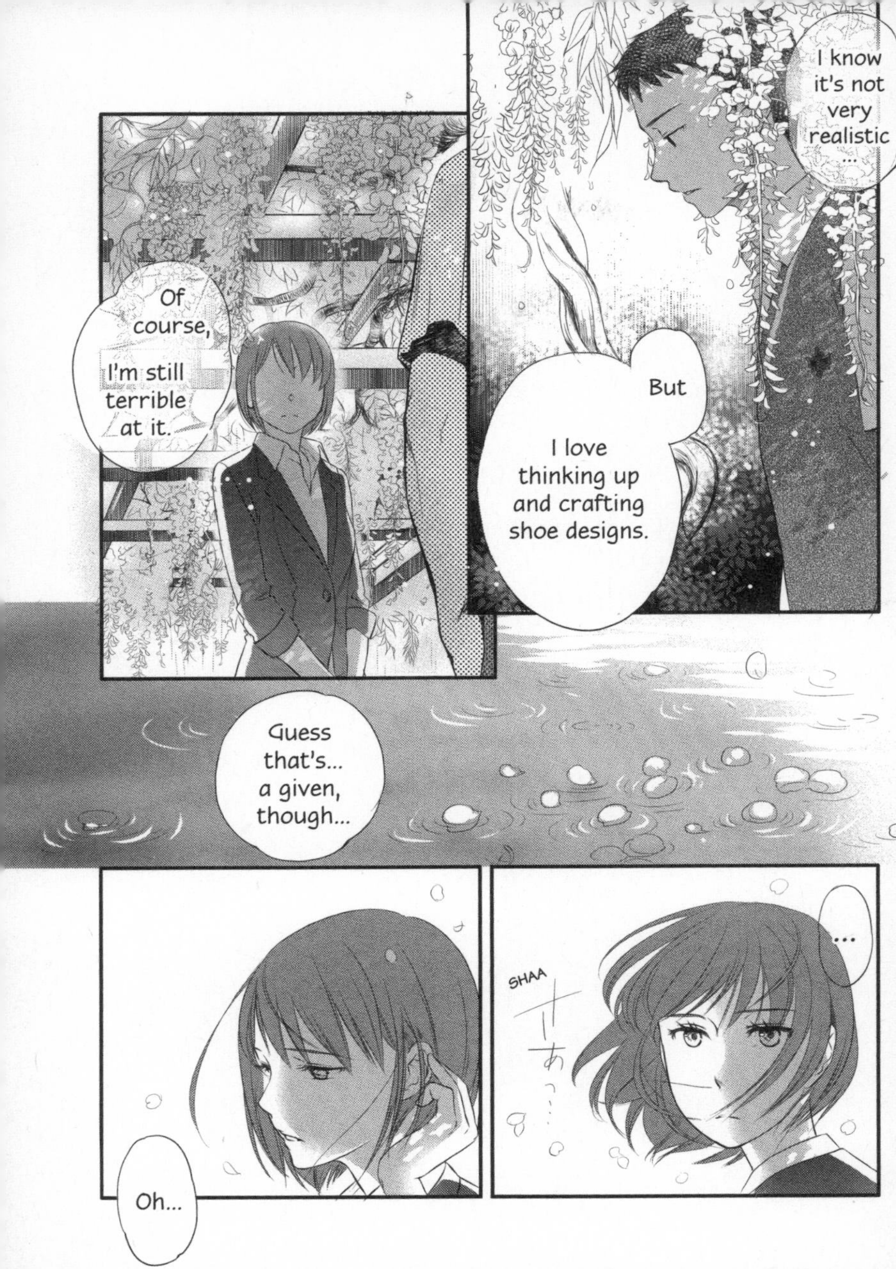
I know it's not very realistic ...
But
I love thinking up and crafting shoe designs.
Of course,
I'm still terrible at it.
Guess that's... a given, though...
...
SHAA
Oh...

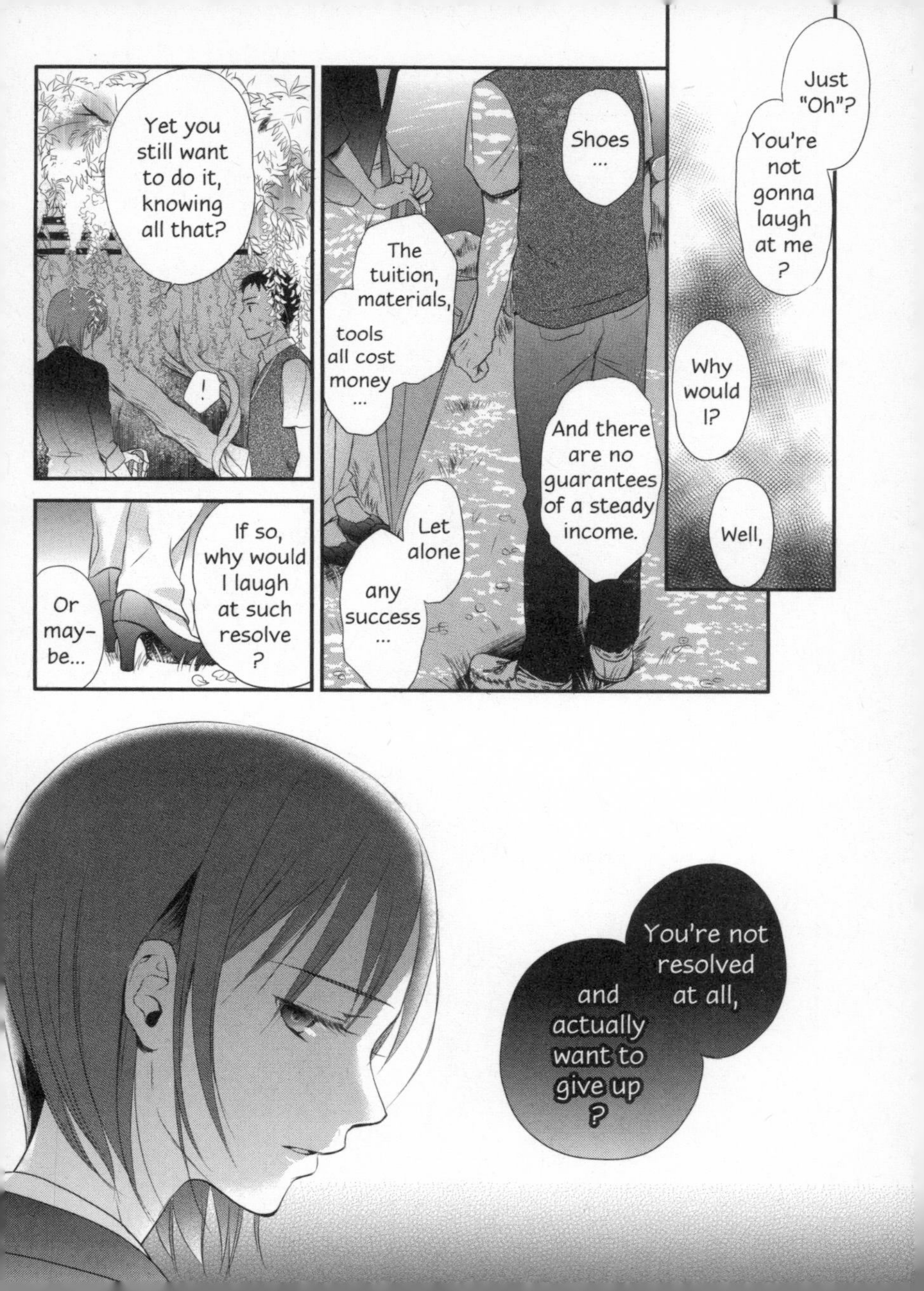
Just "Oh"?
You're not gonna laugh at me ?
Why would I?
Well,
Shoes ...
The tuition, materials,
tools all cost money ...
And there are no guarantees of a steady income.
Let alone
any success ...
Yet you still want to do it, knowing all that?
!
If so, why would I laugh at such resolve ?
Or may-be...
You're not resolved at all,
and actually want to give up ?

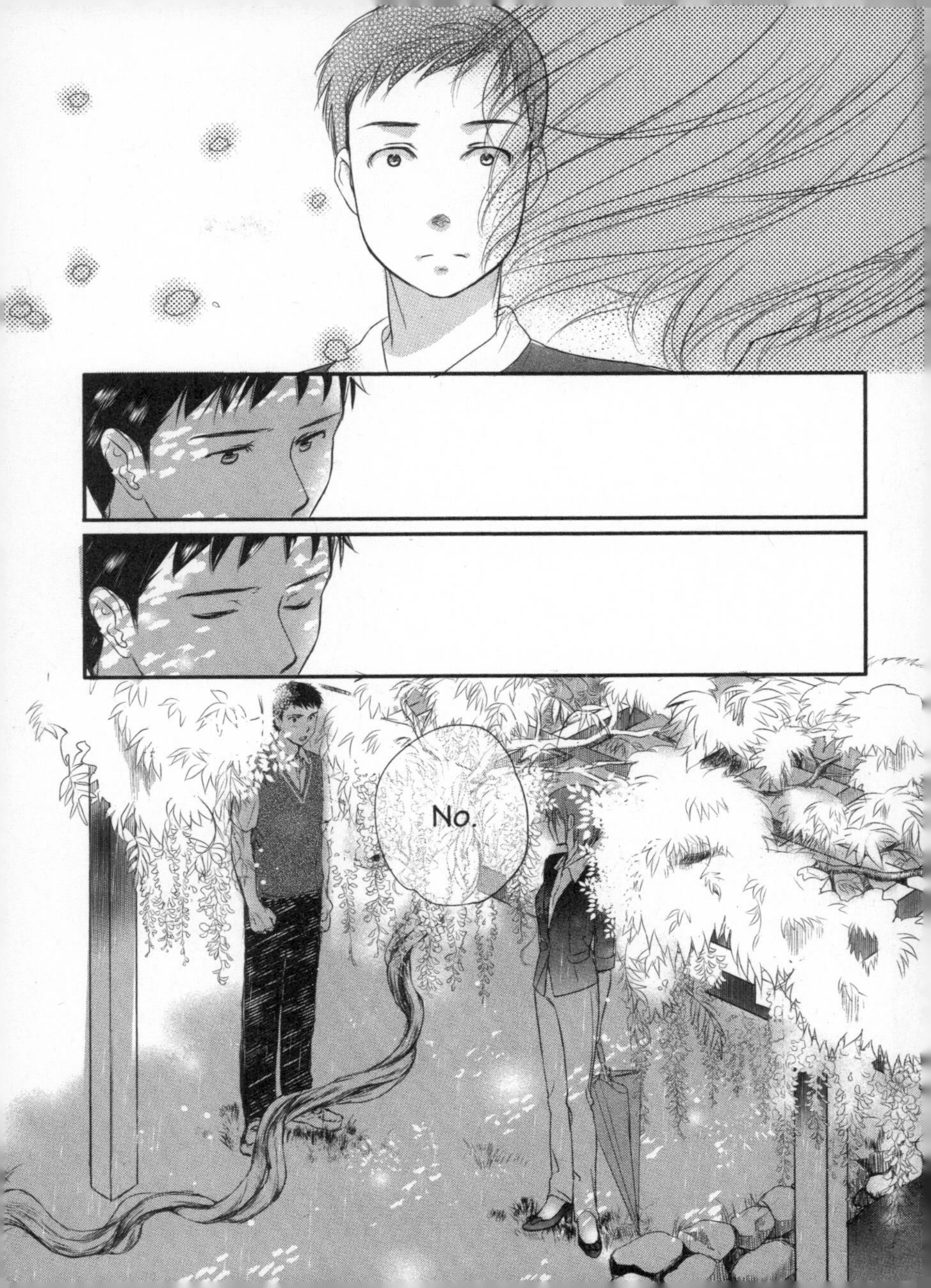
No.

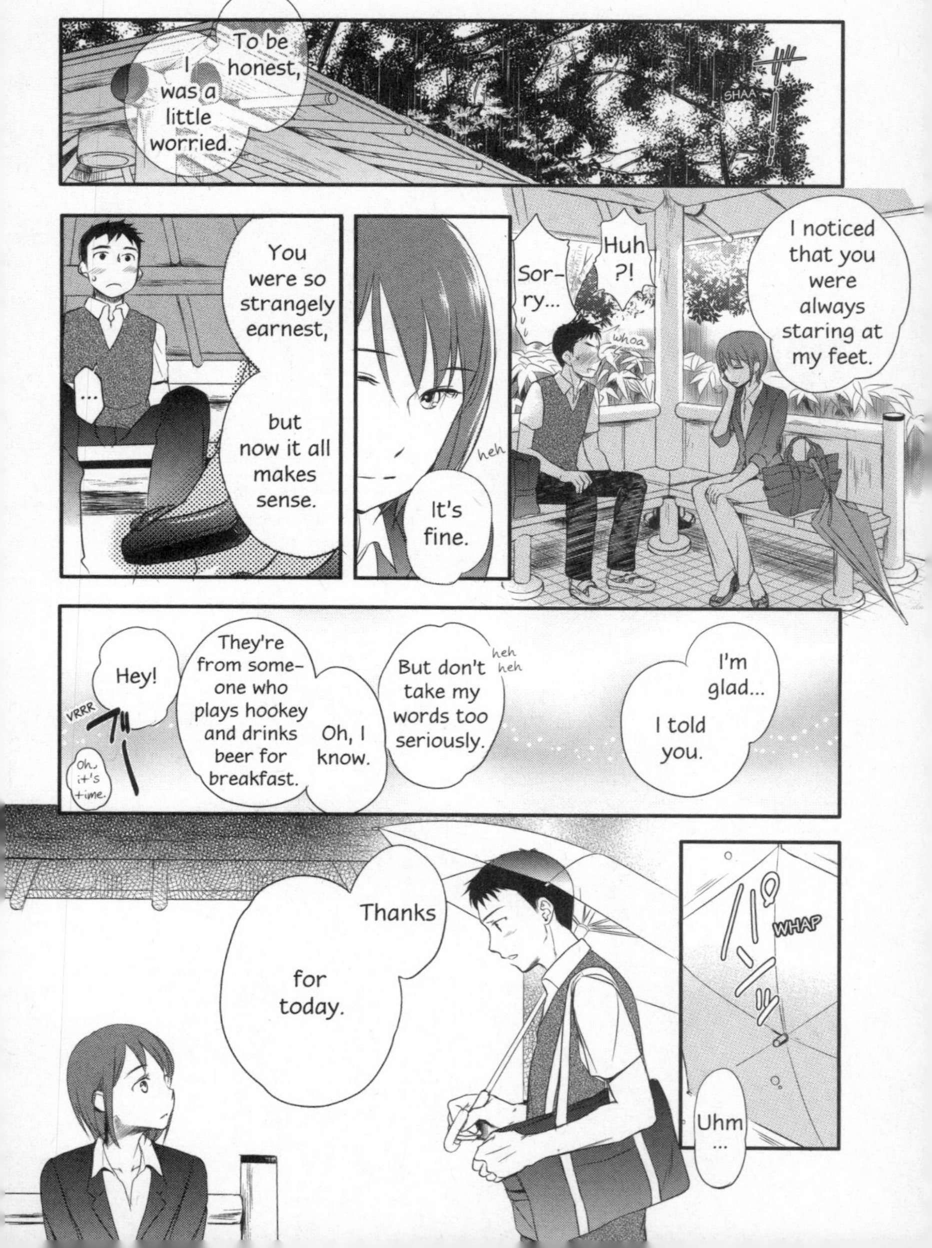
To be honest, I was a little worried.
SHAA
I noticed that you were always staring at my feet.
Huh ?!
Sor-ry...
whoa
heh
It's fine.
You were so strangely earnest,
but now it all makes sense.
...
I'm glad... I told you.
heh heh
But don't take my words too seriously.
Oh, I know.
They're from some-one who plays hookey and drinks beer for breakfast.
Hey!
VRRR
Oh, it's time.
WHAP
Uhm ...
Thanks for today.

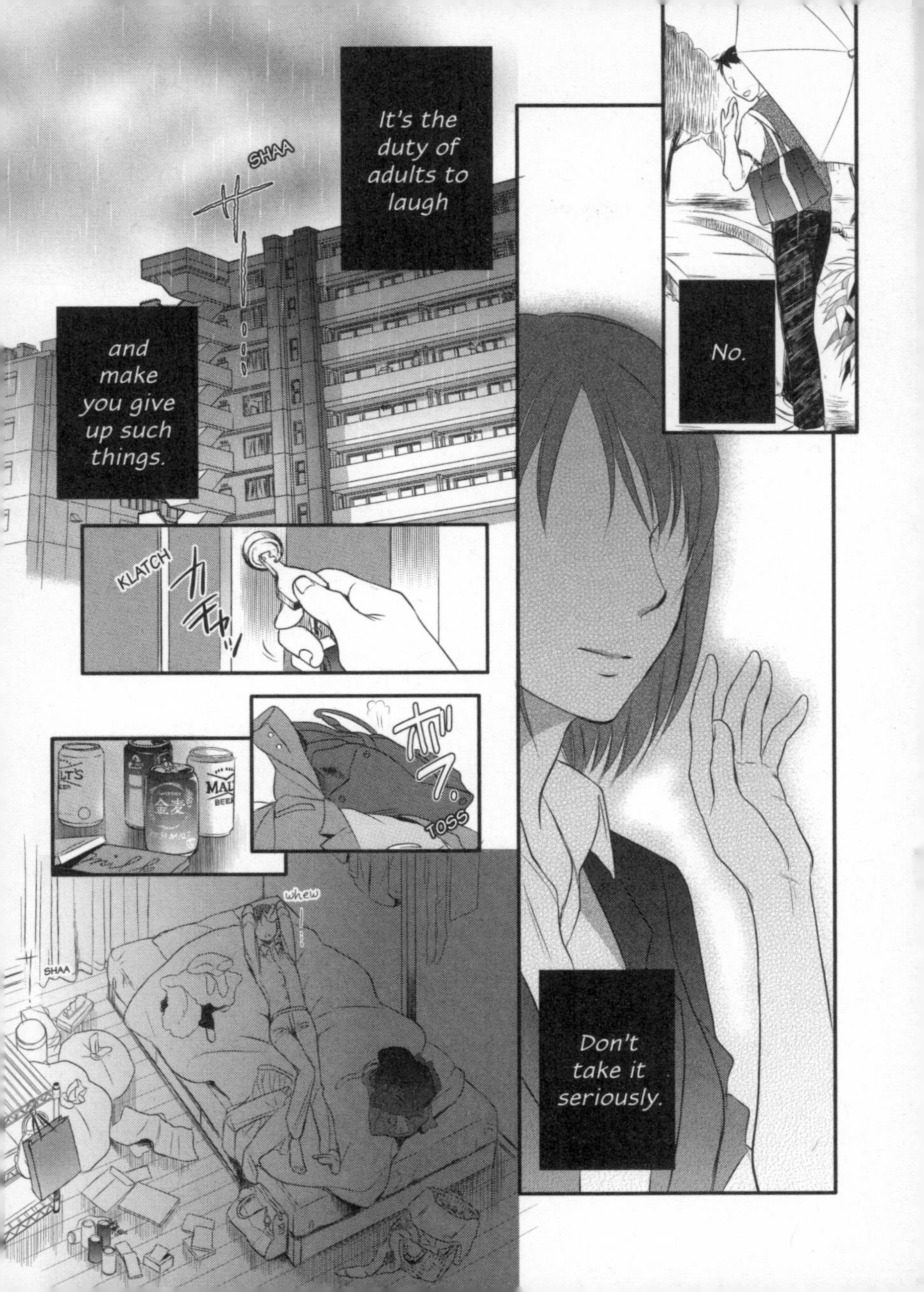
No.
Don't take it seriously.
It's the duty of adults to laugh
SHAA
and make you give up such things.
KLATCH
TOSS
whew
SHAA

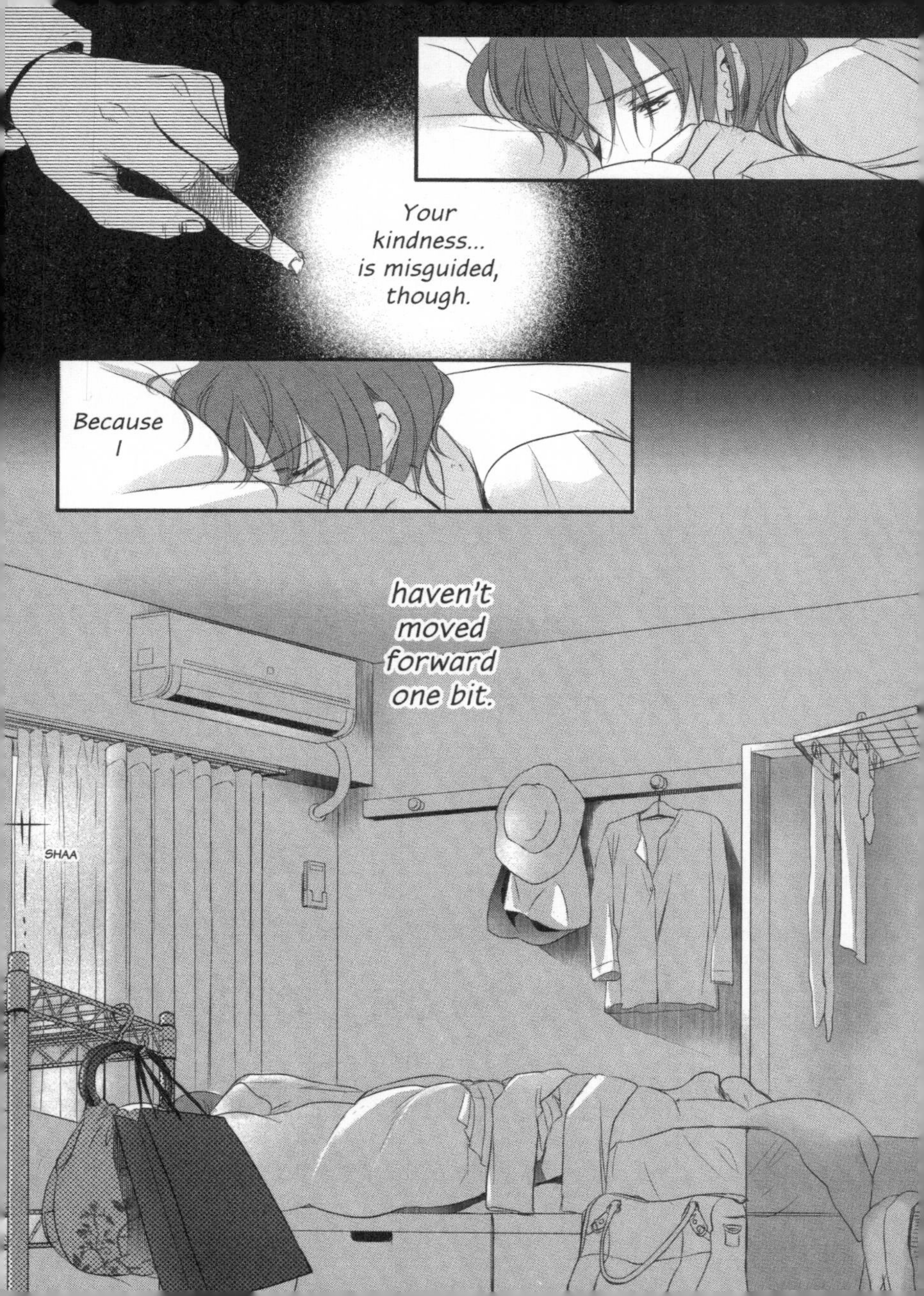
Your kindness... is misguided, though.
Because I
haven't moved forward one bit.
SHAA

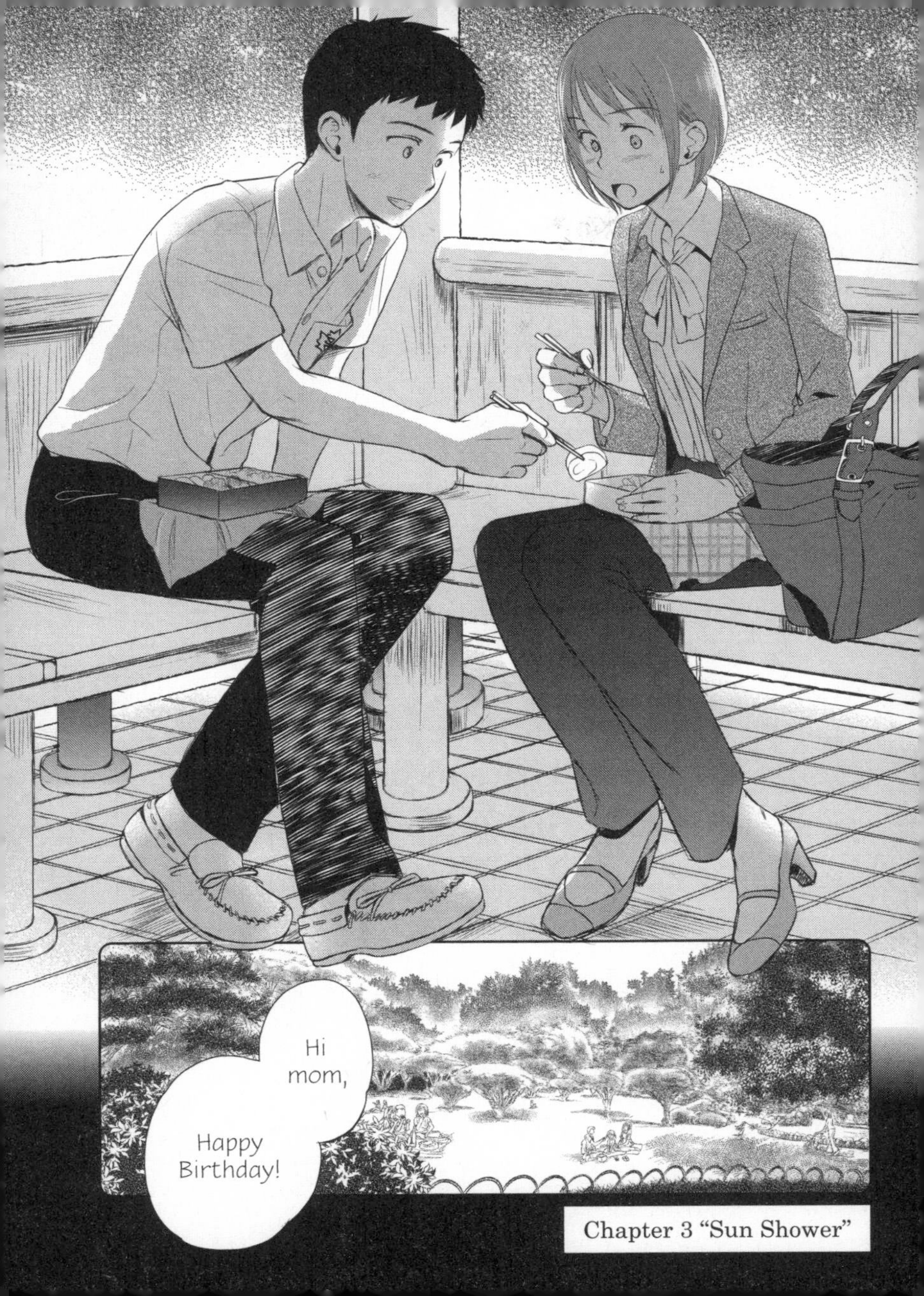
Hi mom,
Happy Birthday!

Chapter 3 "Sun Shower"

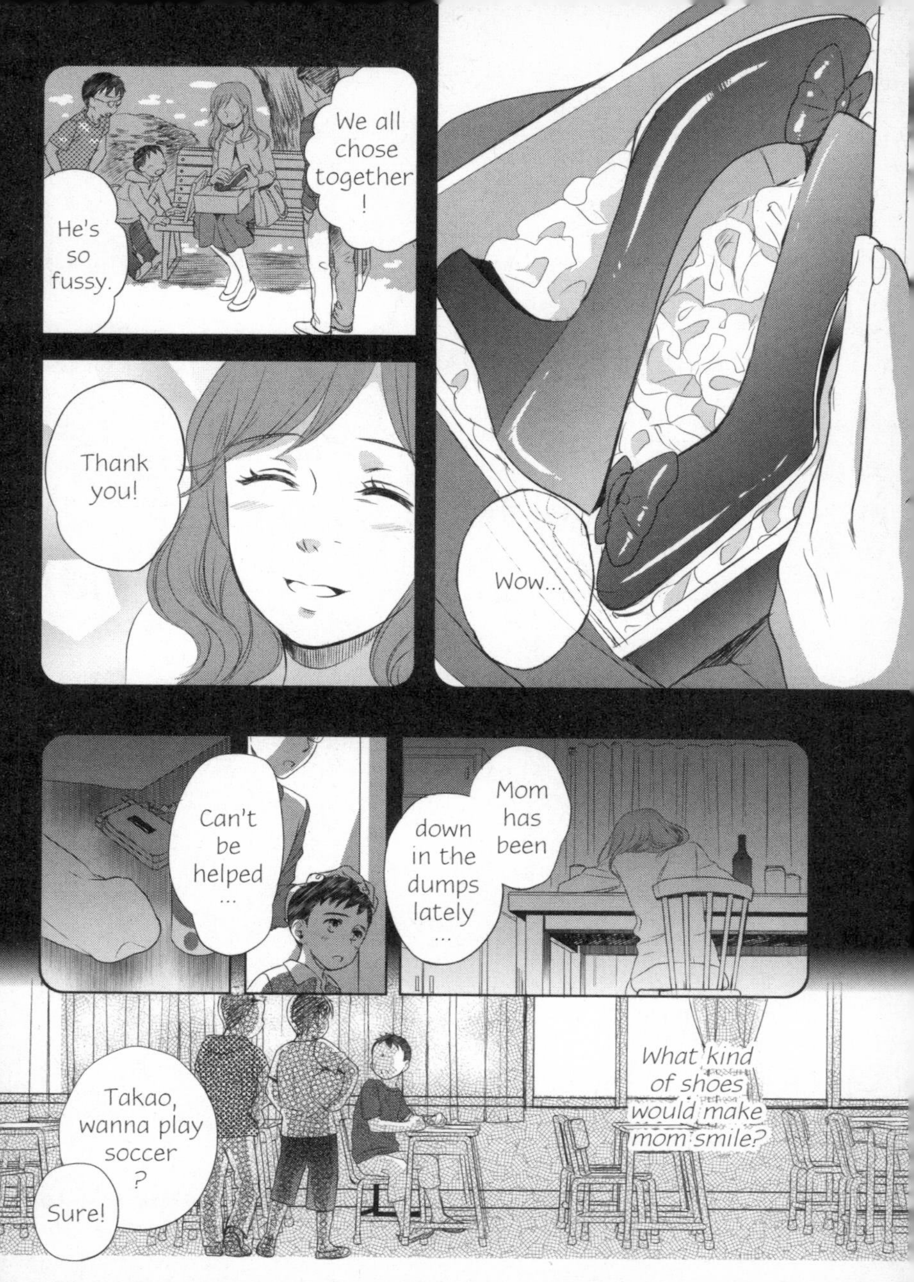
Wow...
We all chose together!
He's so fussy.
Thank you!
Mom has been down in the dumps lately...
Can't be helped...
What kind of shoes would make mom smile?
Takao, wanna play soccer?
Sure!

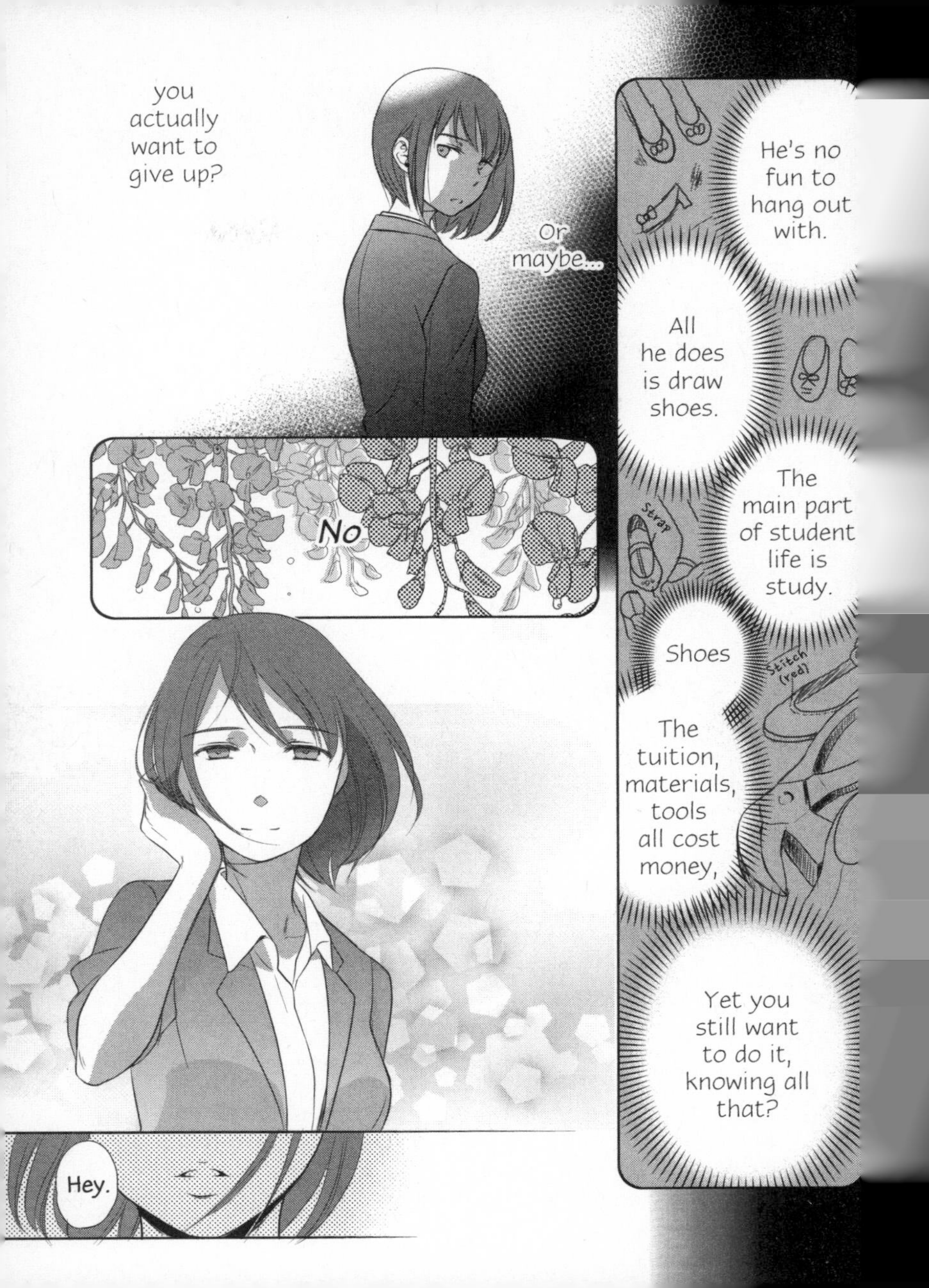
He's no fun to hang out with.
All he does is draw shoes.
Strap
The main part of student life is study.
Shoes
Stitch (red)
The tuition, materials, tools all cost money,
Yet you still want to do it, knowing all that?
Or maybe...
you actually want to give up?
No
Hey.

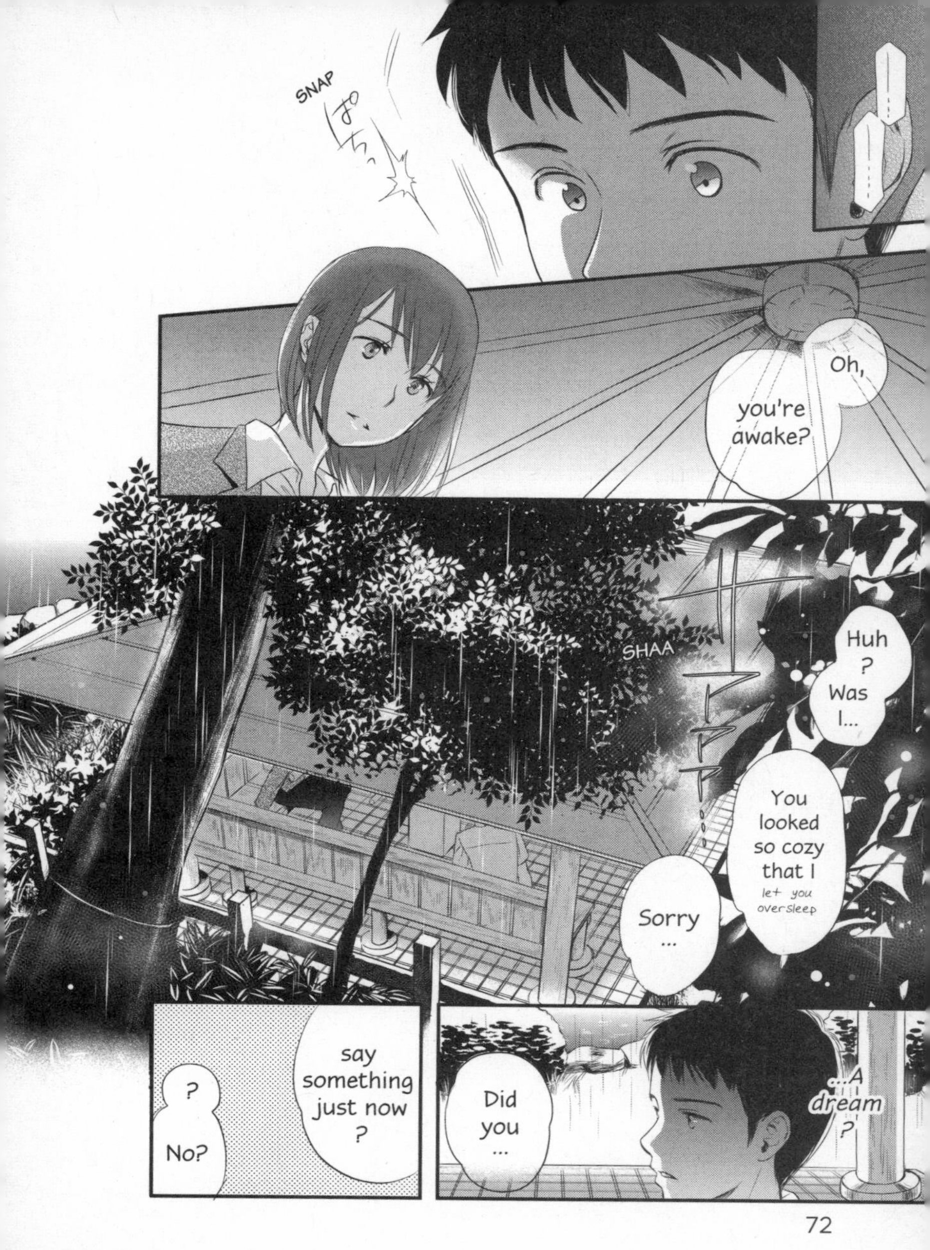
SNAP
ぱち、
Oh, you're awake?
SHAA
サァァァ…
Huh? Was I...
You looked so cozy that I let you oversleep
Sorry ...
...A dream?
Did you ...
say something just now?
?
No?

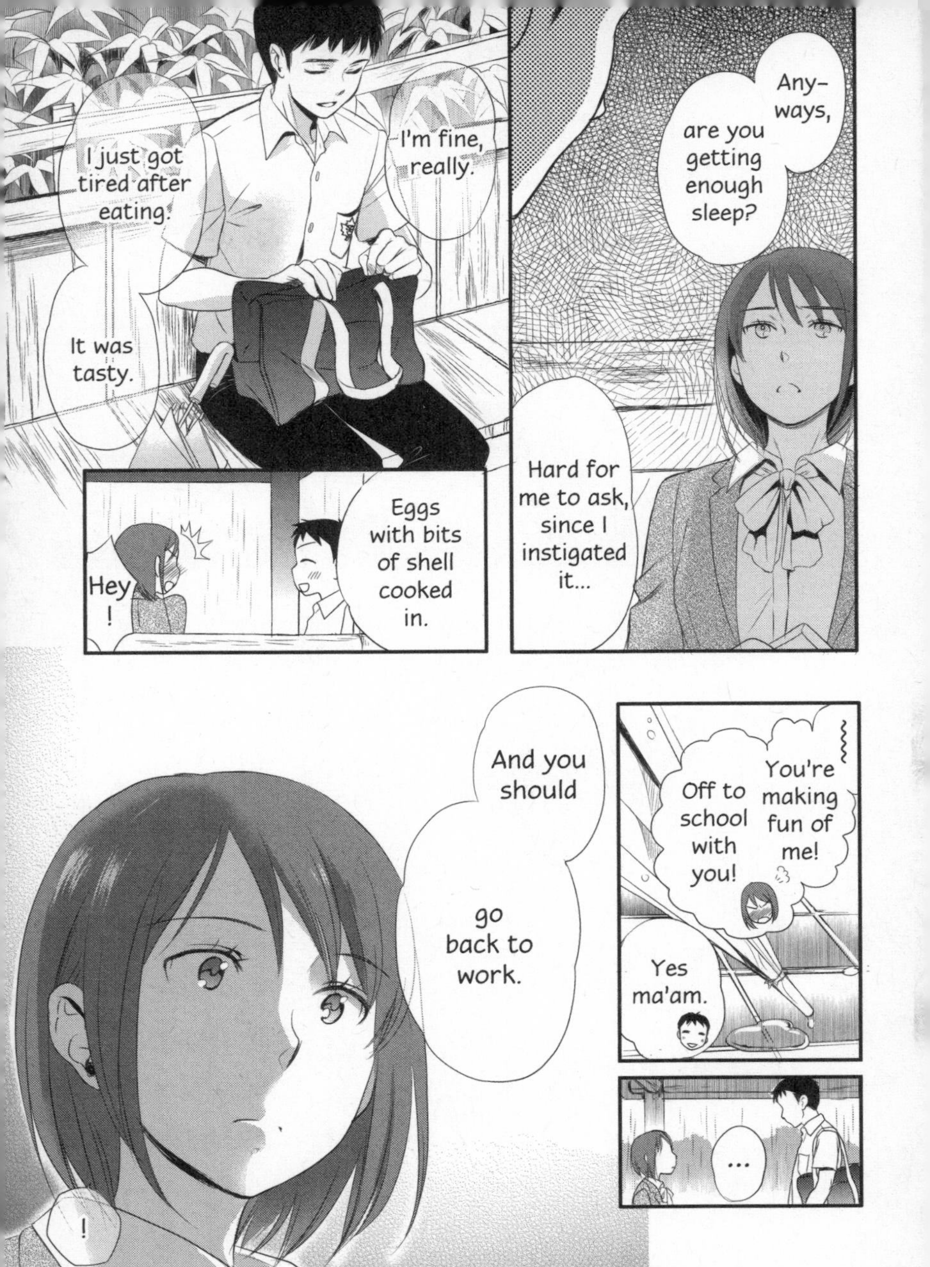
Any-ways,
are you getting enough sleep?
Hard for me to ask, since I instigated it...
I'm fine, really.
I just got tired after eating.
It was tasty.
Eggs with bits of shell cooked in.
Hey!
You're making fun of me!
Off to school with you!
Yes ma'am.
...
And you should
go back to work.
!

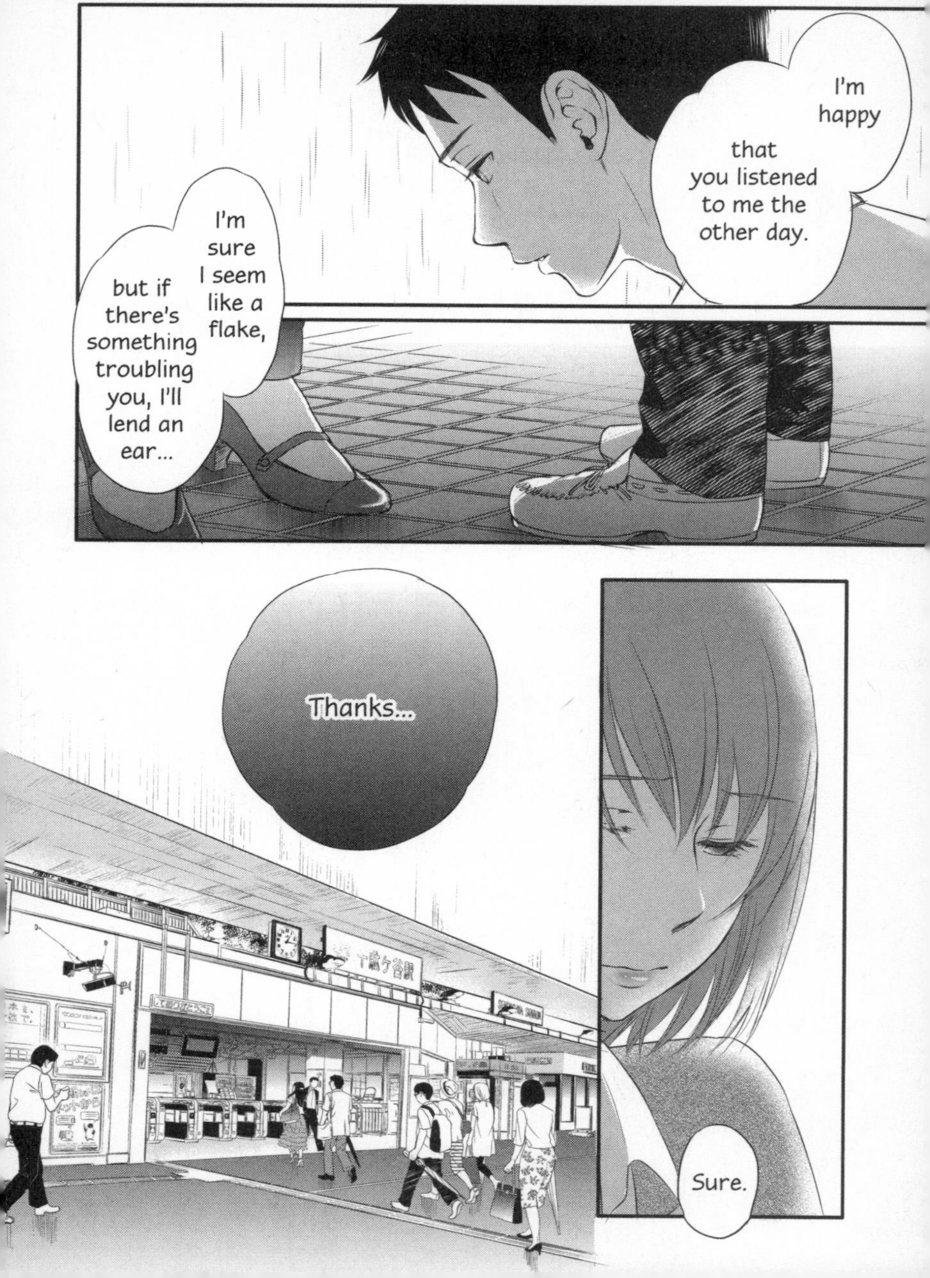
I'm happy that you listened to me the other day.
I'm sure I seem like a flake, but if there's something troubling you, I'll lend an ear...
Sure.
Thanks...

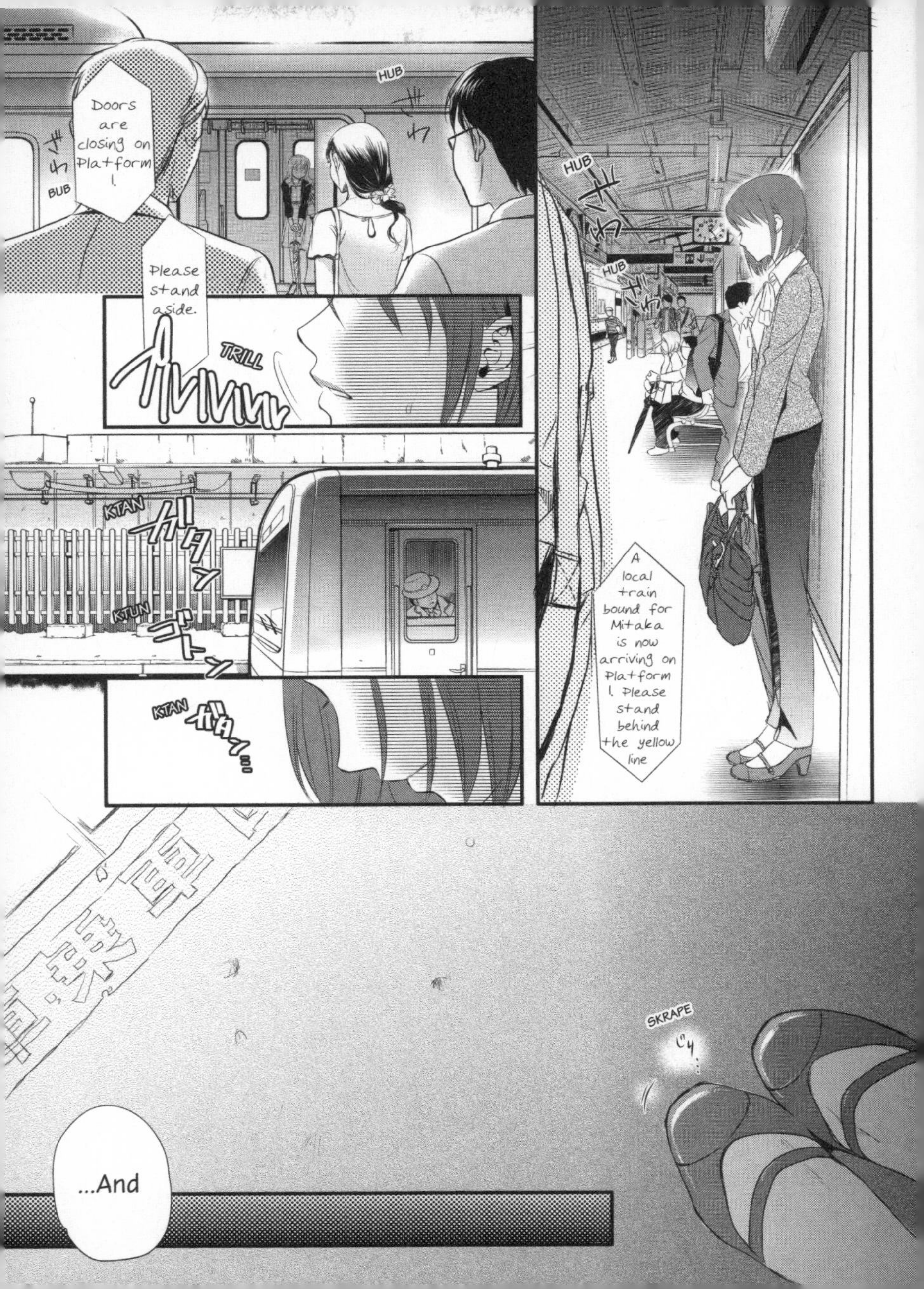
HUB
HUB
A local train bound for Mitaka is now arriving on Platform 1. Please stand behind the yellow line
HUB
Doors are closing on Platform 1.
BUB
Please stand aside.
TRILL
KTAN
KTUN
KTAN
SKRAPE
...And

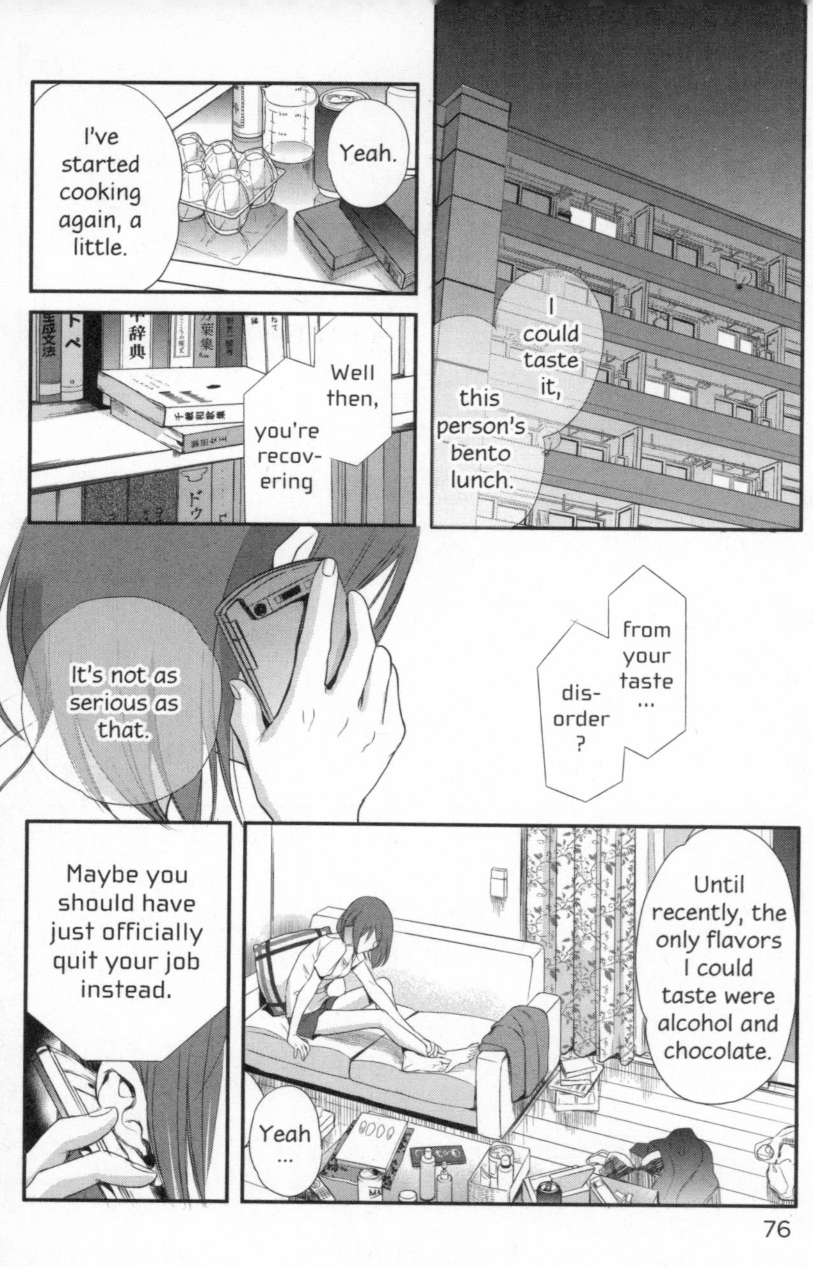
I could taste it,
this person's bento lunch.
Yeah.
I've started cooking again, a little.
Well then, you're recovering
from your taste ...
dis-order ?
It's not as serious as that.
Until recently, the only flavors I could taste were alcohol and chocolate.
Yeah ...
Maybe you should have just officially quit your job instead.

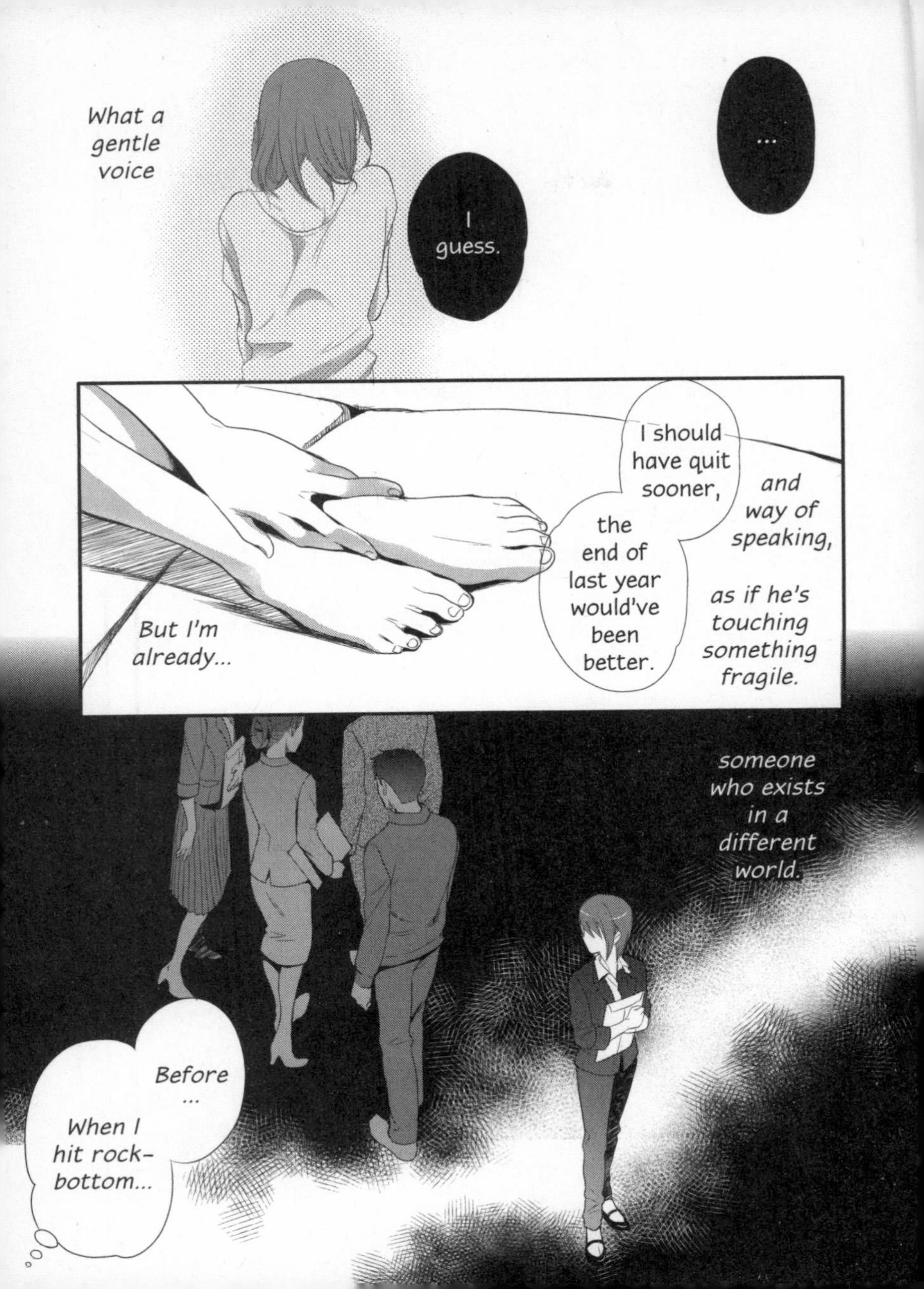
...
I guess.
What a gentle voice
and way of speaking,
as if he's touching something fragile.
I should have quit sooner,
the end of last year would've been better.
But I'm already...
someone who exists in a different world.
Before ...
When I hit rock-bottom...

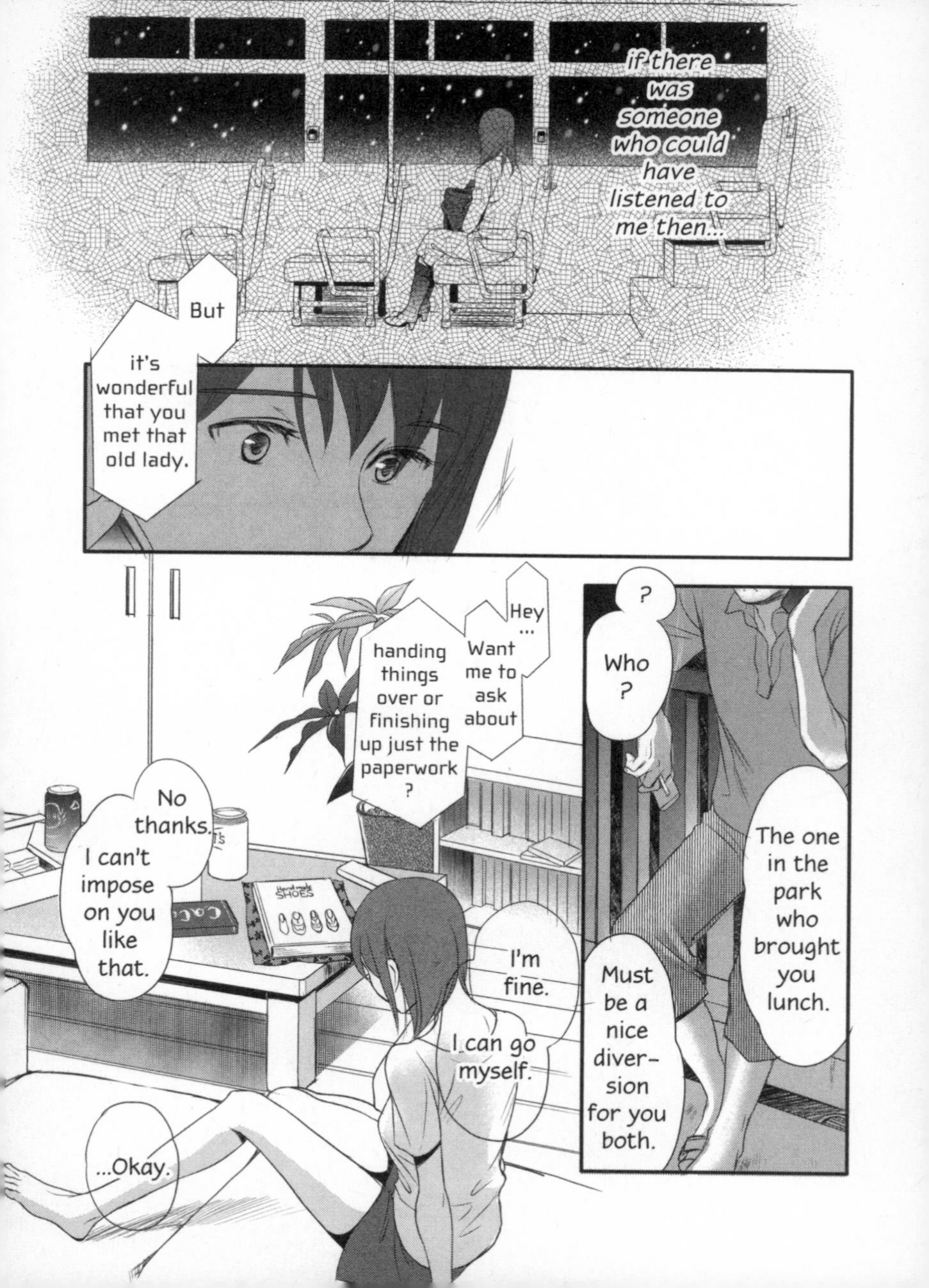
if there was someone who could have listened to me then...
But
it's wonderful that you met that old lady.
?
Who ?
The one in the park who brought you lunch.
Must be a nice diversion for you both.
Hey ...
Want me to ask about handing things over or finishing up just the paperwork ?
No thanks.
I can't impose on you like that.
I'm fine.
I can go myself.
...Okay.
Handmade SHOES

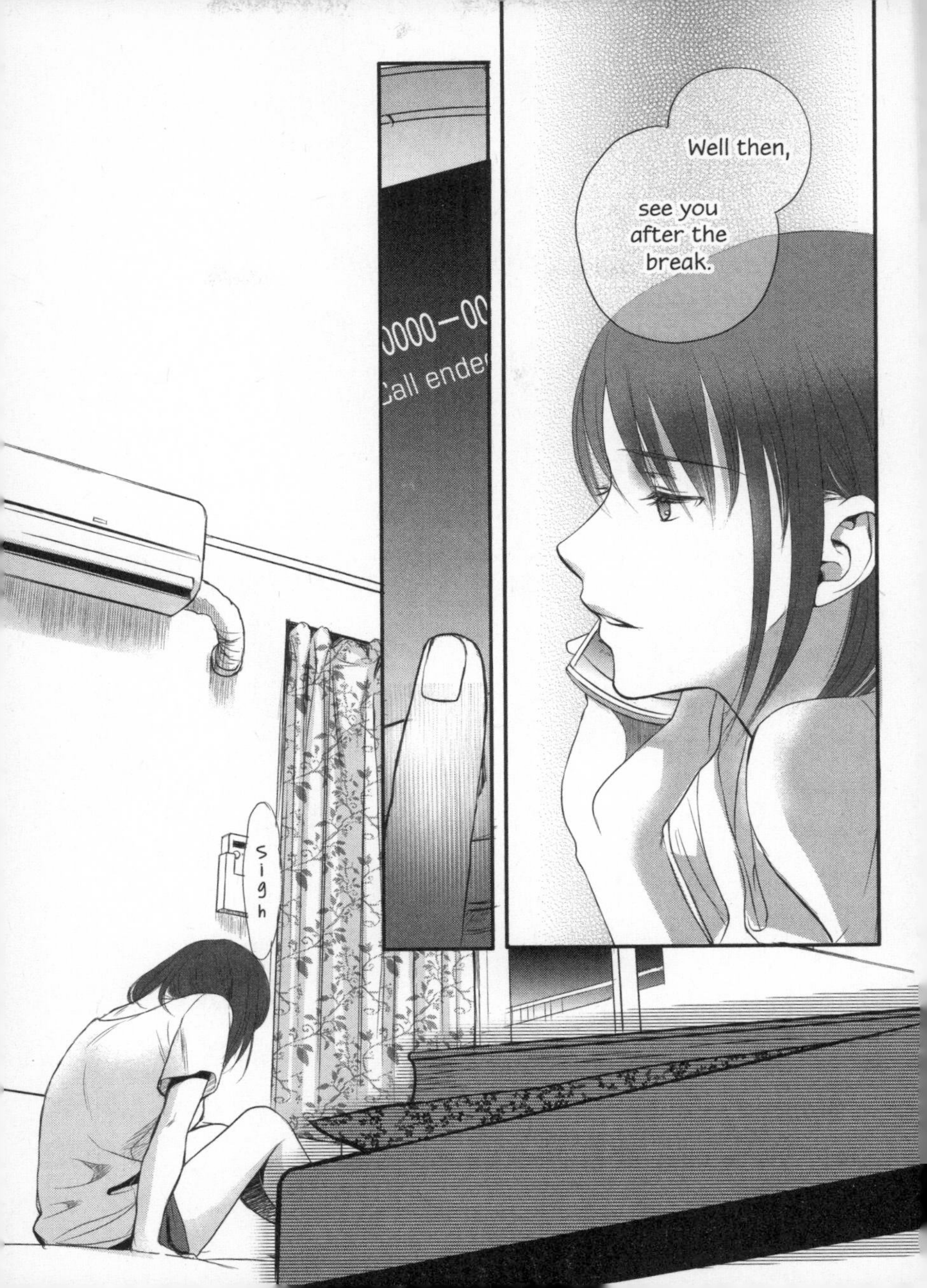
Well then,
see you after the break.
Sigh

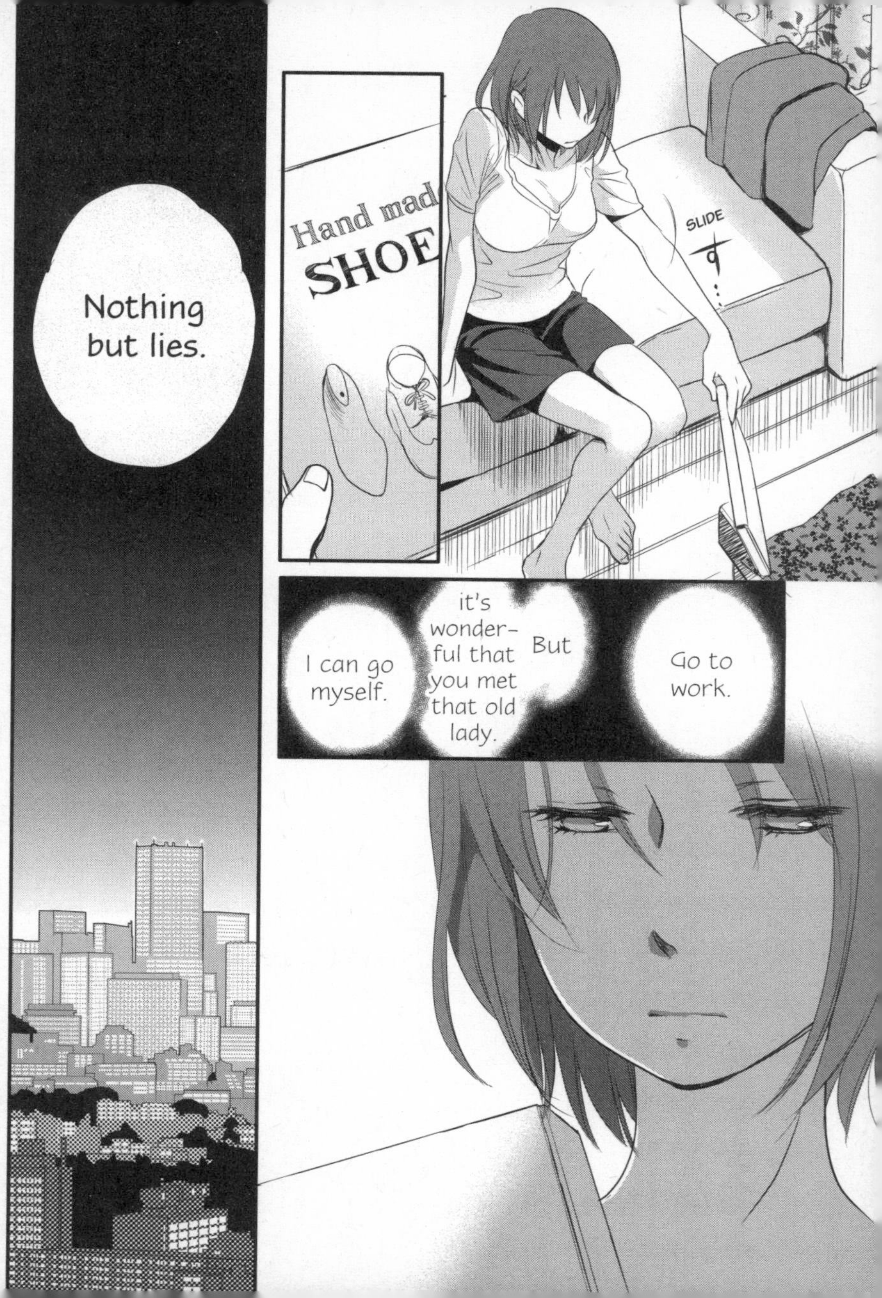
SLIDE
す
Hand mad
SHOE
Go to work.
But
it's wonderful that you met that old lady.
I can go myself.
Nothing but lies.

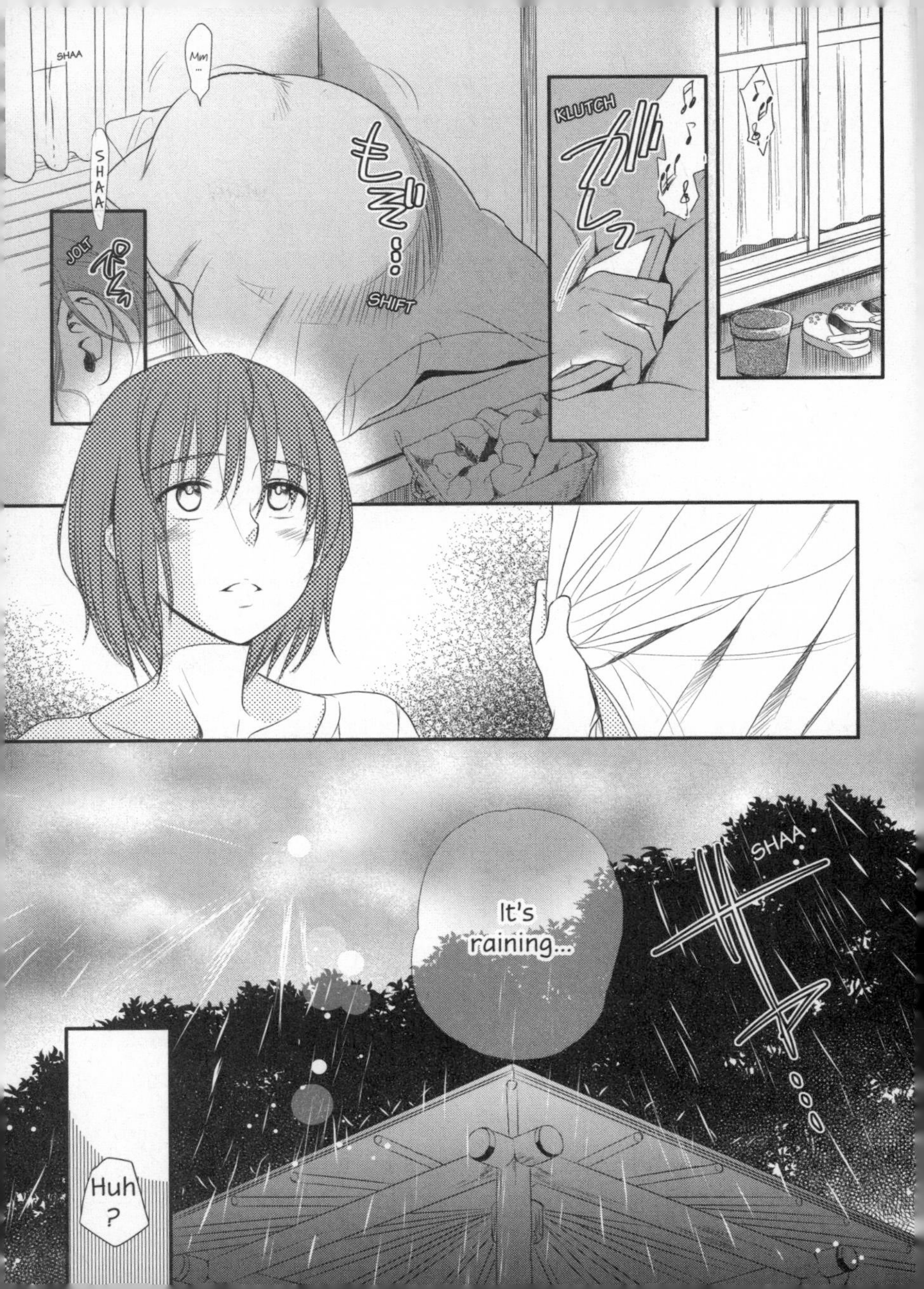
KLUTCH
Mm...
SHAA
SHAA
SHIFT
JOLT
SHAA
It's raining...
Huh?

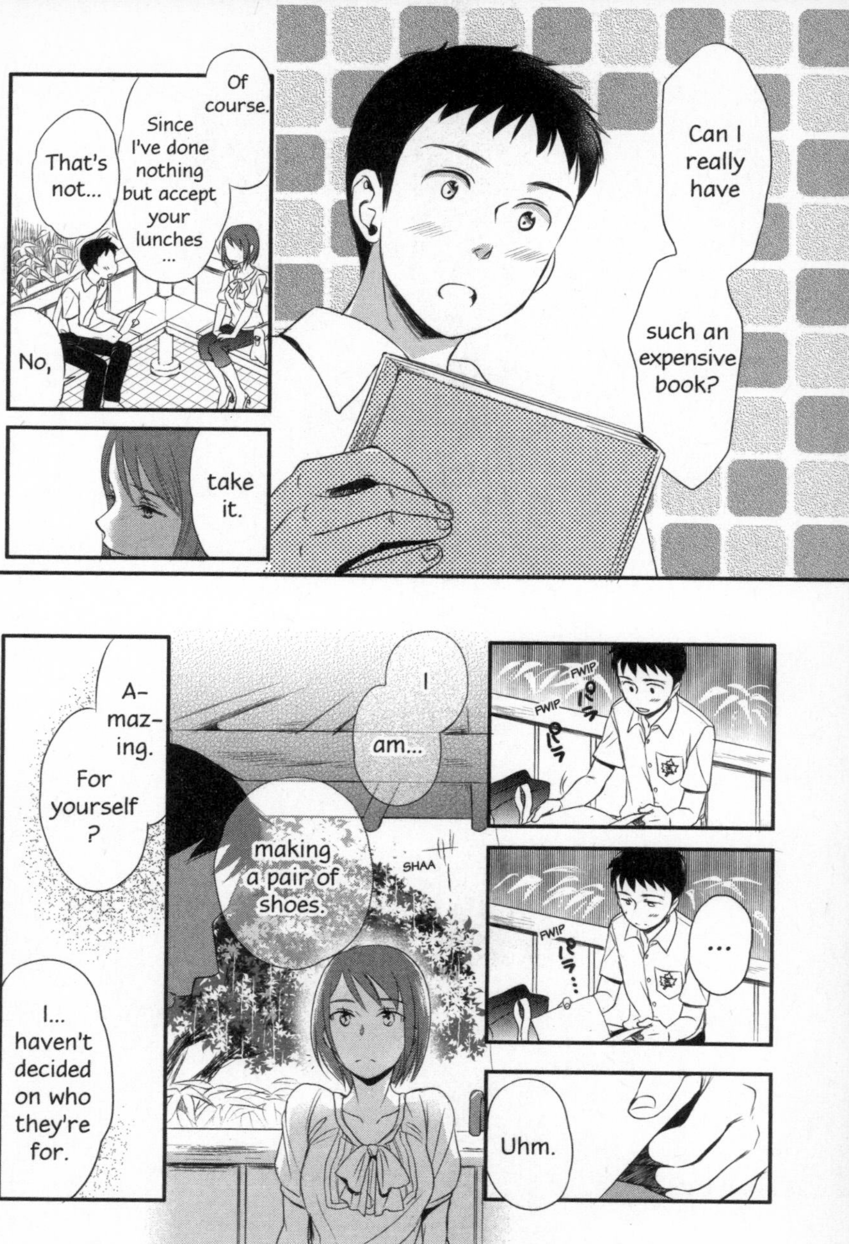
Can I really have such an expensive book?
Of course.
Since I've done nothing but accept your lunches ...
That's not...
No,
take it.
FWIP
FWIP
FWIP
...
Uhm.
I am...
making a pair of shoes.
SHAA
A-maz-ing. For yourself ?
I... haven't decided on who they're for.

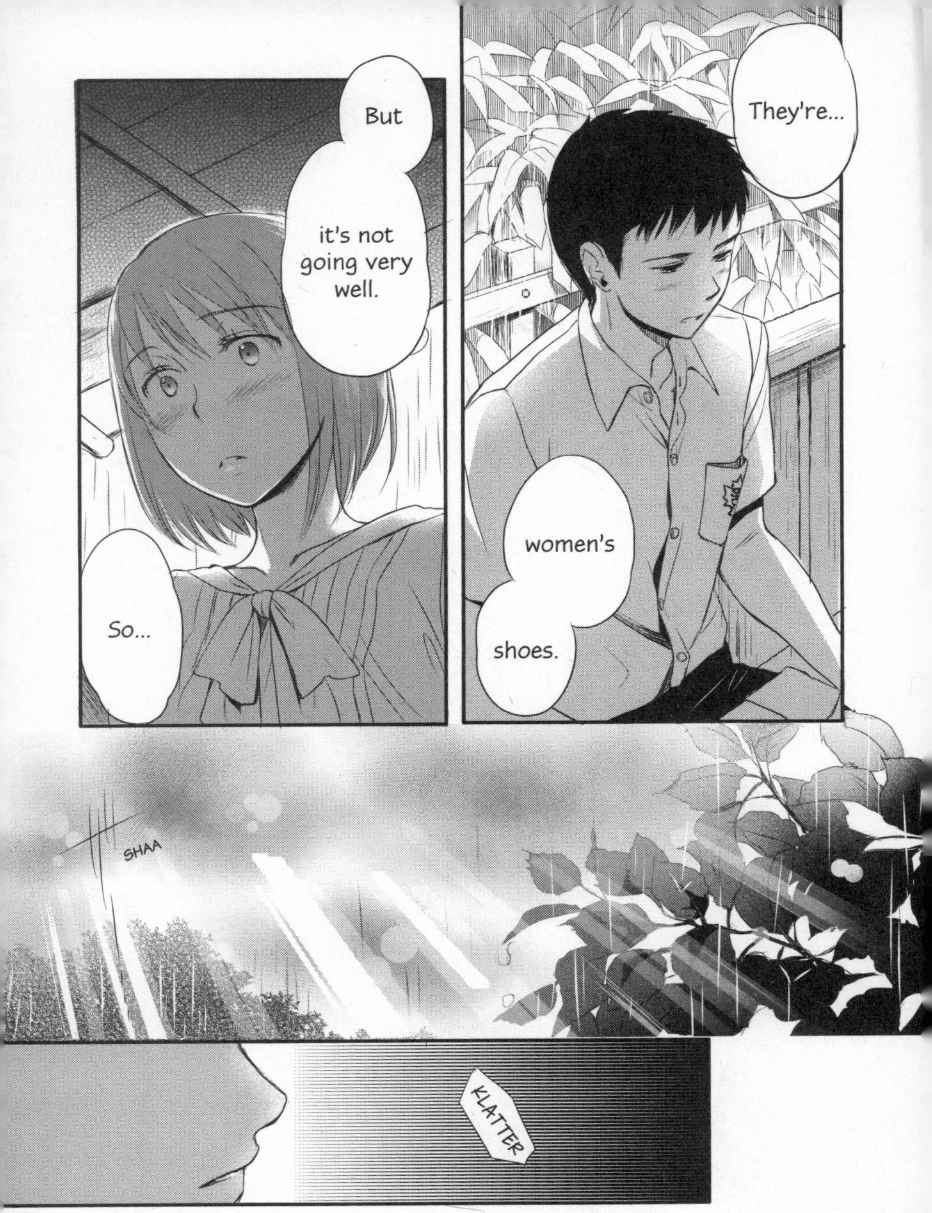
They're...
women's
shoes.
But
it's not going very well.
So...
SHAA
KLATTER

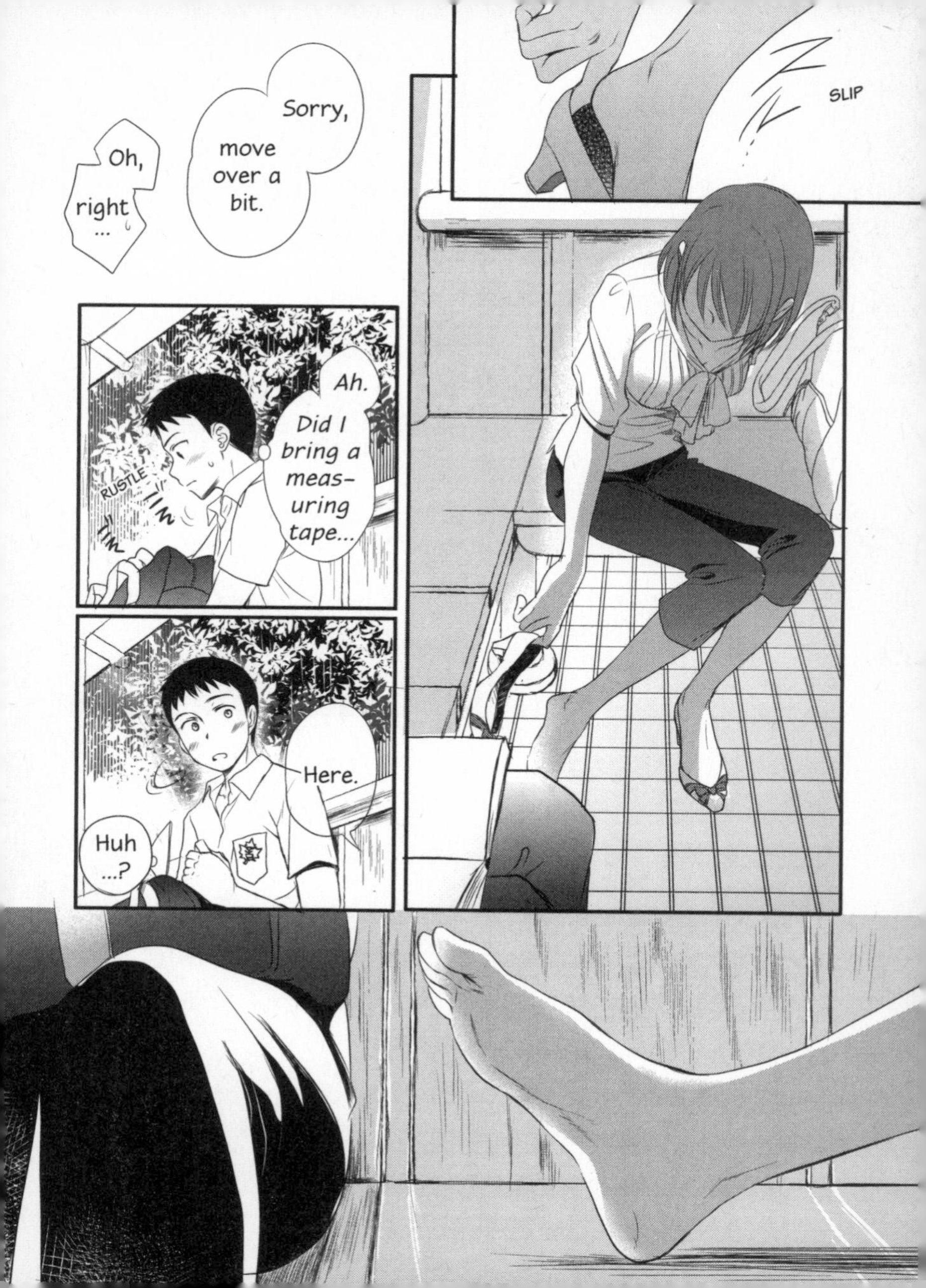
SLIP
Sorry, move over a bit.
Oh, right...
Ah. Did I bring a meas-uring tape...
RUSTLE
Here.
Huh...?

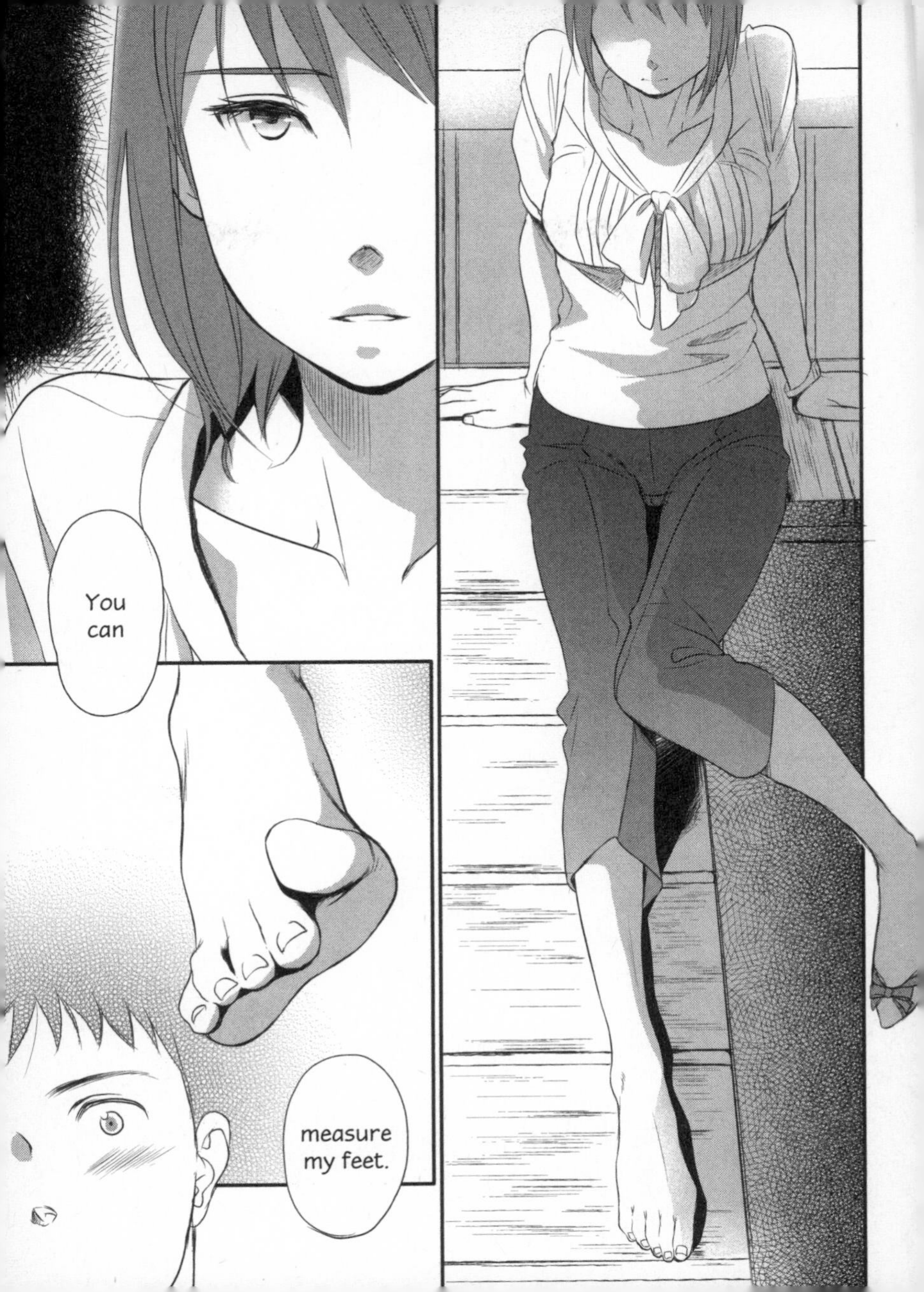
You can
measure my feet.

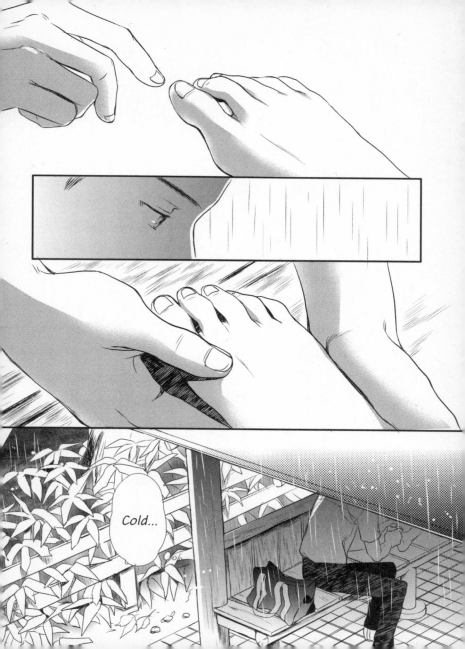

Cold...

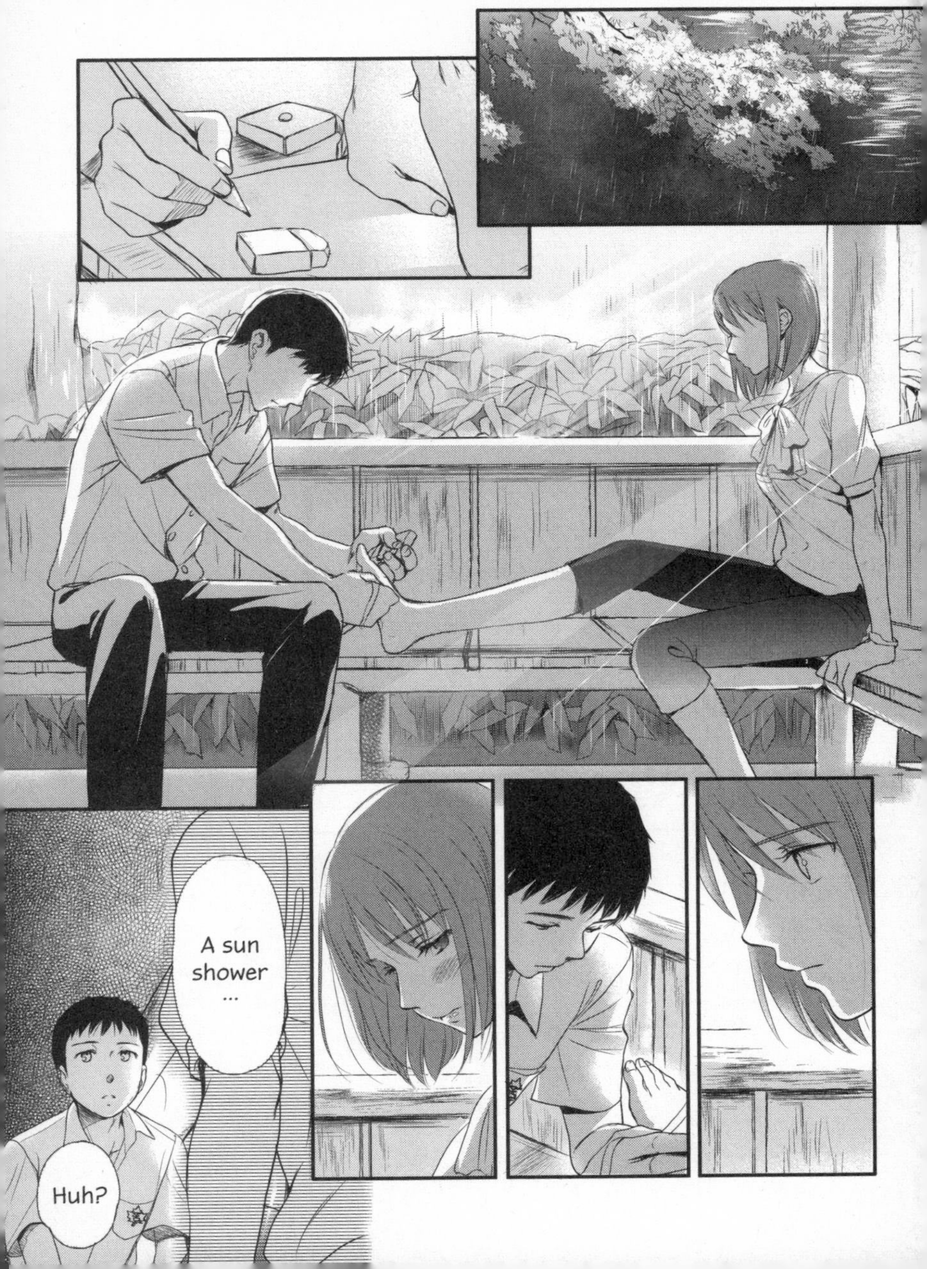
A sun shower ...
Huh?

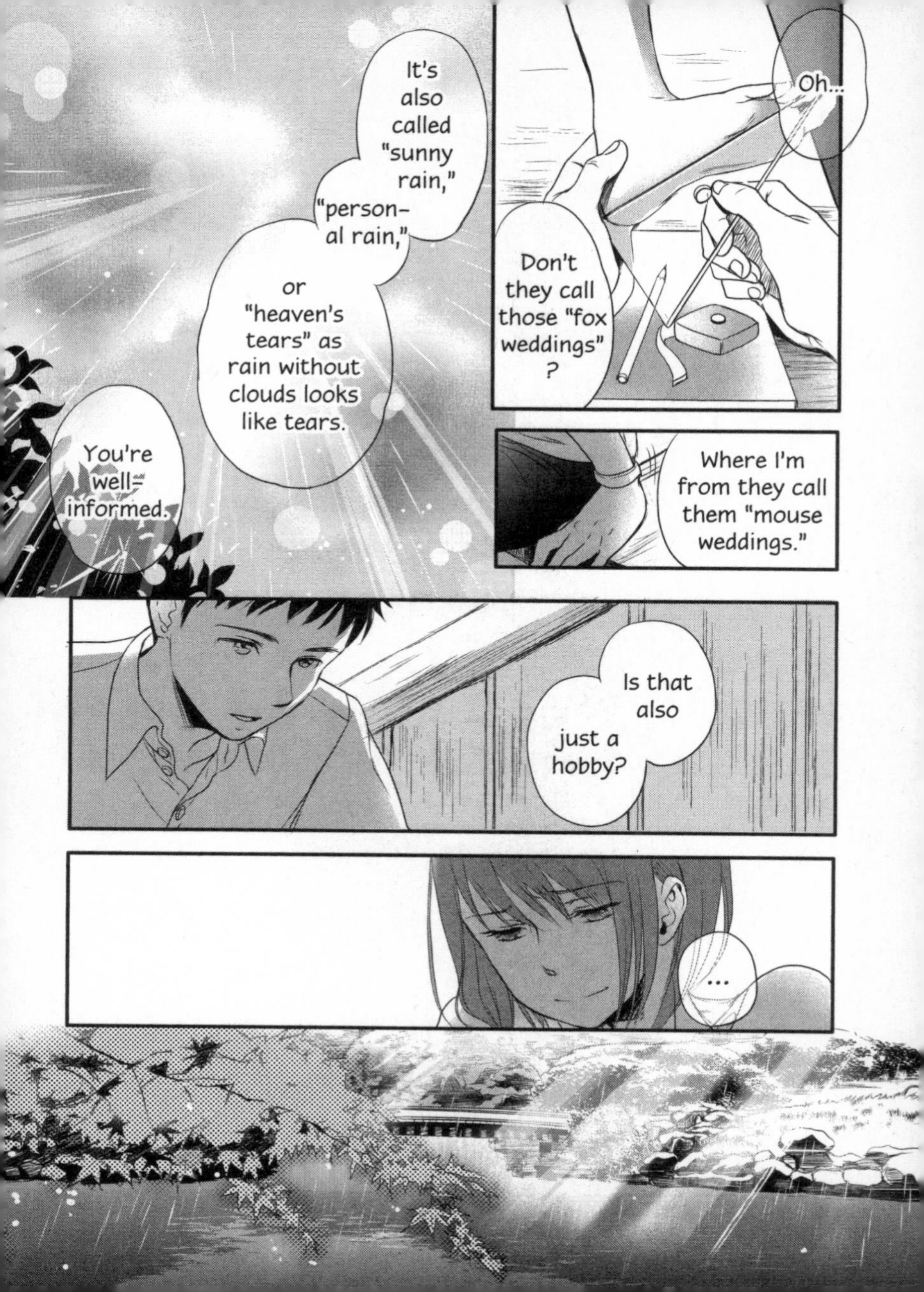
Oh...
Don't they call those "fox weddings"?
Where I'm from they call them "mouse weddings."
It's also called "sunny rain," "person-al rain," or "heaven's tears" as rain without clouds looks like tears.
You're well-informed.
Is that also just a hobby?
...

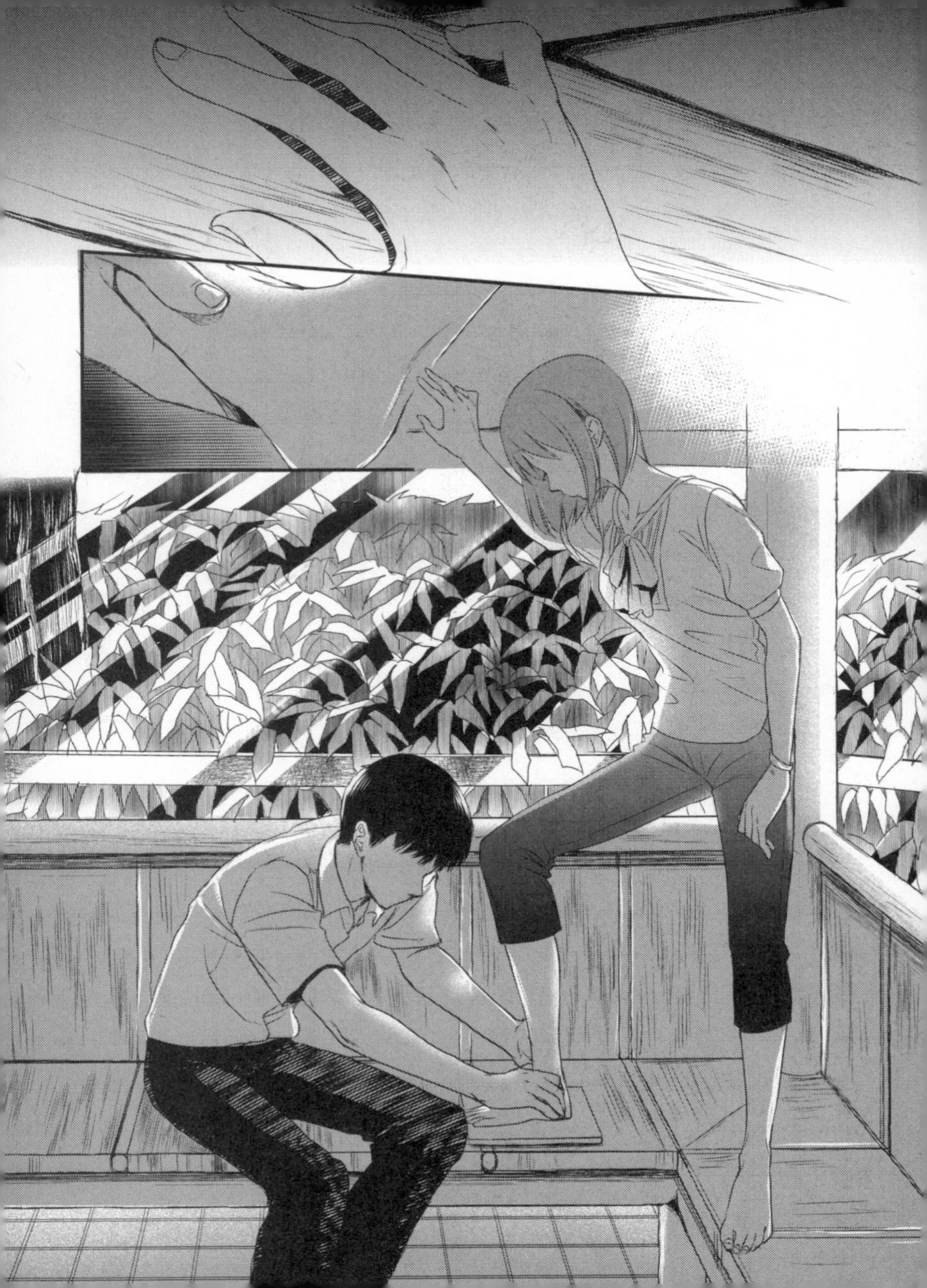

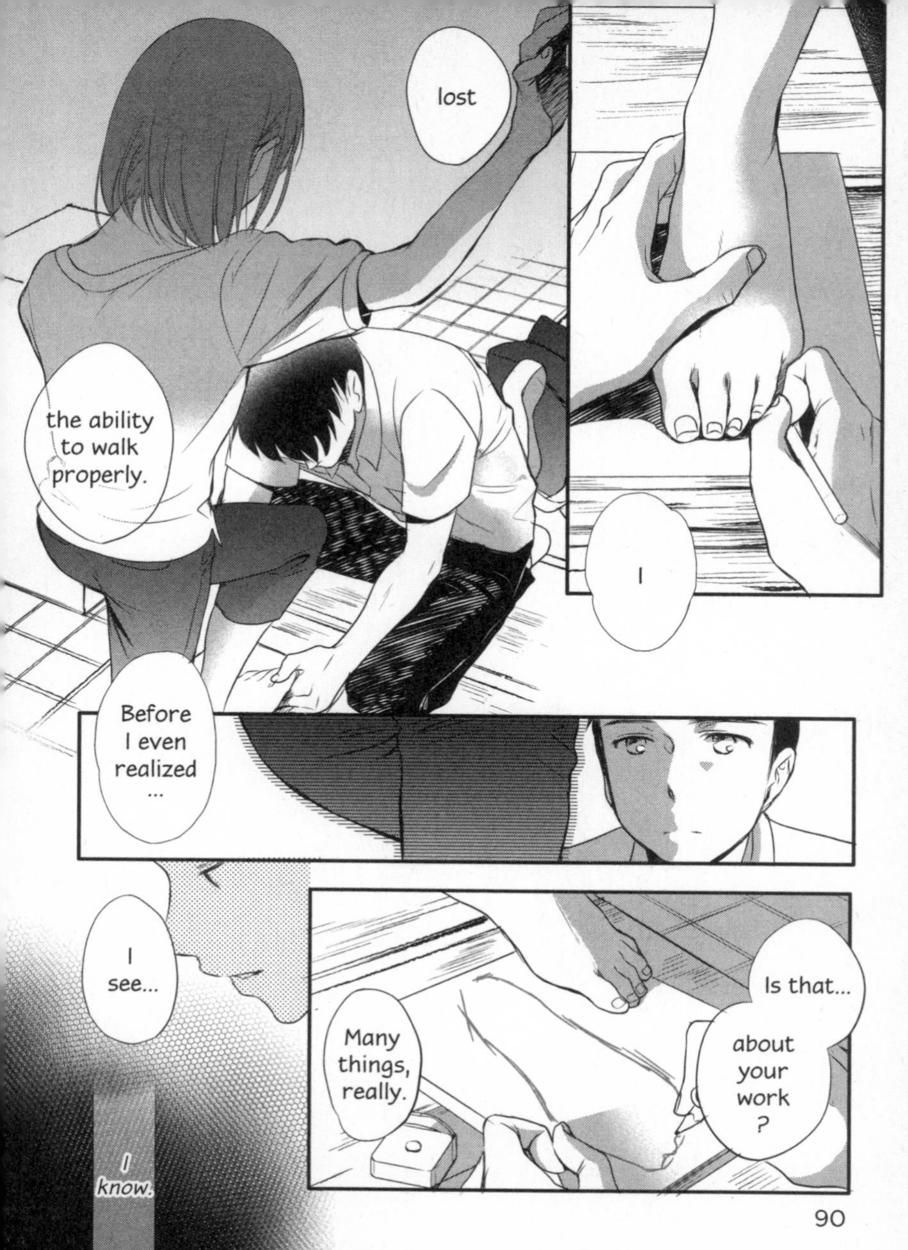
I
lost
the ability to walk properly.
Before I even realized ...
Is that... about your work ?
Many things, really.
I see...
I know.

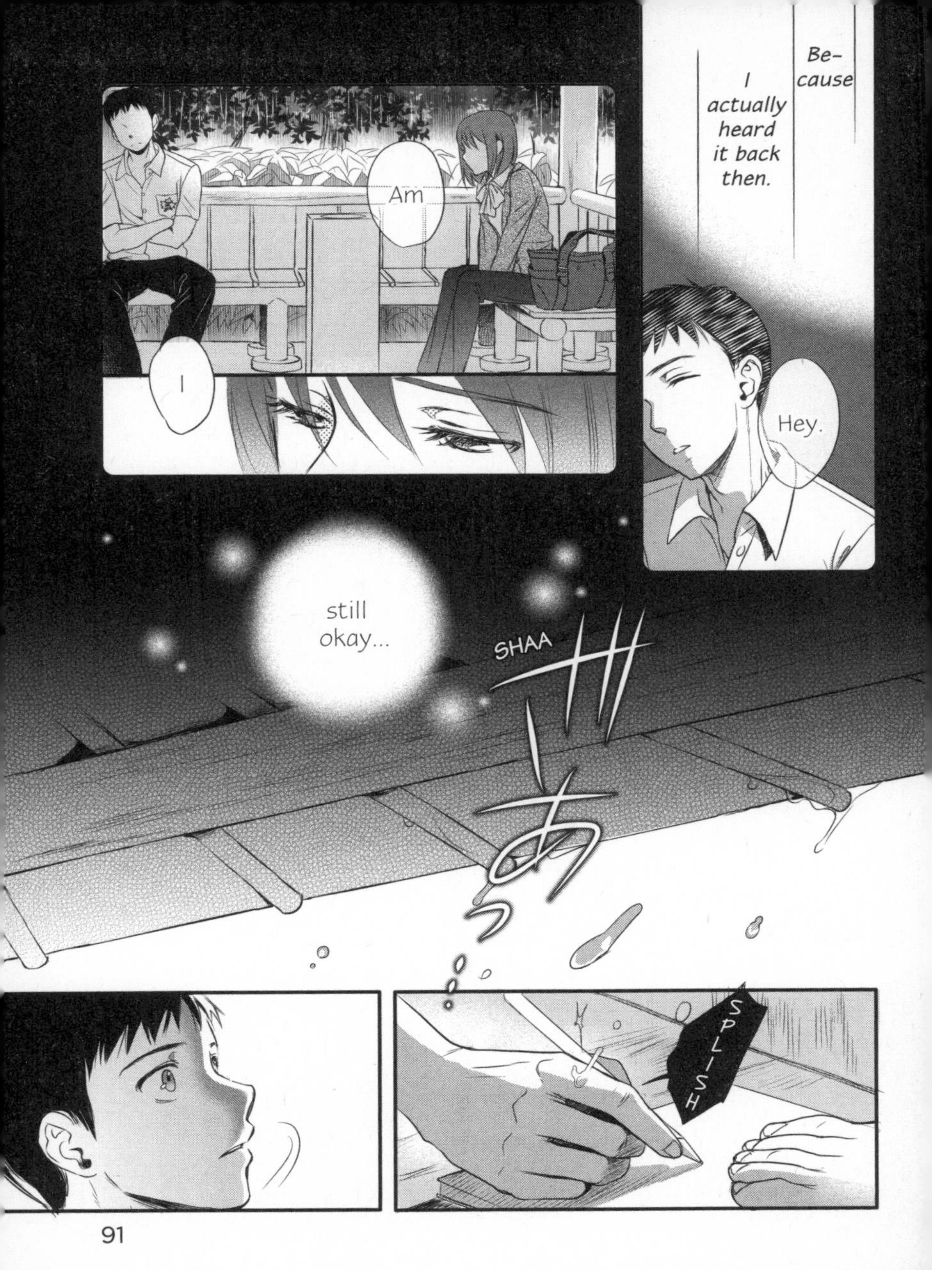
Be-cause
I actually heard it back then.
Hey.
Am
I
still okay...
SHAA
SPLISH

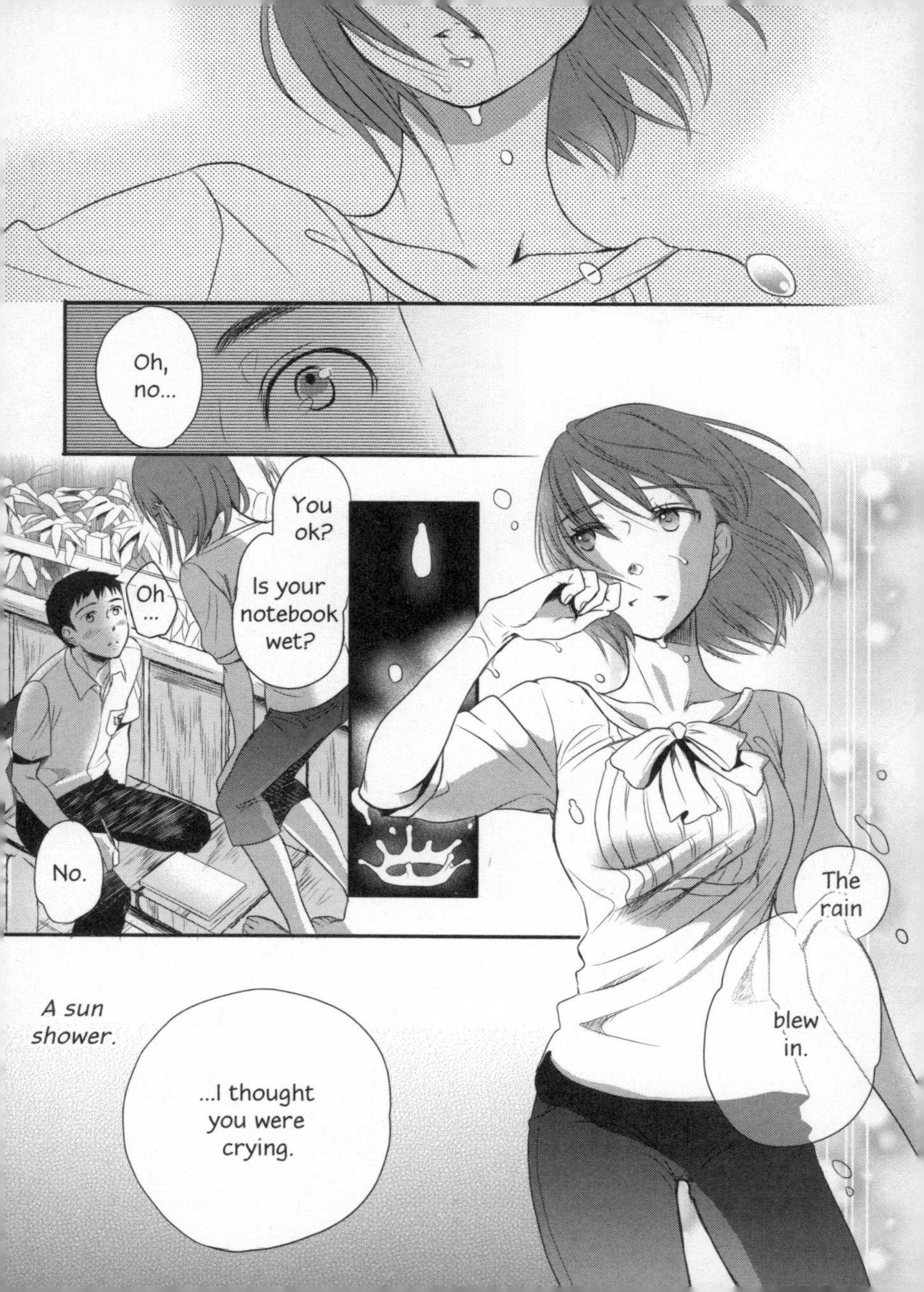
The rain blew in.
Oh, no...
You ok? Is your notebook wet?
Oh ...
No.
A sun shower.
...I thought you were crying.

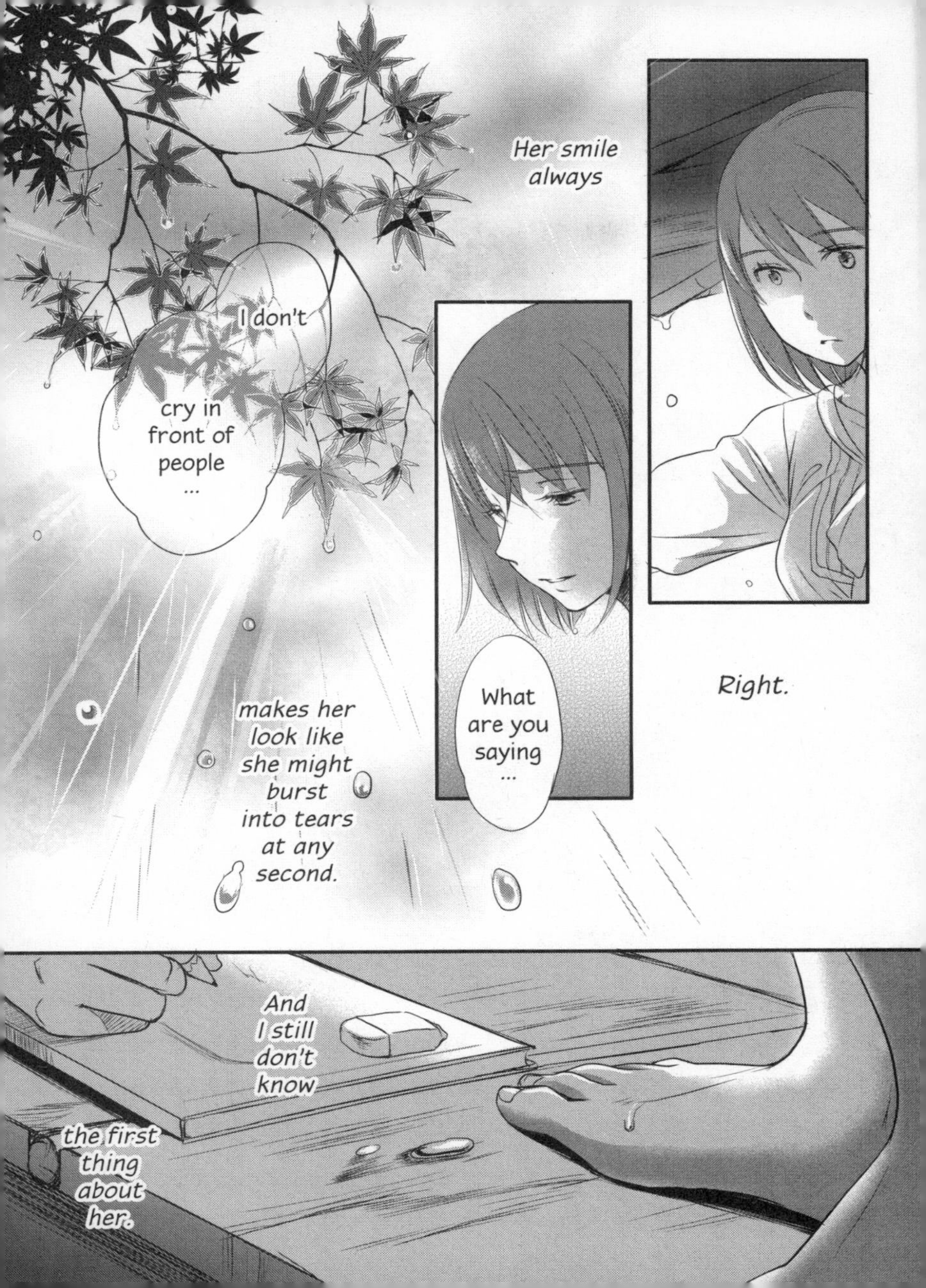
Her smile always
I don't cry in front of people ...
What are you saying ...
Right.
makes her look like she might burst into tears at any second.
And I still don't know
the first thing about her.

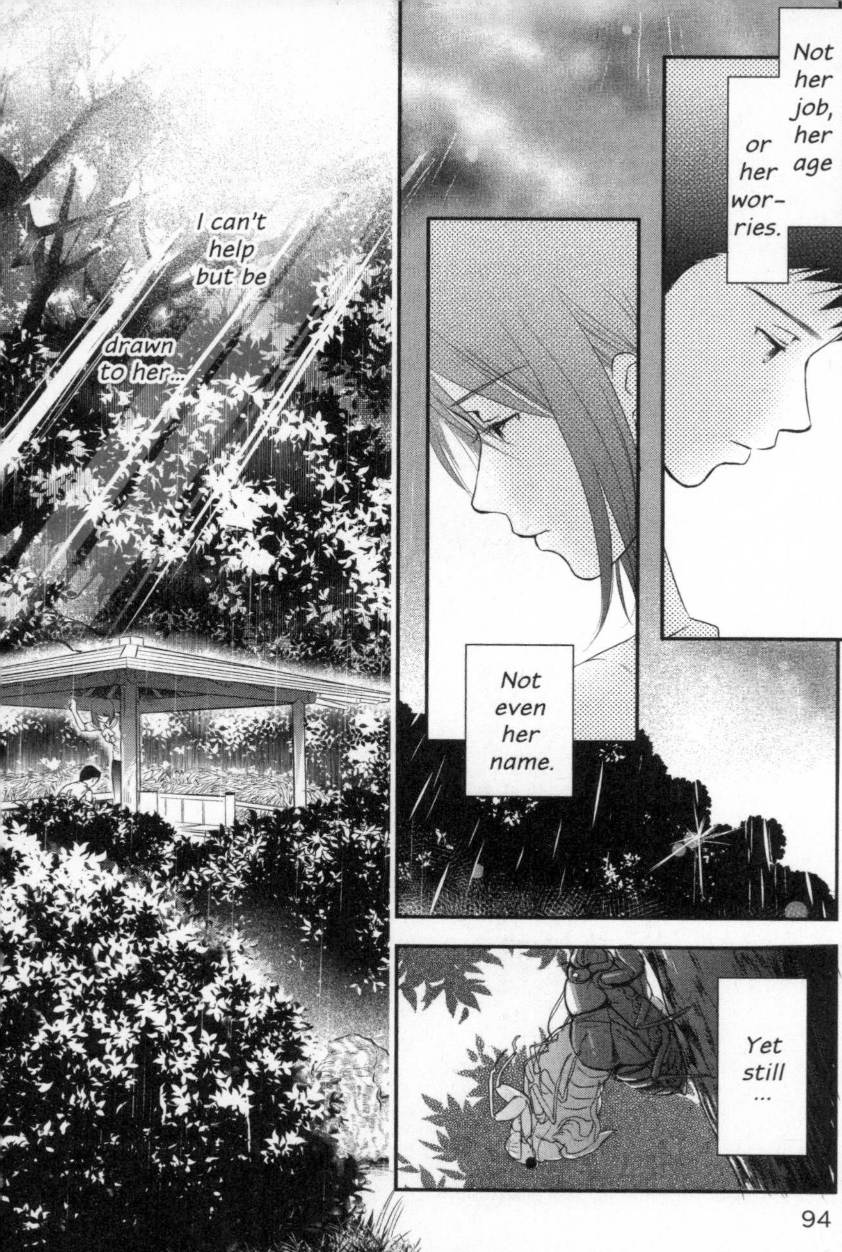
Not her job, her age
or her worries.
Not even her name.
Yet still ...
I can't help but be
drawn to her...

Chapter 4 “Westward Moon”

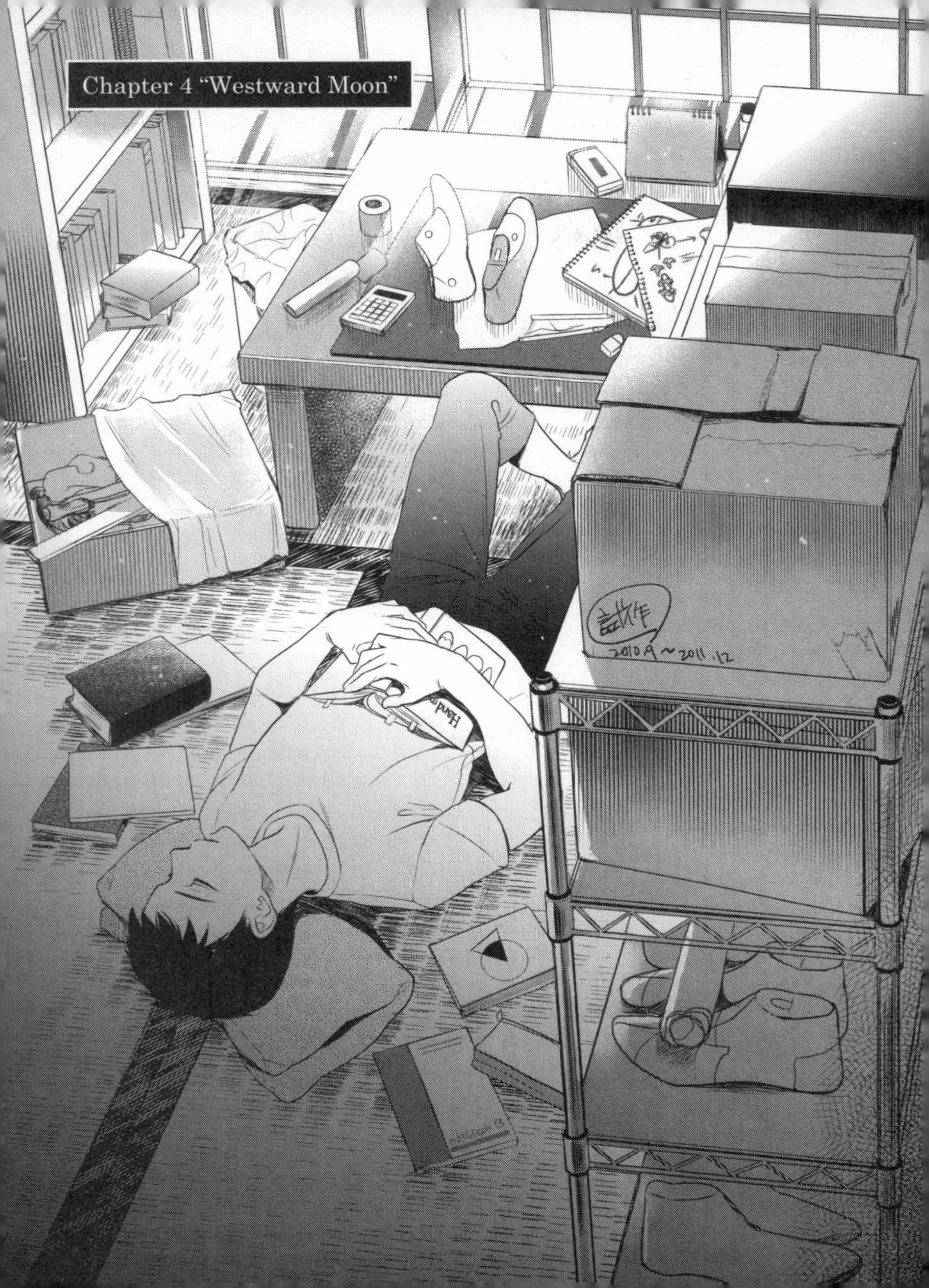

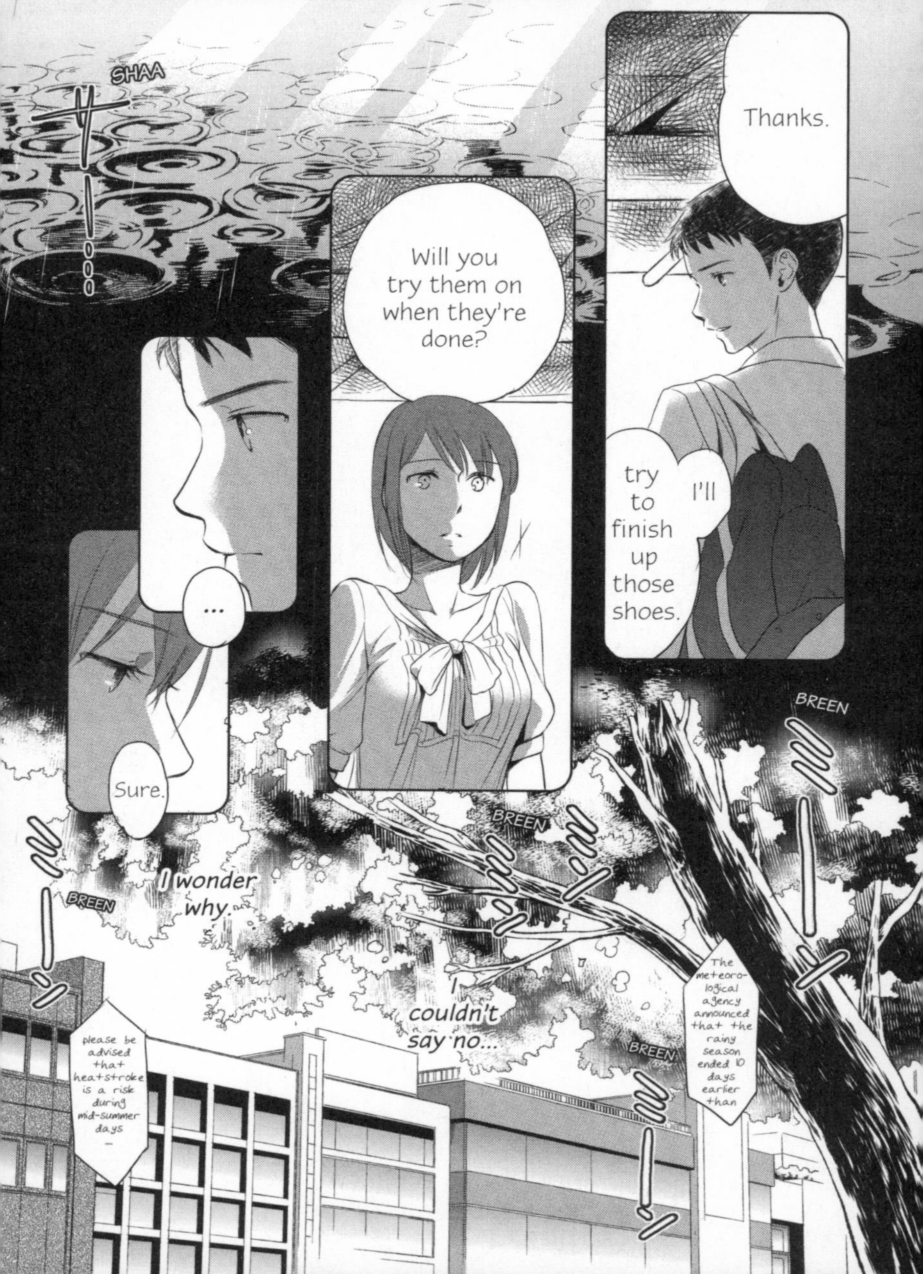
SHAA
Thanks.
I'll try to finish up those shoes.
Will you try them on when they're done?
...
Sure.
BREEN
BREEN
BREEN
I wonder why.
I couldn't say no...
The meteorological agency announced that the rainy season ended 10 days earlier than
BREEN
please be advised that heatstroke is a risk during mid-summer days ...

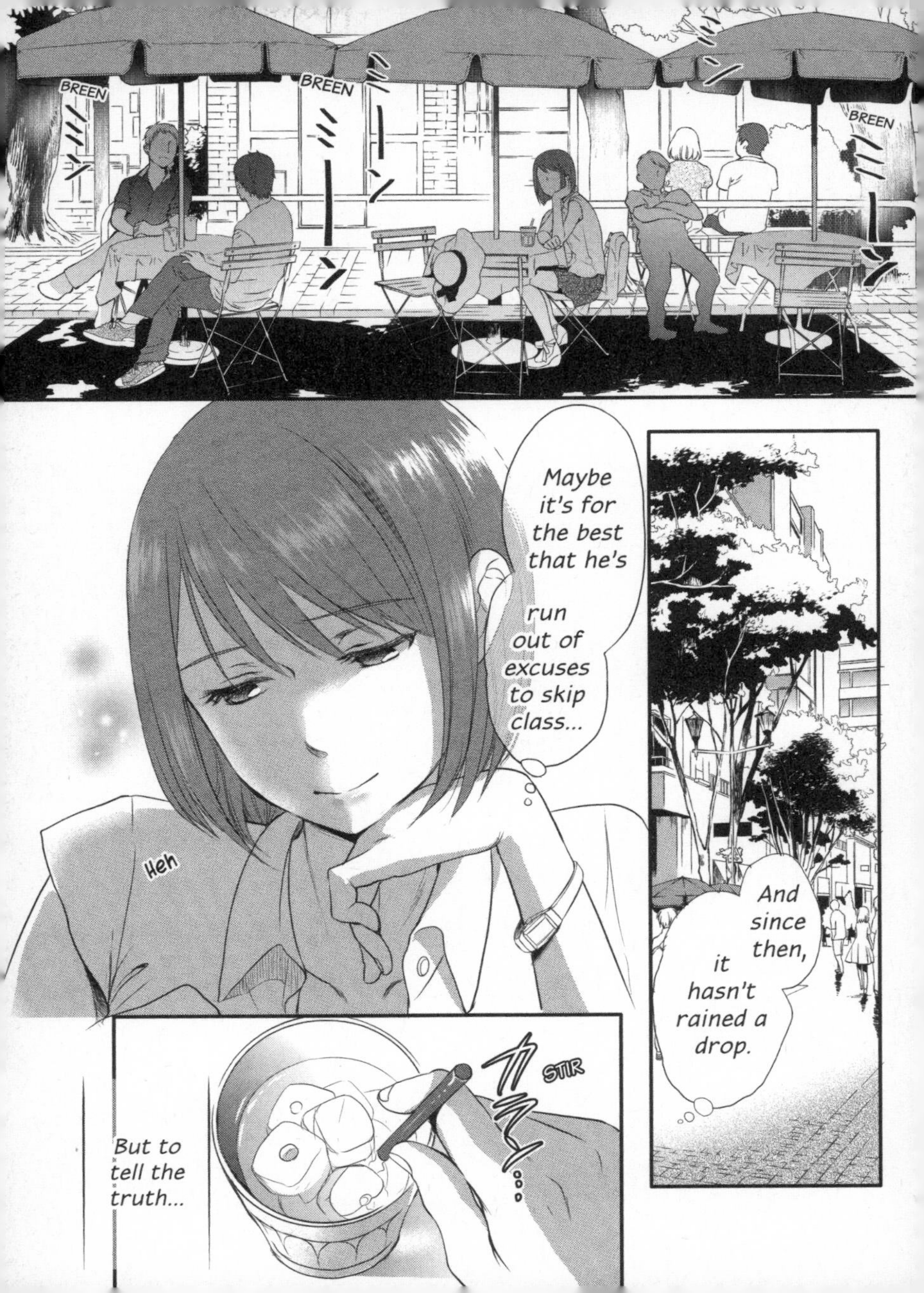
BREEN
BREEN
BREEN
And since then, it hasn't rained a drop.
Maybe it's for the best that he's run out of excuses to skip class...
Heh
STIR
But to tell the truth...

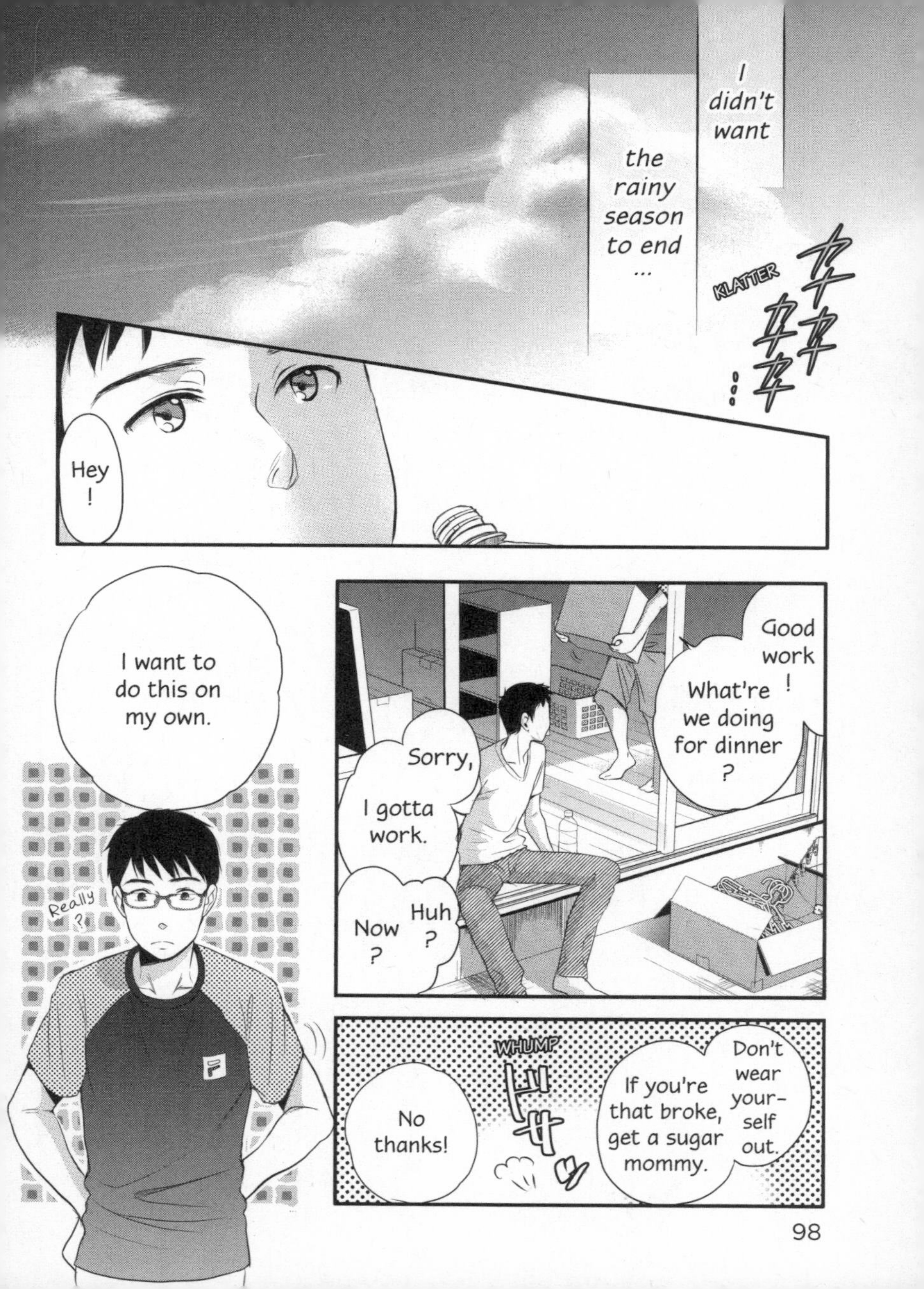
I didn't want
the rainy season to end ...
KLATTER
Hey!
Good work!
What're we doing for dinner?
Sorry,
I gotta work.
Huh?
Now?
Don't wear your-self out.
If you're that broke, get a sugar mommy.
WHUMP
No thanks!
I want to do this on my own.
Really?

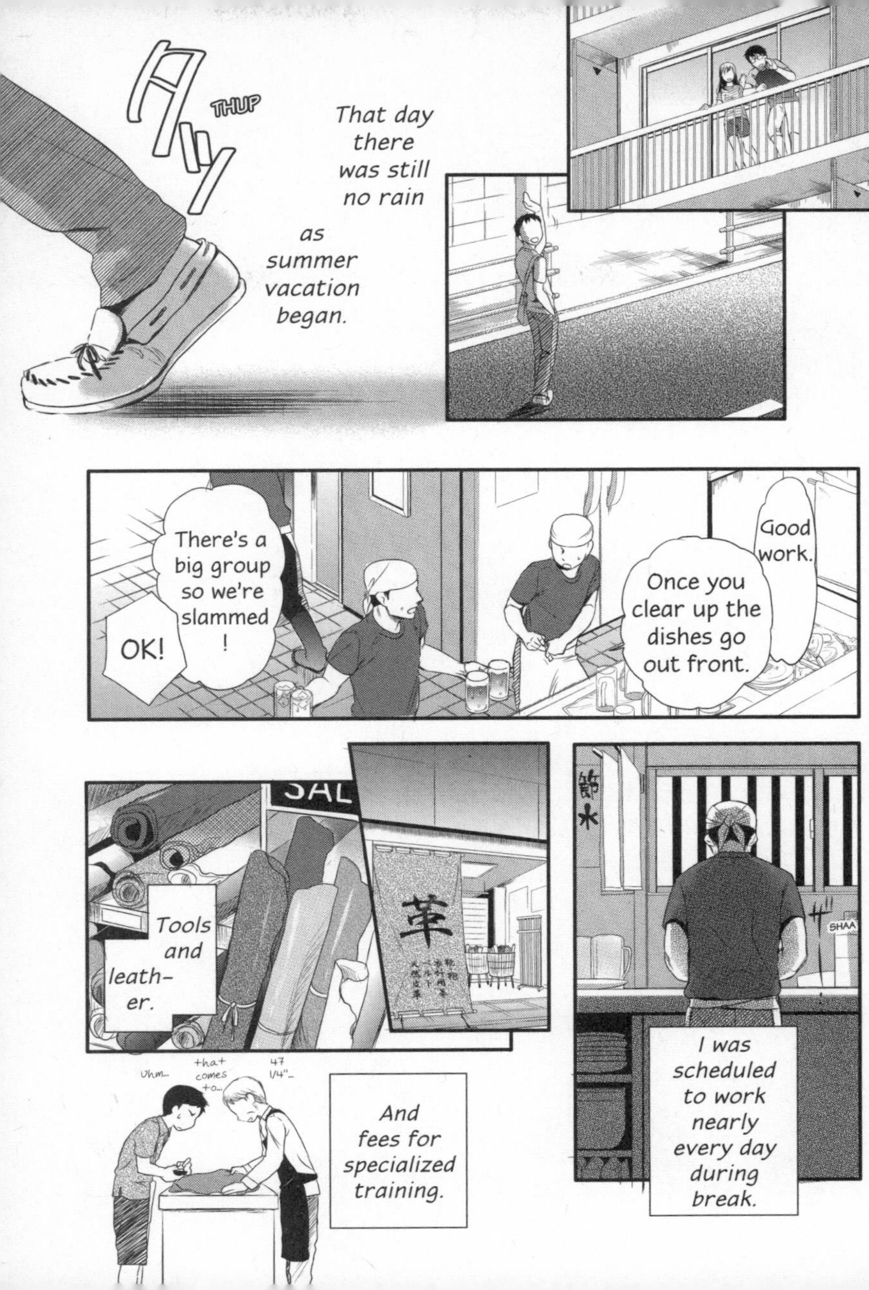
THUP
That day there was still no rain
as summer vacation began.
Good work.
Once you clear up the dishes go out front.
There's a big group so we're slammed!
OK!
節水
SHAA
I was scheduled to work nearly every day during break.
SAL
革
Tools and leather.
47 1/4"...
that comes to...
Uhm...
And fees for specialized training.

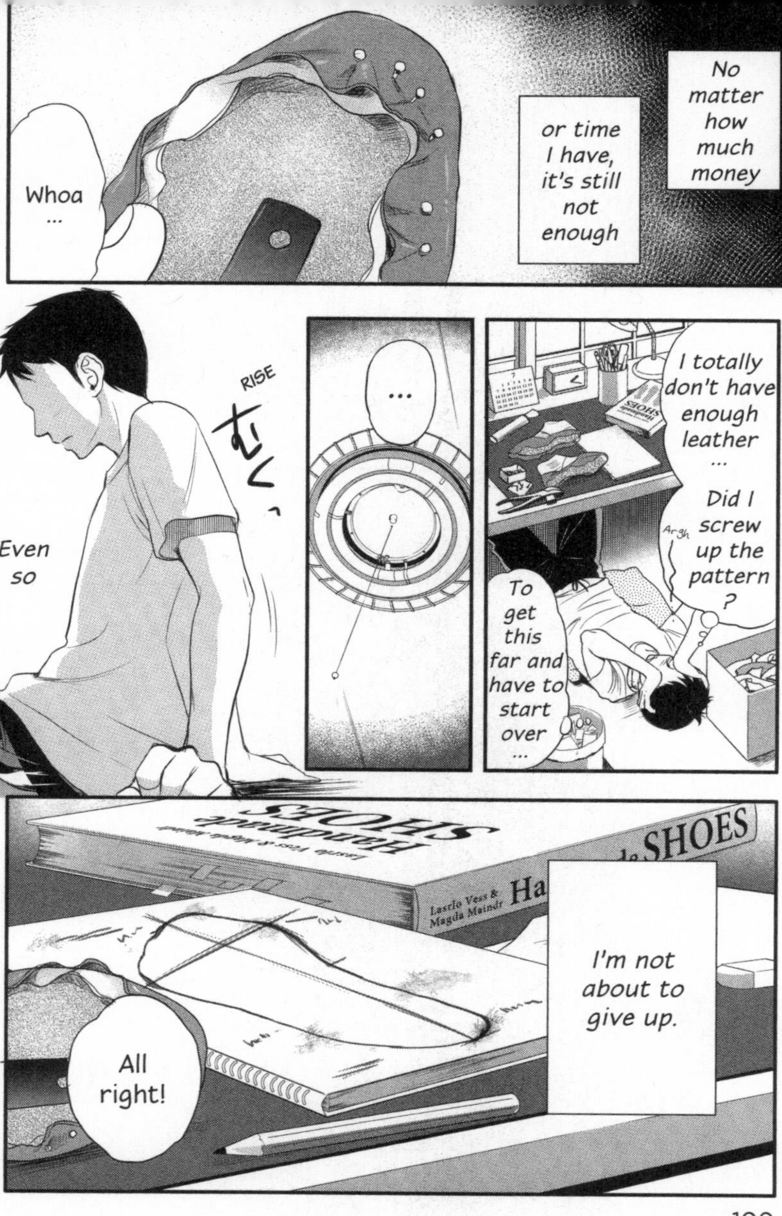
No matter how much money
or time I have, it's still not enough
Whoa ...
I totally don't have enough leather ...
Did I screw up the pattern ?
Argh
To get this far and have to start over ...
...
RISE
むく
Even so
I'm not about to give up.
All right!

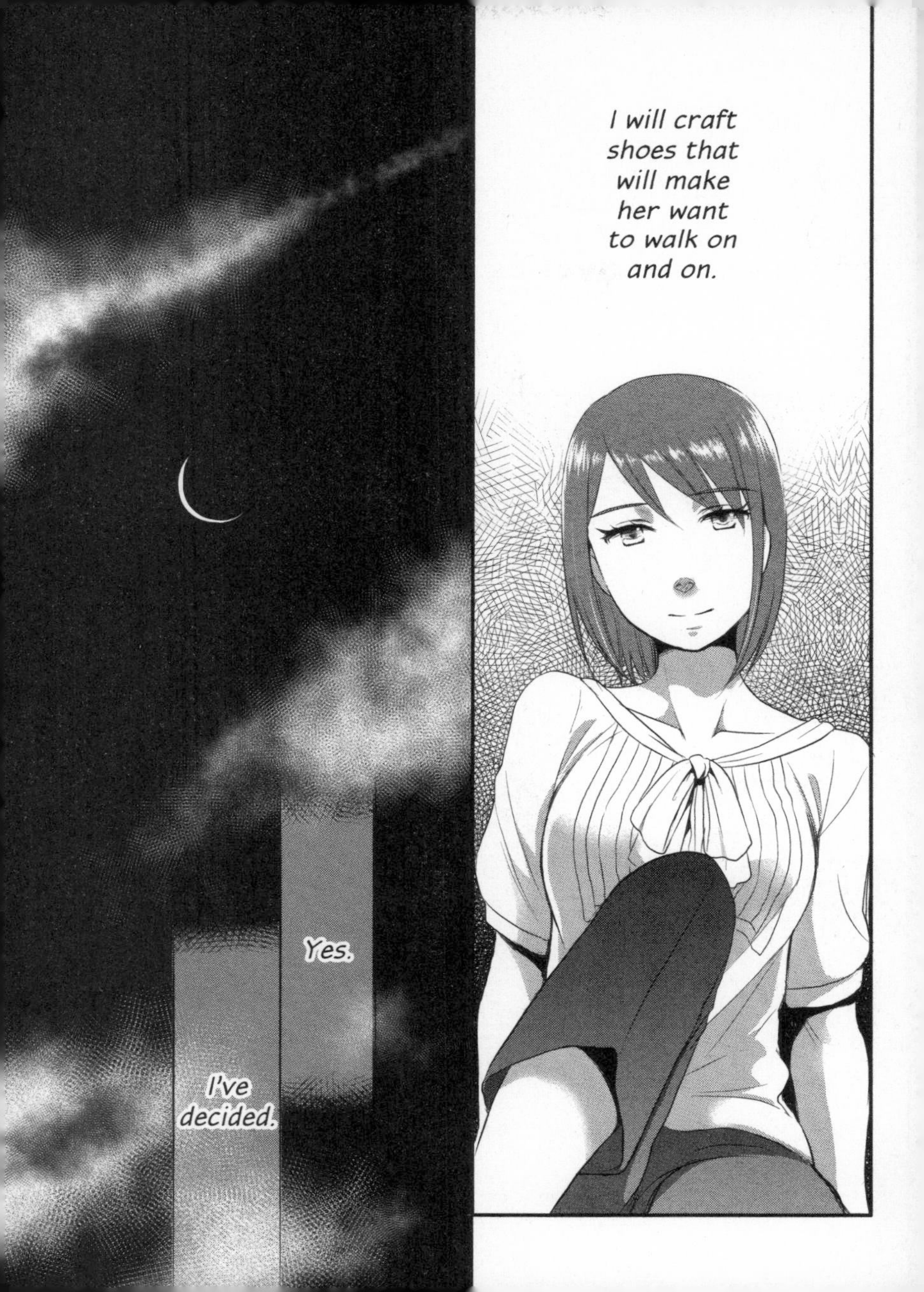
I will craft shoes that will make her want to walk on and on.
Yes.
I've decided.

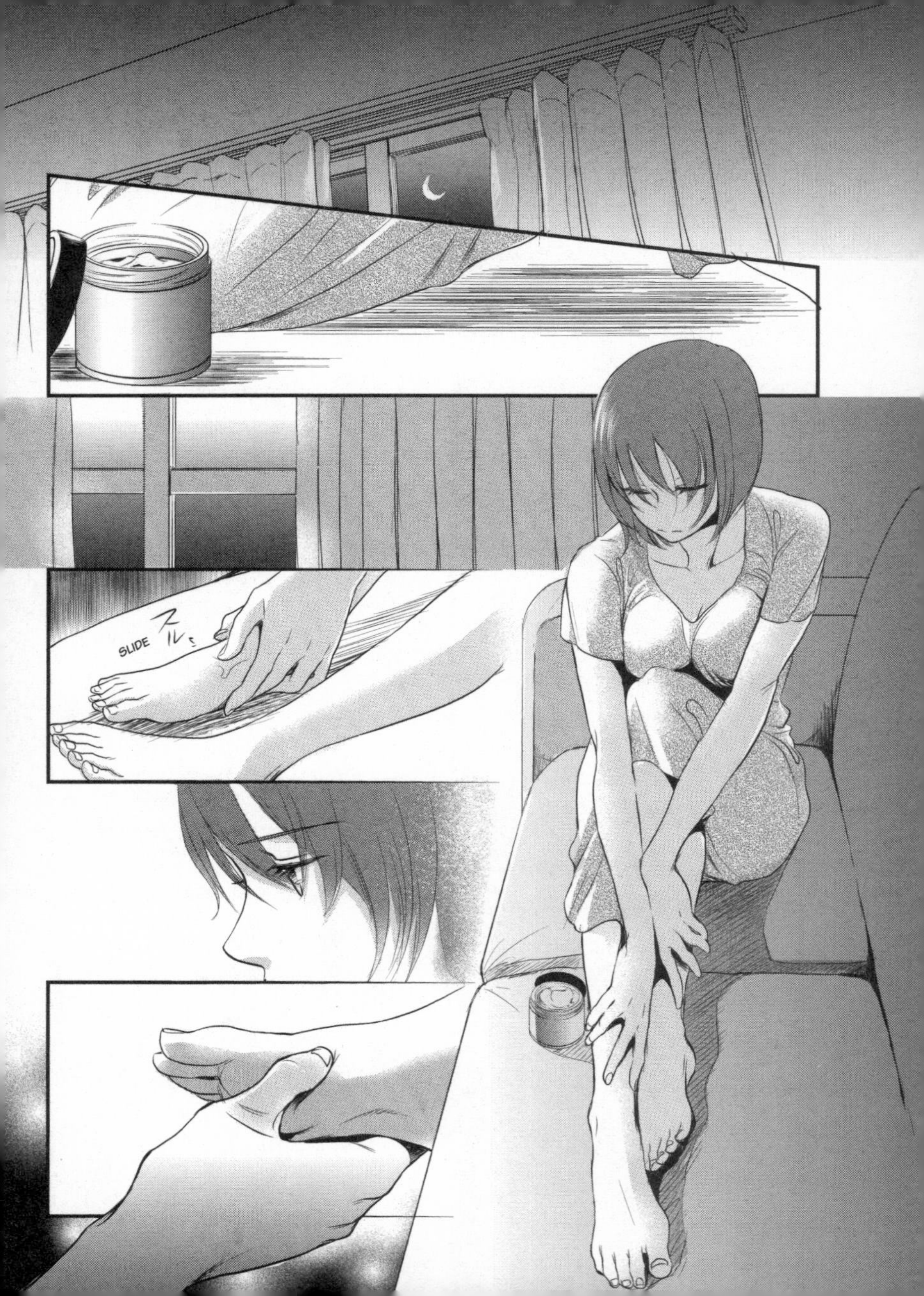
SLIDE スルッ

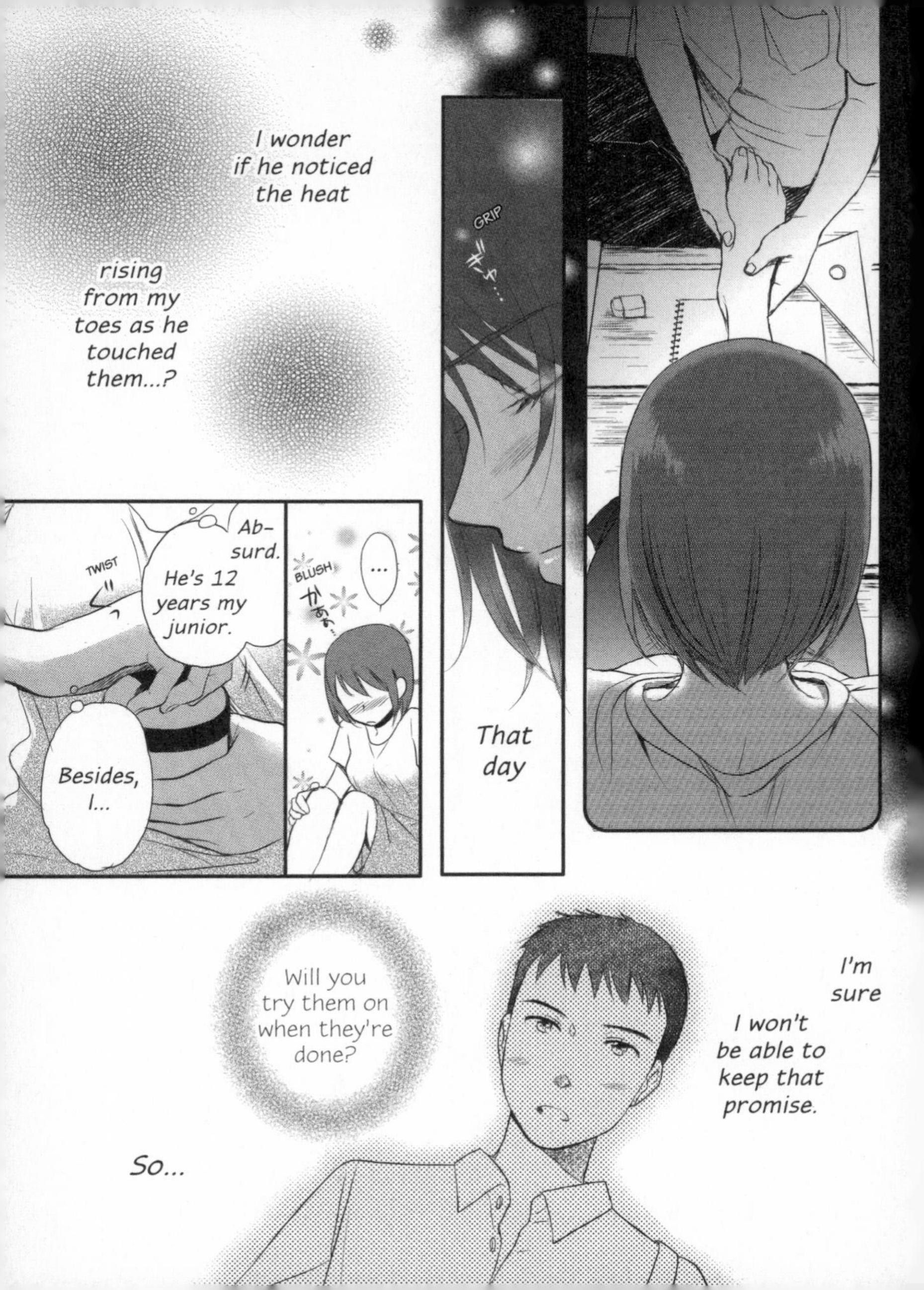
GRIP
That day
I wonder if he noticed the heat
rising from my toes as he touched them...?
BLUSH
...
TWIST
Ab-surd.
He's 12 years my junior.
Besides, I...
I'm sure I won't be able to keep that promise.
Will you try them on when they're done?
So...

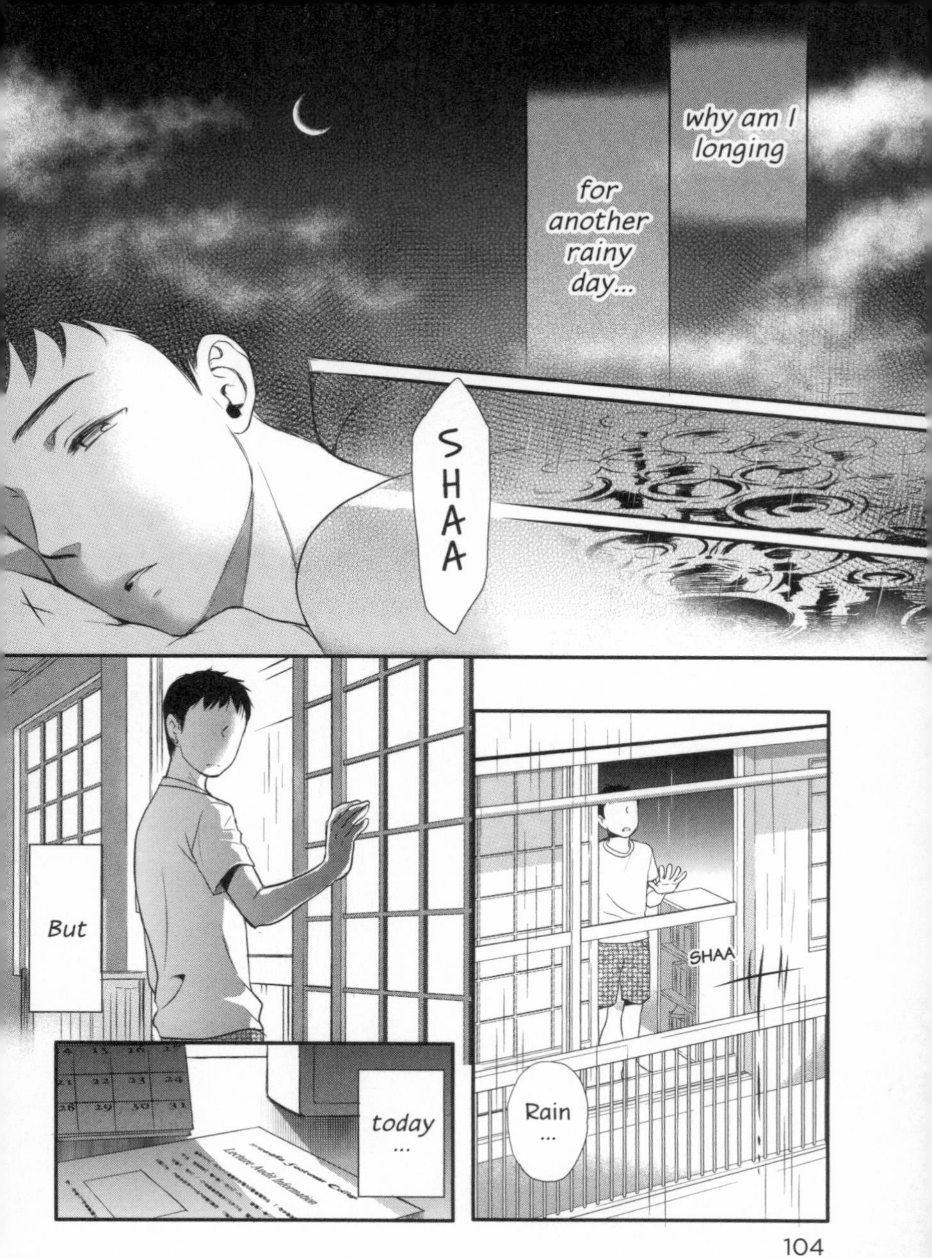
why am I longing
for another rainy day...
SHAA
SHAA
Rain ...
But
today ...

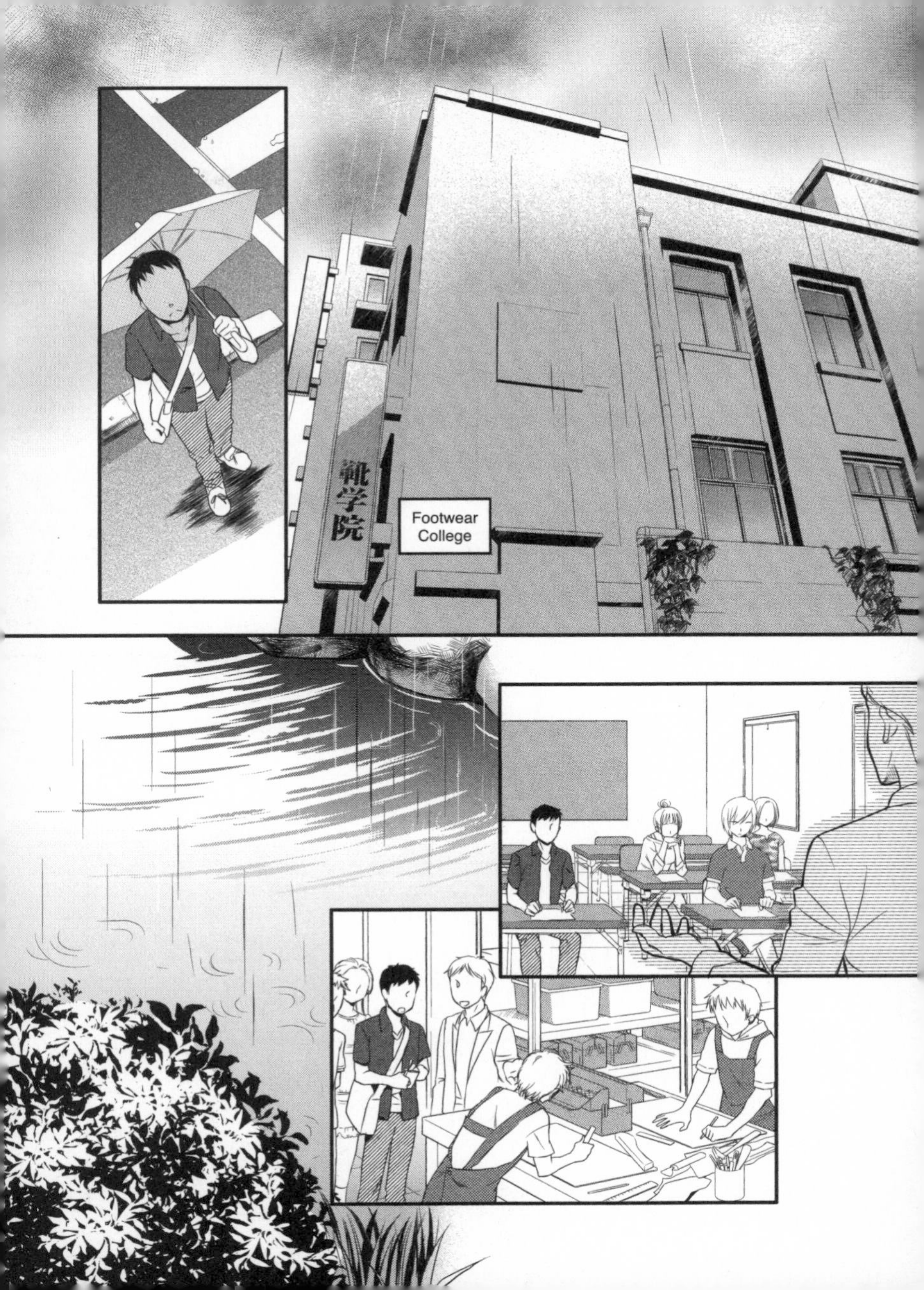
靴学院
Footwear College

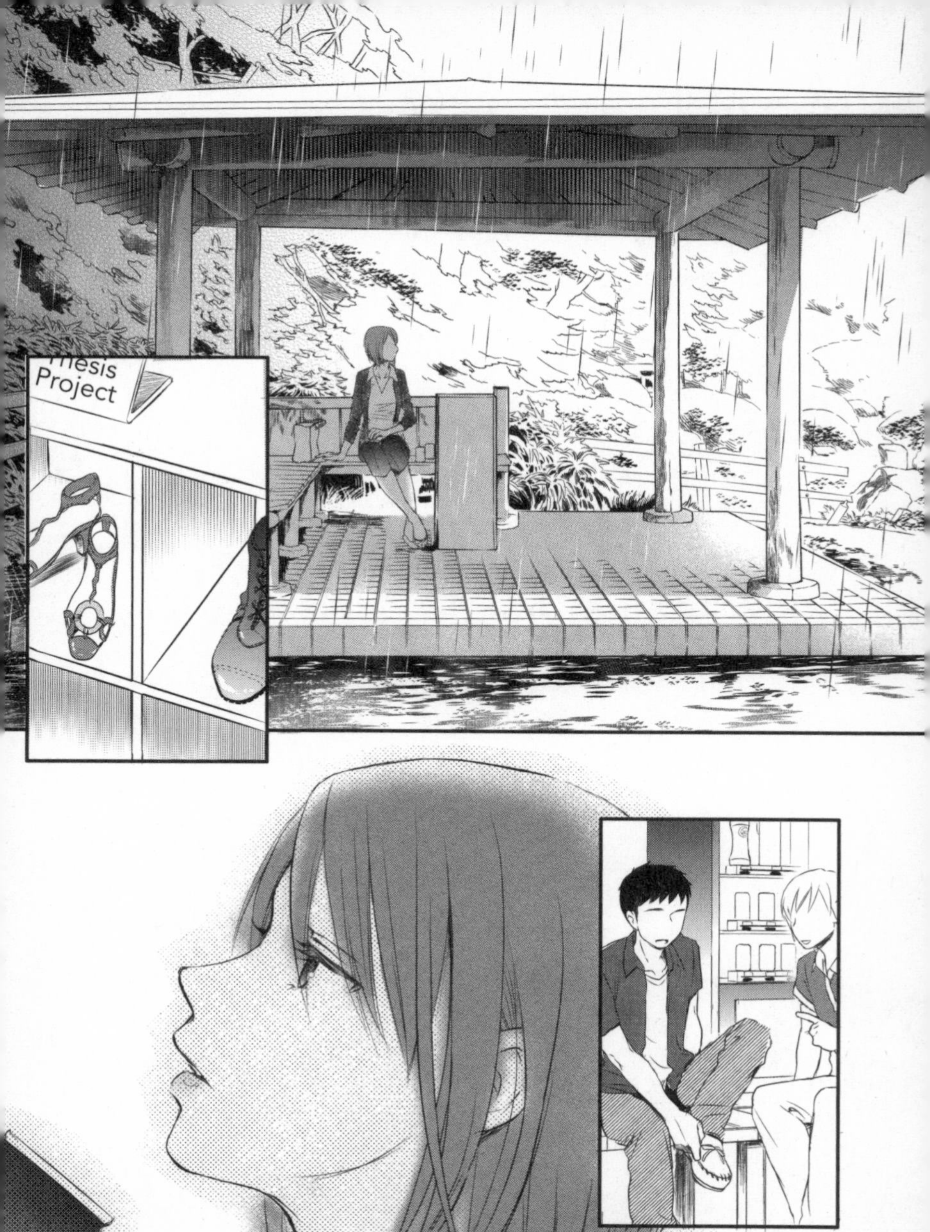
Thesis Project

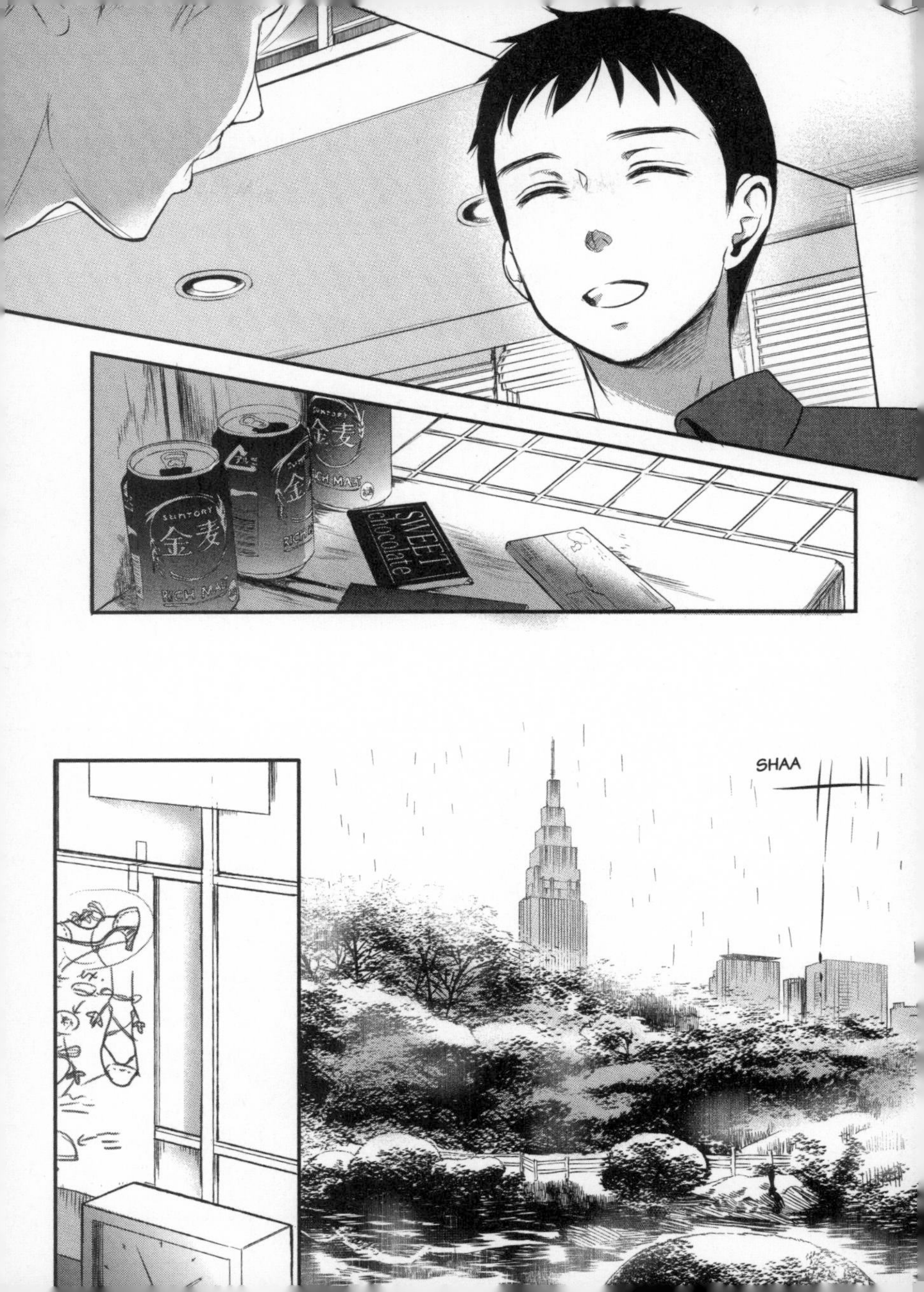
SUNTORY
金麦
RICH MALT
SWEET chocolate
SHAA

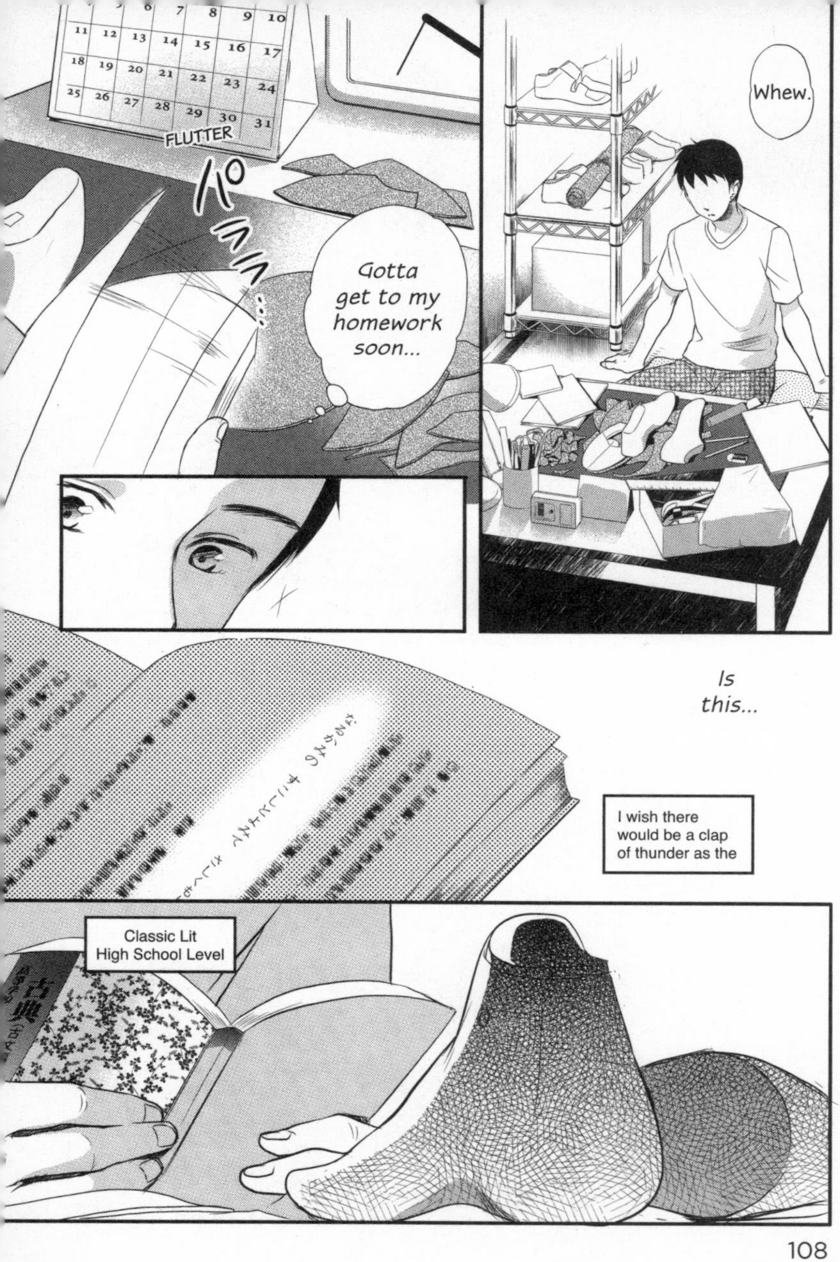
Whew.
FLUTTER
Gotta get to my homework soon...
Is this...
I wish there would be a clap of thunder as the
Classic Lit High School Level

*Thoughts
of her come
to mind
unexpectedly,
every day.*

CLOSE

パタ...

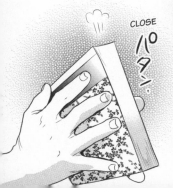

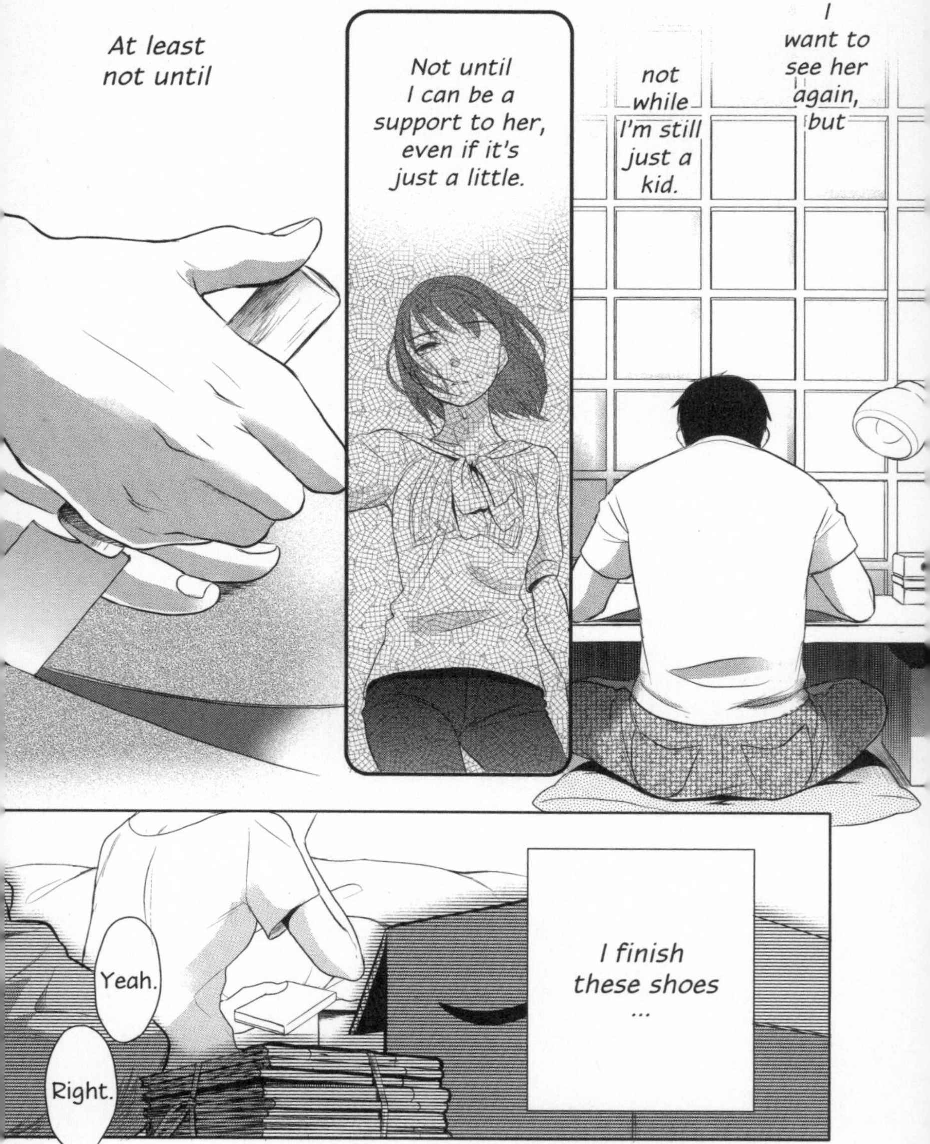
I want to see her again, but
not while I'm still just a kid.
Not until I can be a support to her, even if it's just a little.
At least not until
I finish these shoes ...
Yeah.
Right.

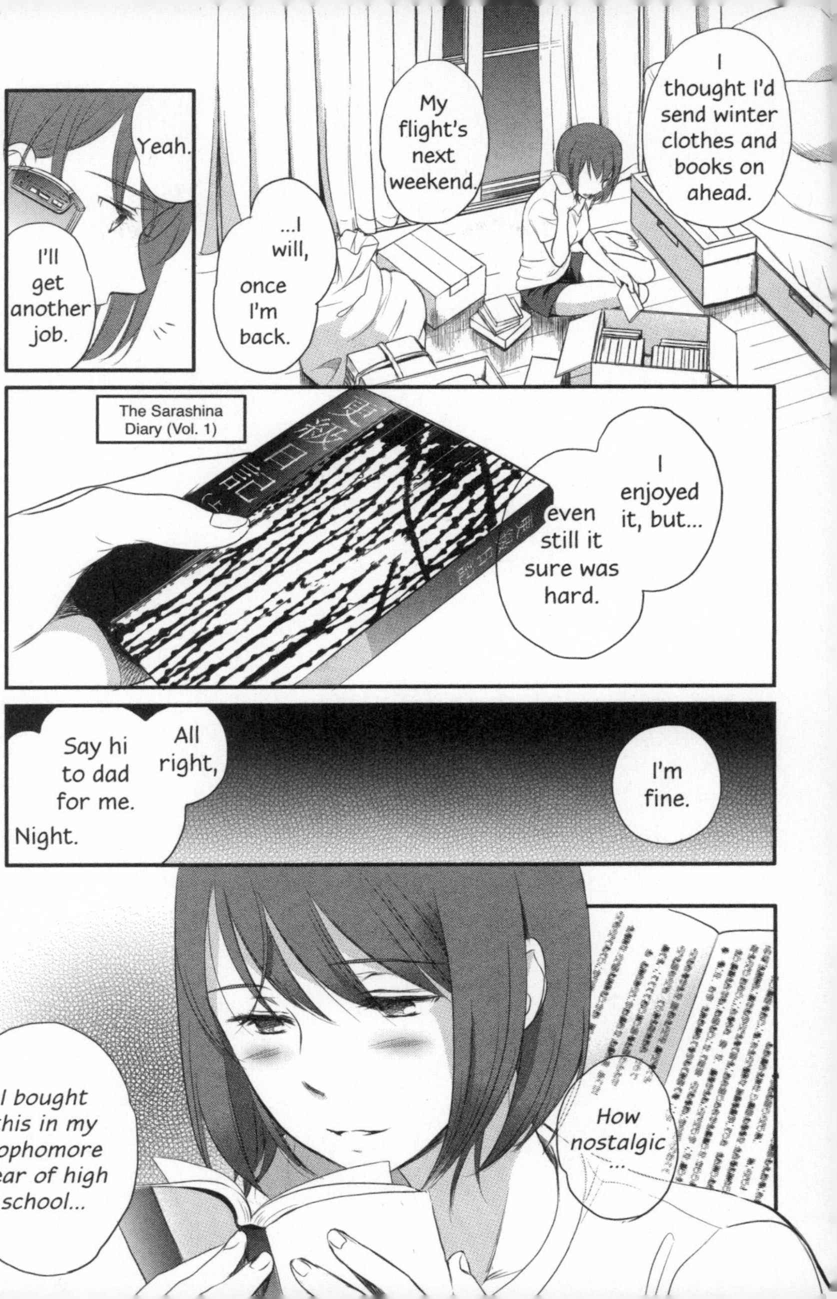
I thought I'd send winter clothes and books on ahead.
My flight's next weekend.
...I will, once I'm back.
Yeah.
I'll get another job.
The Sarashina Diary (Vol. 1)
I enjoyed it, but... even still it sure was hard.
I'm fine.
All right,
Say hi to dad for me.
Night.
How nostalgic...
I bought this in my sophomore year of high school...

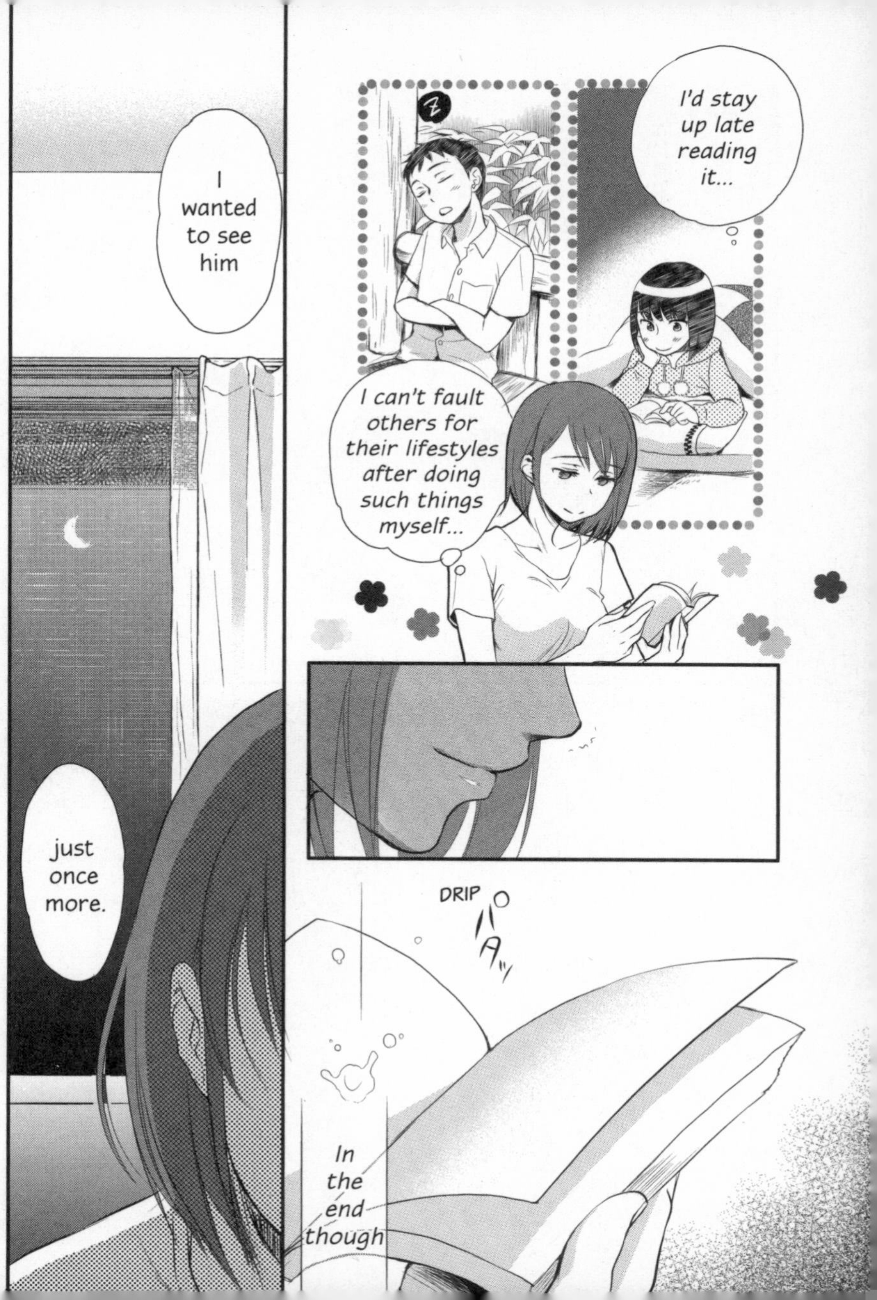
I'd stay up late reading it...
I can't fault others for their lifestyles after doing such things myself...
DRIP
In the end though
I wanted to see him
just once more.

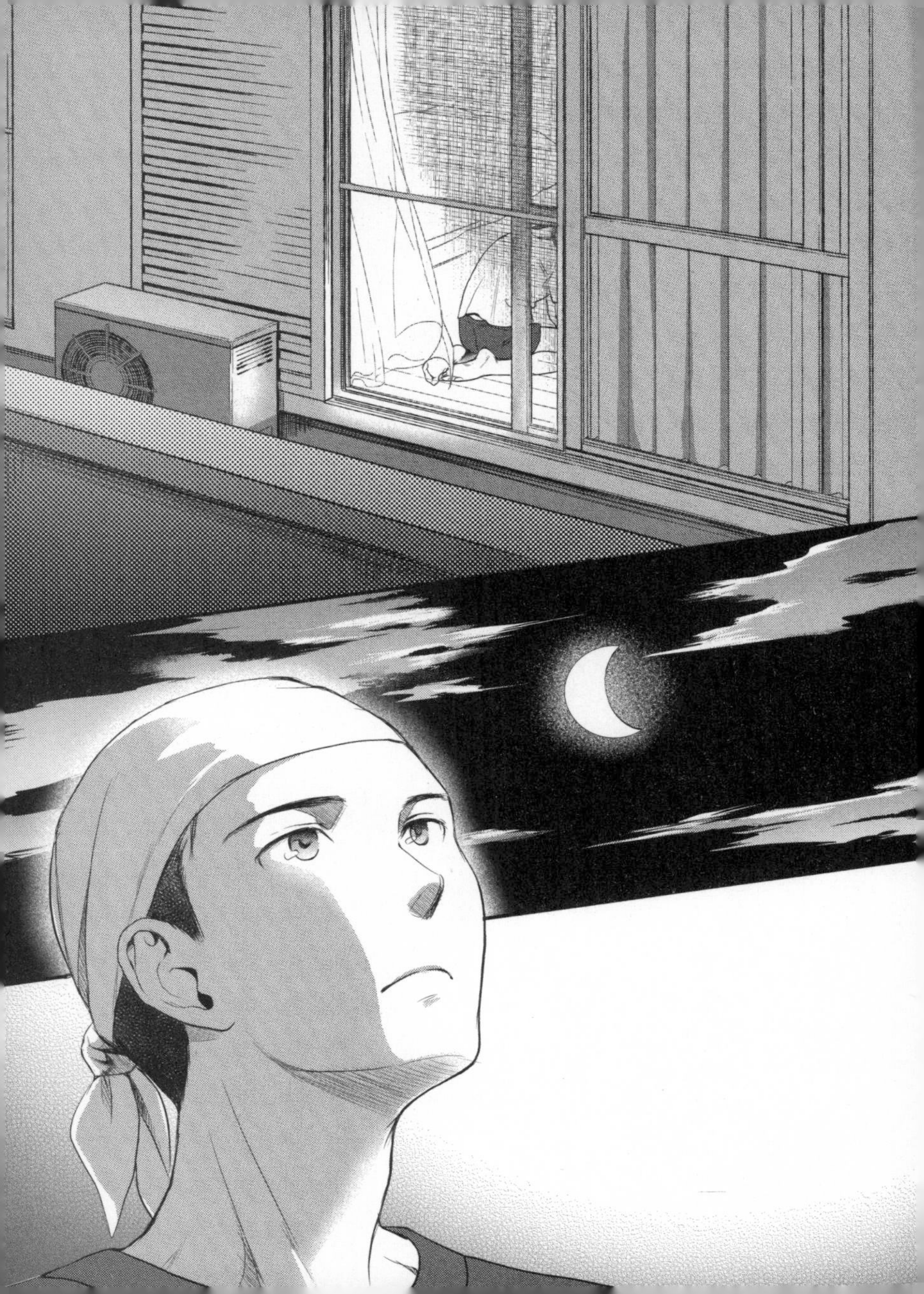

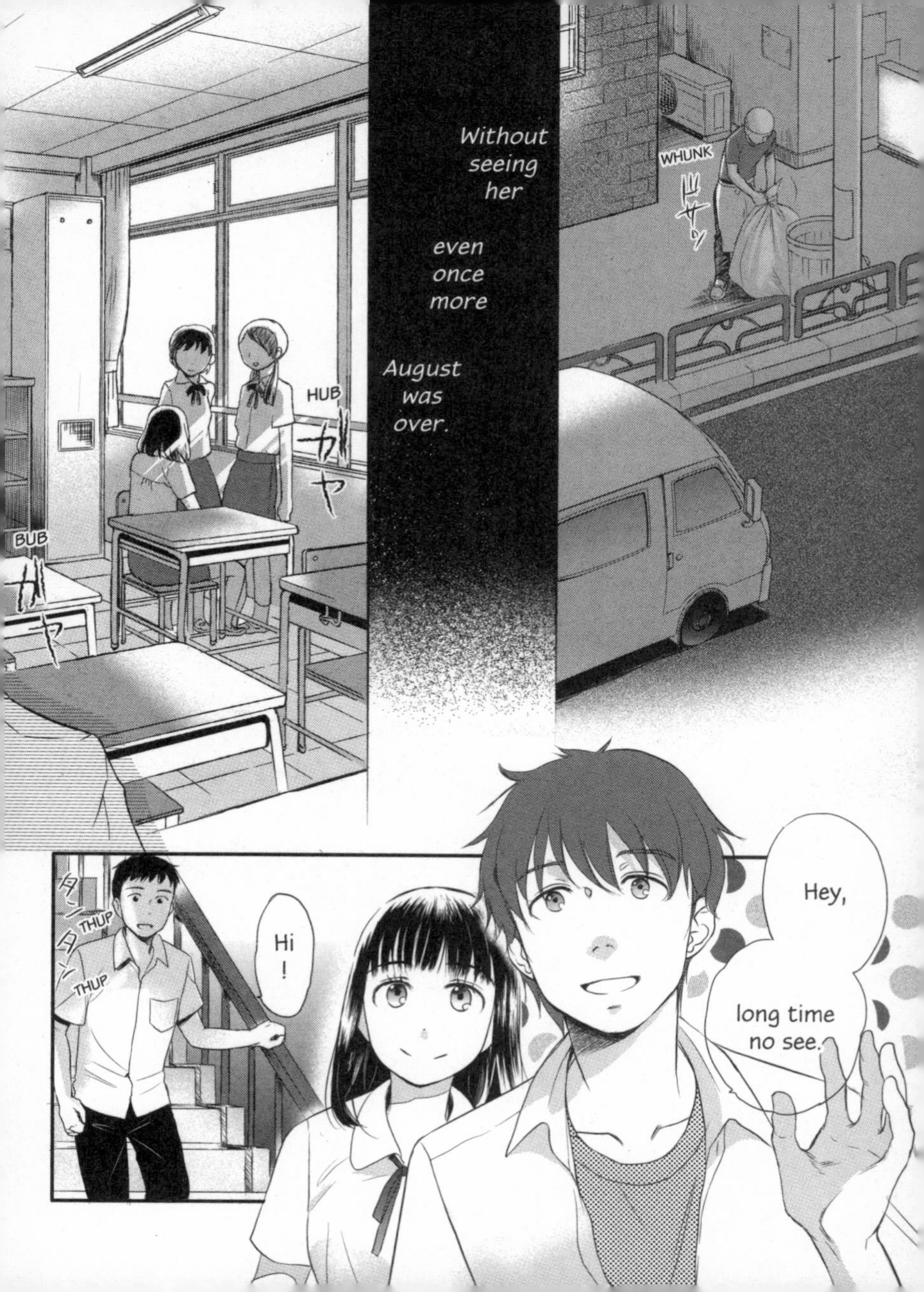

WHUNK
Without seeing her
even once more
August was over.
HUB
BUB
Hey,
long time no see.
Hi!
THUP
THUP

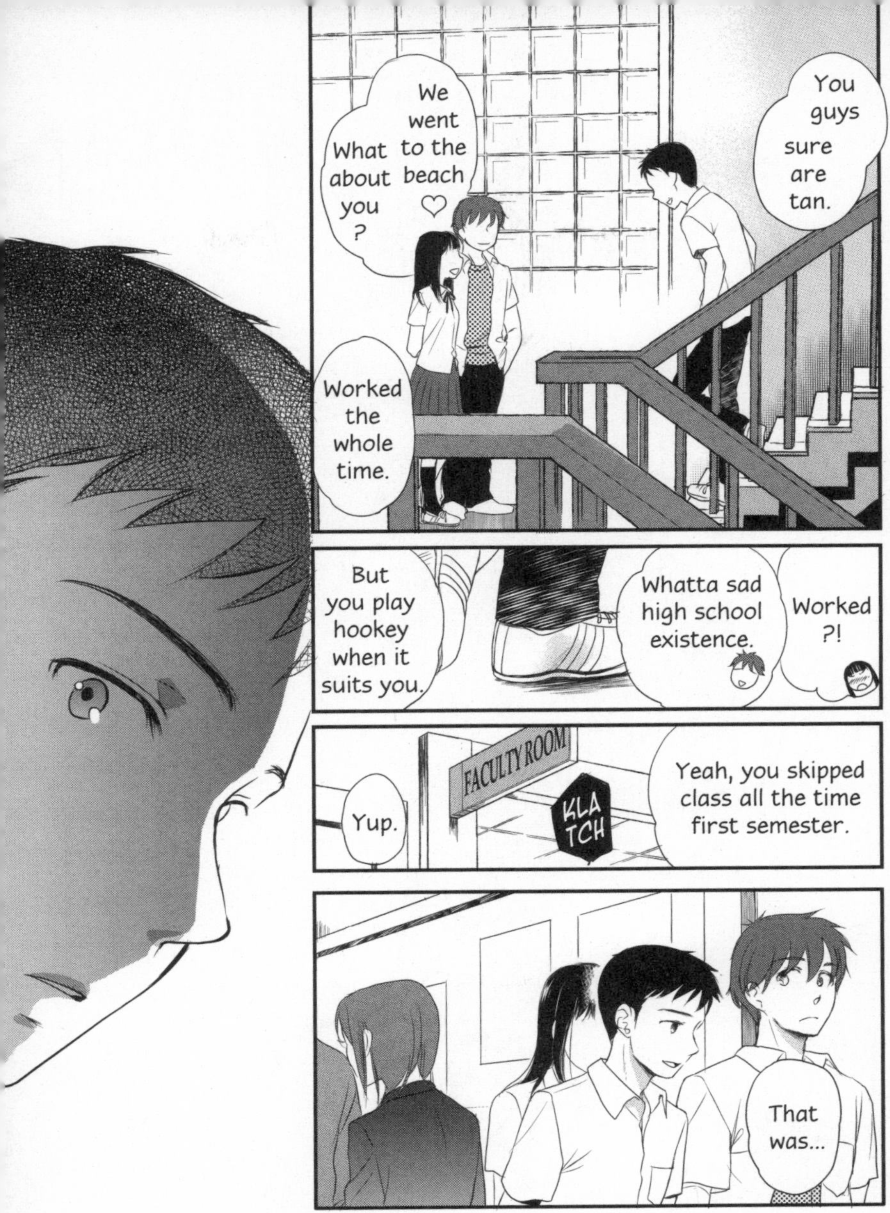

You guys sure are tan.
We went to the beach ♡
What about you?
Worked the whole time.
Worked?!
Whatta sad high school existence.
But you play hookey when it suits you.
Yeah, you skipped class all the time first semester.
KLATCH
FACULTY ROOM
Yup.
That was...

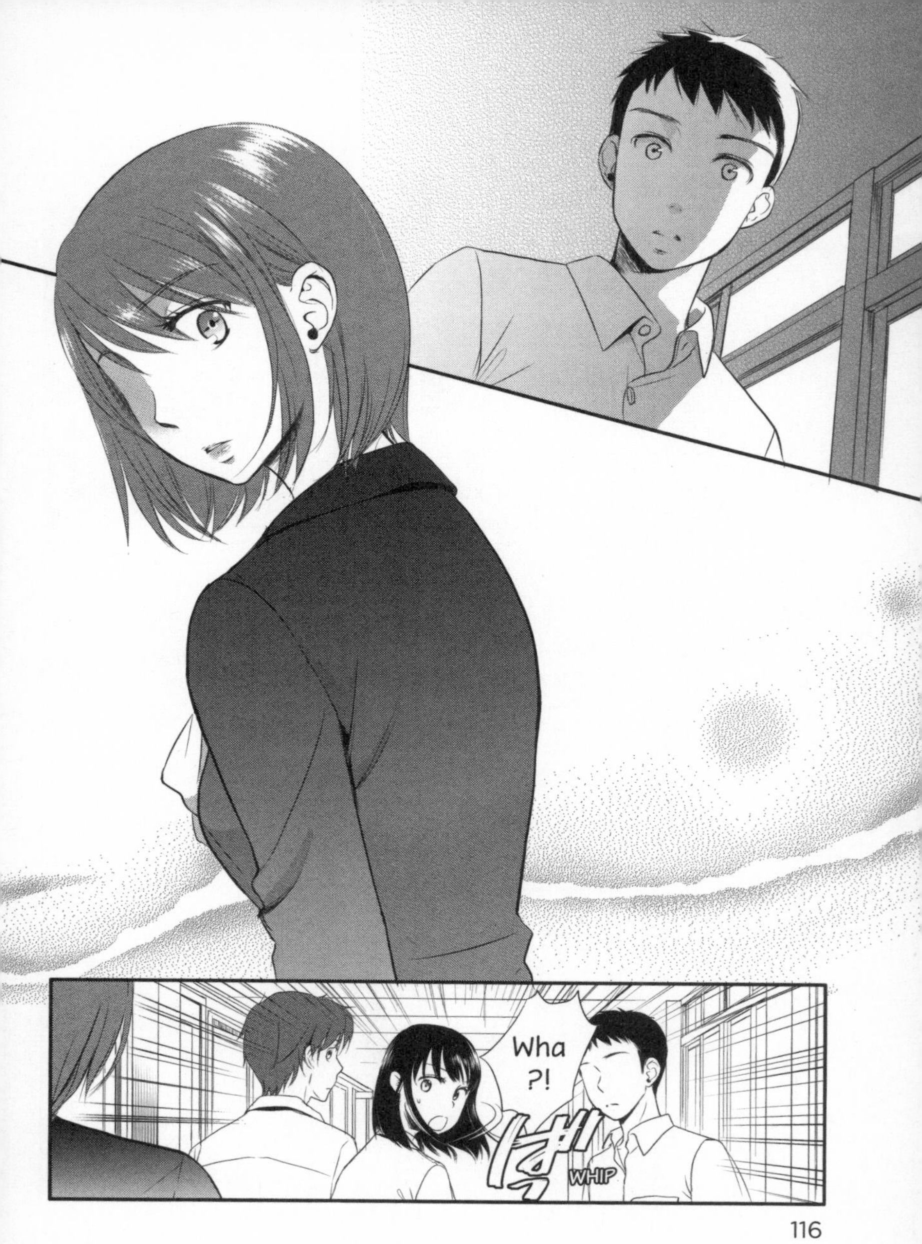
Wha ?!
WHIP

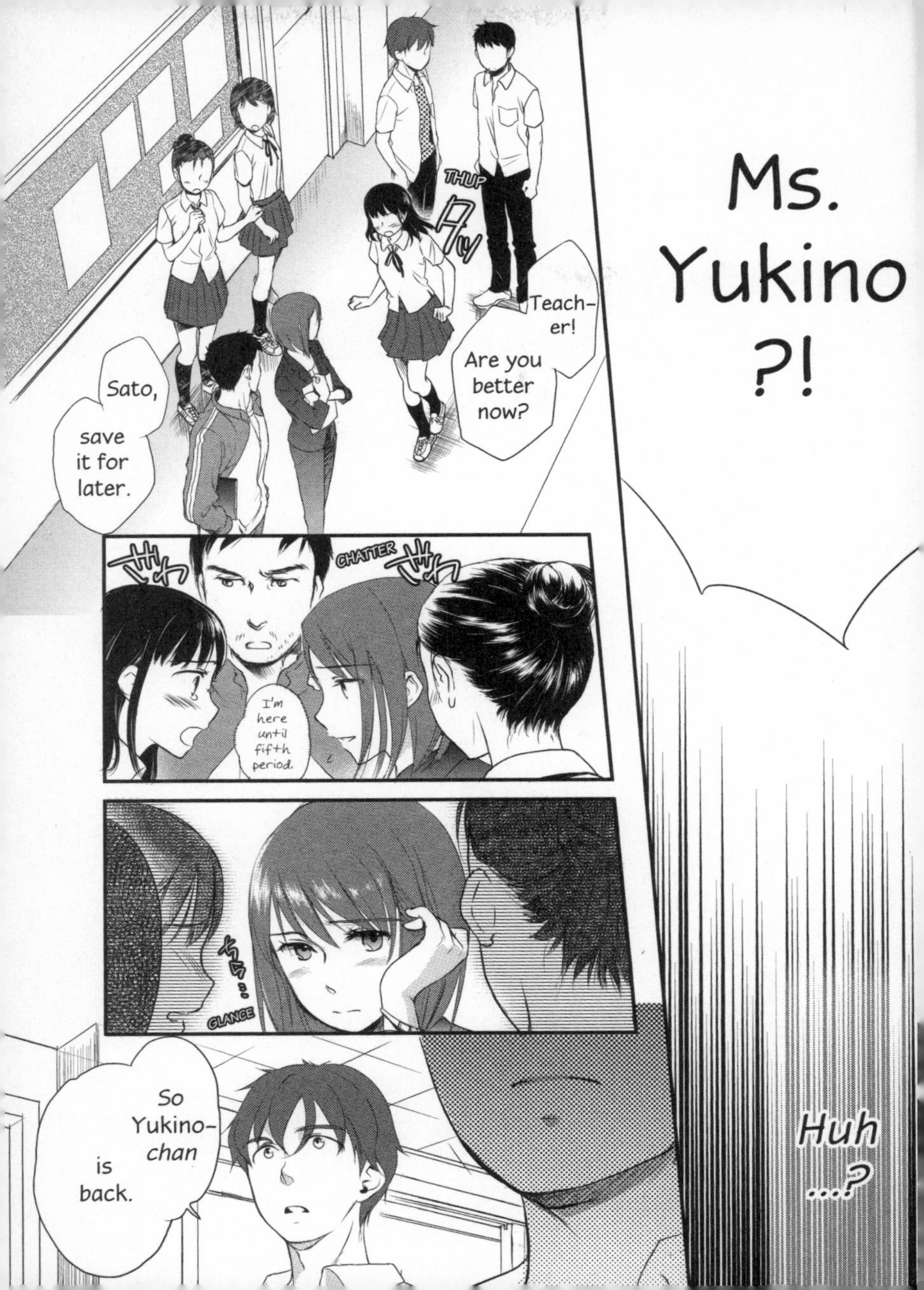

Ms. Yukino ?!
THUP
Teacher! Are you better now?
Sato, save it for later.
CHATTER
I'm here until fifth period.
GLANCE
So Yukino-chan is back.
Huh ...?

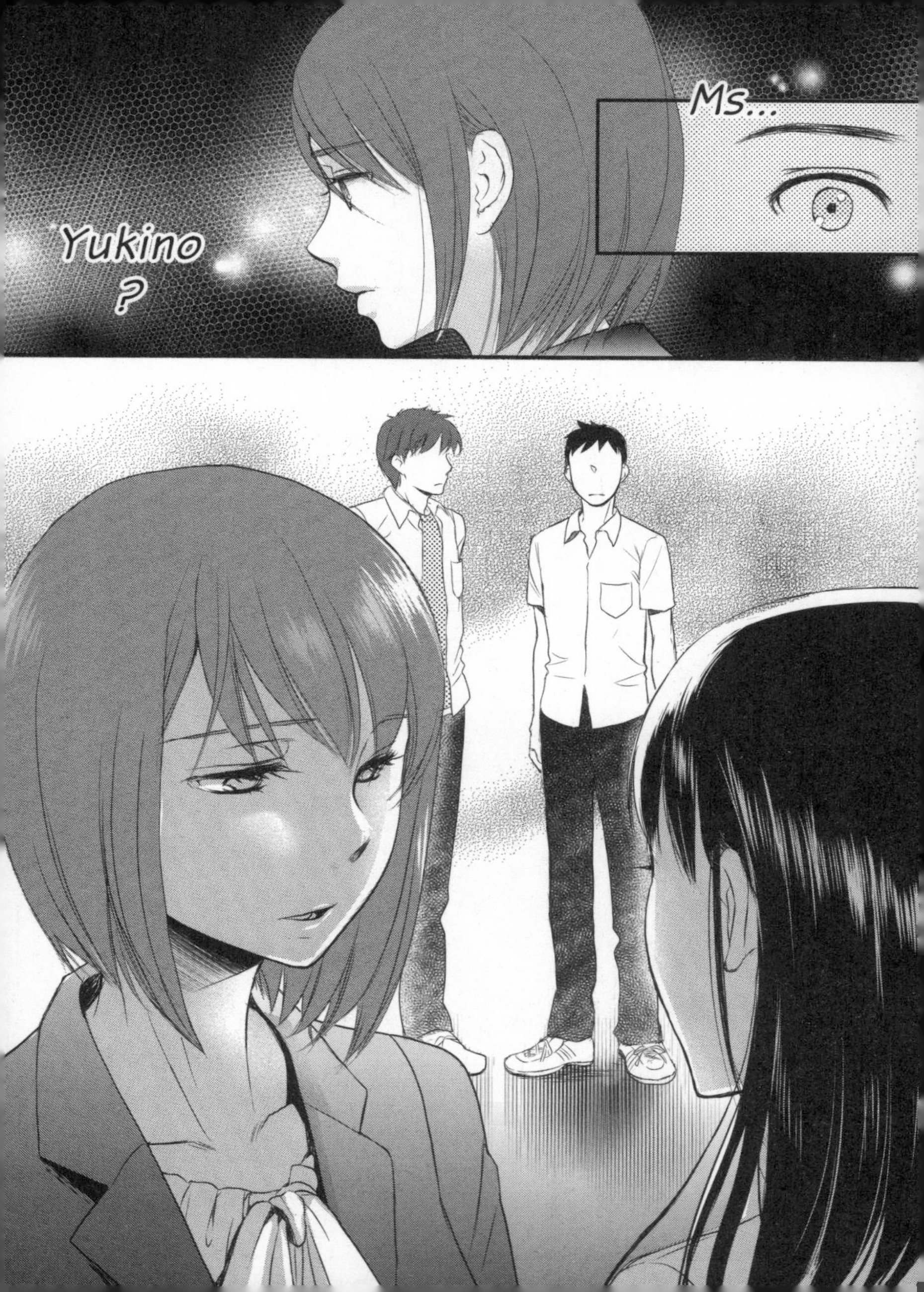
Ms...
Yukino ?

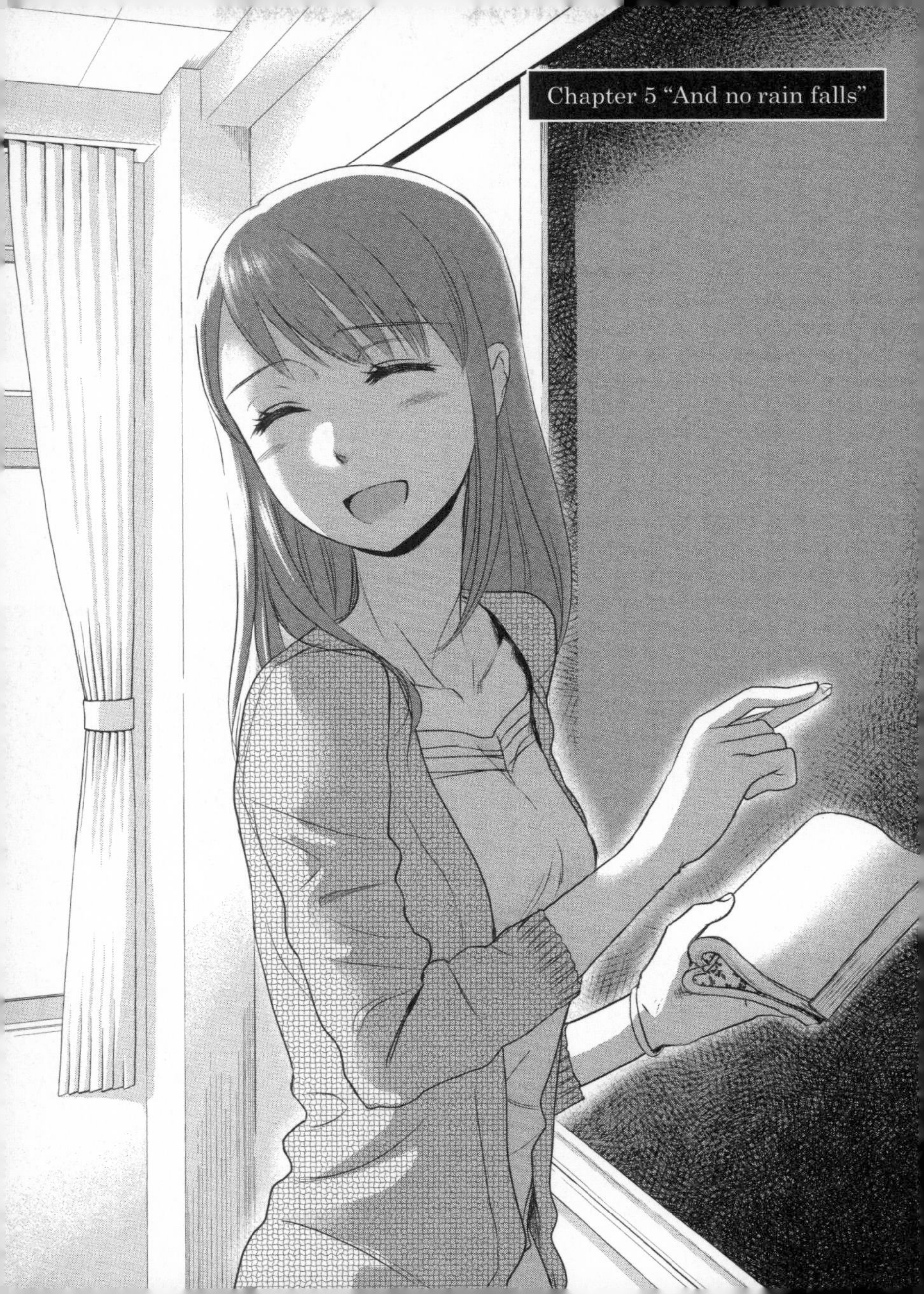
Chapter 5 “And no rain falls”

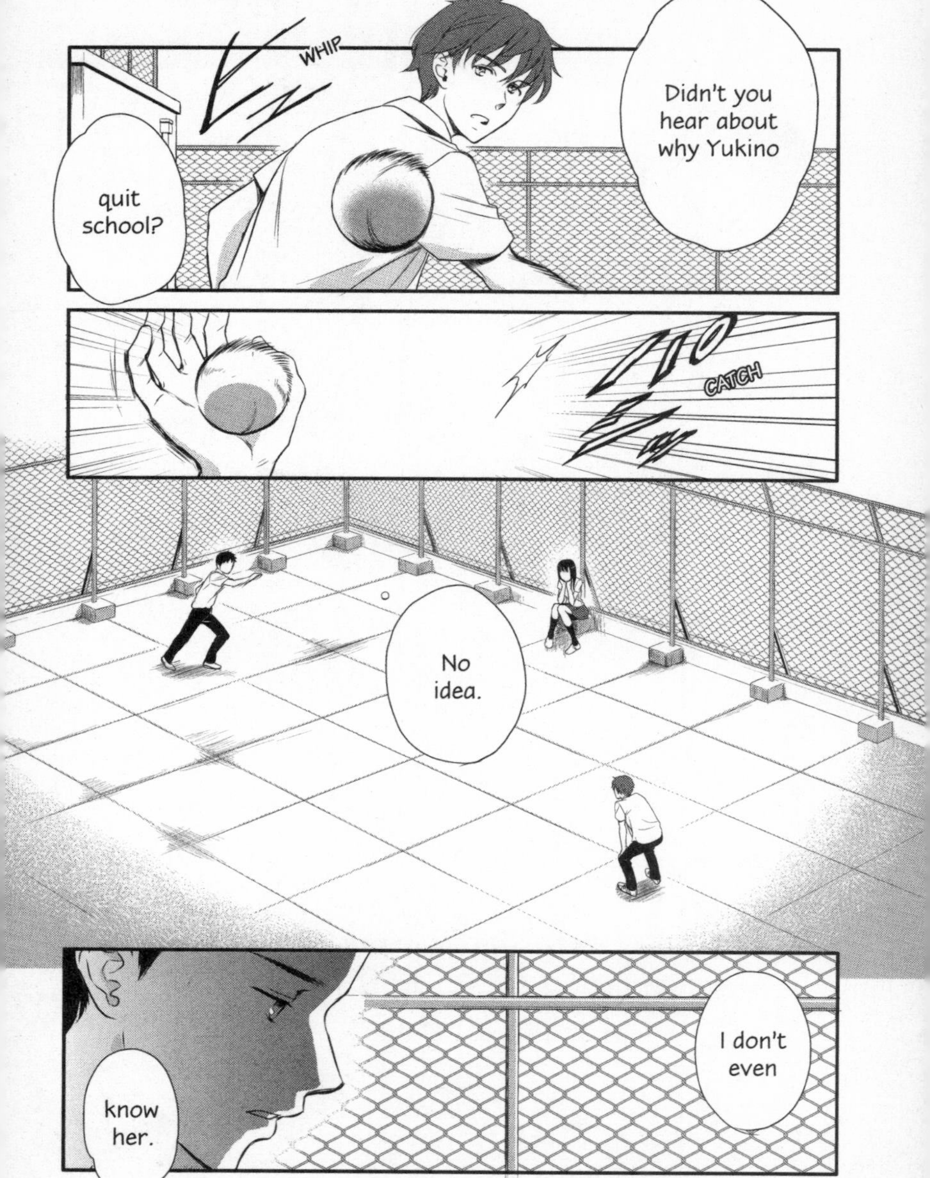
Didn't you hear about why Yukino
WHIP
quit school?
CATCH
No idea.
I don't even
know her.

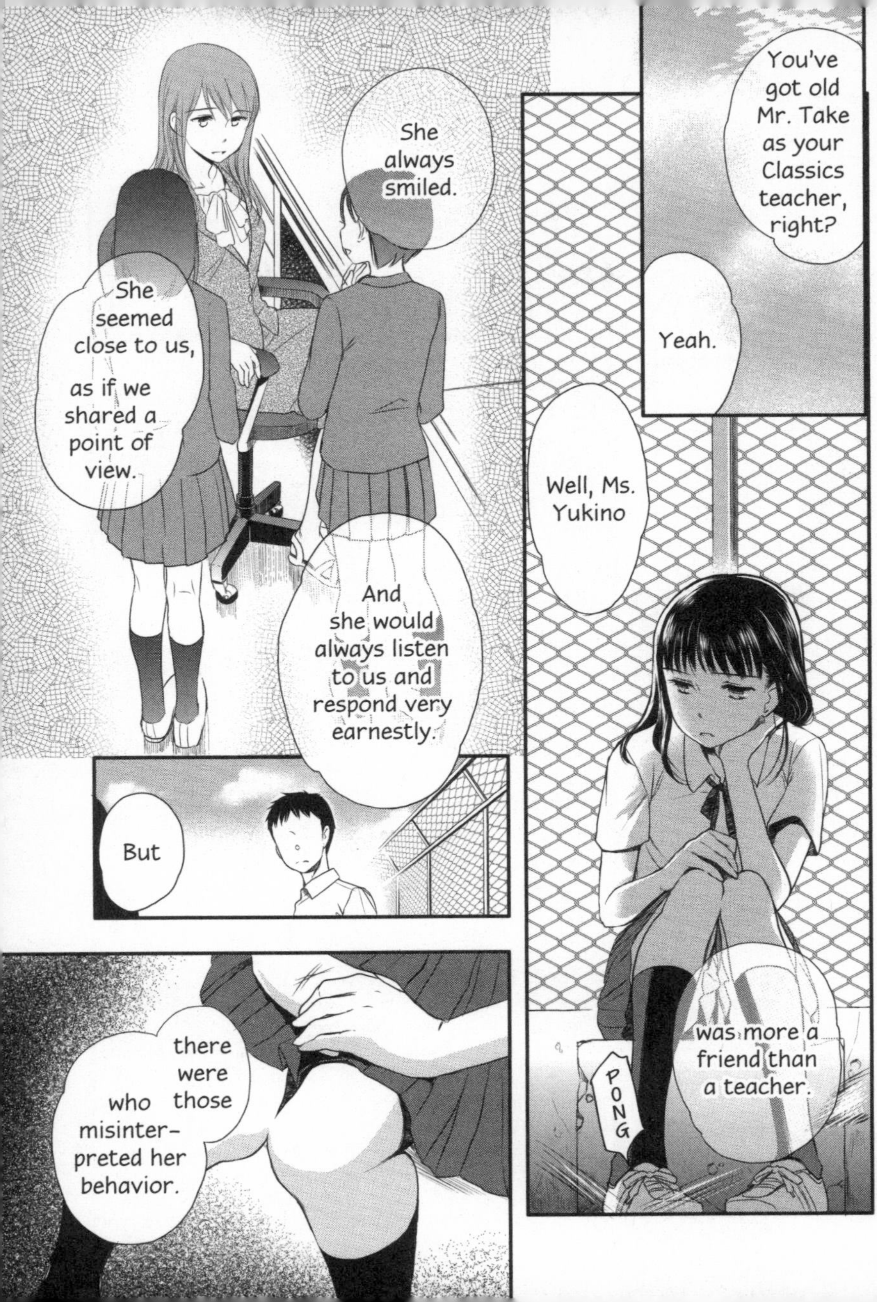
You've got old Mr. Take as your Classics teacher, right?
Yeah.
Well, Ms. Yukino
was more a friend than a teacher.
PONG
She always smiled.
She seemed close to us,
as if we shared a point of view.
And she would always listen to us and respond very earnestly.
But
there were those who misinter-preted her behavior.

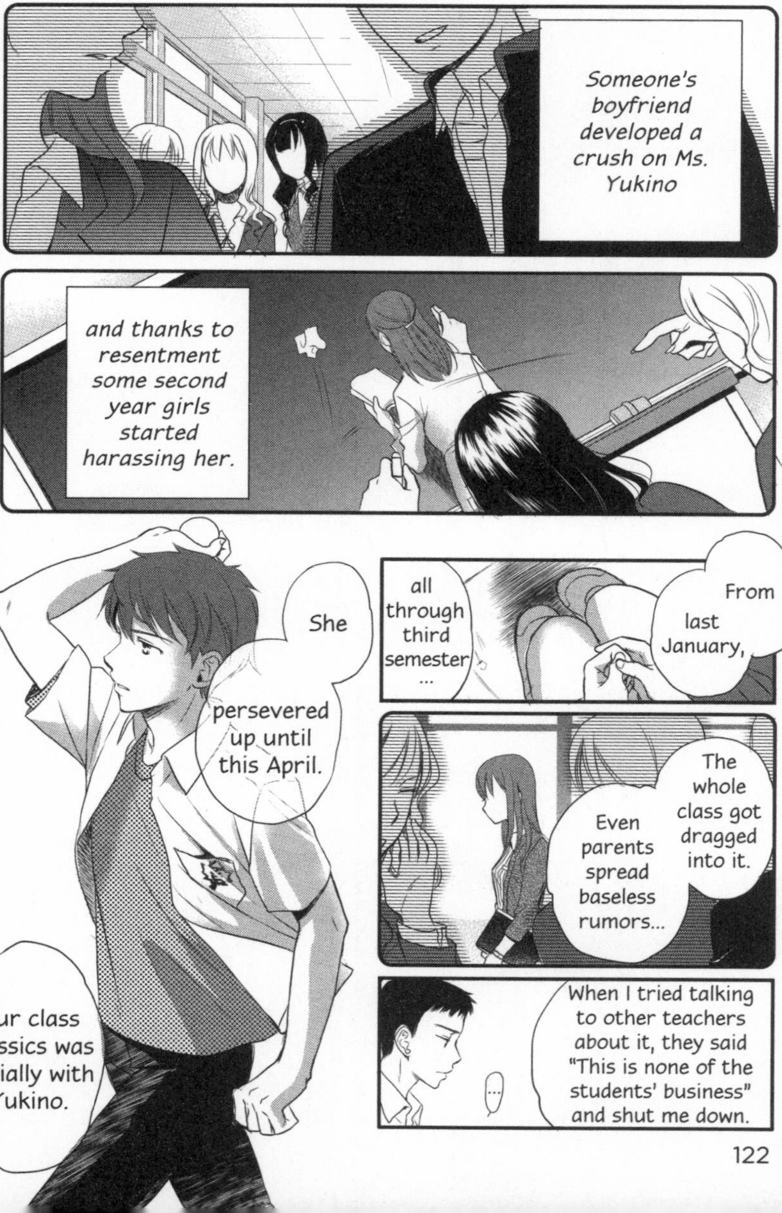

Someone's boyfriend developed a crush on Ms. Yukino
and thanks to resentment some second year girls started harassing her.
From last January,
all through third semester ...
The whole class got dragged into it.
Even parents spread baseless rumors...
When I tried talking to other teachers about it, they said "This is none of the students' business" and shut me down.
...
She
persevered up until this April.
Our class Classics was initially with Yukino.

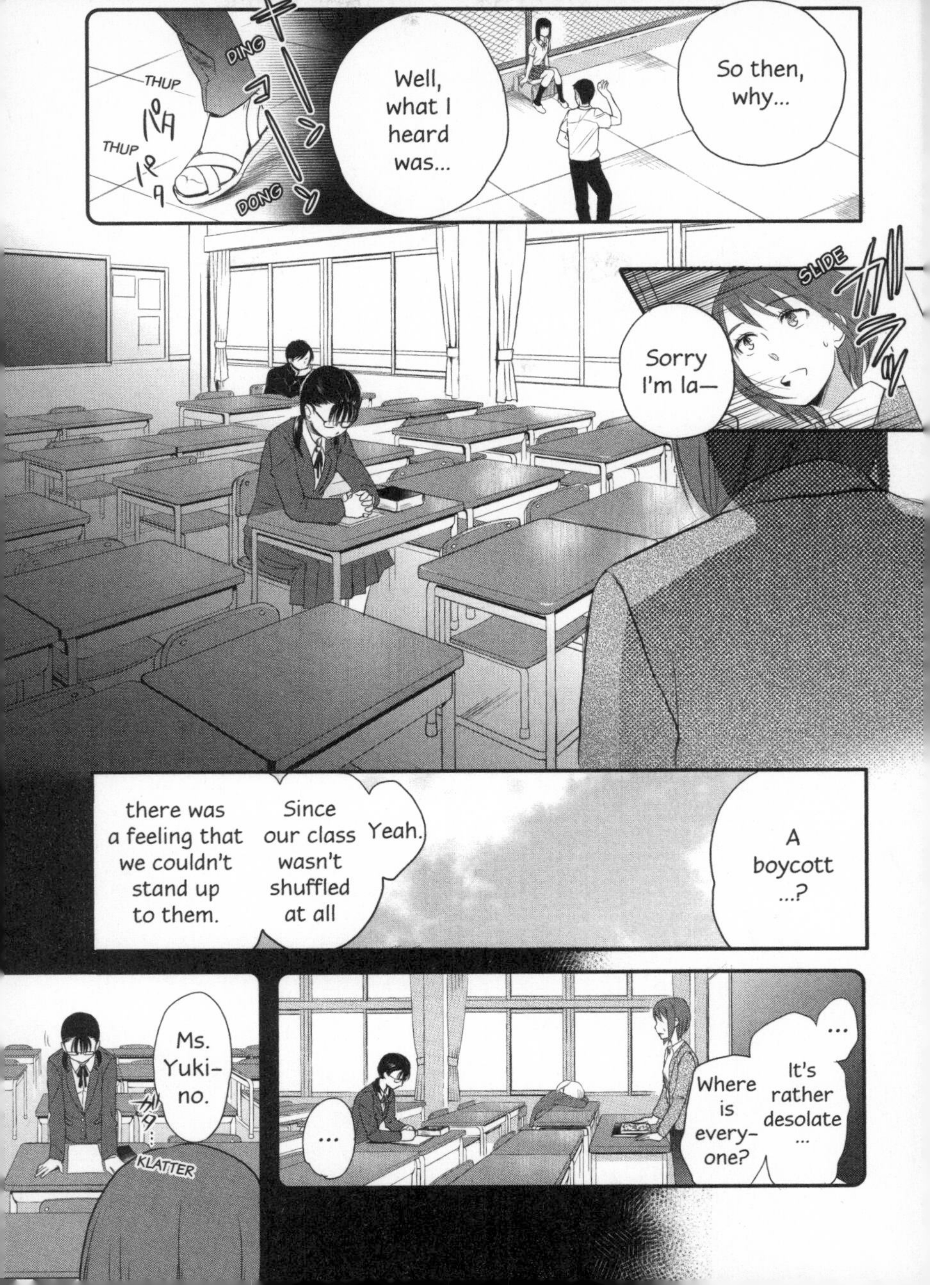
So then, why...
Well, what I heard was...
DING
DONG
THUP
THUP
SLIDE
Sorry I'm la—
A boycott ...?
Yeah.
Since our class wasn't shuffled at all
there was a feeling that we couldn't stand up to them.
...
It's rather desolate ...
Where is every-one?
...
Ms. Yuki-no.
KLATTER

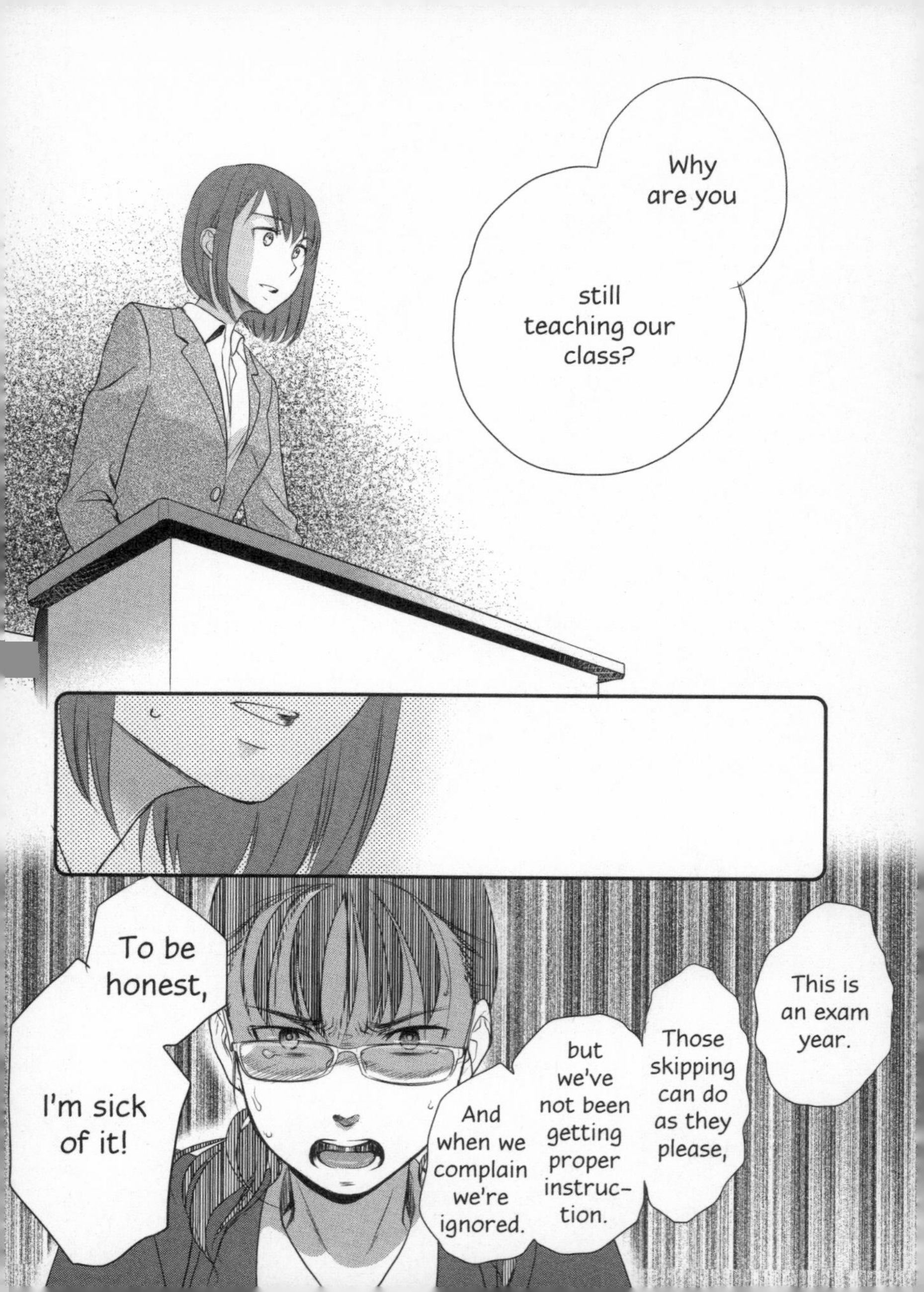

Why are you still teaching our class?
This is an exam year.
Those skipping can do as they please,
but we've not been getting proper instruction.
And when we complain we're ignored.
To be honest, I'm sick of it!

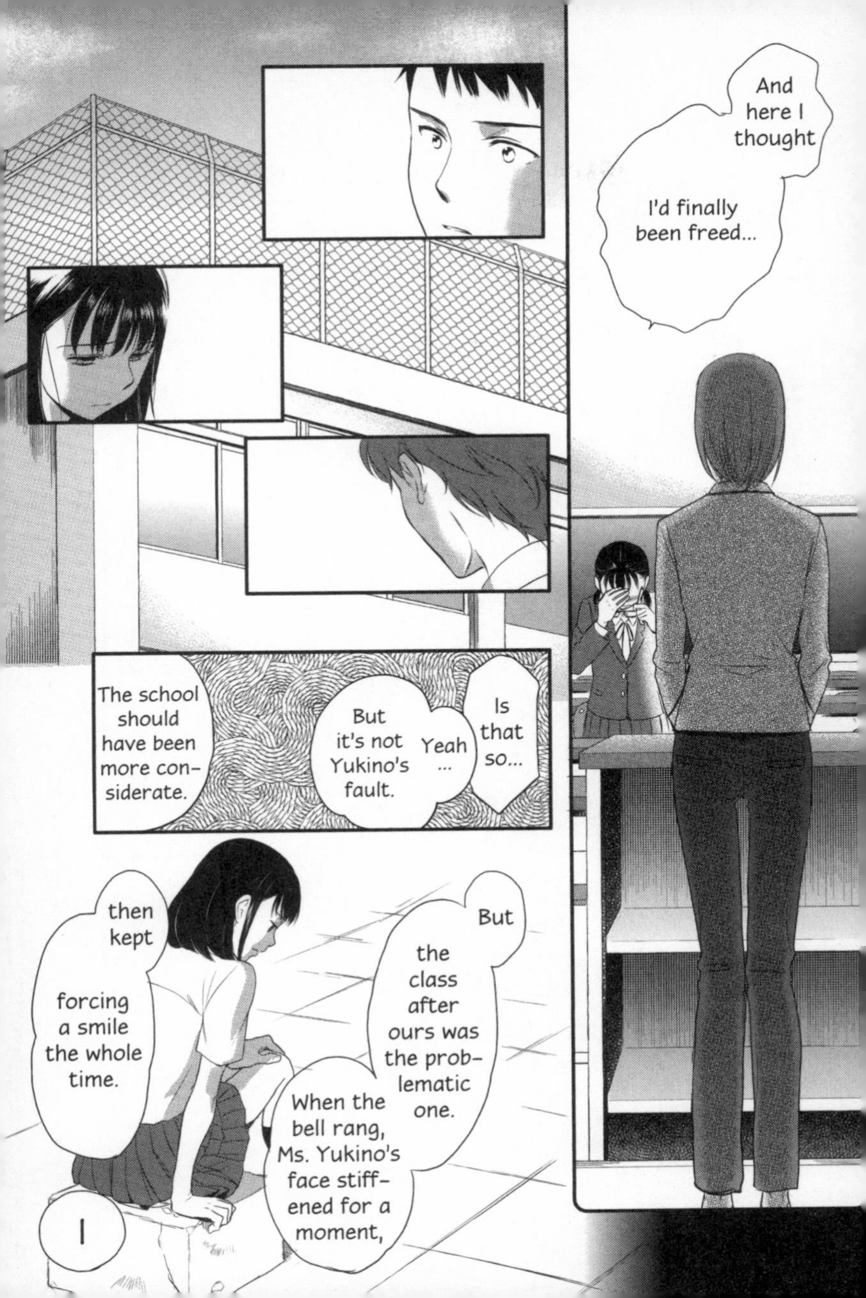
And here I thought
I'd finally been freed...
Is that so...
Yeah...
But it's not Yukino's fault.
The school should have been more considerate.
But the class after ours was the problematic one.
When the bell rang, Ms. Yukino's face stiffened for a moment,
then kept forcing a smile the whole time.

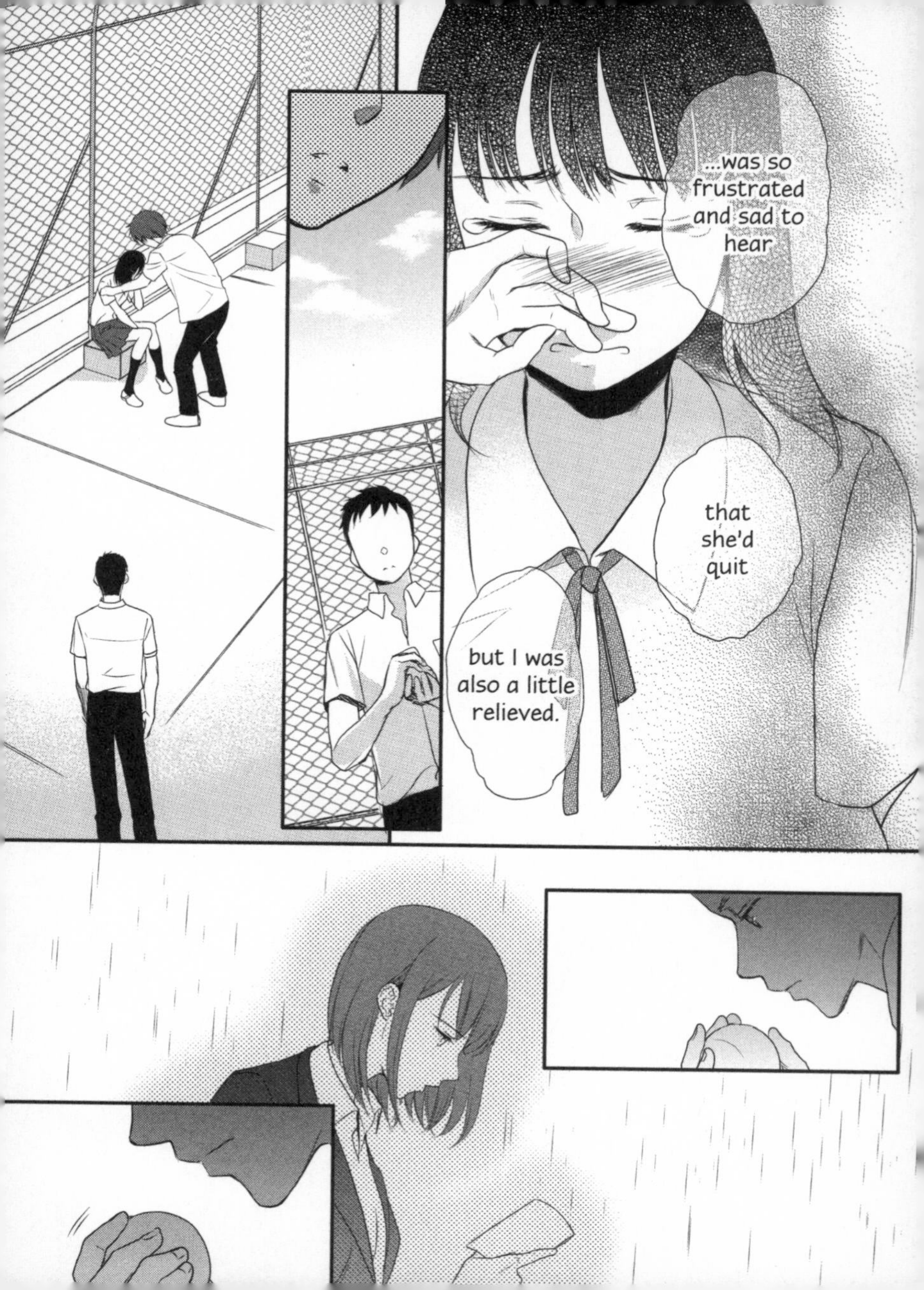
...was so frustrated and sad to hear
that she'd quit
but I was also a little relieved.

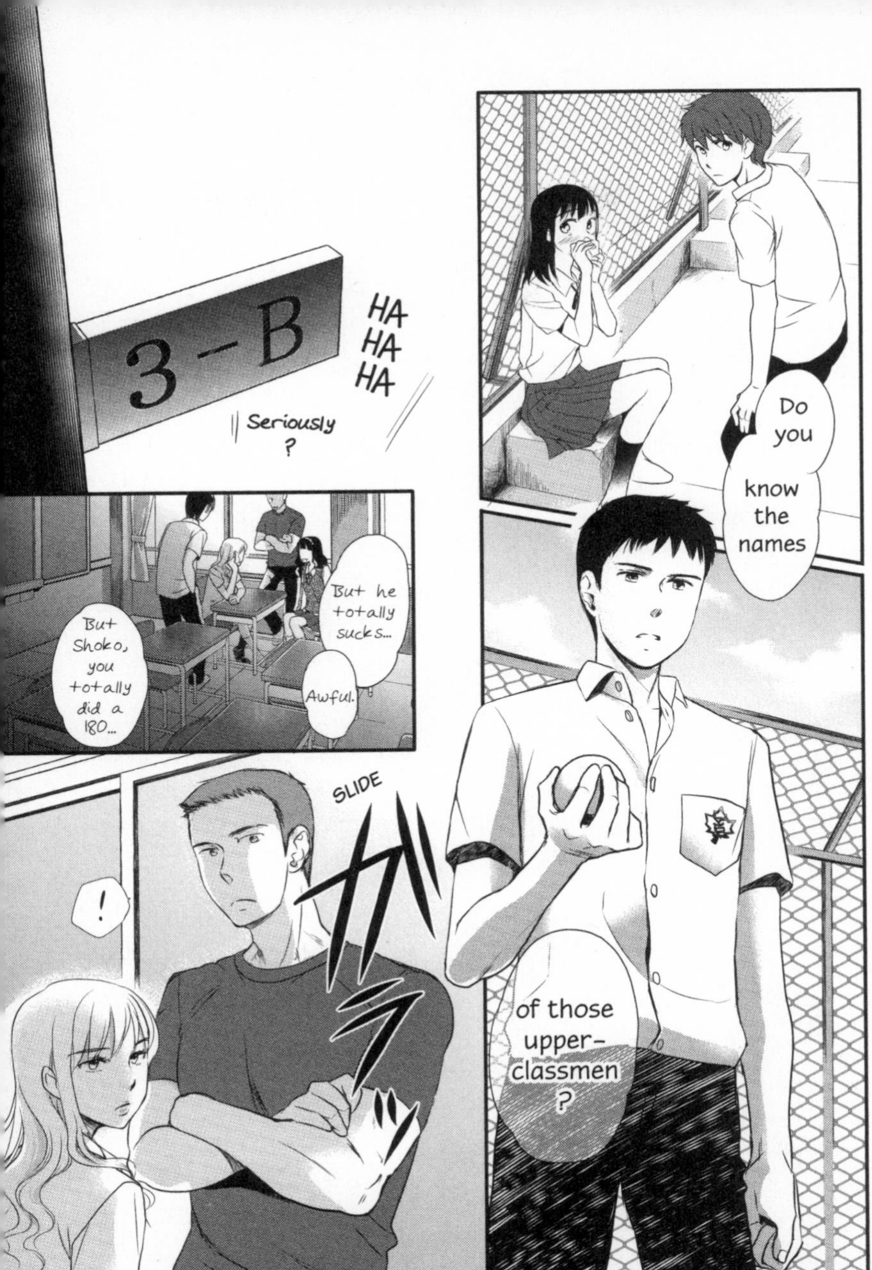
Do you know the names
of those upper-classmen?
HA HA HA
Seriously?
But he totally sucks...
Awful.
But Shoko, you totally did a 180...
SLIDE
!

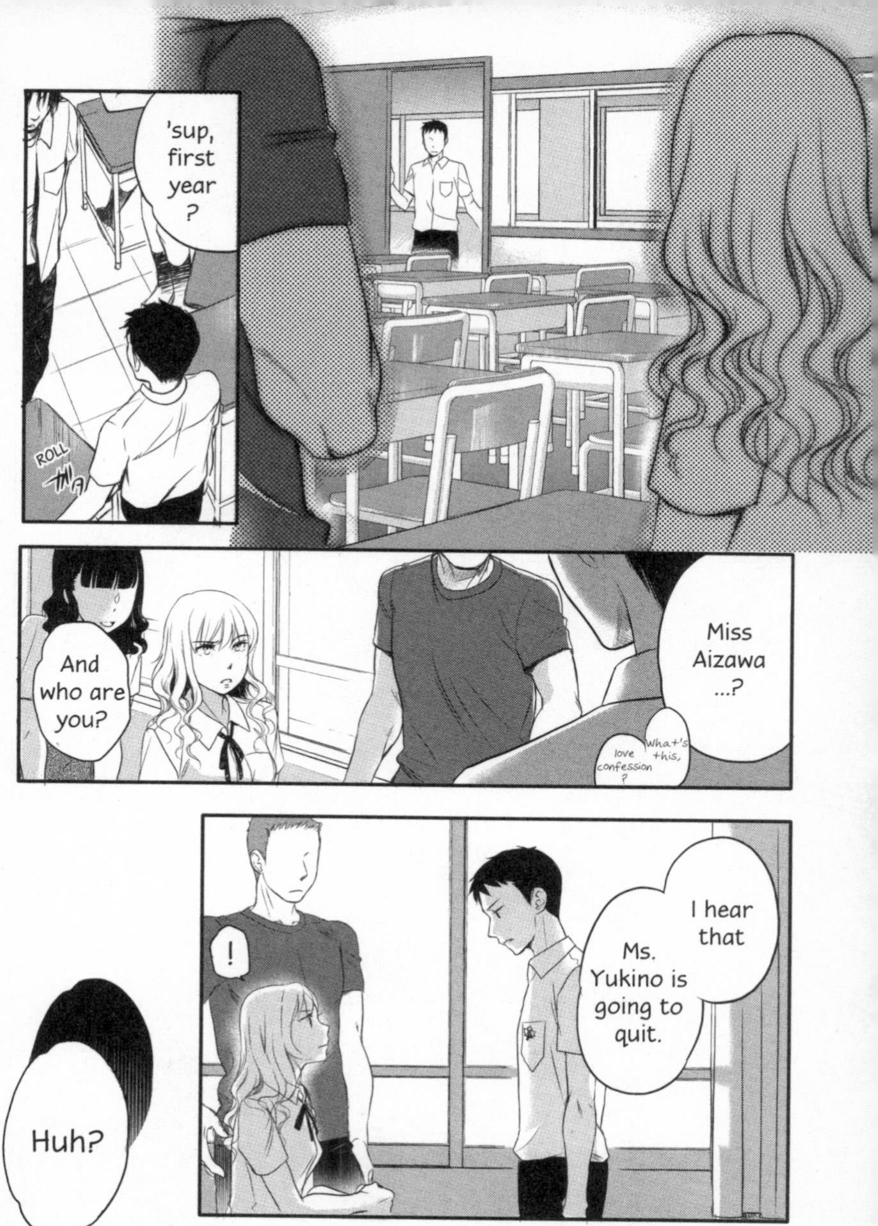
'sup, first year?
ROLL
Miss Aizawa ...?
What's this, love confession?
And who are you?
I hear that Ms. Yukino is going to quit.
!
Huh?

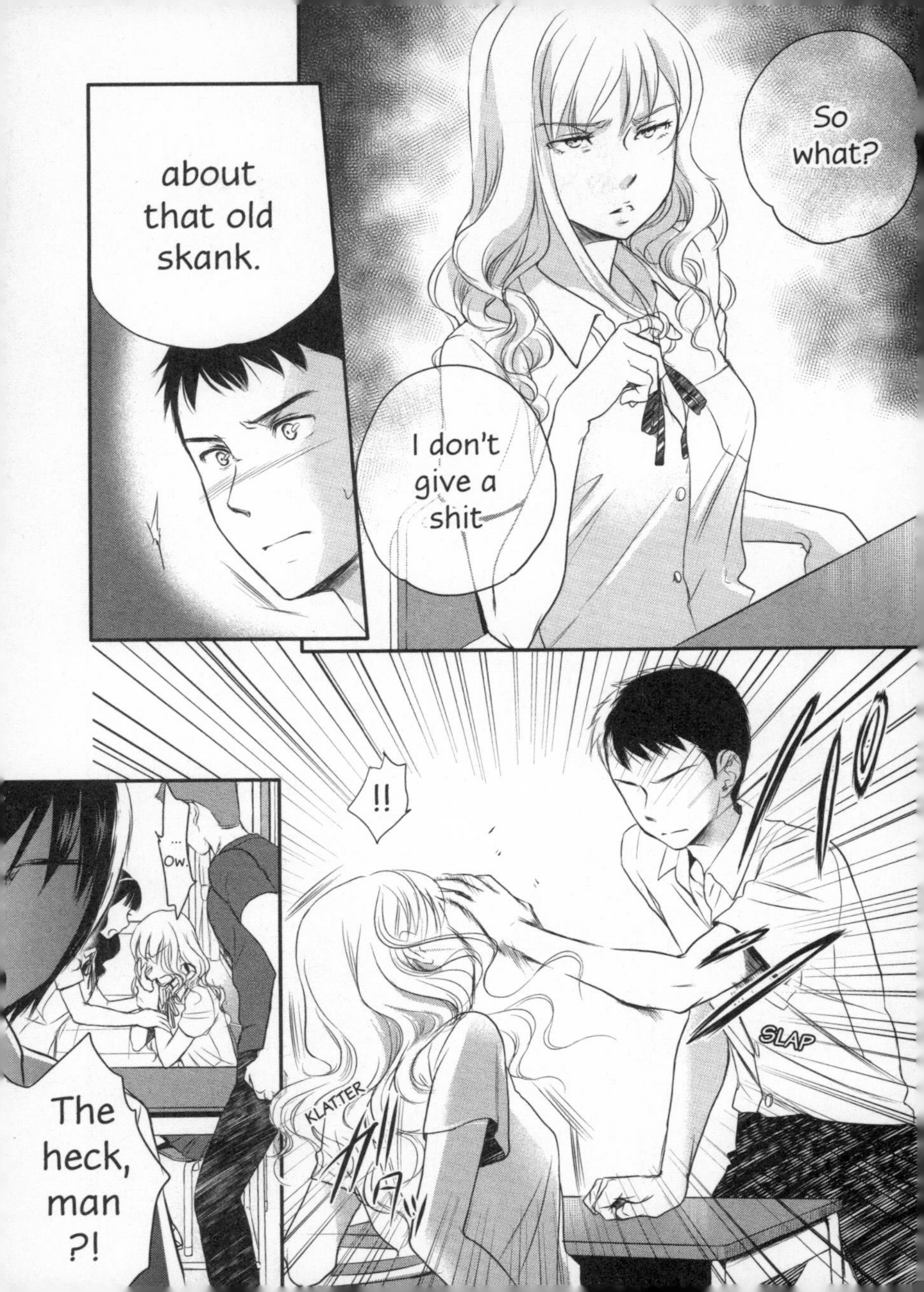
So what?
I don't give a shit
about that old skank.
!!
SLAP
KLATTER
... OW.
The heck, man ?!

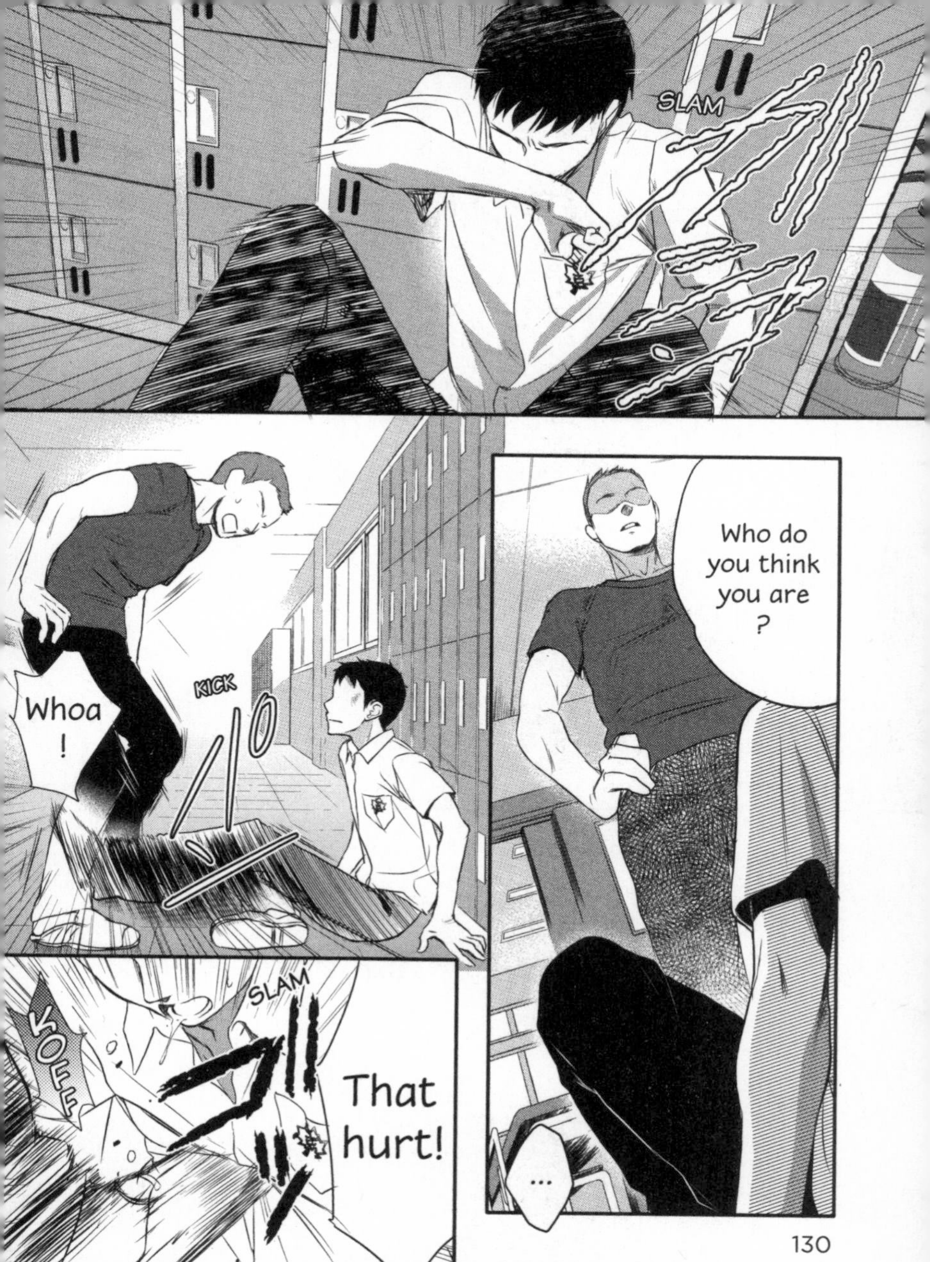
SLAM
Who do you think you are ?
...
KICK
Whoa !
SLAM
KOFF
That hurt!

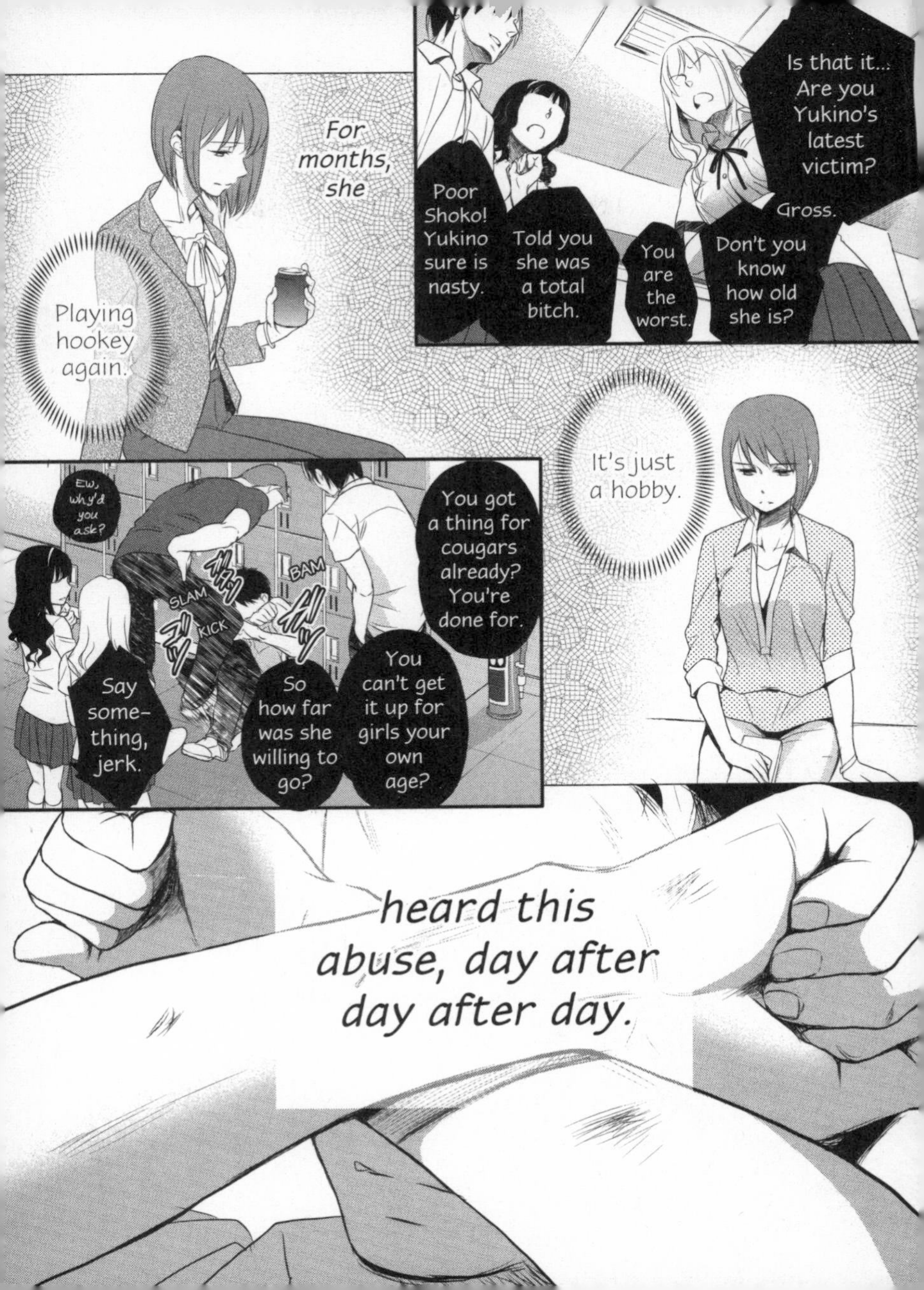
Is that it... Are you Yukino's latest victim?
Gross.
Don't you know how old she is?
You are the worst.
Told you she was a total bitch.
Poor Shoko! Yukino sure is nasty.
For months, she
Playing hookey again.
It's just a hobby.
You got a thing for cougars already? You're done for.
BAM
You can't get it up for girls your own age?
So how far was she willing to go?
SLAM
KICK
Ew, why'd you ask?
Say some-thing, jerk.
heard this abuse, day after day after day.

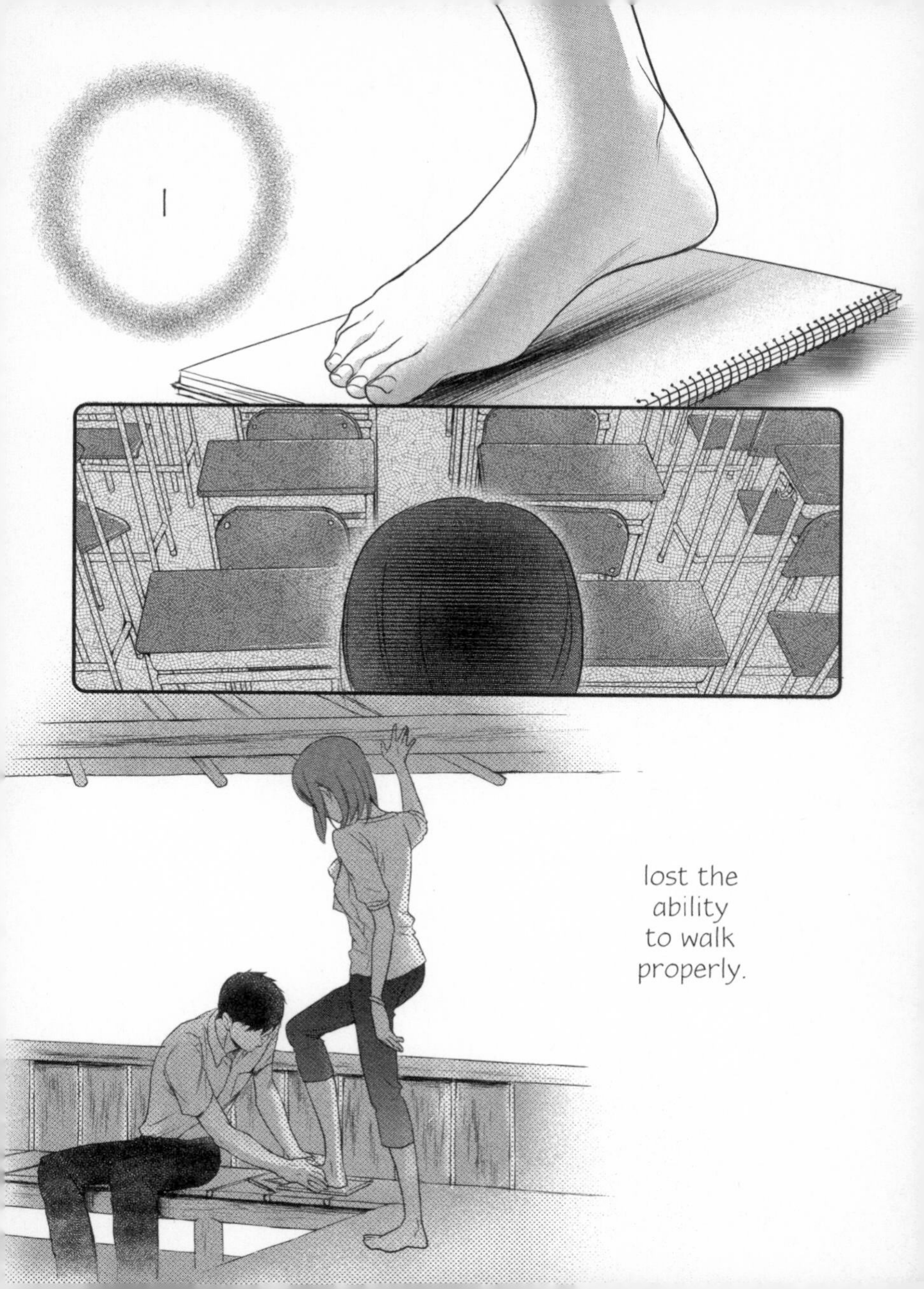
I
lost the ability to walk properly.

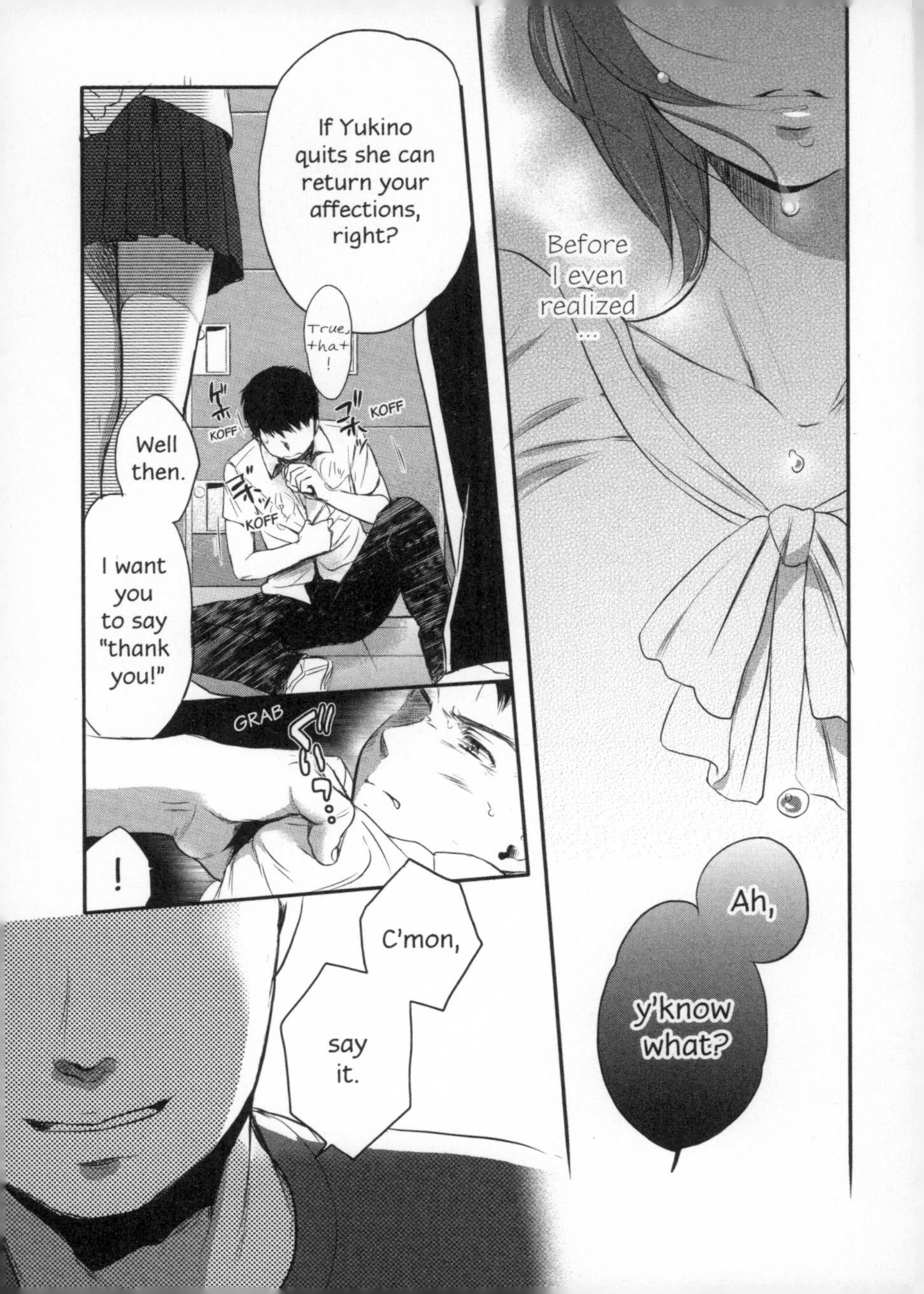
Before I even realized ...
Ah, y'know what?
If Yukino quits she can return your affections, right?
True, that!
KOFF
KOFF
KOFF
Well then.
I want you to say "thank you!"
GRAB
!
C'mon, say it.

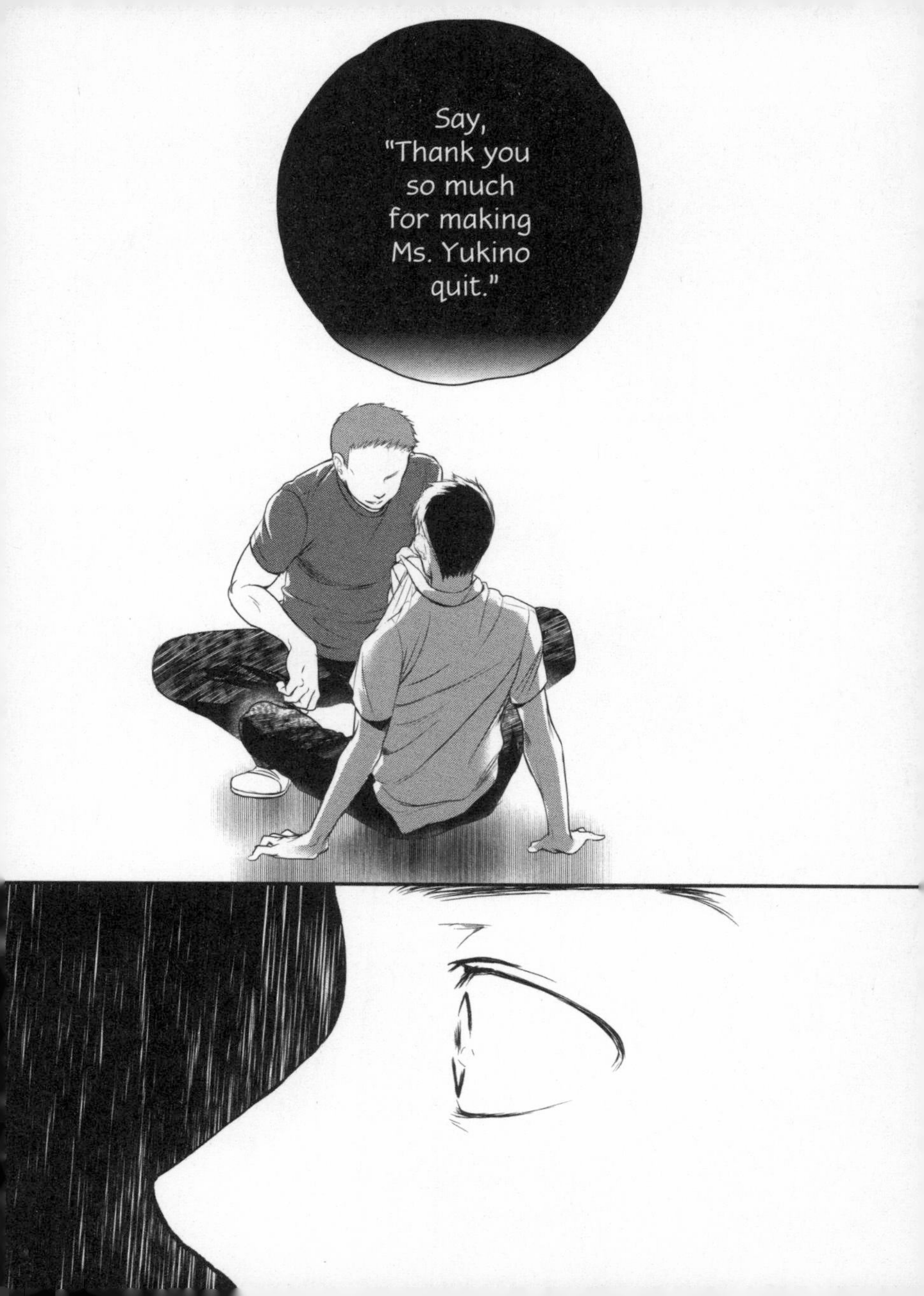
Say, "Thank you so much for making Ms. Yukino quit."

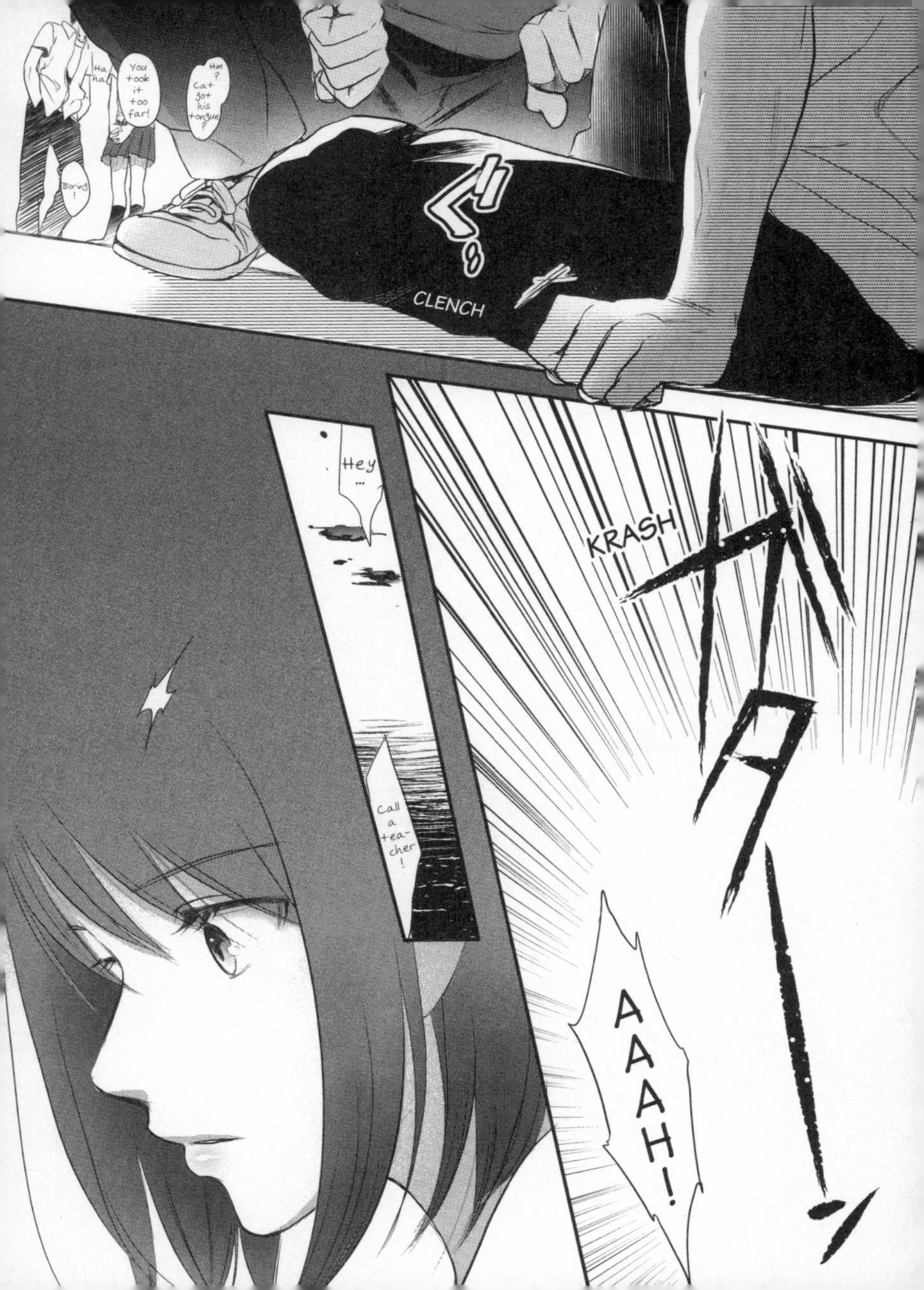
Hm? Cat got his tongue?
You took it too far!
Ha ha
Boring!
CLENCH
KRASH
AAAH!
Hey...
Call a teacher!

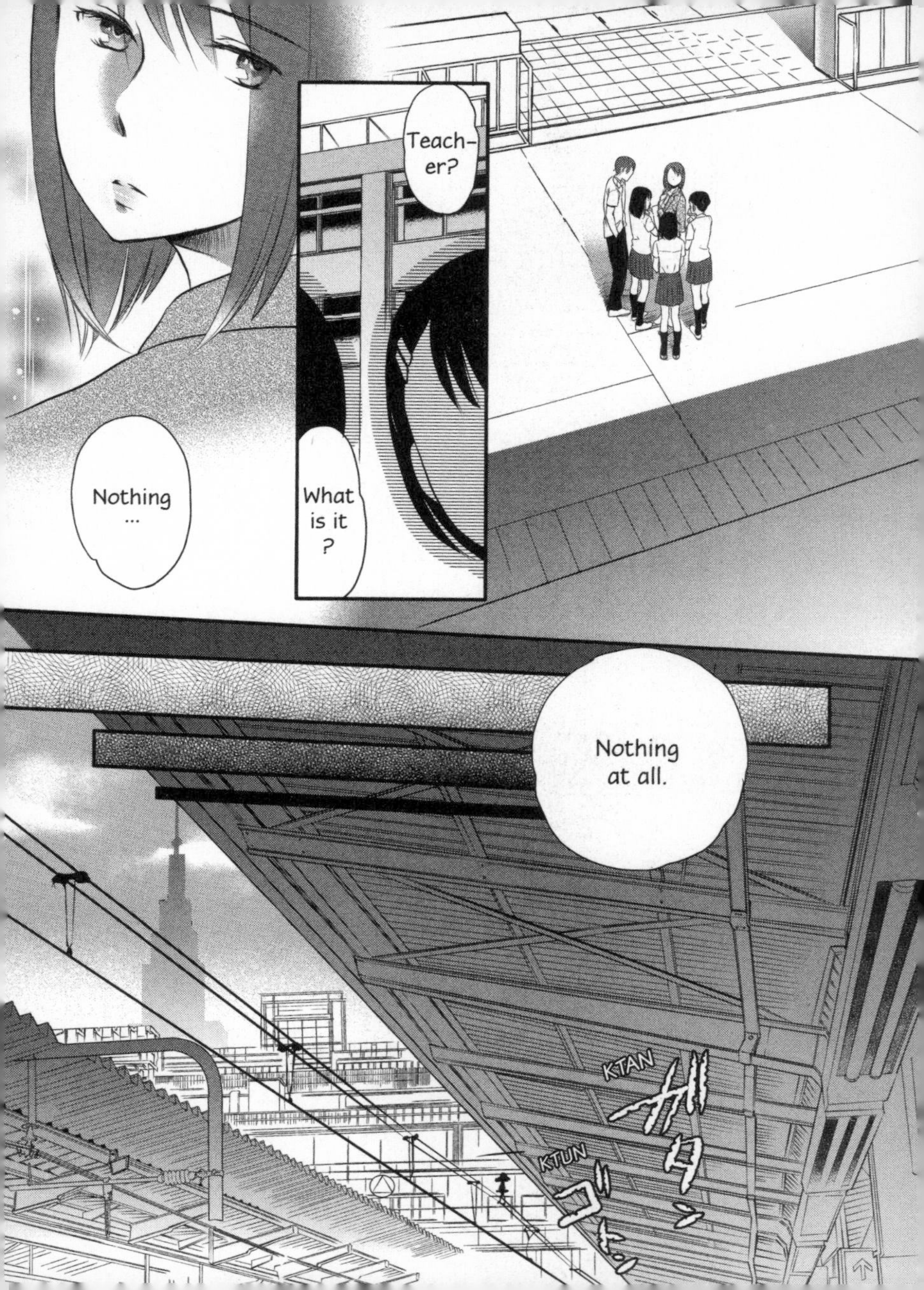
Teach-er?
What is it ?
Nothing ...
Nothing at all.
KTAN
KTUN

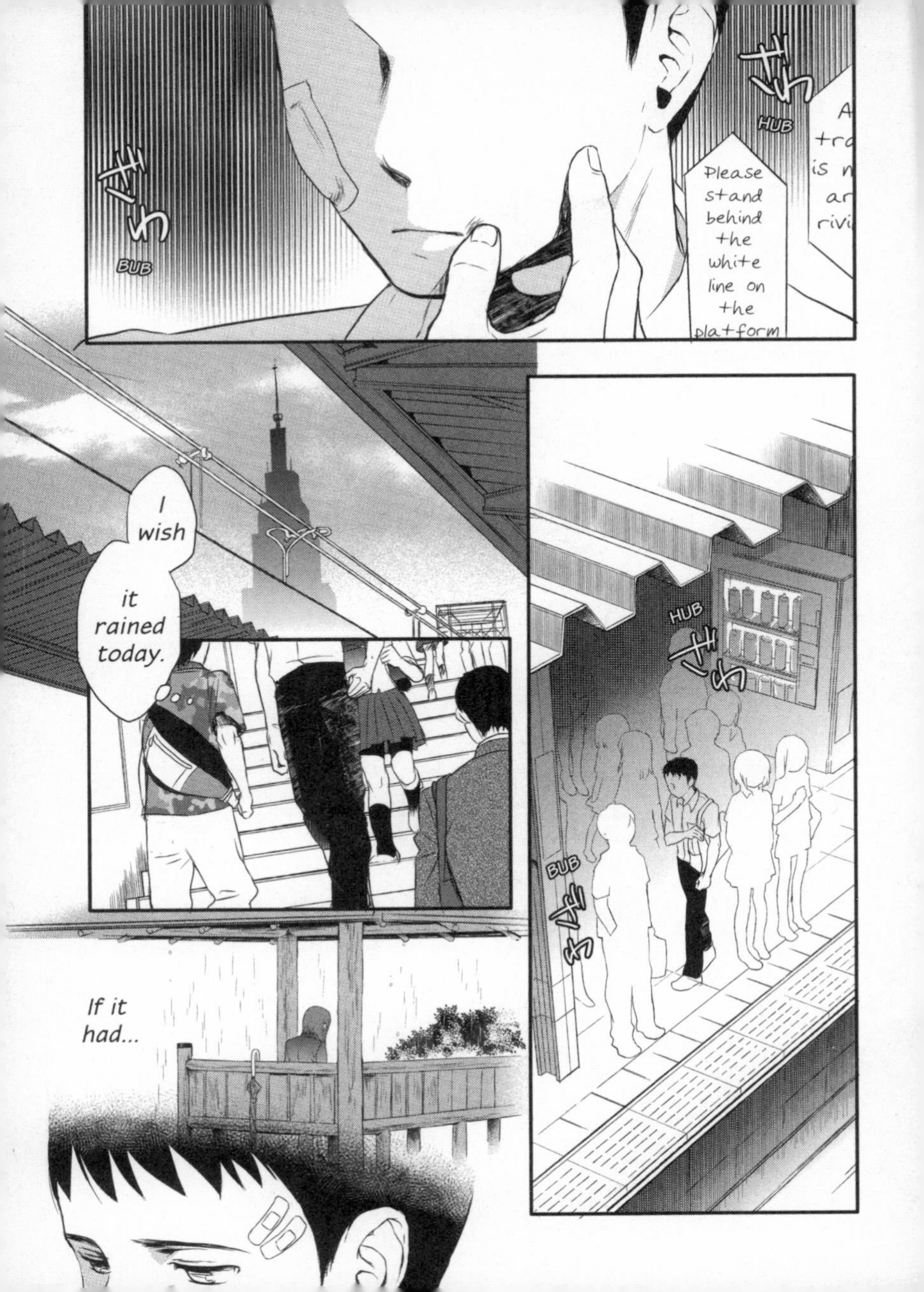
ざわ
HUB
Please stand behind the white line on the platform
ざわ
BUB
HUB
ざわ
BUB
ざわ
I wish it rained today.
If it had...

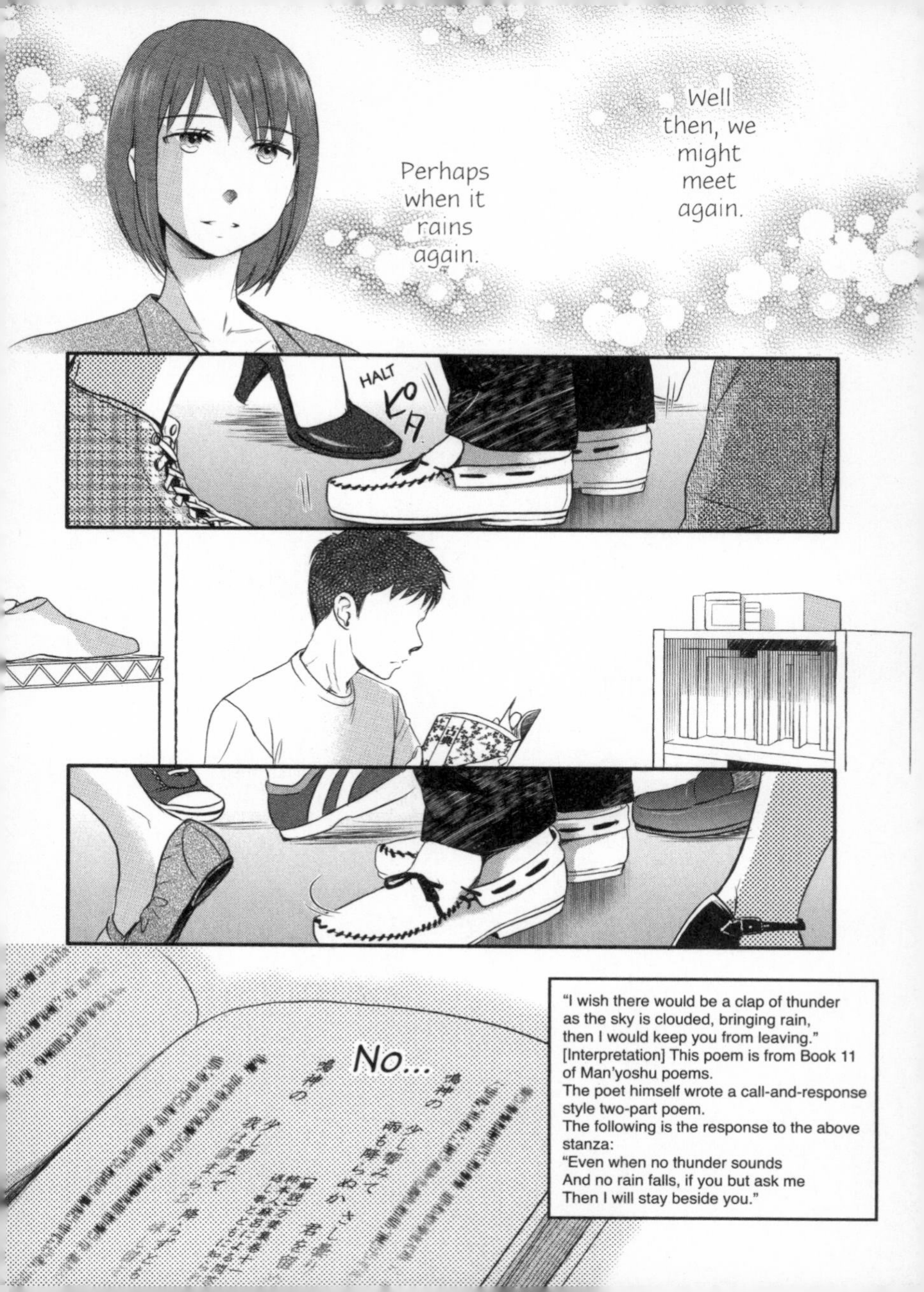
Well then, we might meet again.
Perhaps when it rains again.
HALT
"I wish there would be a clap of thunder as the sky is clouded, bringing rain, then I would keep you from leaving."
[Interpretation] This poem is from Book 11 of Man'yoshu poems.
The poet himself wrote a call-and-response style two-part poem.
The following is the response to the above stanza:
"Even when no thunder sounds
And no rain falls, if you but ask me
Then I will stay beside you."
No...

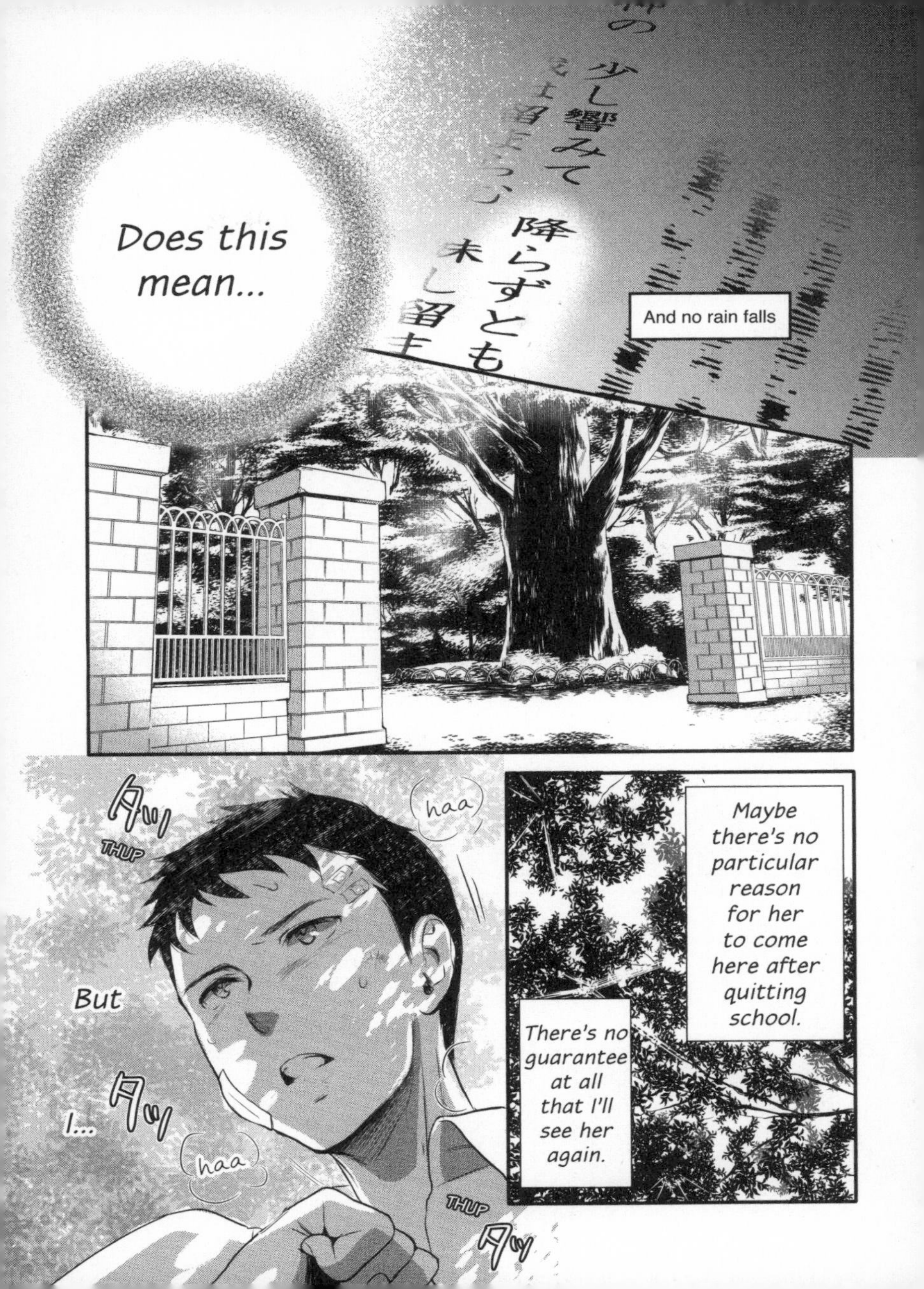
少し響みて
降らずとも
And no rain falls
Does this mean...
Maybe there's no particular reason for her to come here after quitting school.
There's no guarantee at all that I'll see her again.
haa
タッ
THUP
But
I...
タッ
haa
THUP
タッ

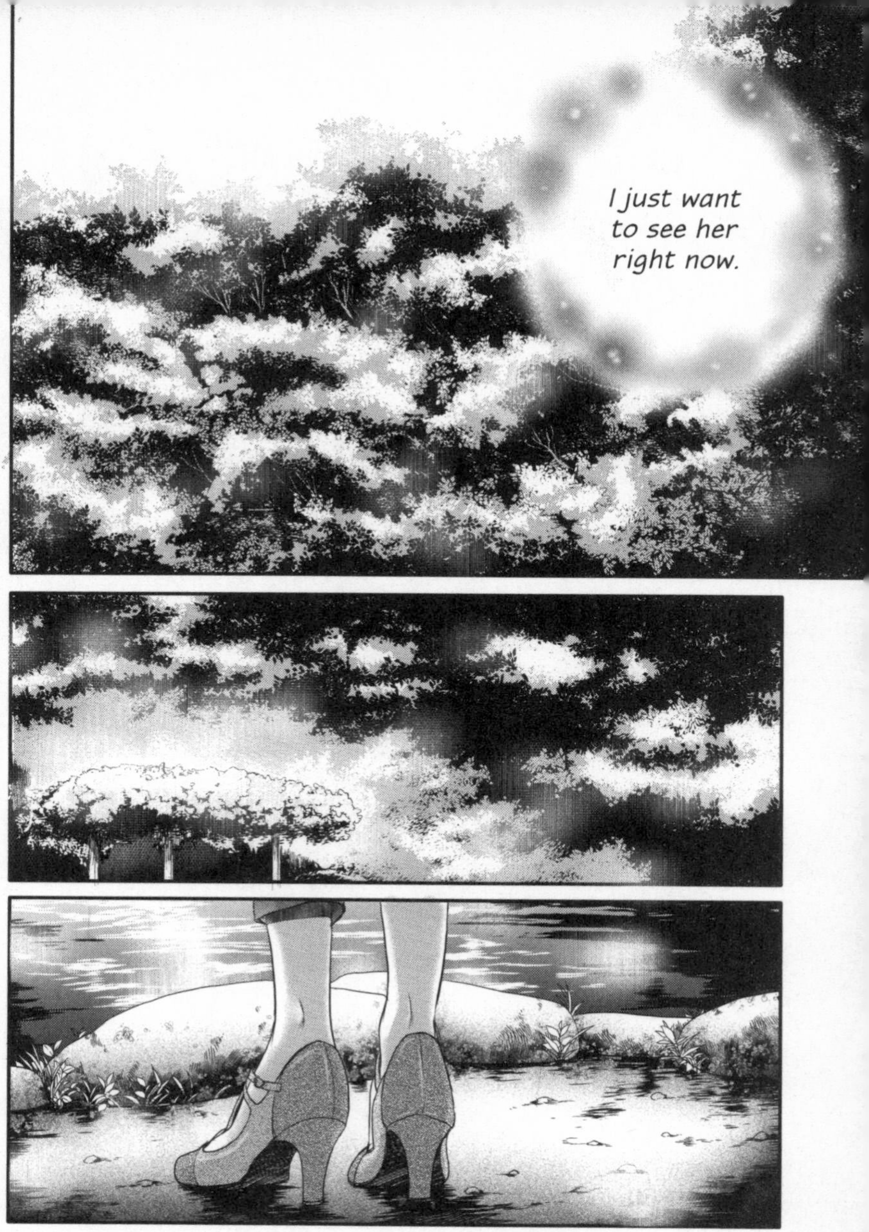
I just want to see her right now.

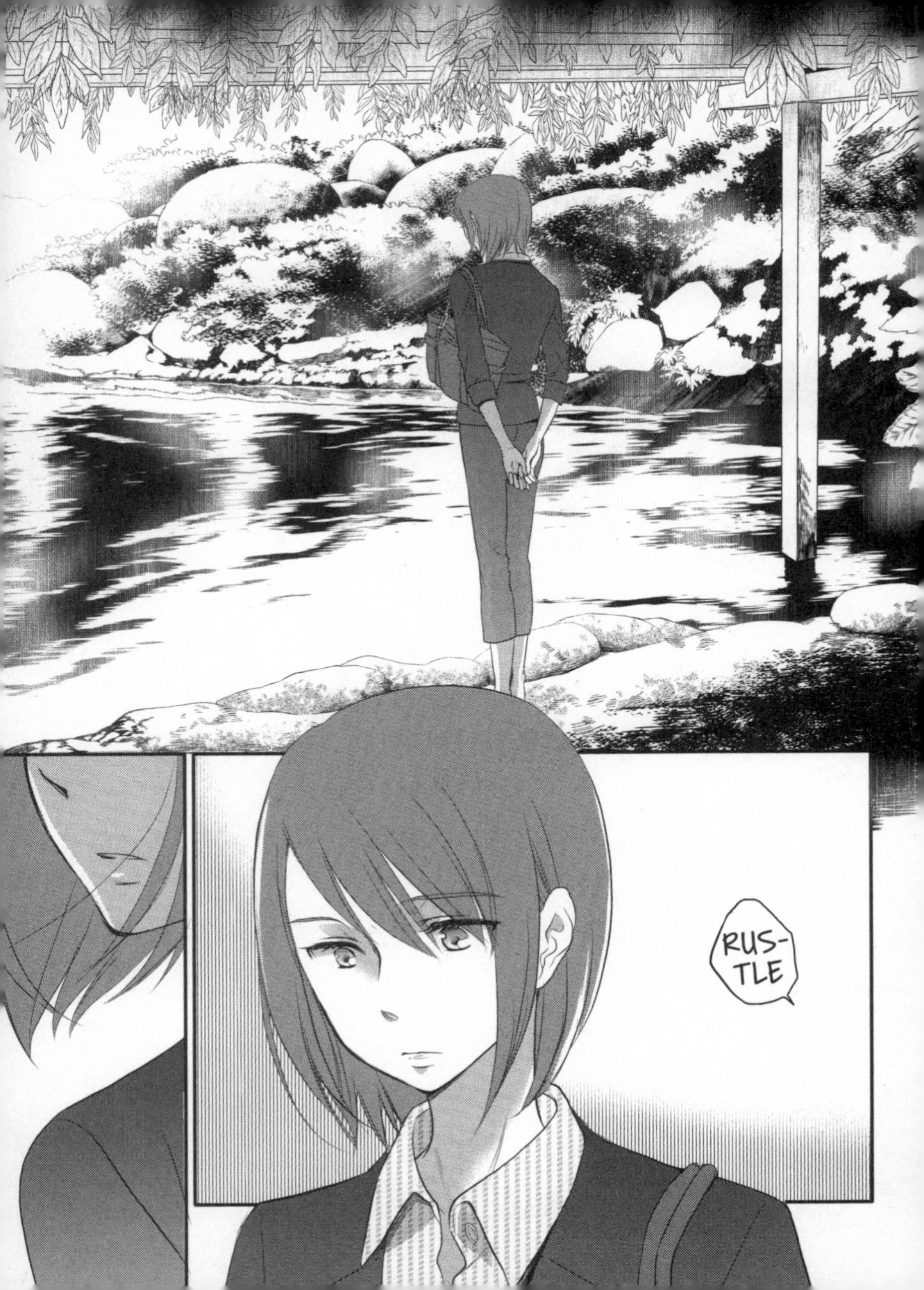
RUS-
TLE

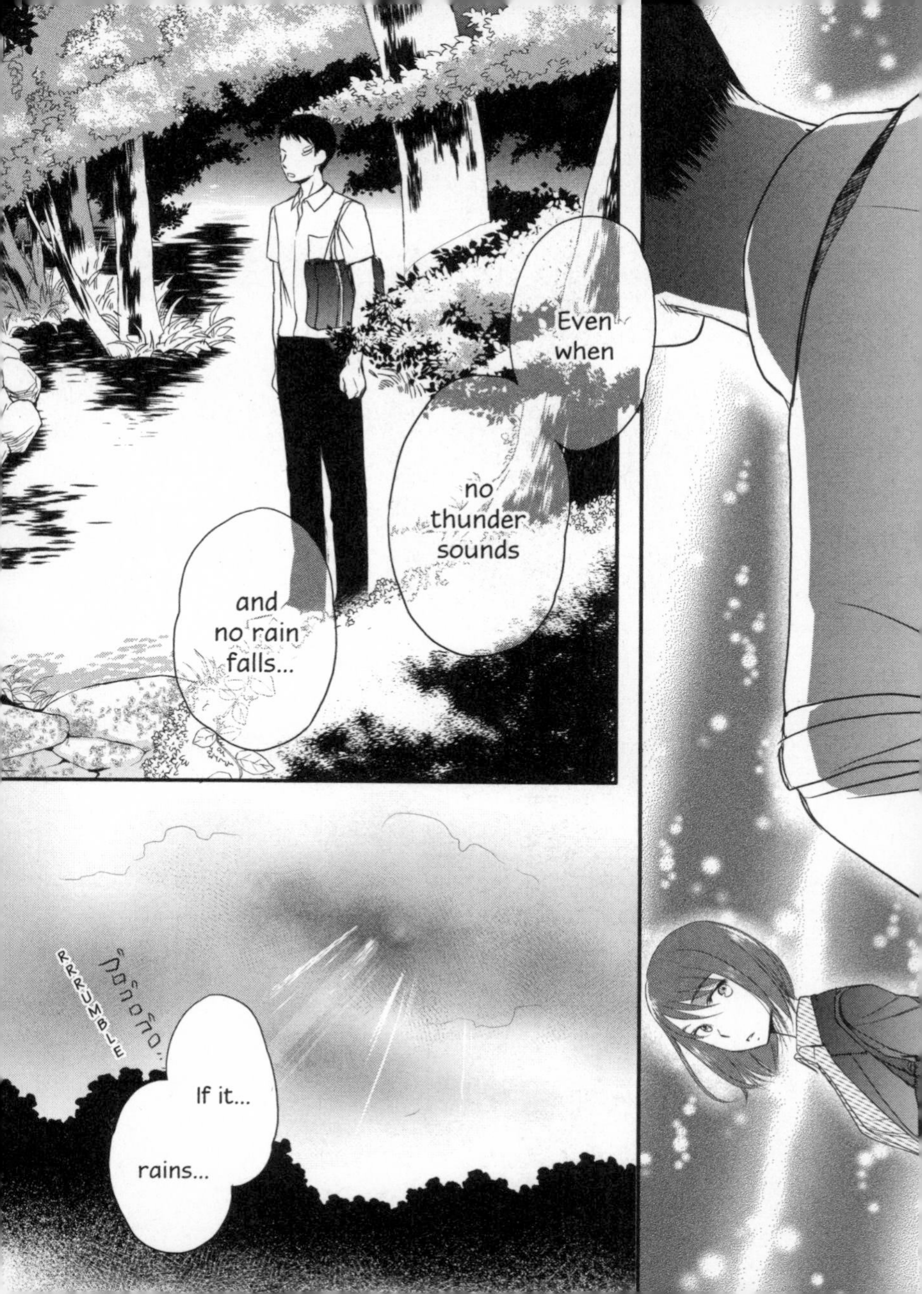
Even when
no thunder sounds
and no rain falls...
RRRUMBLE
If it...
rains...

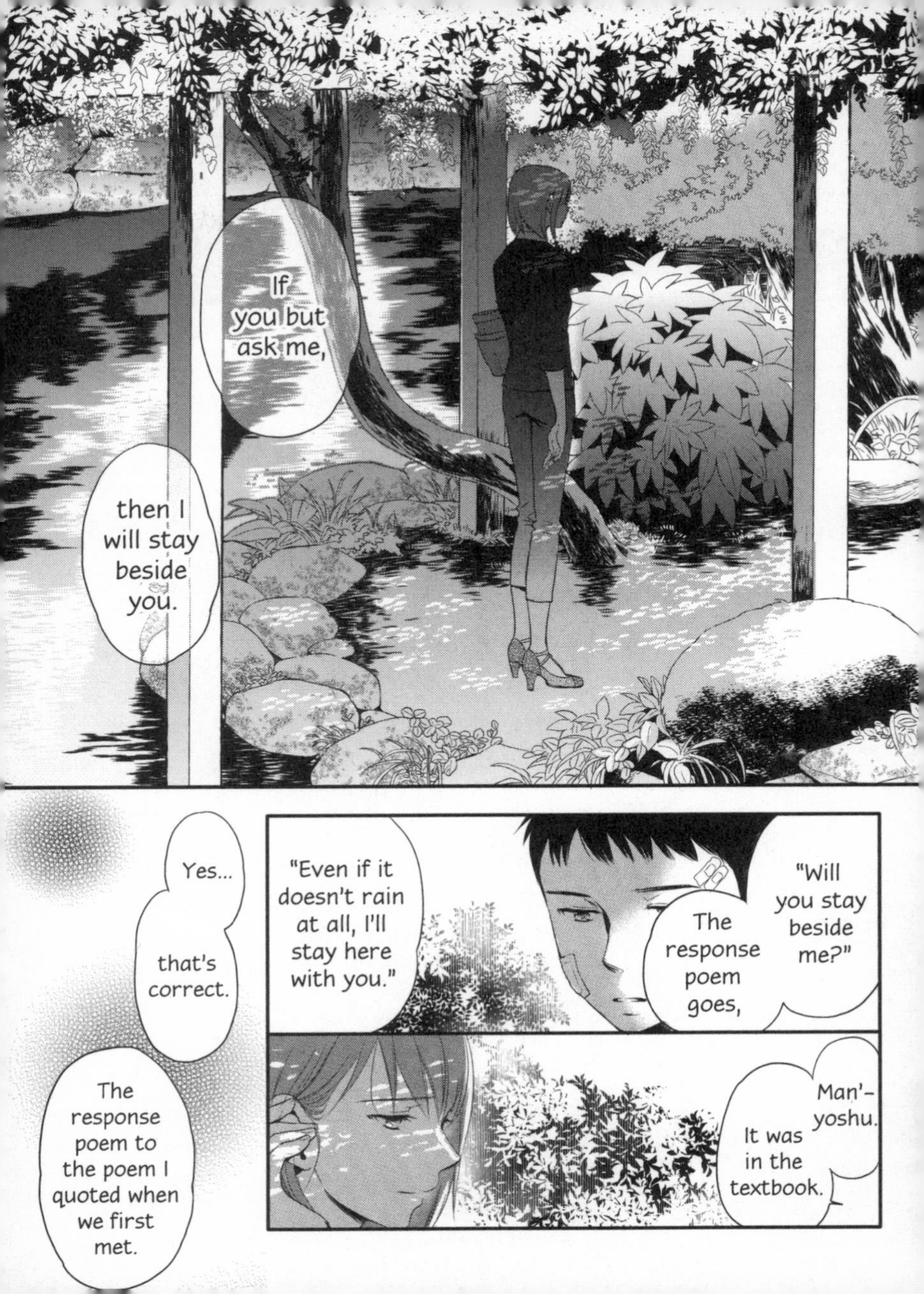
If you but ask me,
then I will stay beside you.
"Will you stay beside me?"
The response poem goes,
"Even if it doesn't rain at all, I'll stay here with you."
Yes...
that's correct.
Man'-yoshu.
It was in the textbook.
The response poem to the poem I quoted when we first met.

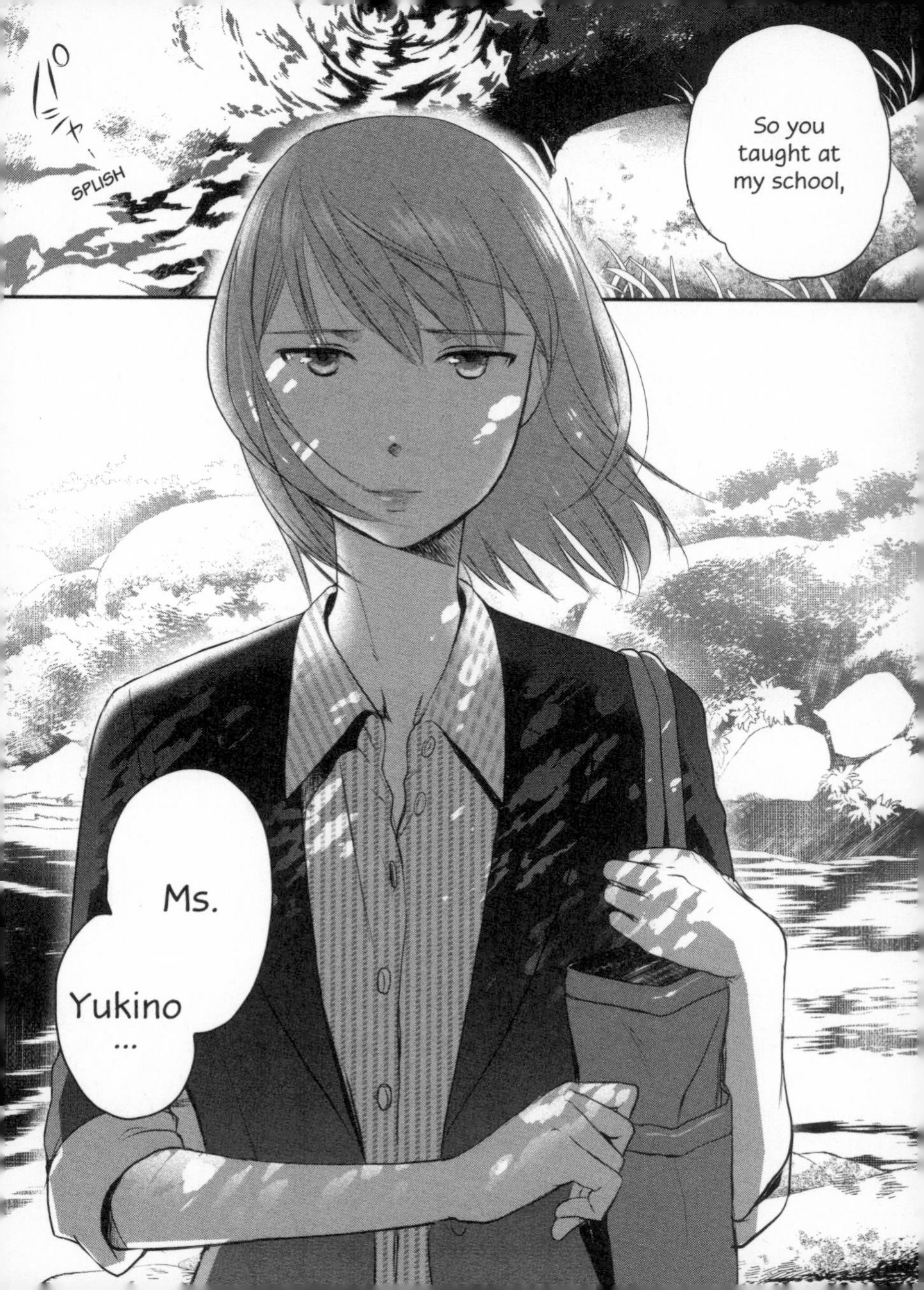
So you taught at my school,
パシャ
SPLISH
Ms. Yukino ...

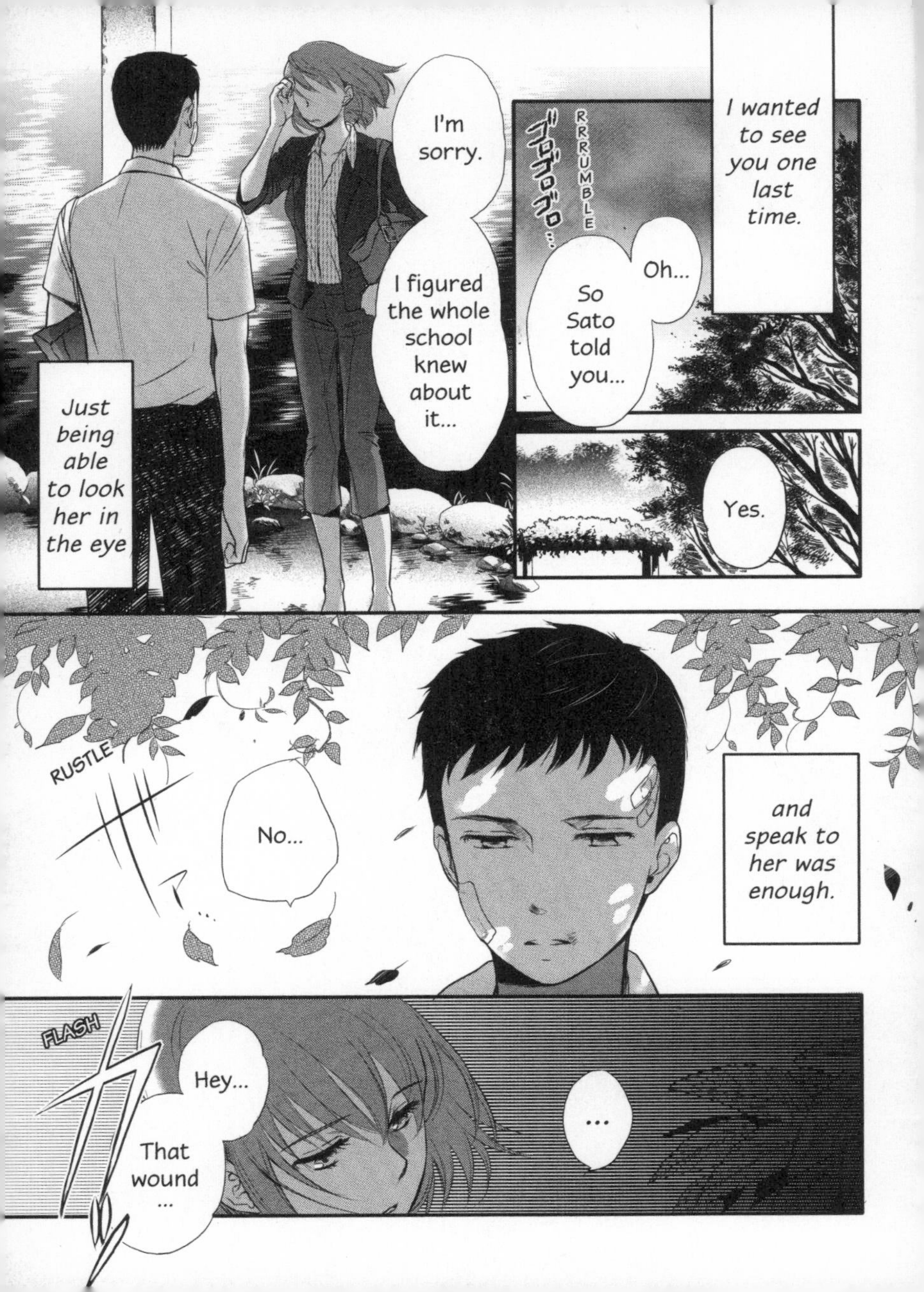
I wanted to see you one last time.
ゴロゴロゴロ…
RRRUMBLE
Oh...
So Sato told you...
Yes.
I'm sorry.
I figured the whole school knew about it...
Just being able to look her in the eye
and speak to her was enough.
No...
RUSTLE
...
Hey...
That wound ...
FLASH

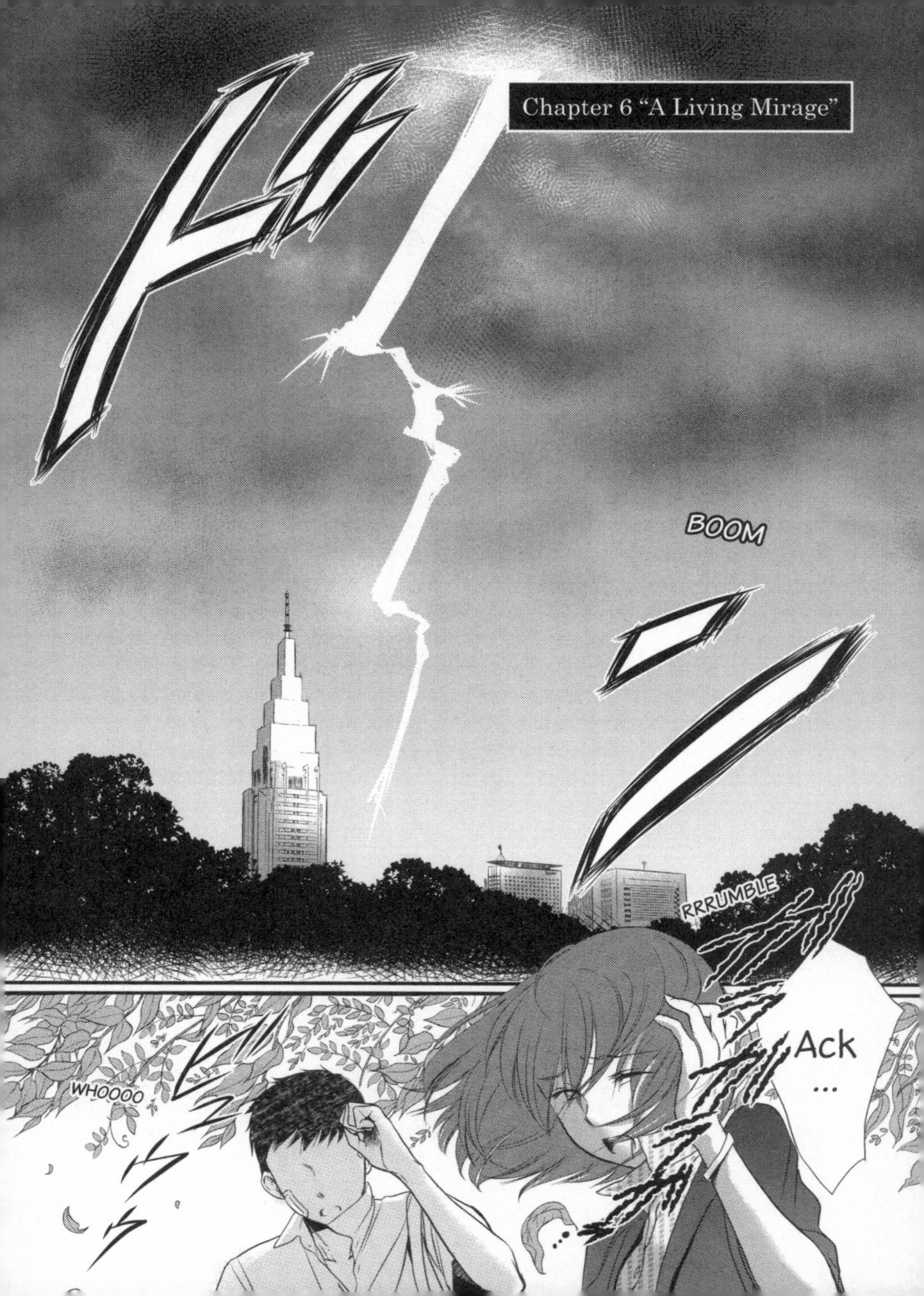
Chapter 6 "A Living Mirage"
BOOM
RRRUMBLE
Ack
...
WHOOOO

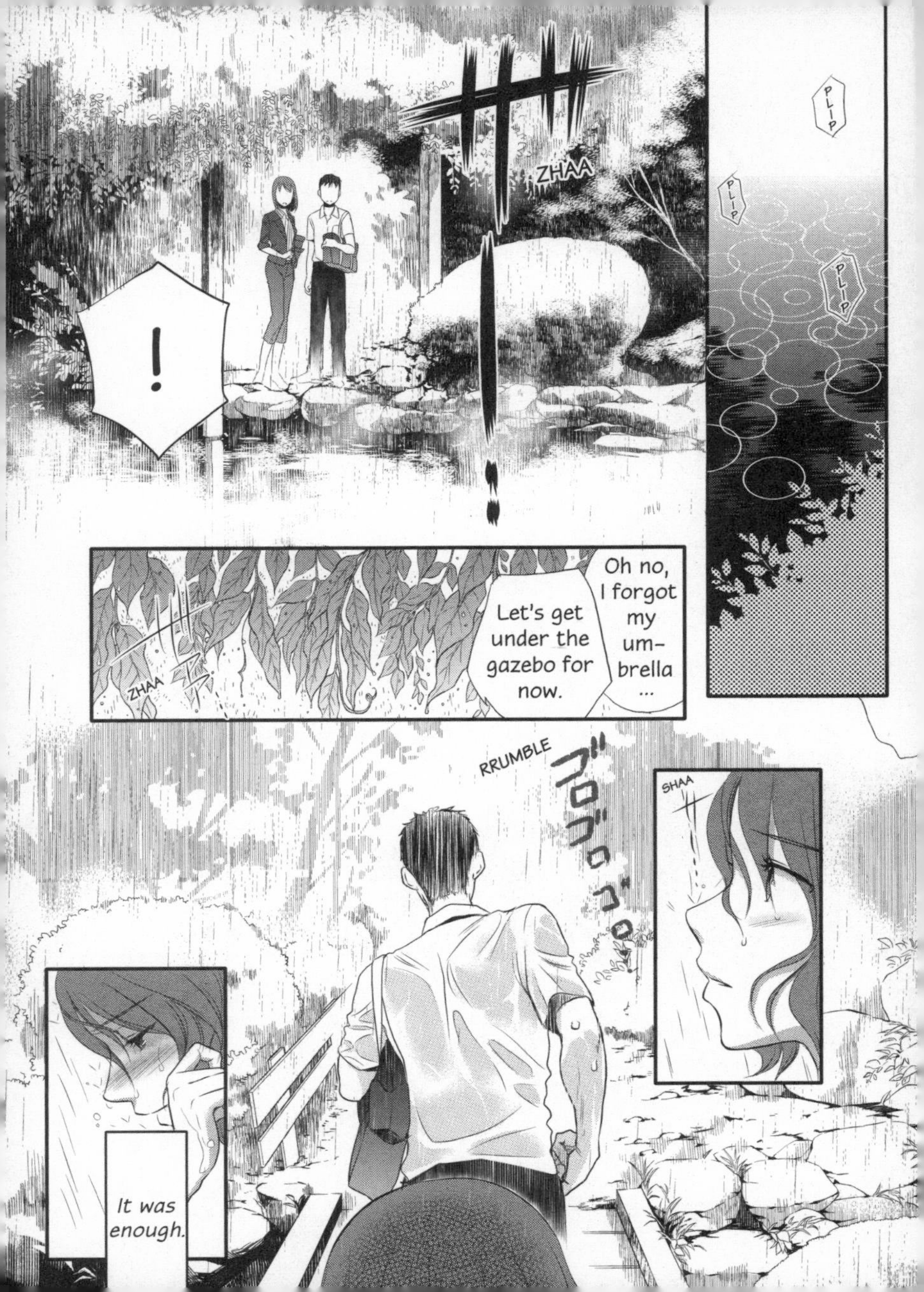
PLIP
PLIP
PLIP
ZHAA
!
Oh no, I forgot my um-brella ...
Let's get under the gazebo for now.
ZHAA
RRUMBLE
ゴロゴロ
SHAA
It was enough.

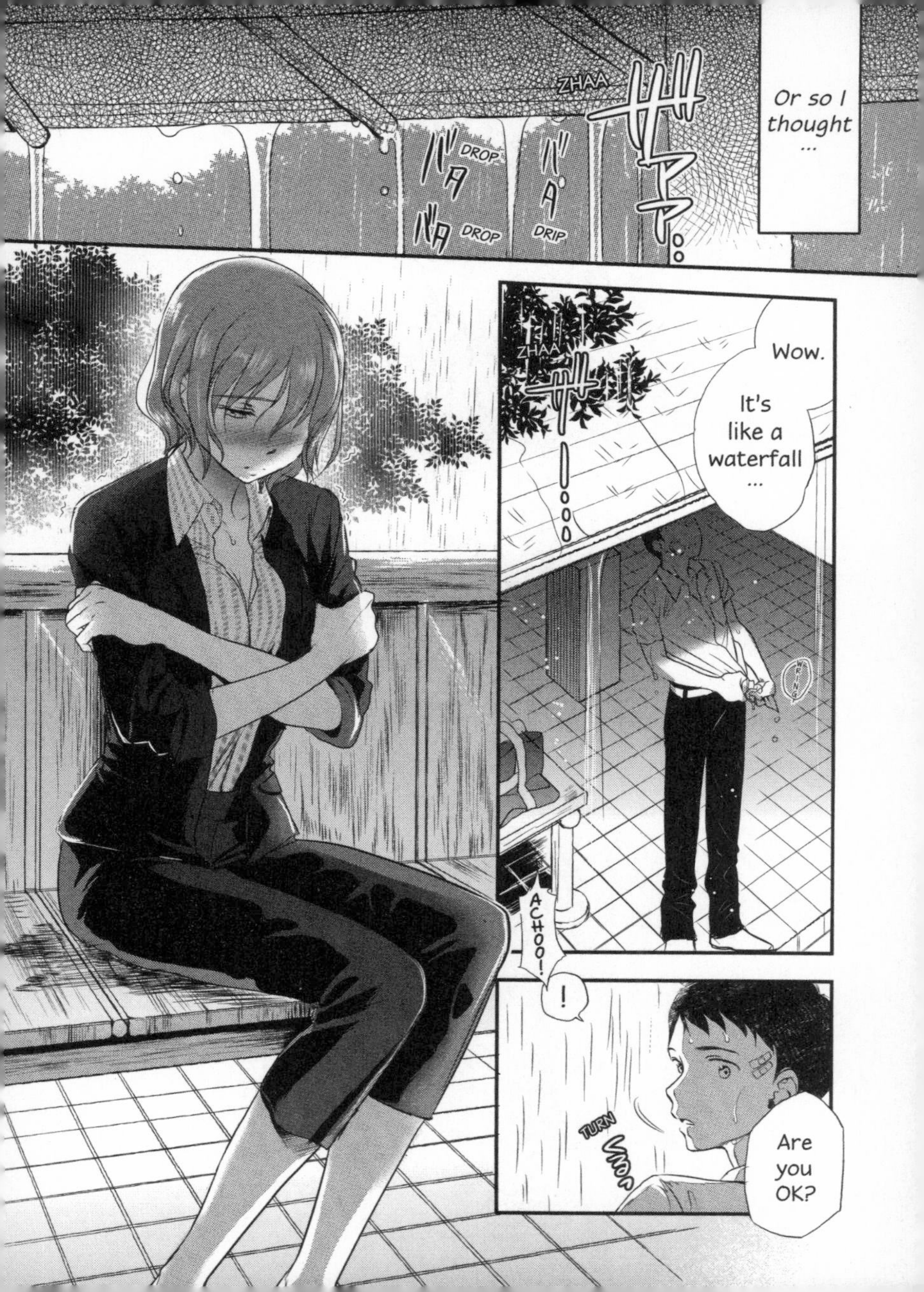
Or so I thought ...
ZHAA
DROP
DRIP
DROP
ZHAA
Wow.
It's like a waterfall ...
WRING
ACHOO!
!
TURN
Are you OK?

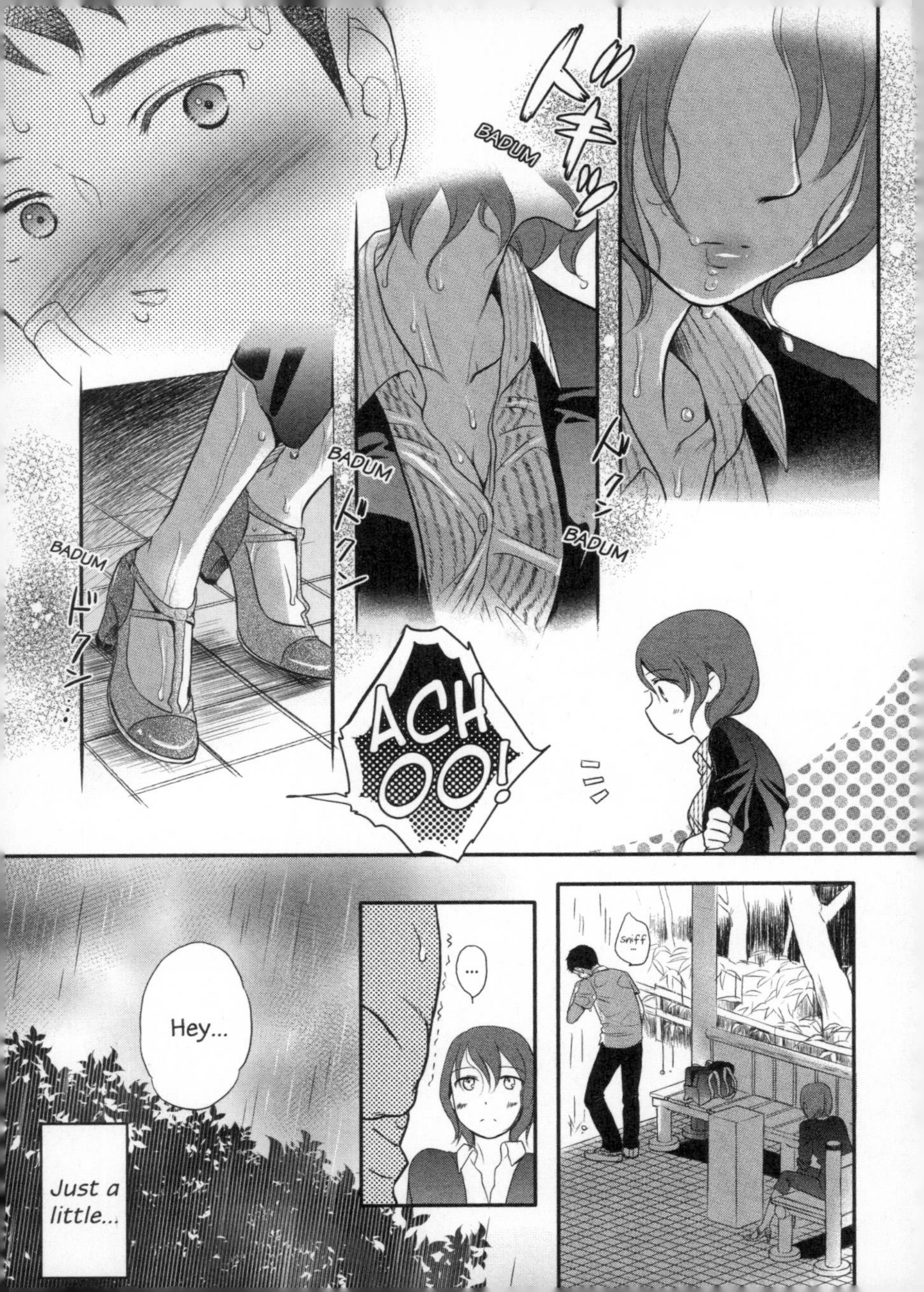

ドキッ
BADUM
ドクン
BADUM
BADUM
ドクン
BADUM
ドクン…
ACHOO!
sniff…
…
Hey…
Just a little…

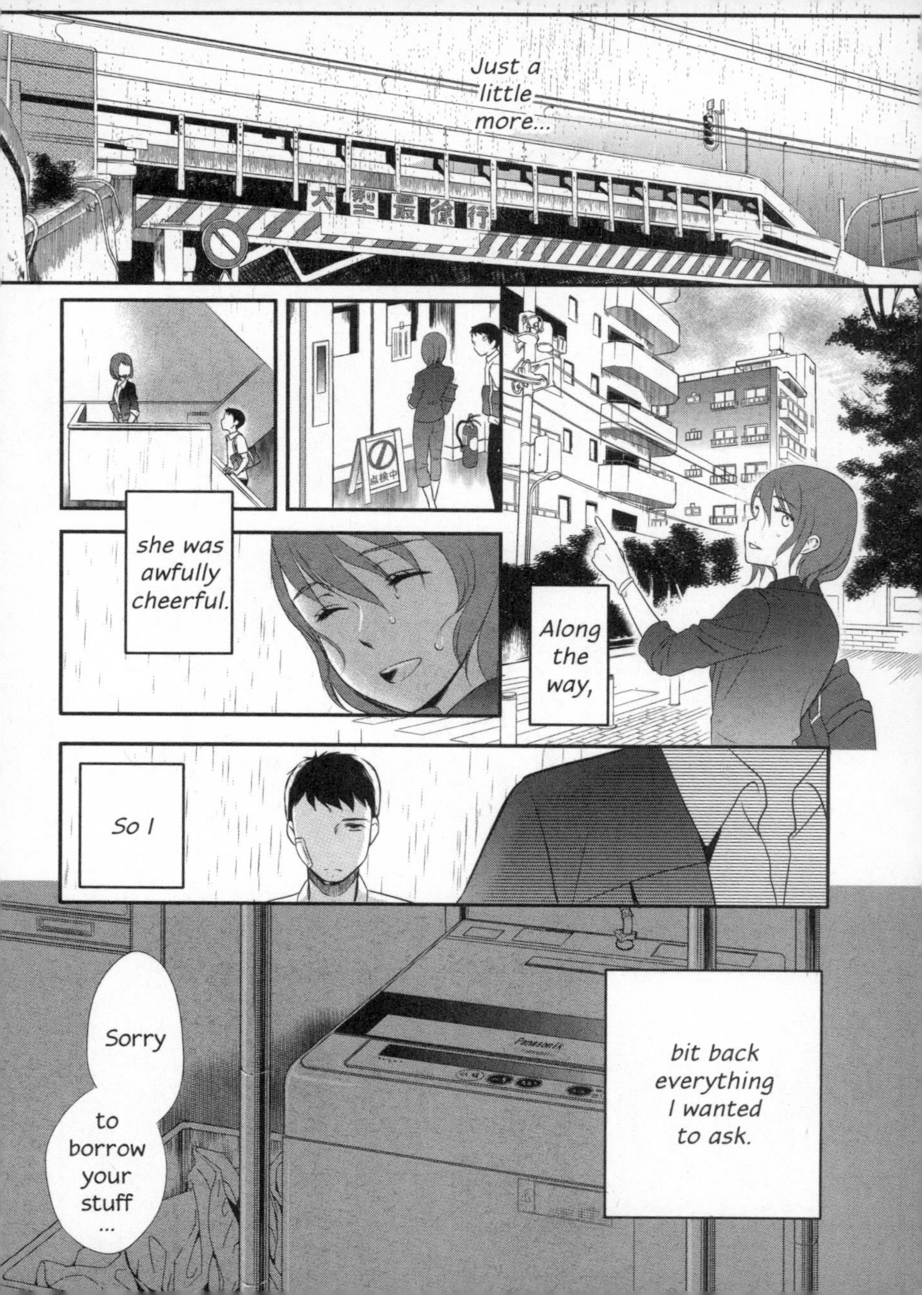
Just a little more...
Along the way,
she was awfully cheerful.
So I
bit back everything I wanted to ask.
Sorry to borrow your stuff...

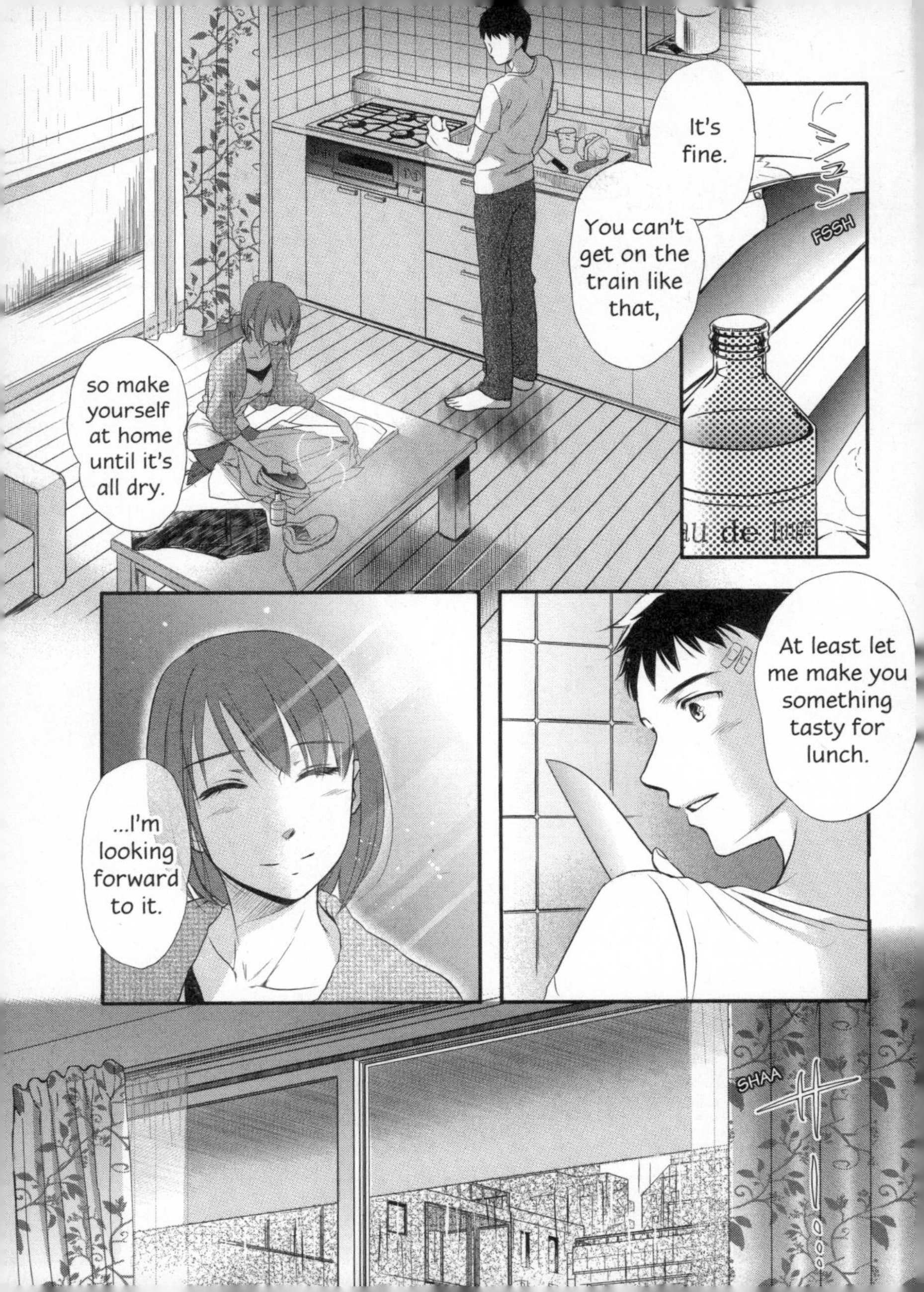
It's fine.
You can't get on the train like that,
FSSH
so make yourself at home until it's all dry.
At least let me make you something tasty for lunch.
...I'm looking forward to it.
SHAA

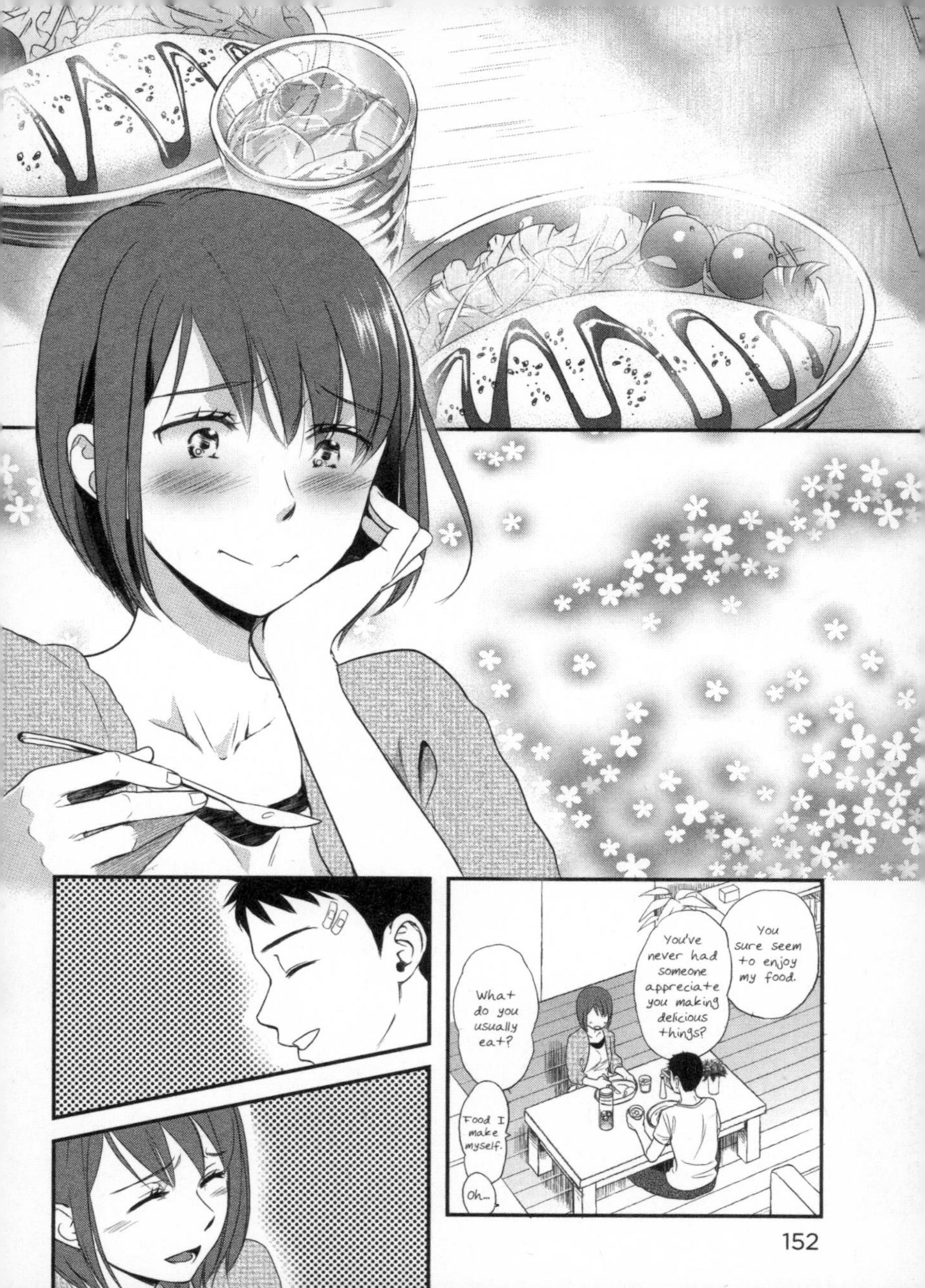
You sure seem to enjoy my food.
You've never had someone appreciate you making delicious things?
What do you usually eat?
Food I make myself.
Oh...

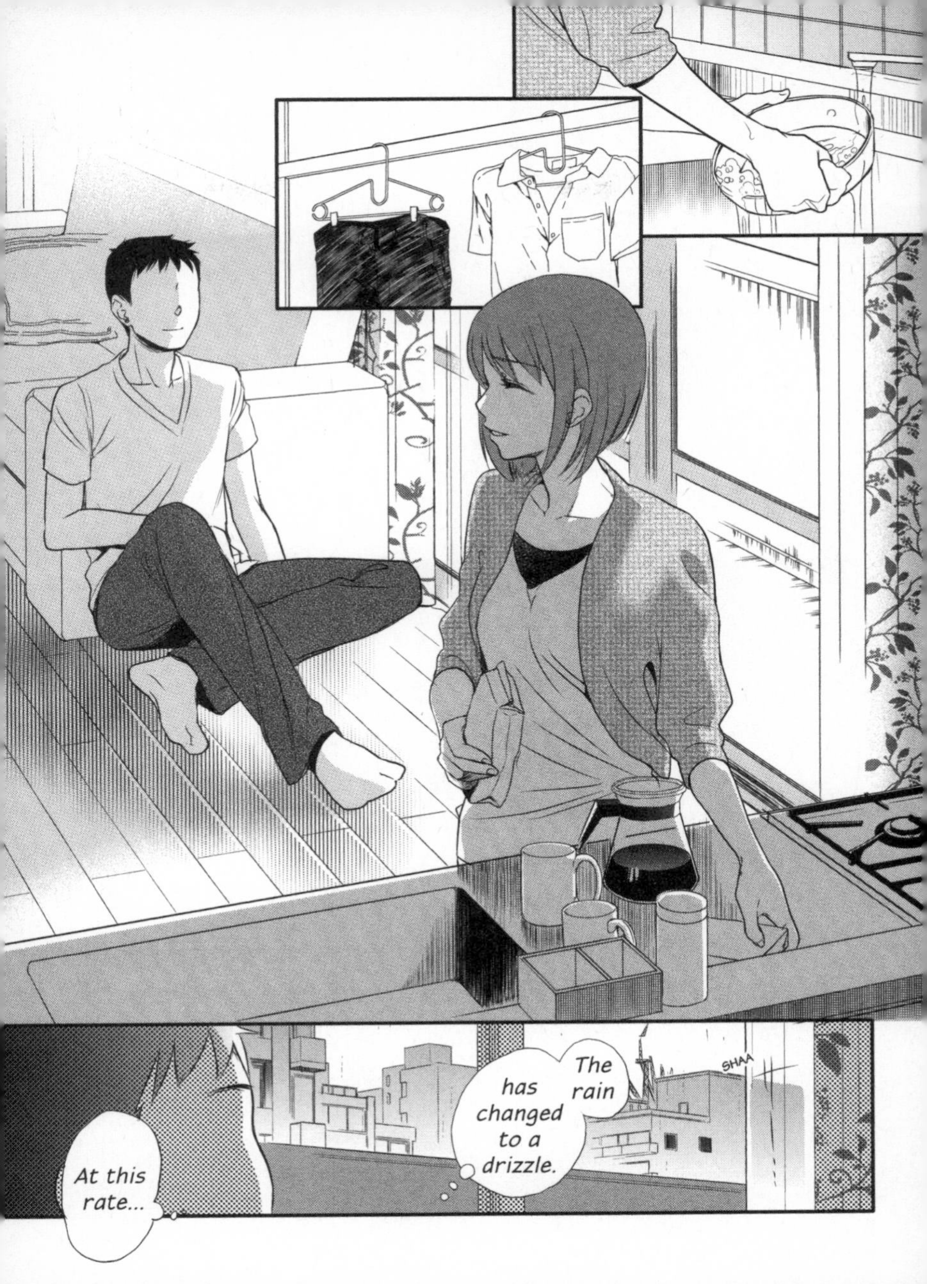
SHAA
The rain has changed to a drizzle.
At this rate...

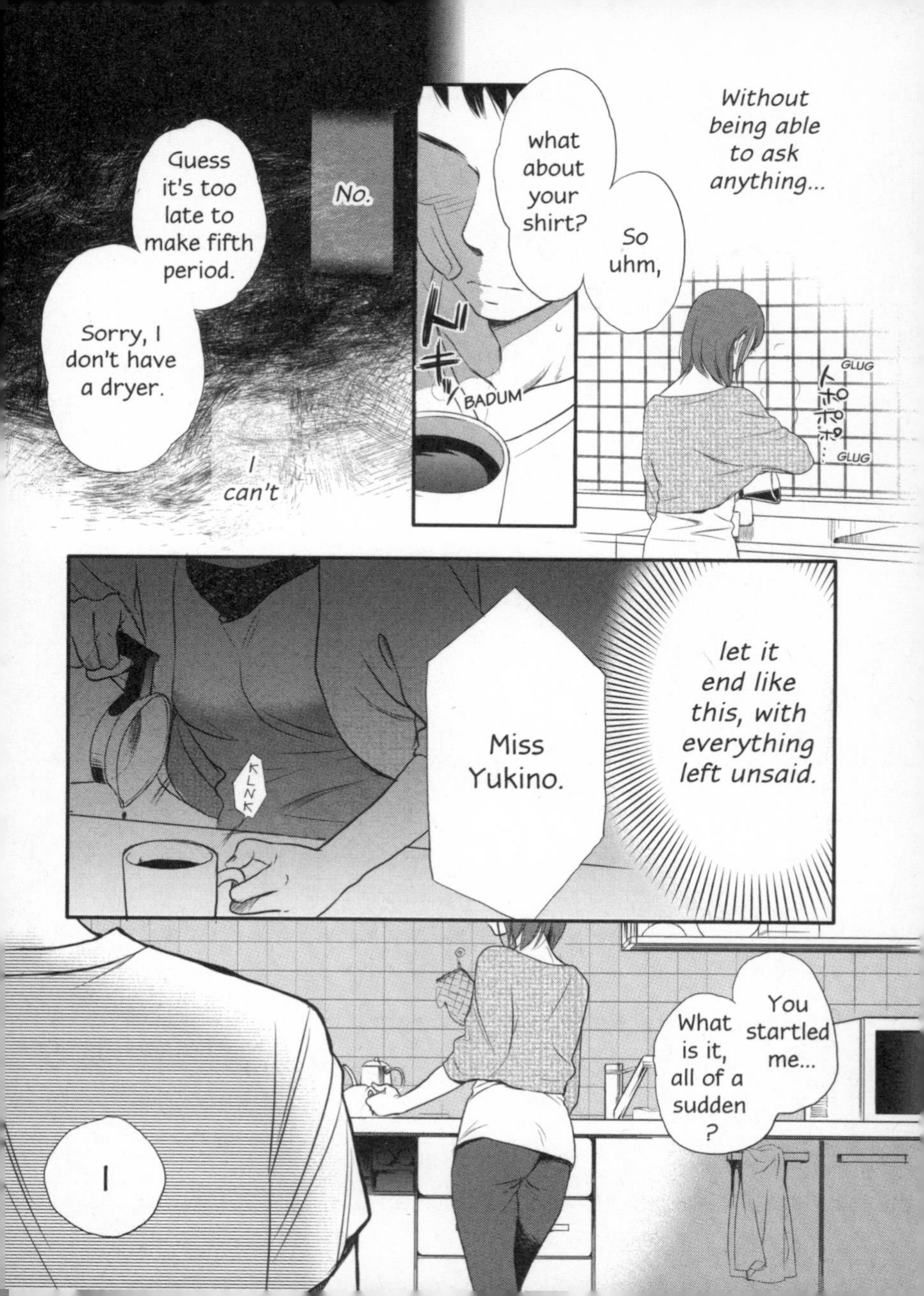
Without being able to ask anything...
GLUG
トポポポ…
GLUG
So uhm,
what about your shirt?
ドキッ
BADUM
No.
Guess it's too late to make fifth period.
Sorry, I don't have a dryer.
I can't
let it end like this, with everything left unsaid.
Miss Yukino.
KLNK
You startled me...
What is it, all of a sudden?
I

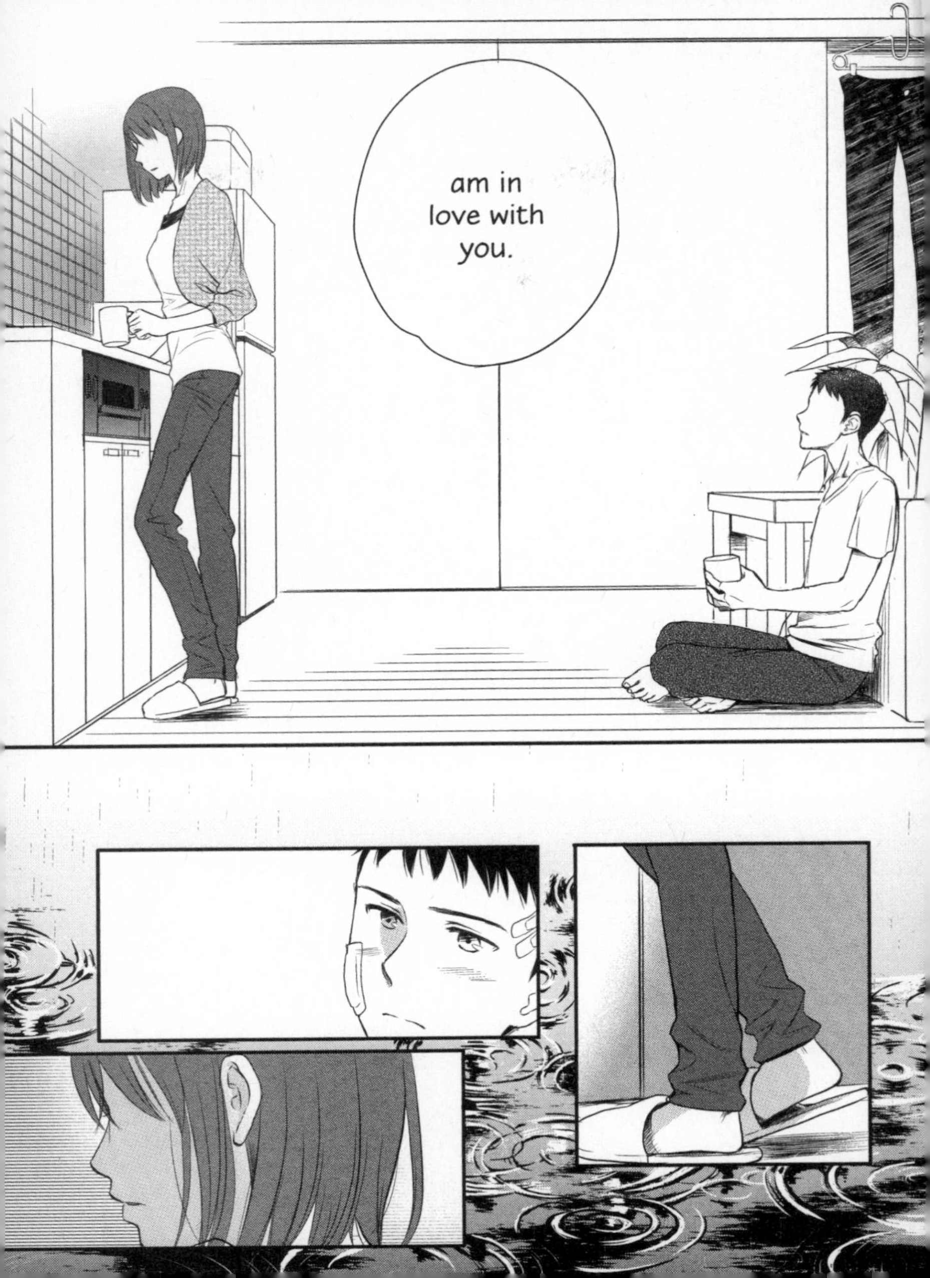
am in love with you.

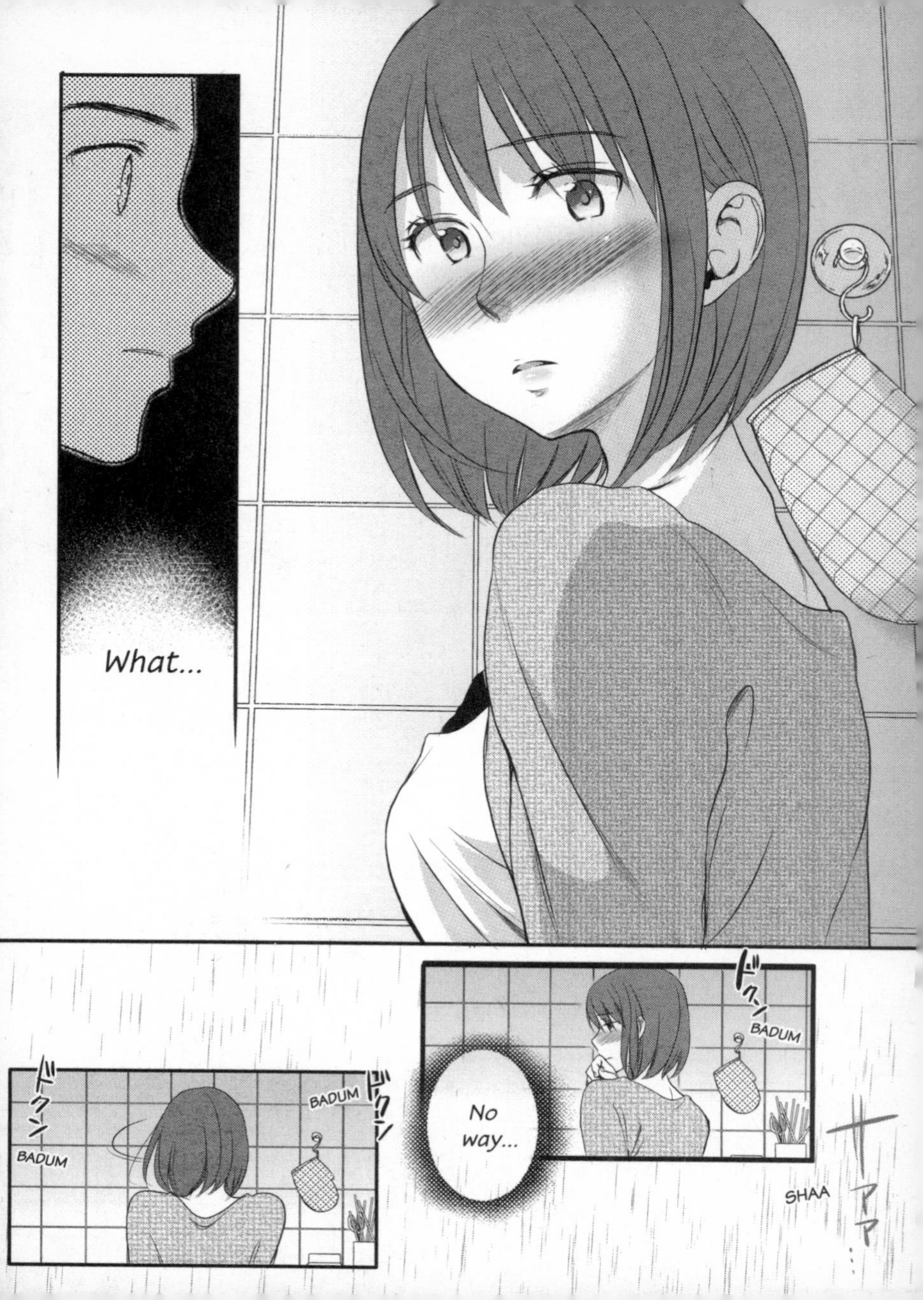
What...
ドクン
BADUM
No way...
サァァ…
SHAA
ドクン
BADUM
ドクン
BADUM

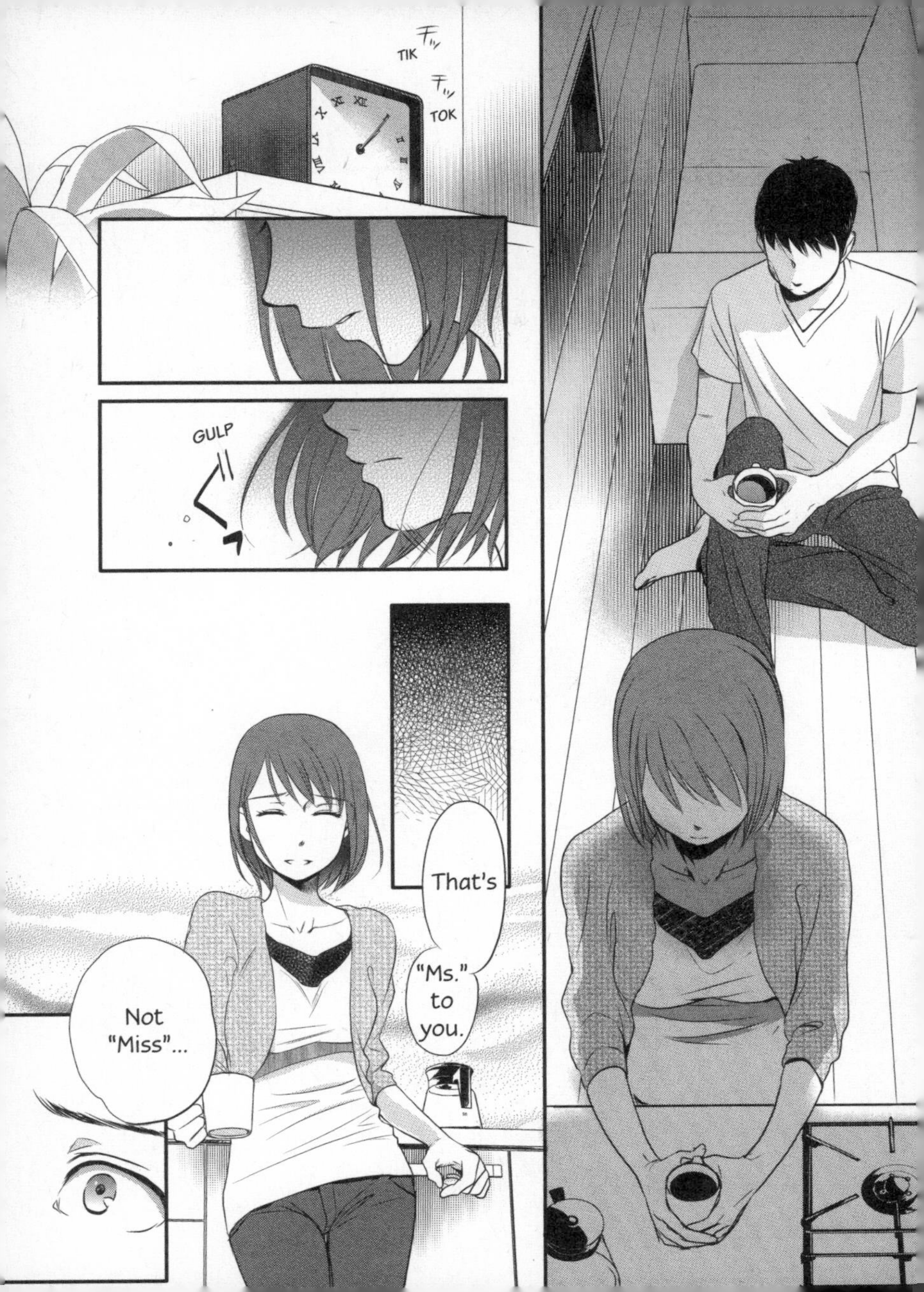
チッ
TIK
チッ
TOK
GULP
That's "Ms." to you.
Not "Miss"...

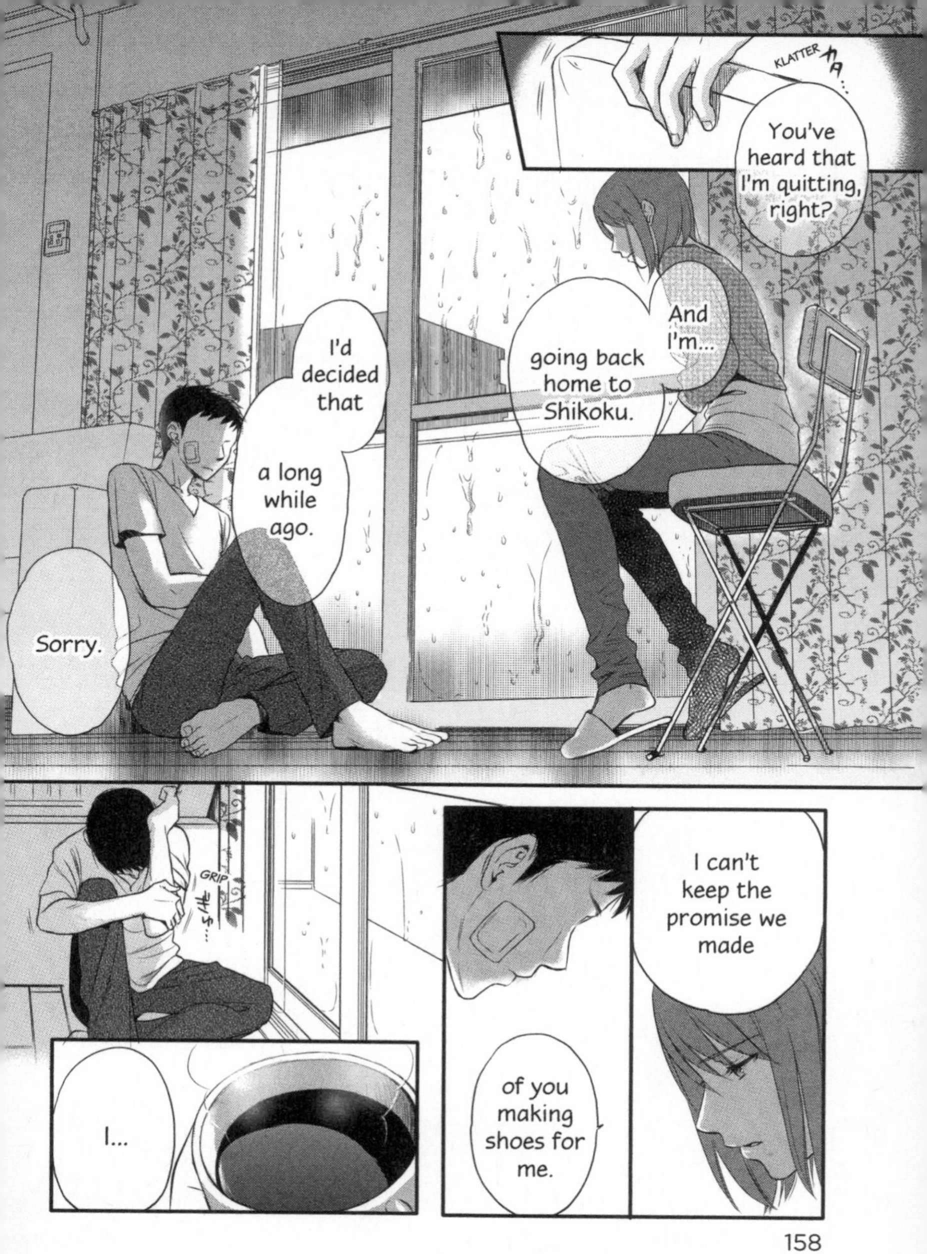
KLATTER
You've heard that I'm quitting, right?
And I'm...
going back home to Shikoku.
I'd decided that
a long while ago.
Sorry.
I can't keep the promise we made
of you making shoes for me.
GRIP
I...

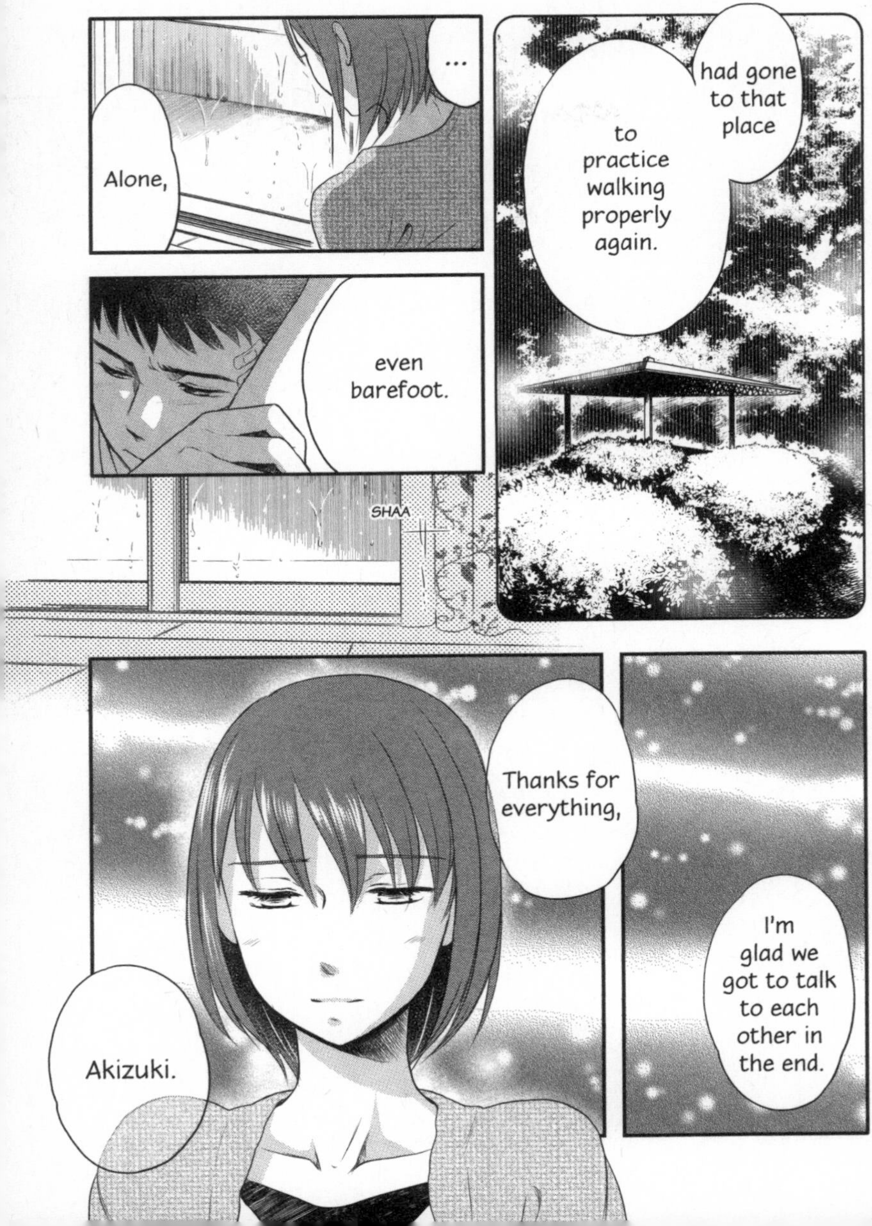
...
Alone,
even barefoot.
SHAA
had gone to that place
to practice walking properly again.
Thanks for everything,
Akizuki.
I'm glad we got to talk to each other in the end.

TMP
コト…
I'm going home.
What?
I'll go change.
Wait...
THUP
SLIP
My shirt was still damp.

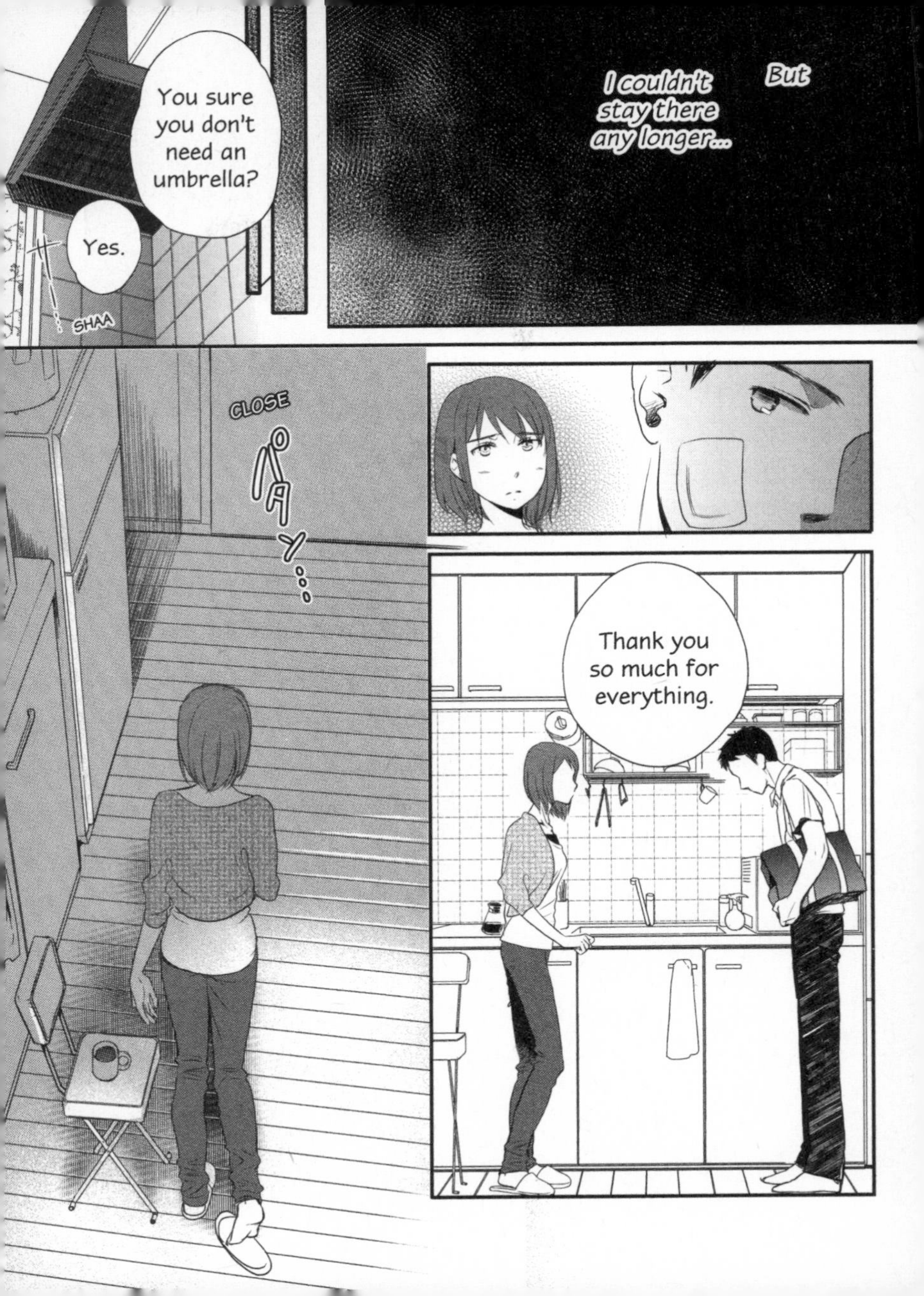
But
I couldn't stay there any longer...
You sure you don't need an umbrella?
Yes.
SHAA
Thank you so much for everything.
CLOSE

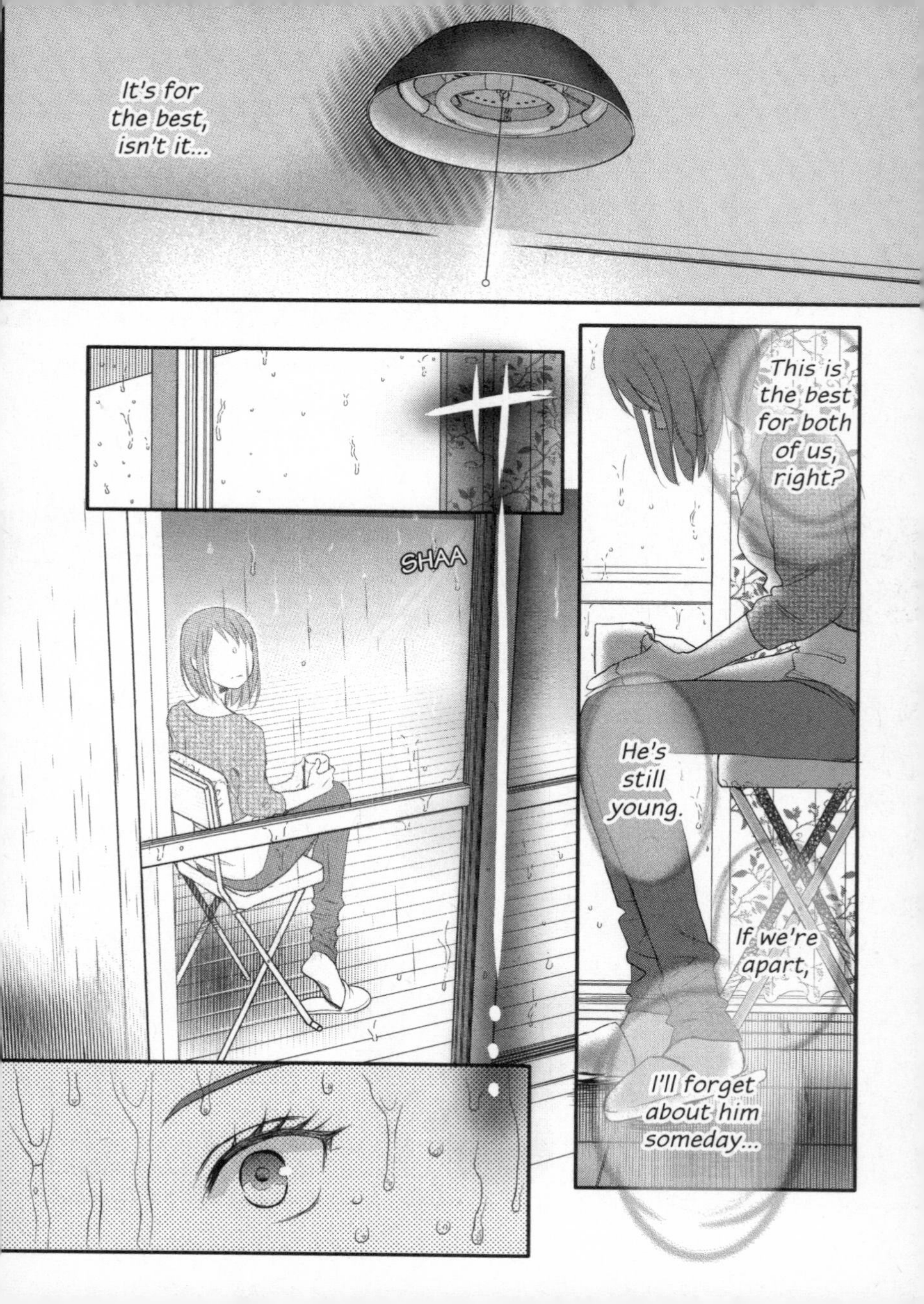
It's for the best, isn't it...
This is the best for both of us, right?
He's still young.
If we're apart,
I'll forget about him someday...
SHAA

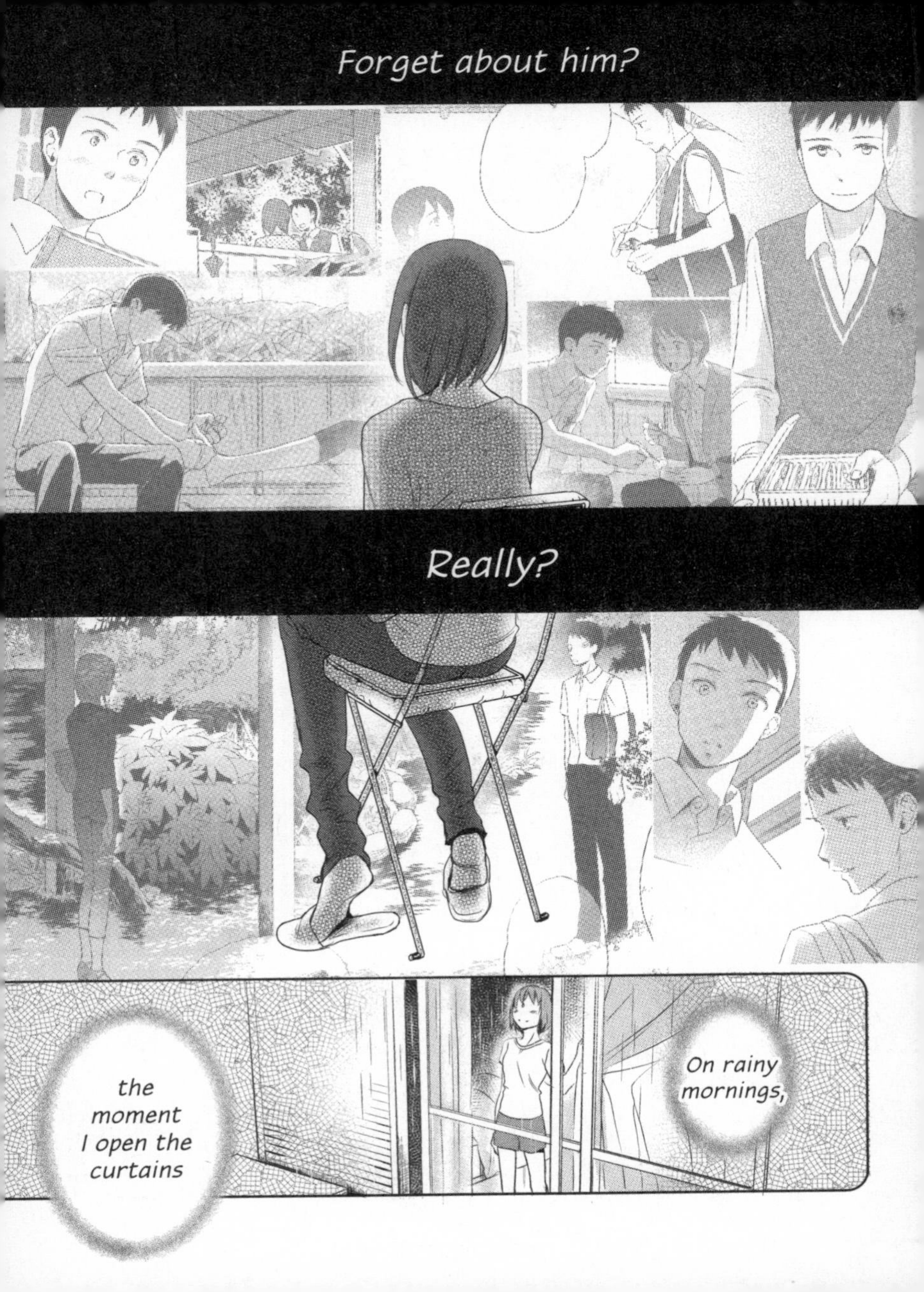

Forget about him?
Really?
On rainy mornings,
the moment I open the curtains

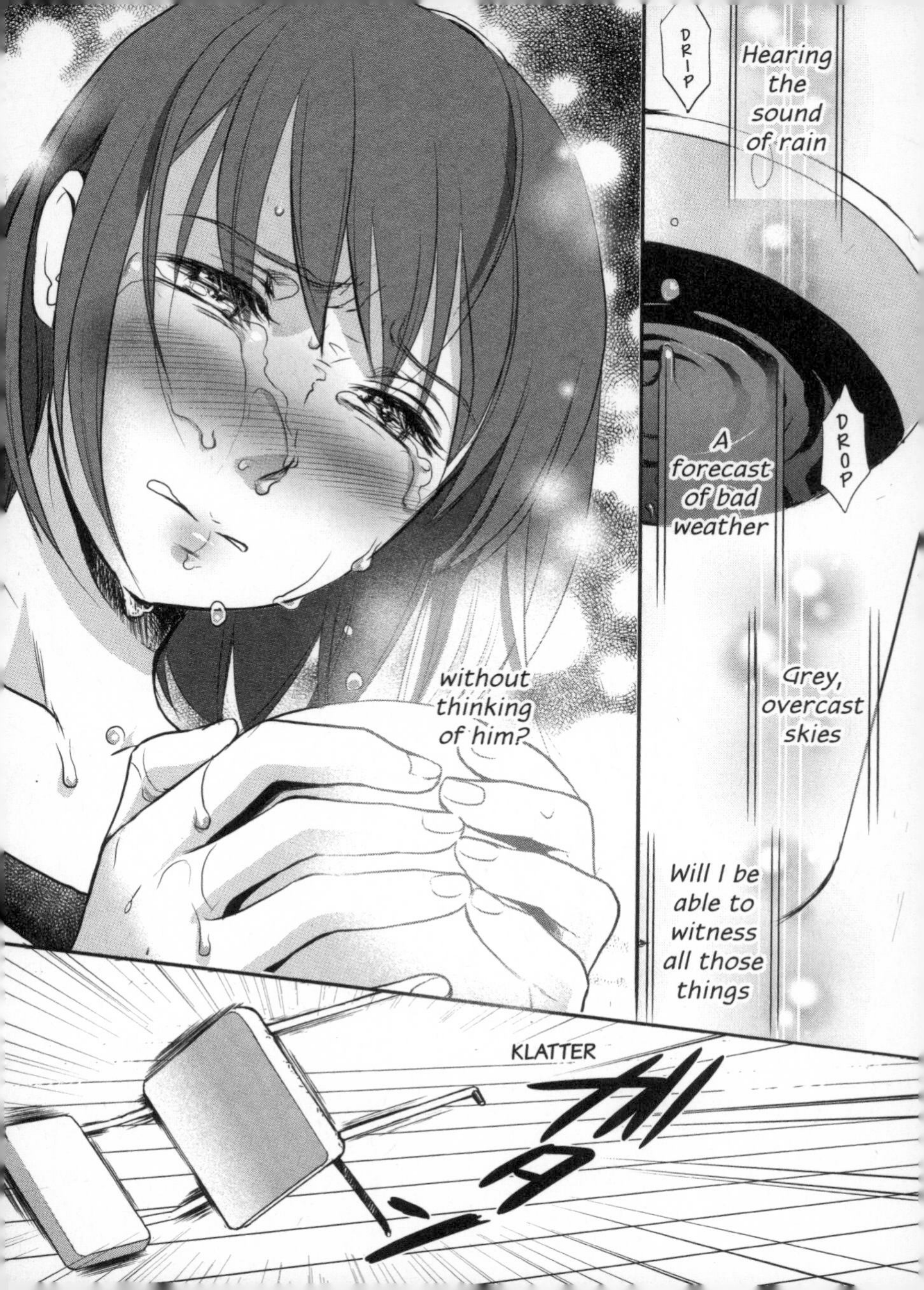
DRIP
Hearing the sound of rain
DROP
A forecast of bad weather
Grey, overcast skies
Will I be able to witness all those things
without thinking of him?
KLATTER

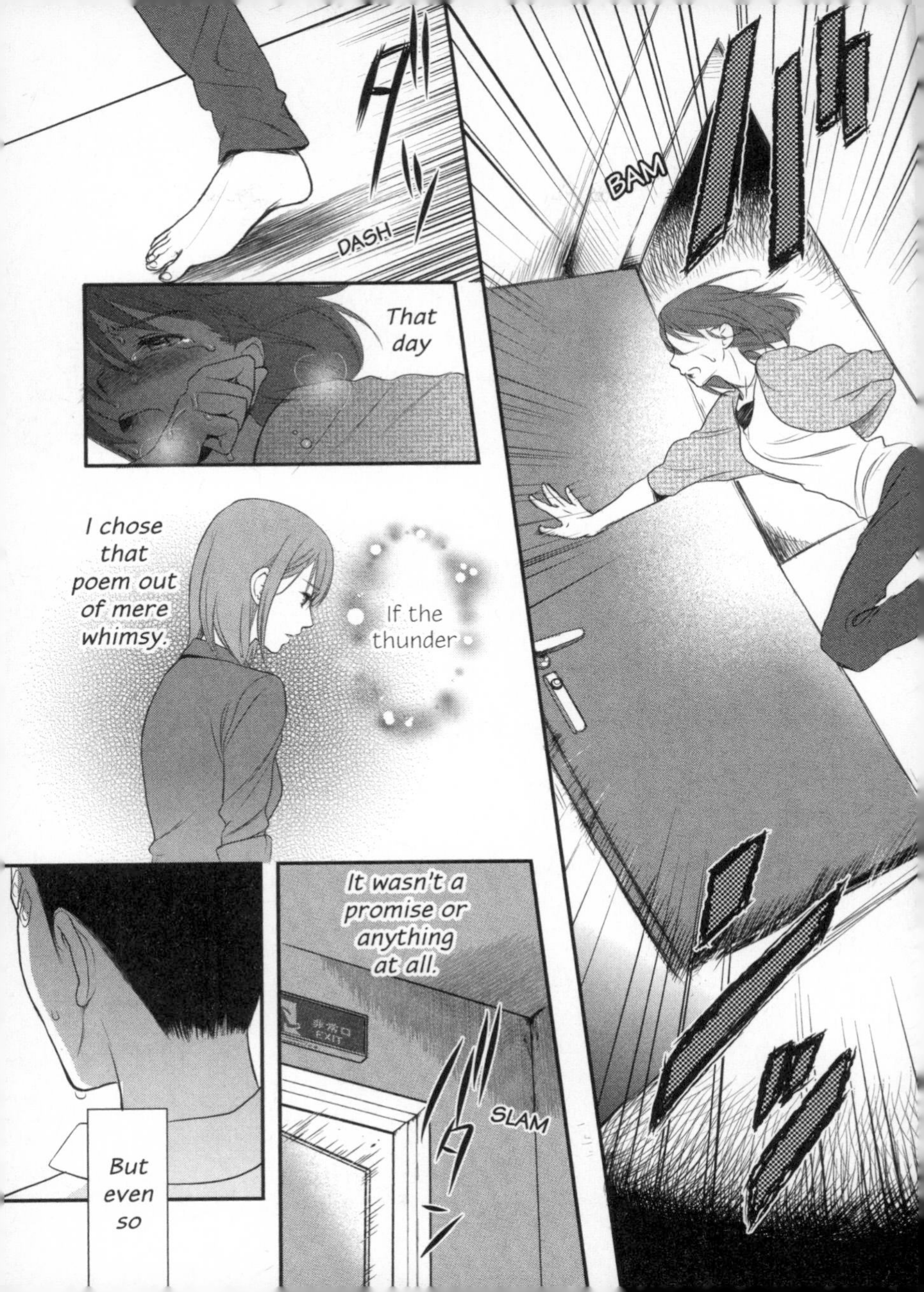
BAM
DASH
That day
I chose that poem out of mere whimsy.
If the thunder
It wasn't a promise or anything at all.
SLAM
But even so

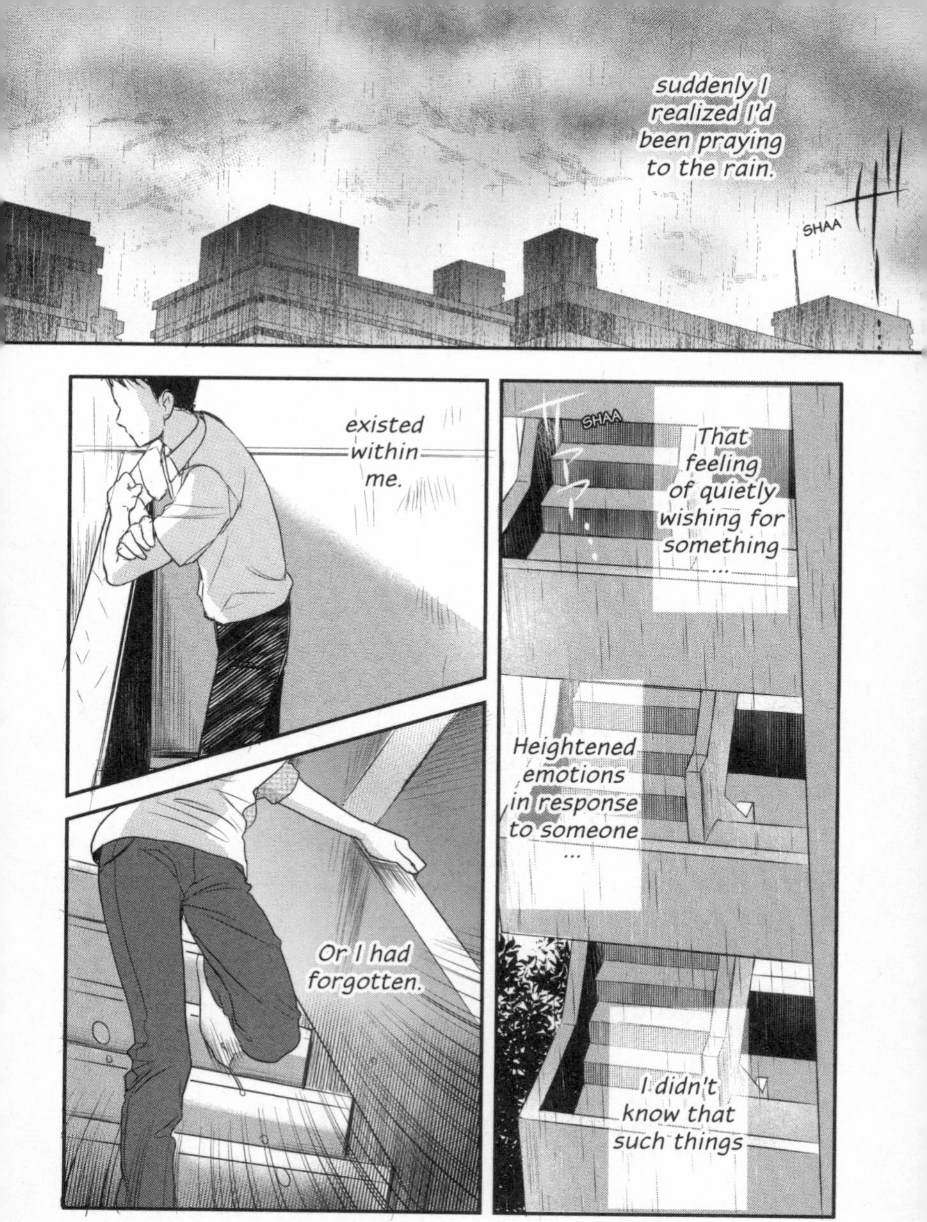
suddenly I realized I'd been praying to the rain.
SHAA
SHAA
That feeling of quietly wishing for something ...
Heightened emotions in response to someone ...
I didn't know that such things
existed within me.
Or I had forgotten.

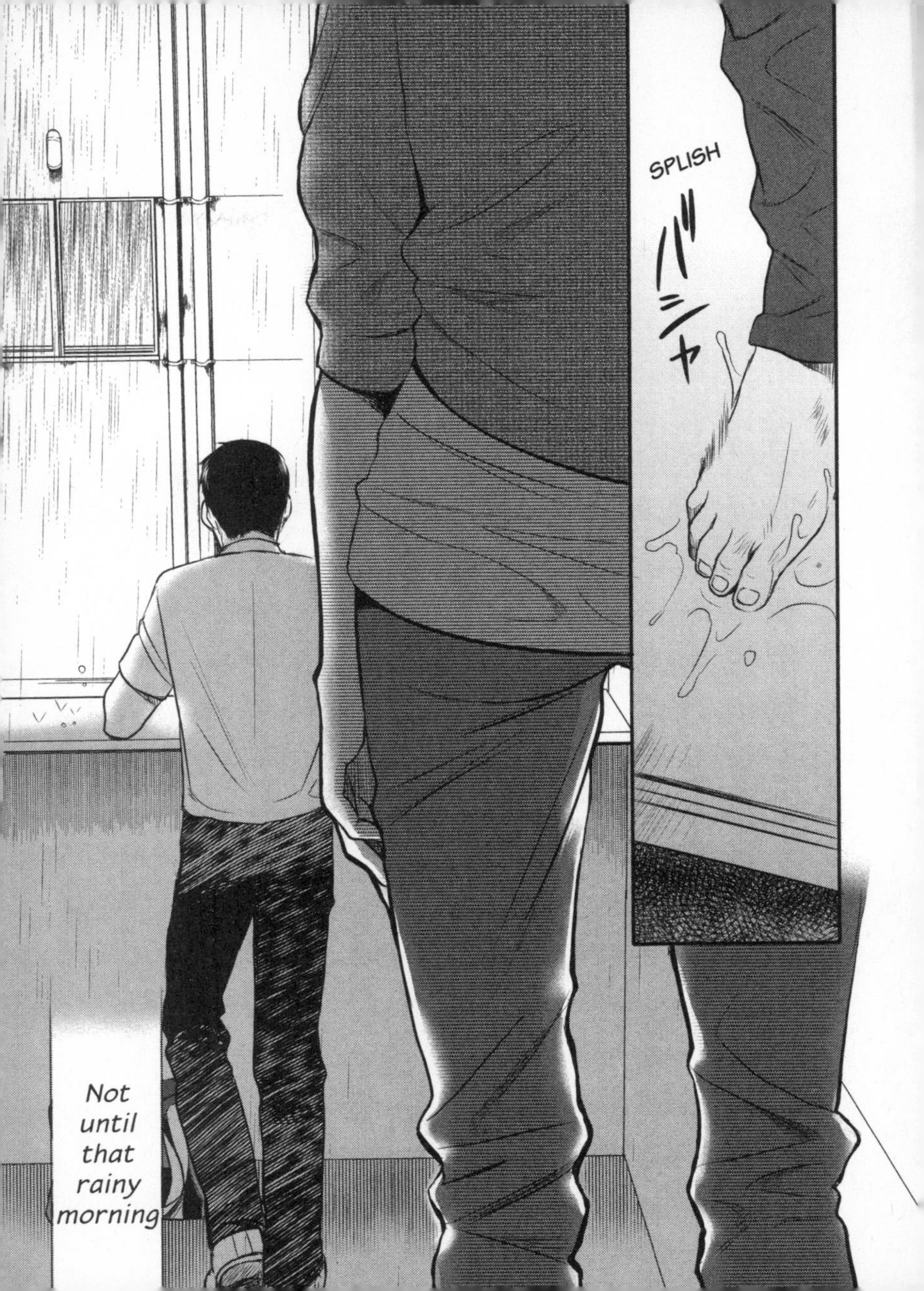
SPLISH
バシャ
Not until that rainy morning

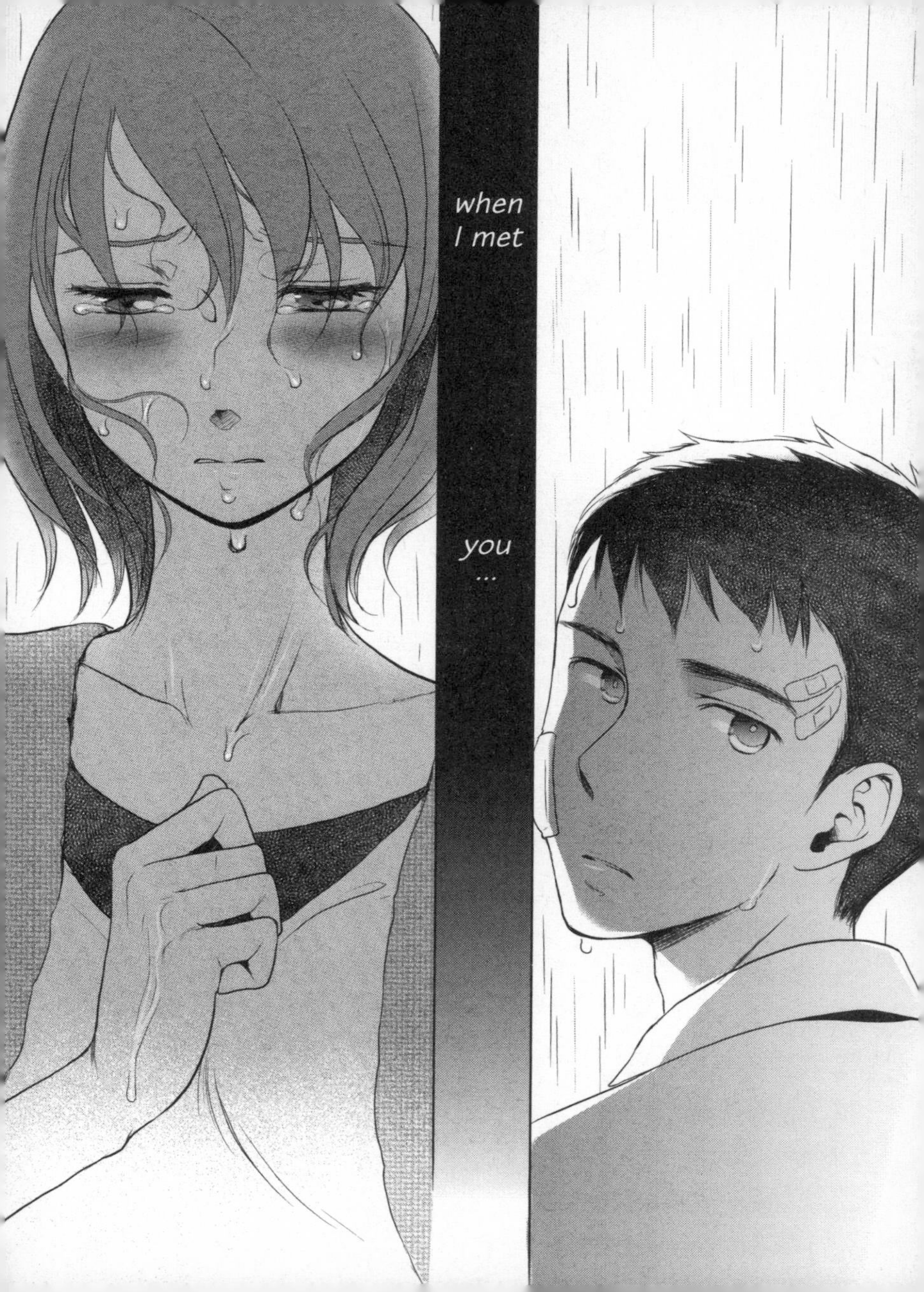
when
I met
you
...

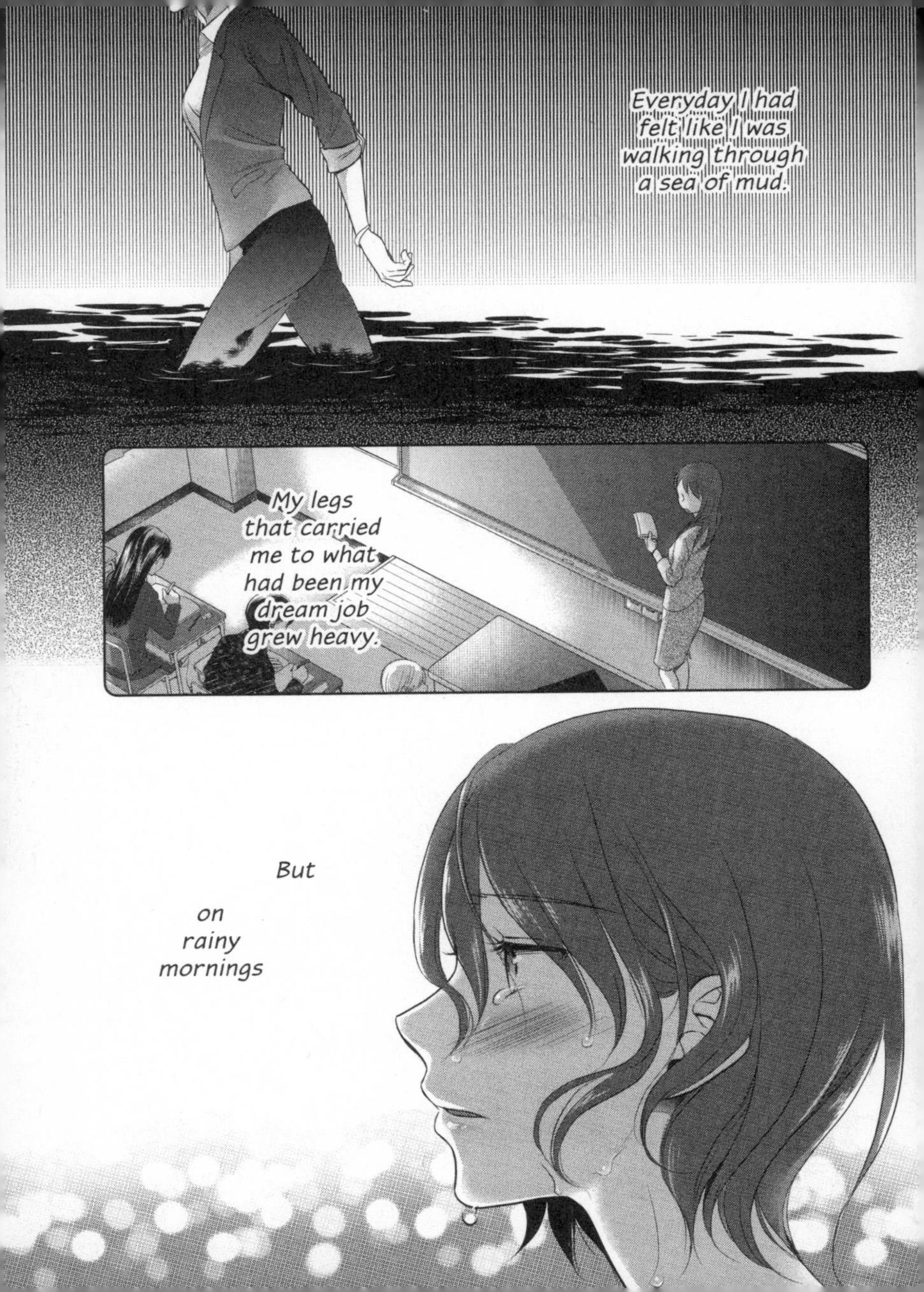

Everyday I had felt like I was walking through a sea of mud.
My legs that carried me to what had been my dream job grew heavy.
But
on rainy mornings

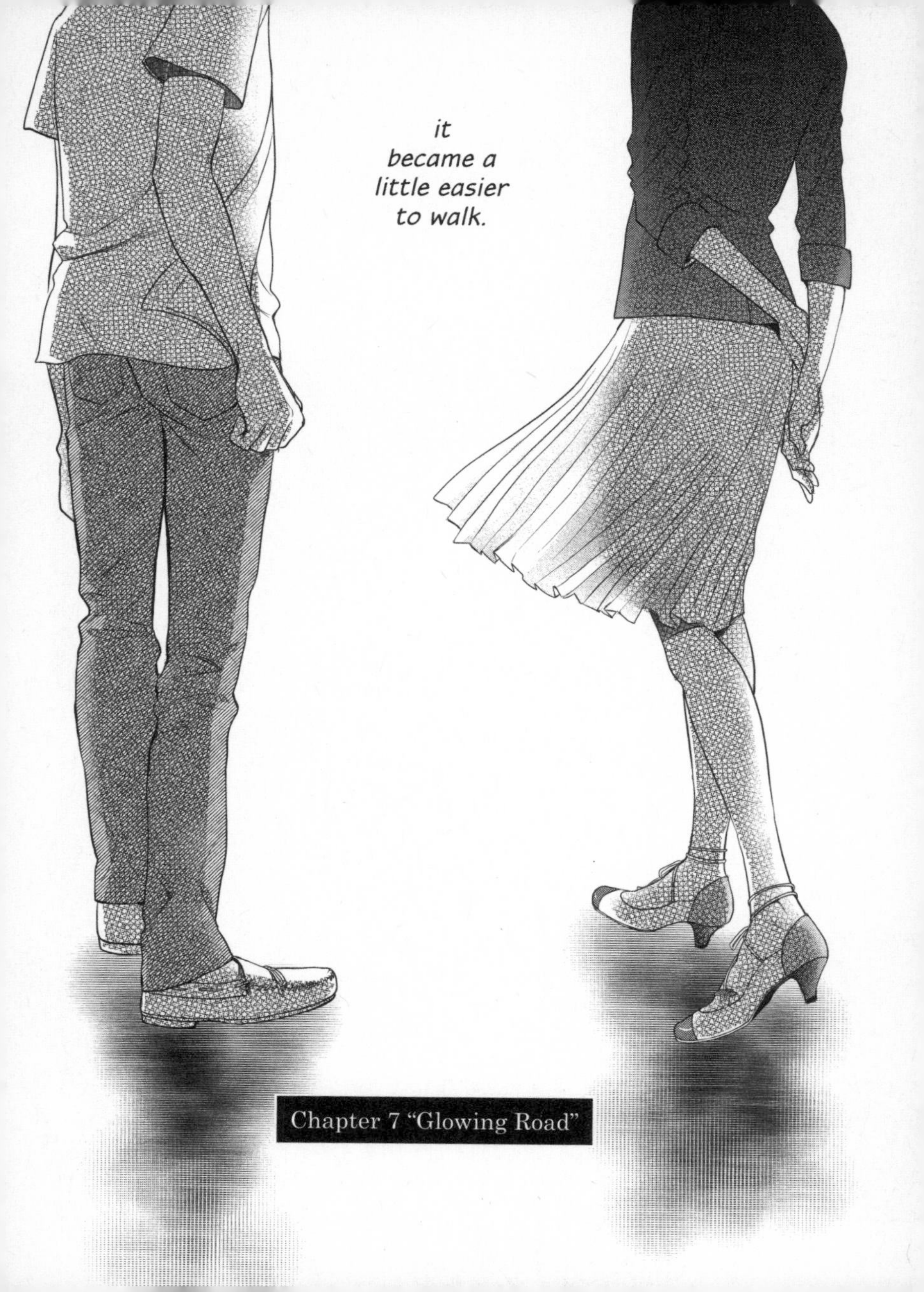
it
became a
little easier
to walk.
Chapter 7 "Glowing Road"

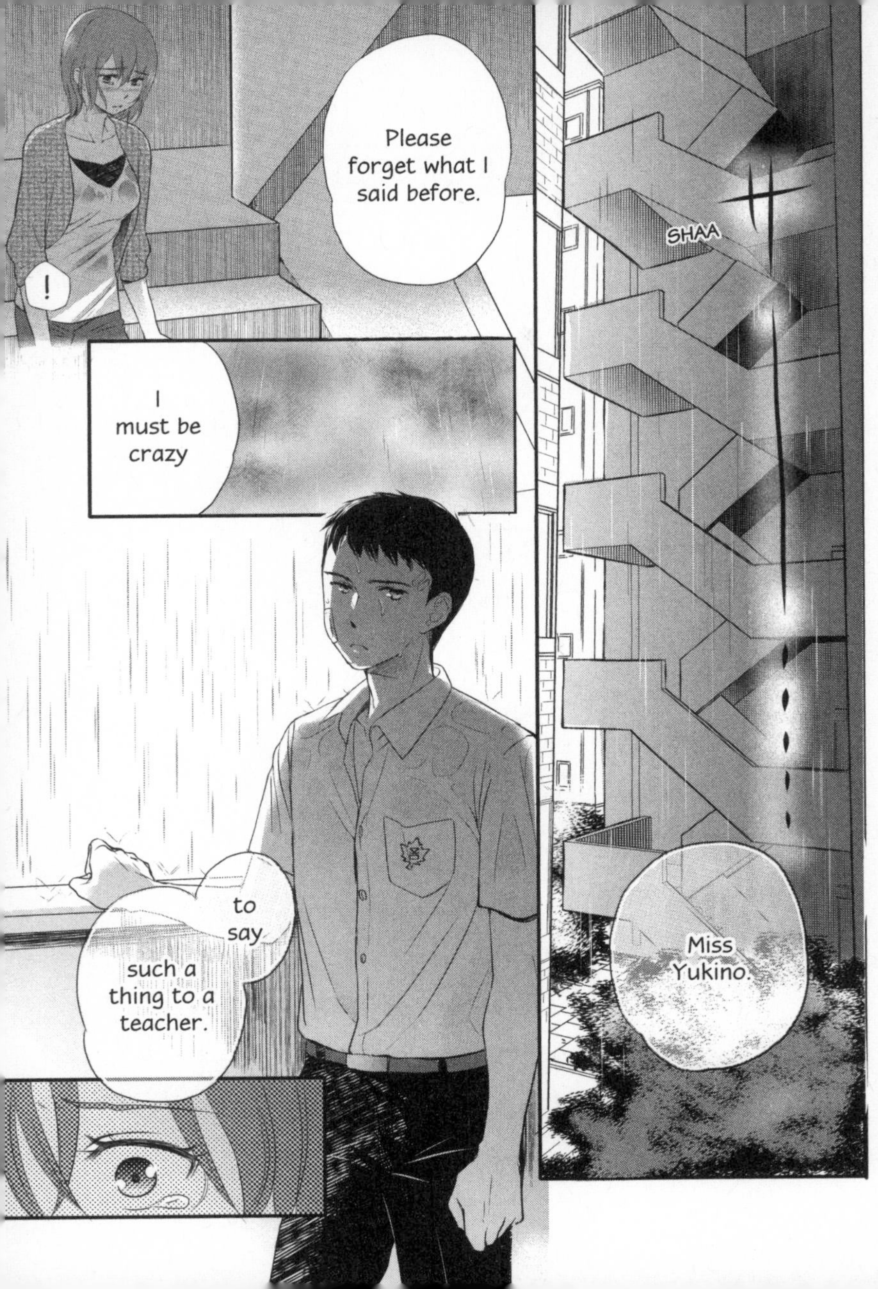
SHAA
Miss Yukino.
Please forget what I said before.
!
I must be crazy
to say such a thing to a teacher.

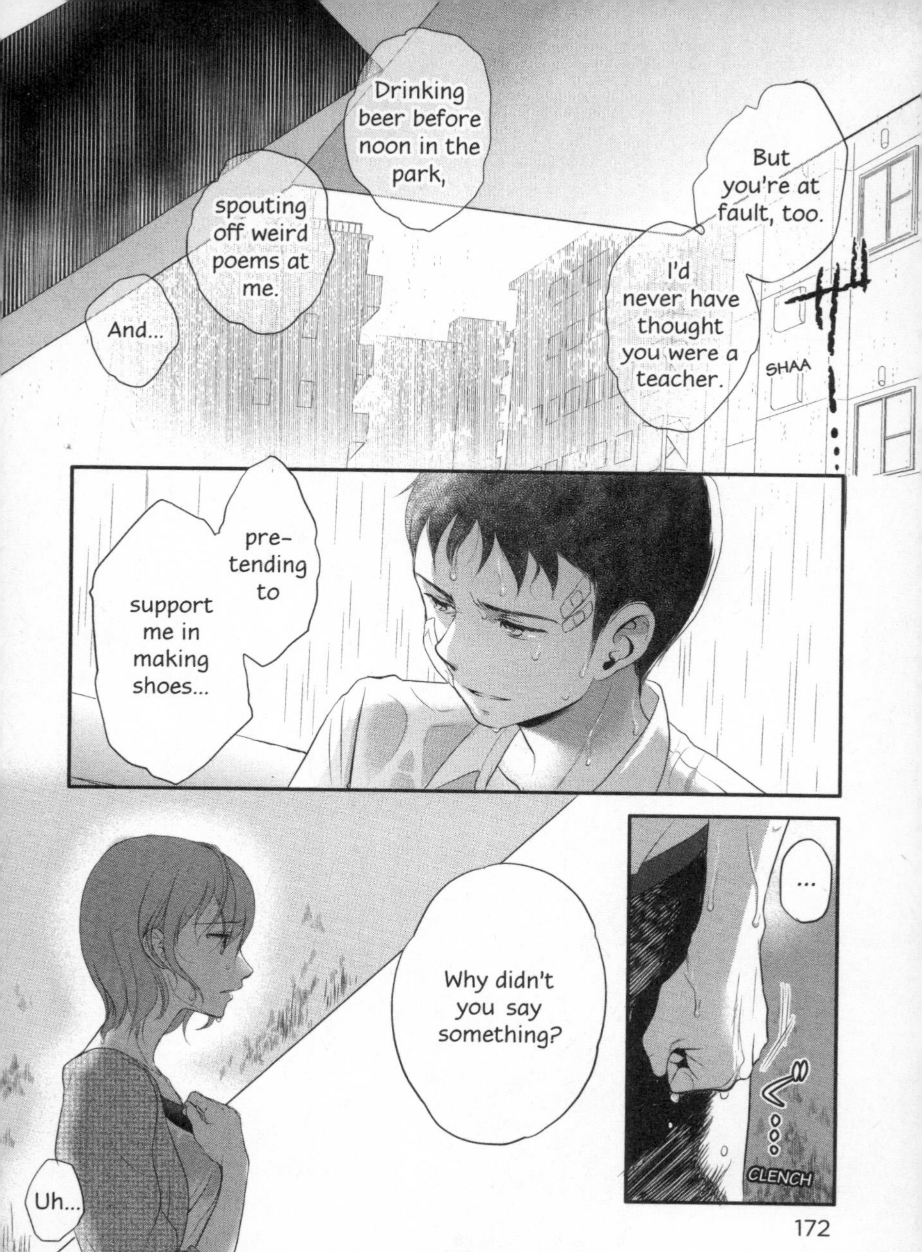
But you're at fault, too.
I'd never have thought you were a teacher.
SHAA
Drinking beer before noon in the park,
spouting off weird poems at me.
And...
pre-tending to
support me in making shoes...
...
CLENCH
Why didn't you say something?
Uh...

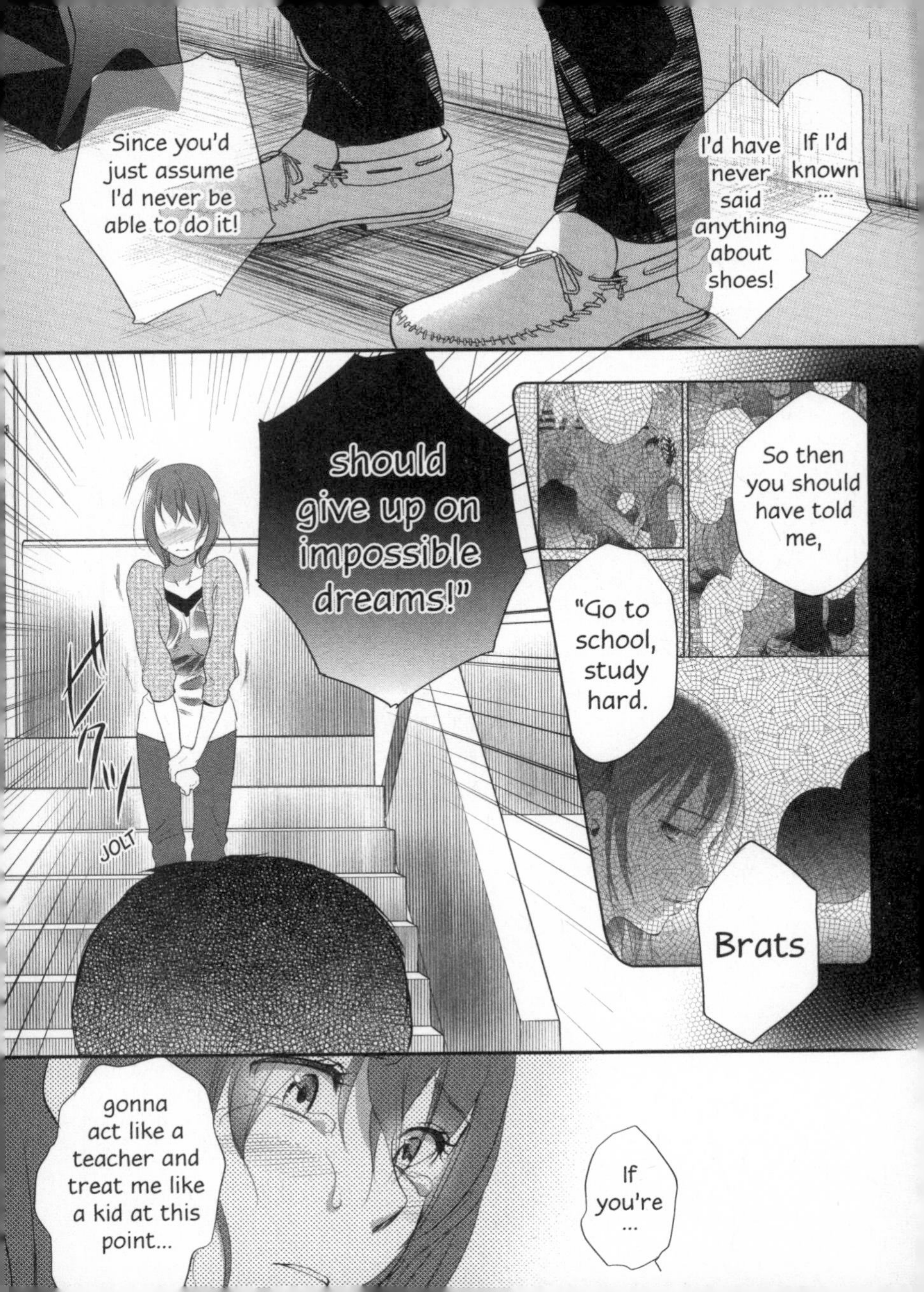
If I'd known ...
I'd have never said anything about shoes!
Since you'd just assume I'd never be able to do it!
So then you should have told me,
"Go to school, study hard.
Brats
should give up on impossible dreams!"
JOLT
If you're ...
gonna act like a teacher and treat me like a kid at this point...

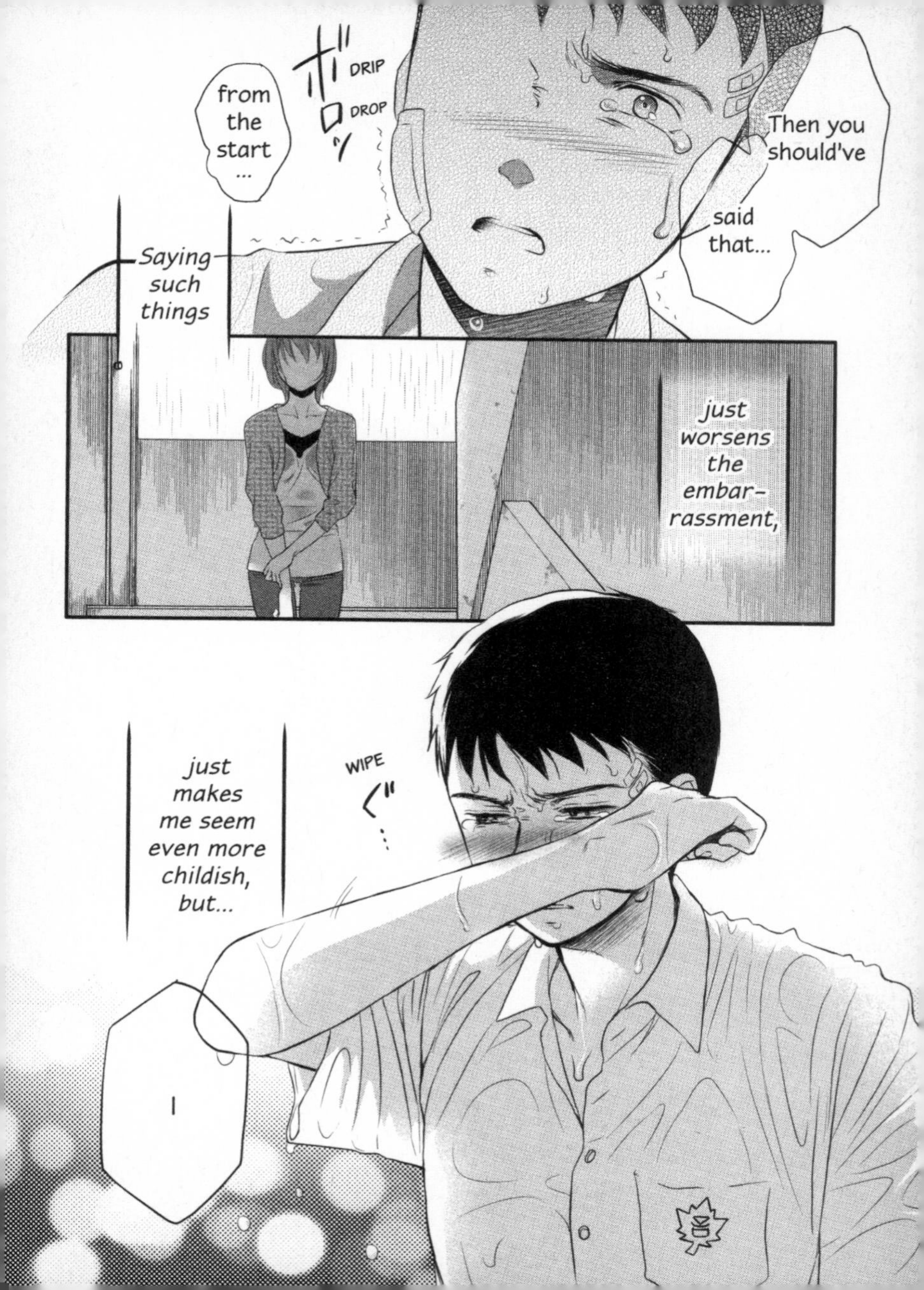

Then you should've
said that...
DRIP
DROP
from the start ...
Saying such things
just worsens the embarrassment,
WIPE
just makes me seem even more childish, but...
I

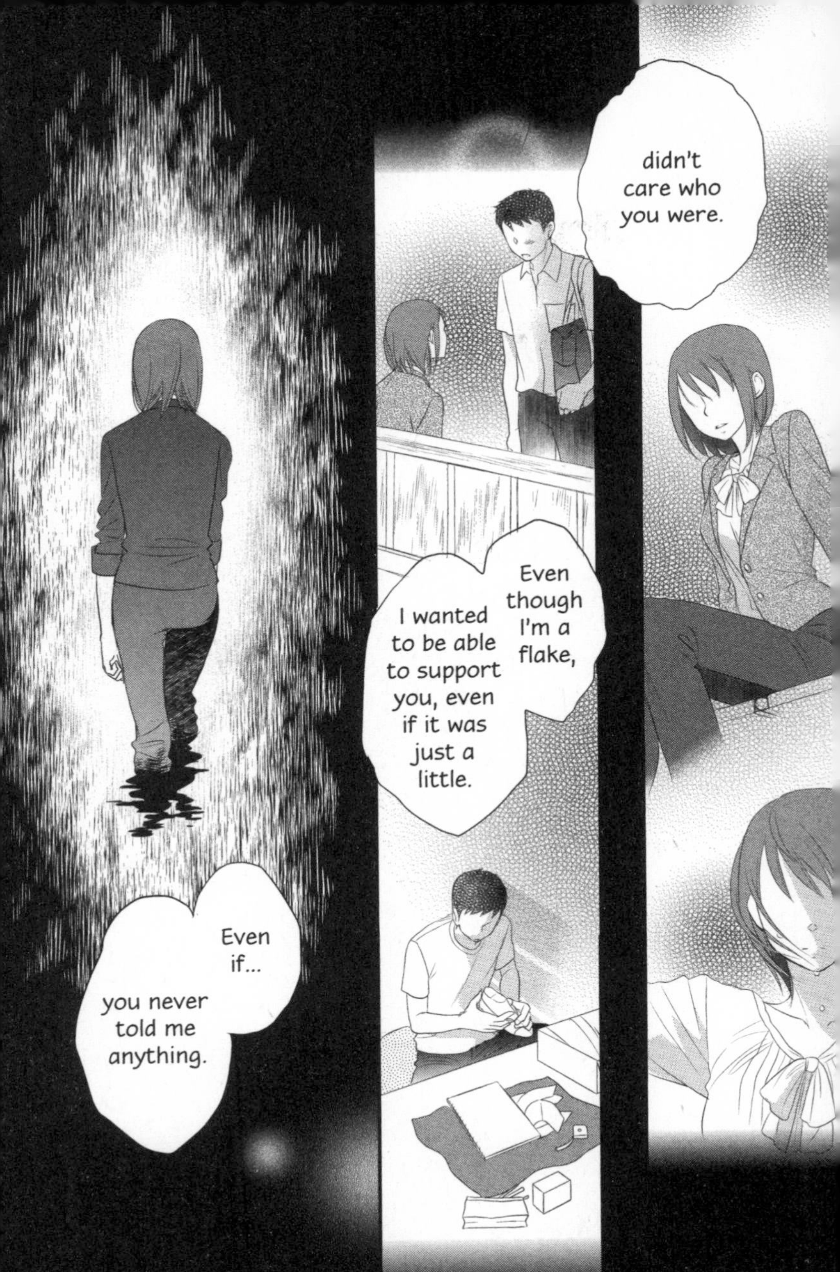
didn't care who you were.
Even though I'm a flake,
I wanted to be able to support you, even if it was just a little.
Even if...
you never told me anything.

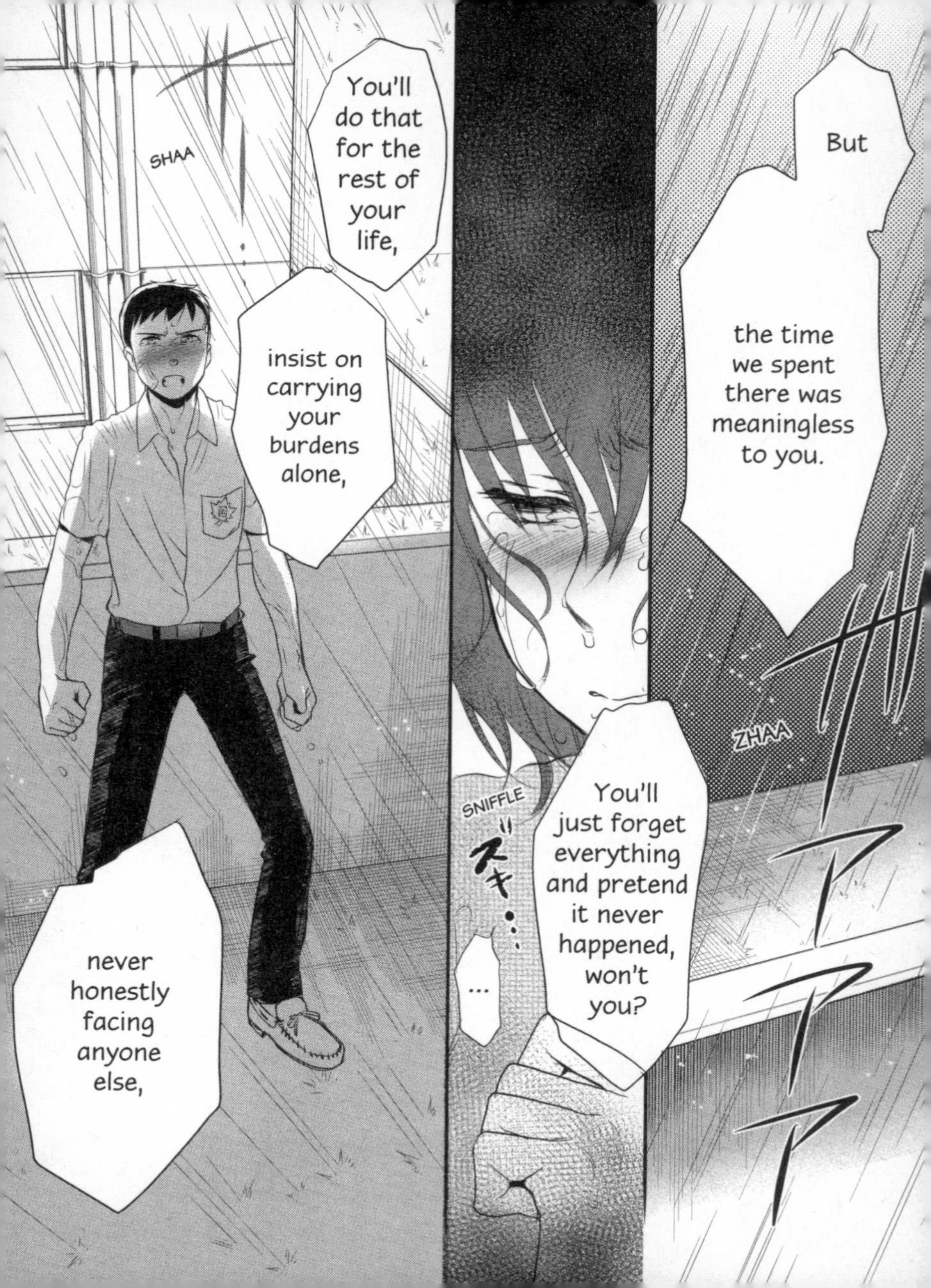
But
the time we spent there was meaningless to you.
ZHAA
You'll just forget everything and pretend it never happened, won't you?
SNIFFLE
...
You'll do that for the rest of your life,
SHAA
insist on carrying your burdens alone,
never honestly facing anyone else,

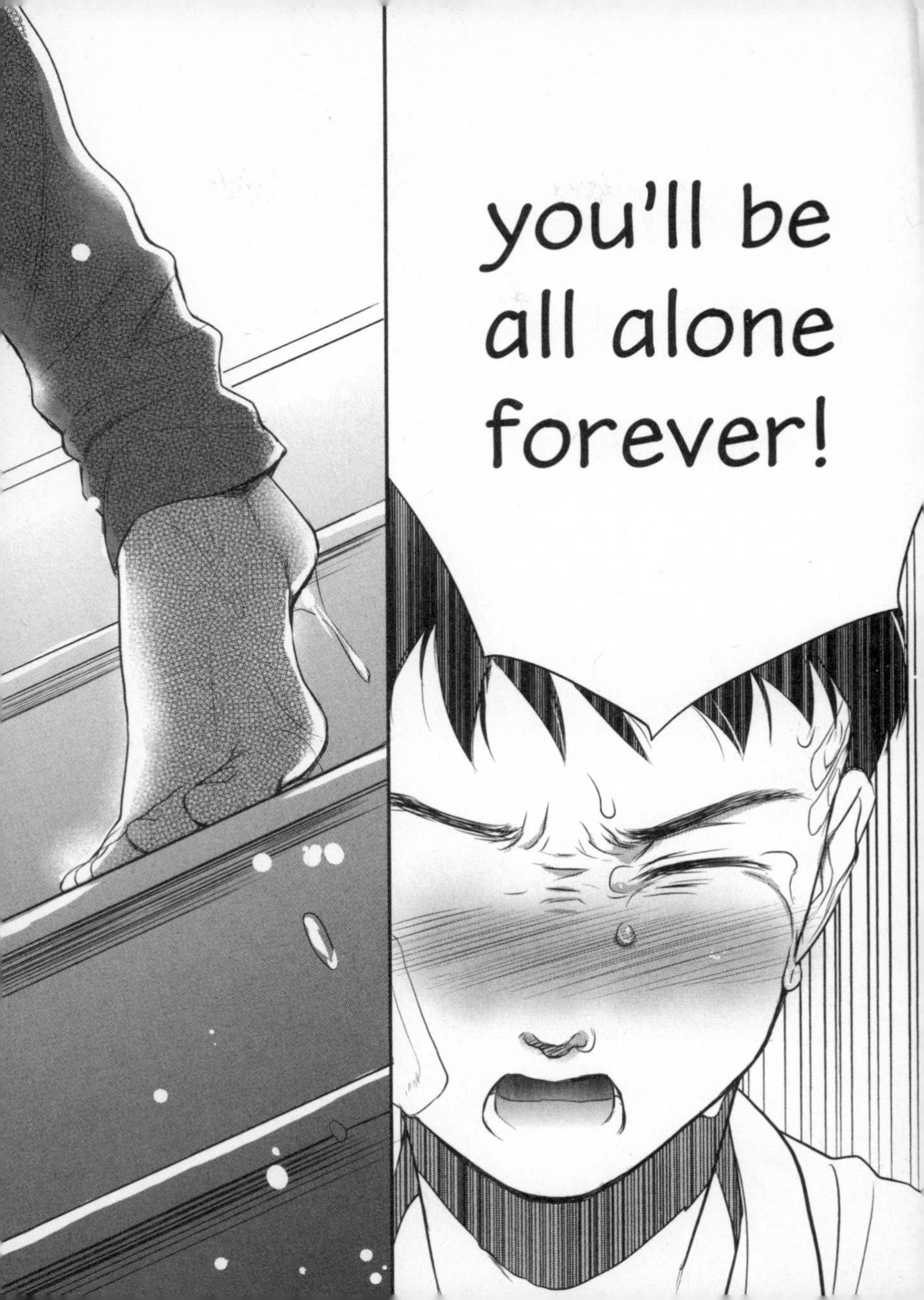
you'll be all alone forever!

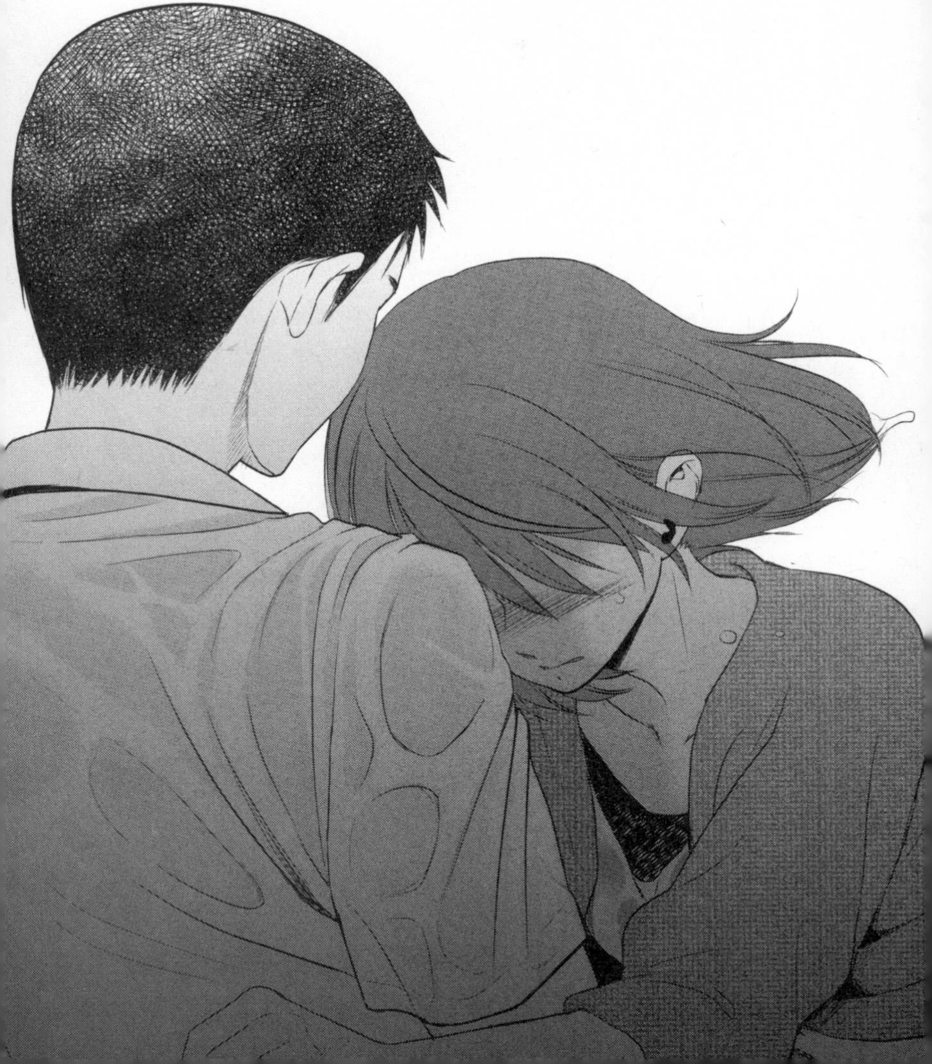

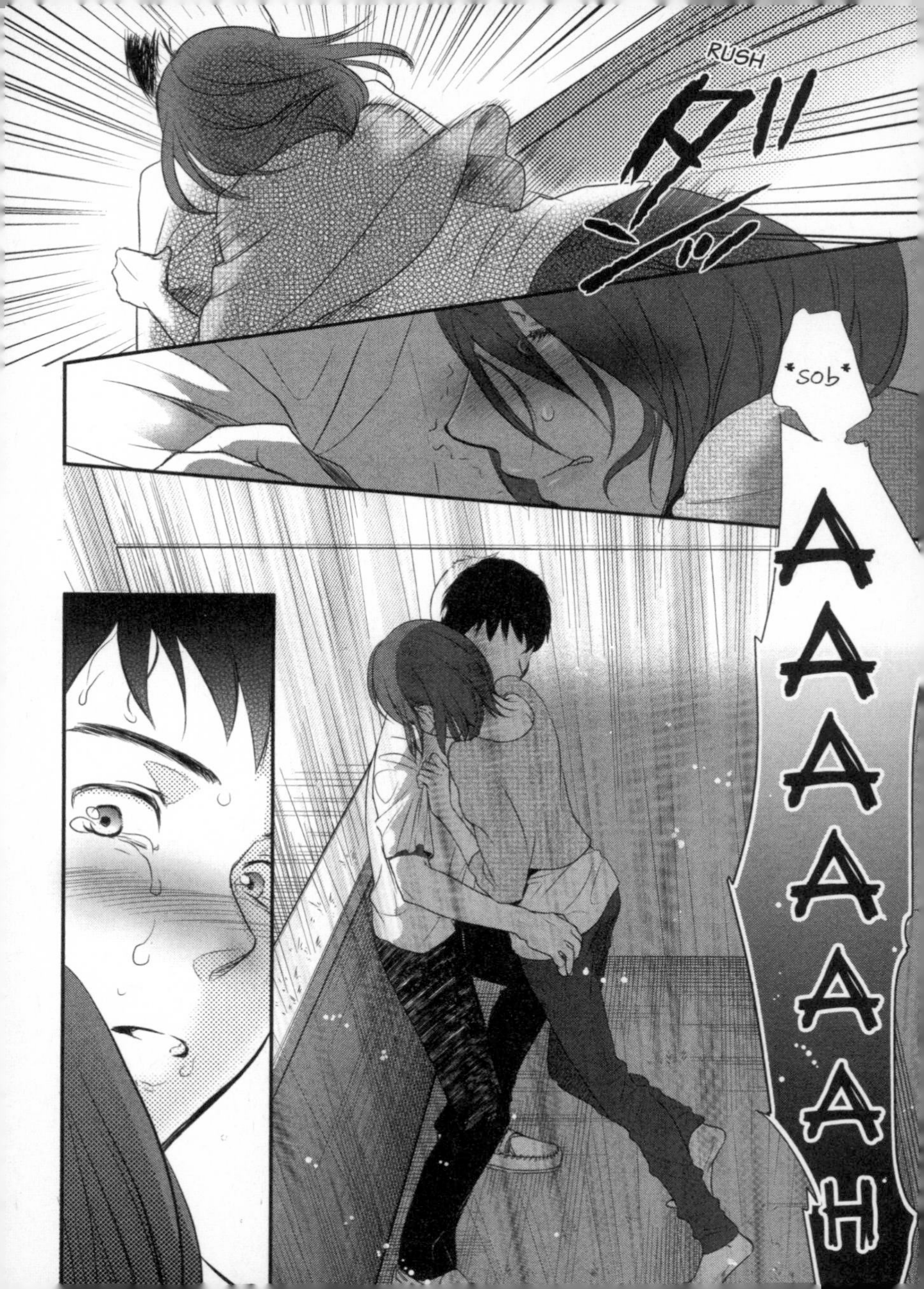
RUSH
ダッ
sob
AAAAAAAH

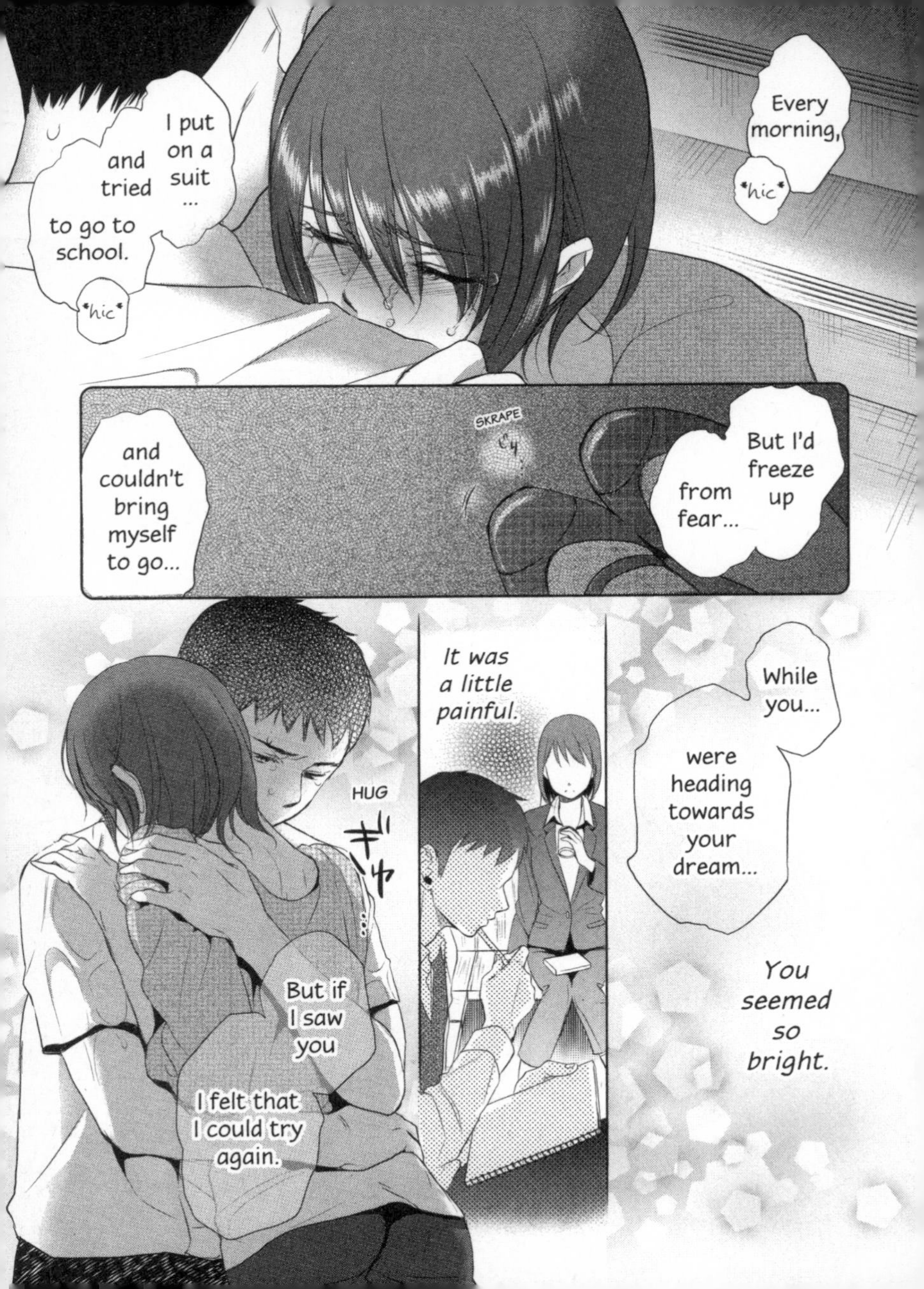
Every morning,
hic
I put on a suit...
and tried to go to school.
hic
But I'd freeze up from fear...
SKRAPE
and couldn't bring myself to go...
While you...
were heading towards your dream...
You seemed so bright.
It was a little painful.
HUG
ギュ…
But if I saw you
I felt that I could try again.

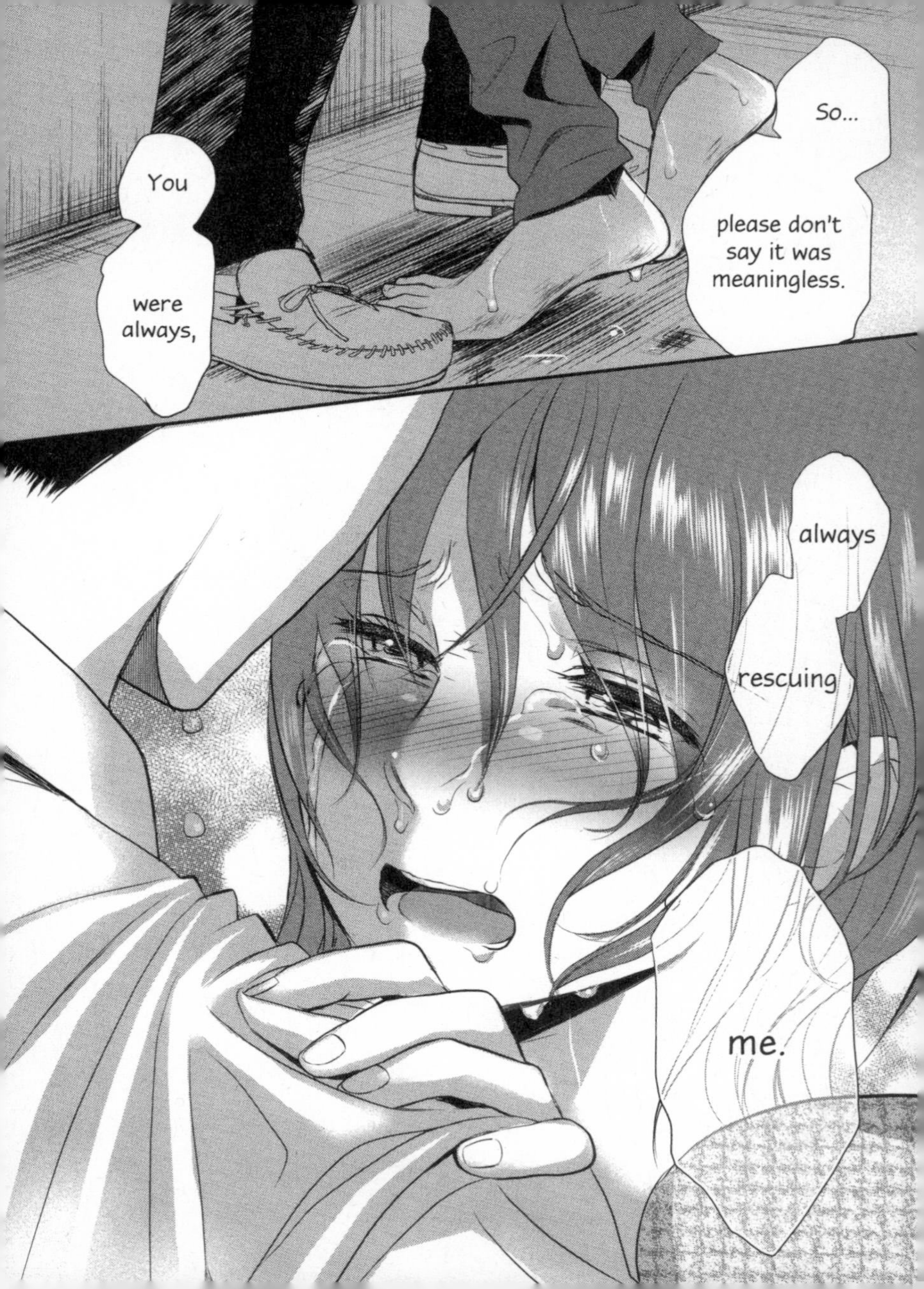
So...
please don't say it was meaningless.
You
were always,
always
rescuing
me.

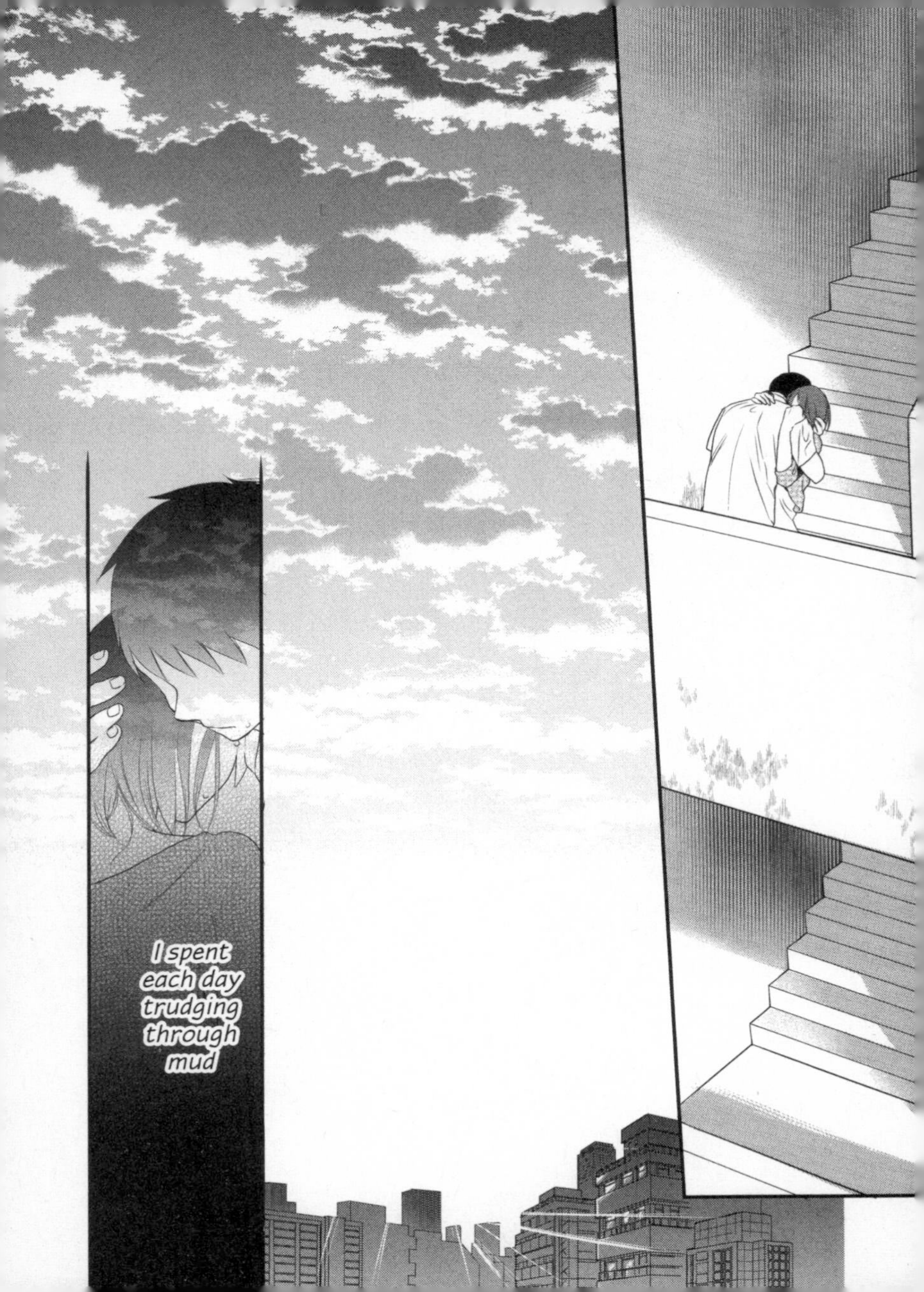
I spent each day trudging through mud

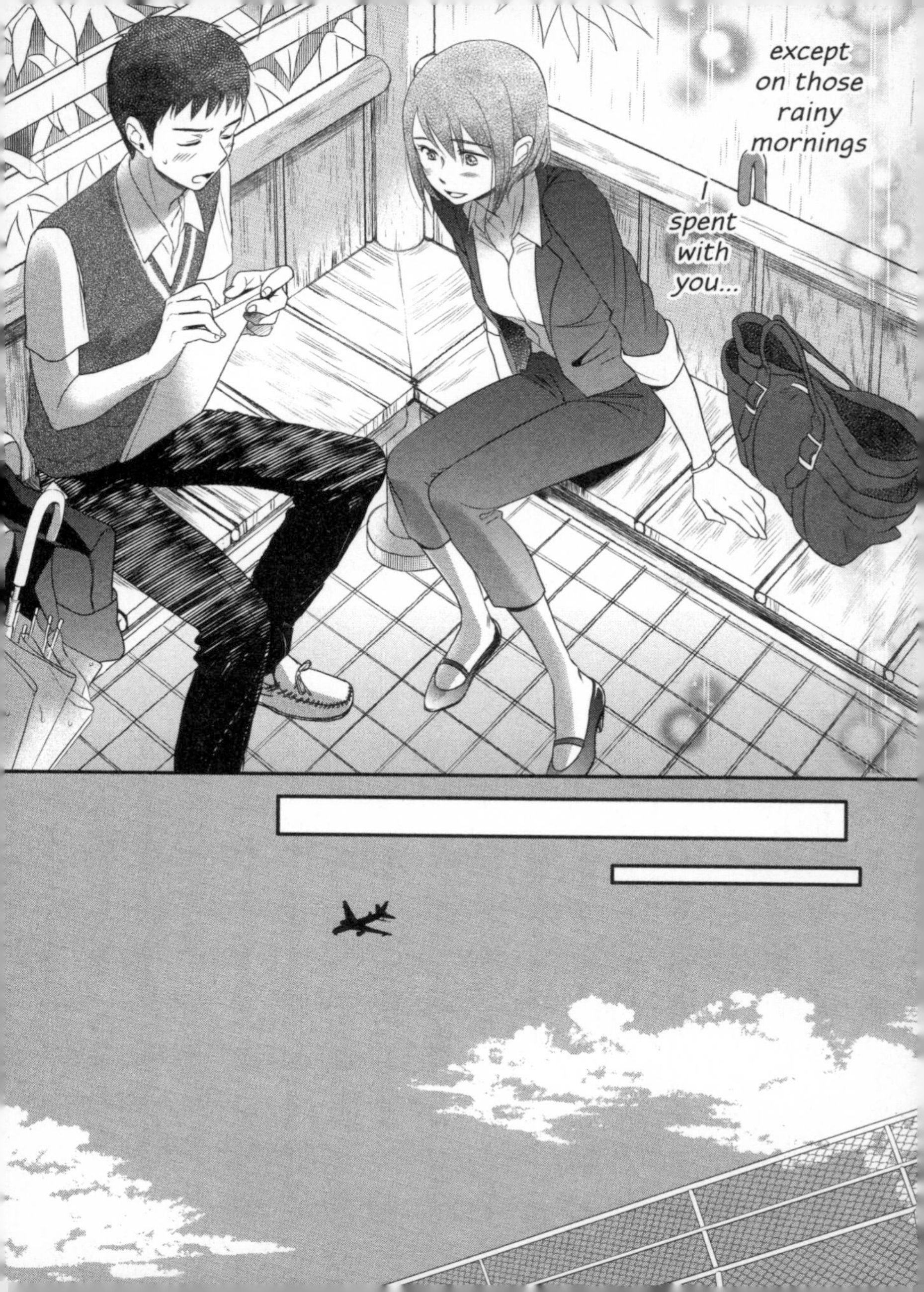
except on those rainy mornings
I spent with you...

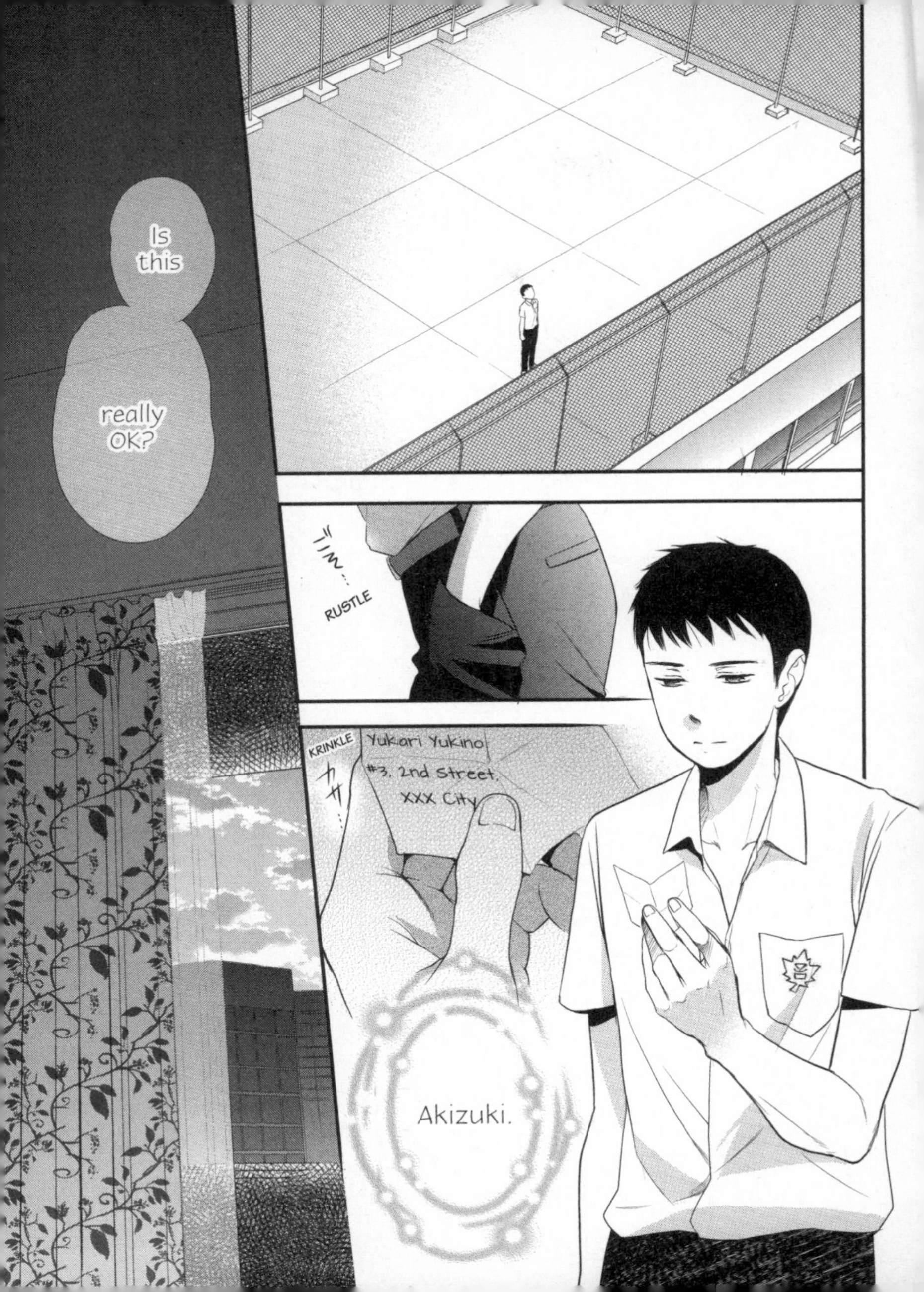

RUSTLE
KRINKLE
Yukari Yukino
#3, 2nd Street,
XXX City
Akizuki.
Is this really OK?

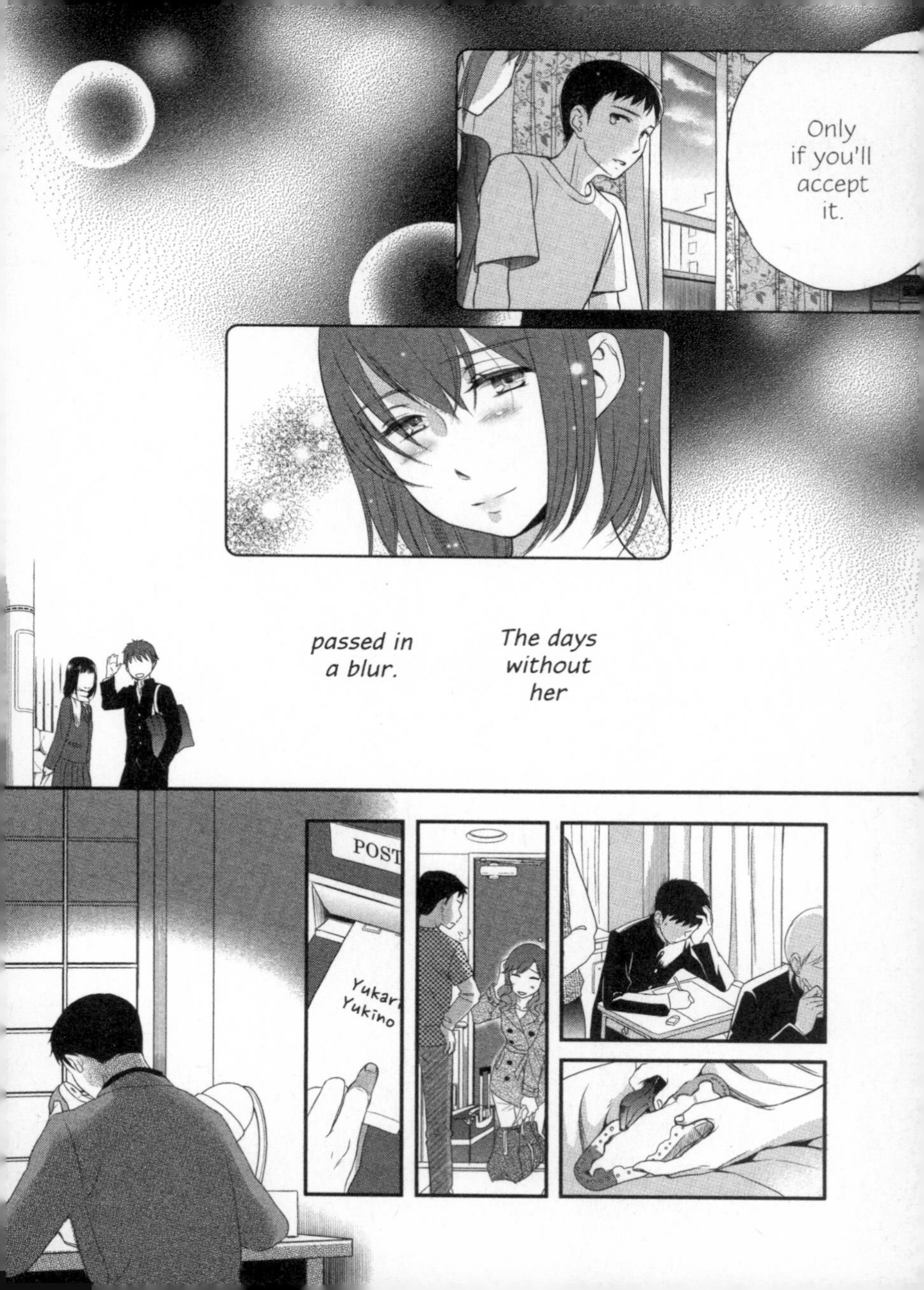
Only if you'll accept it.
The days without her
passed in a blur.
POST
Yukari Yukino

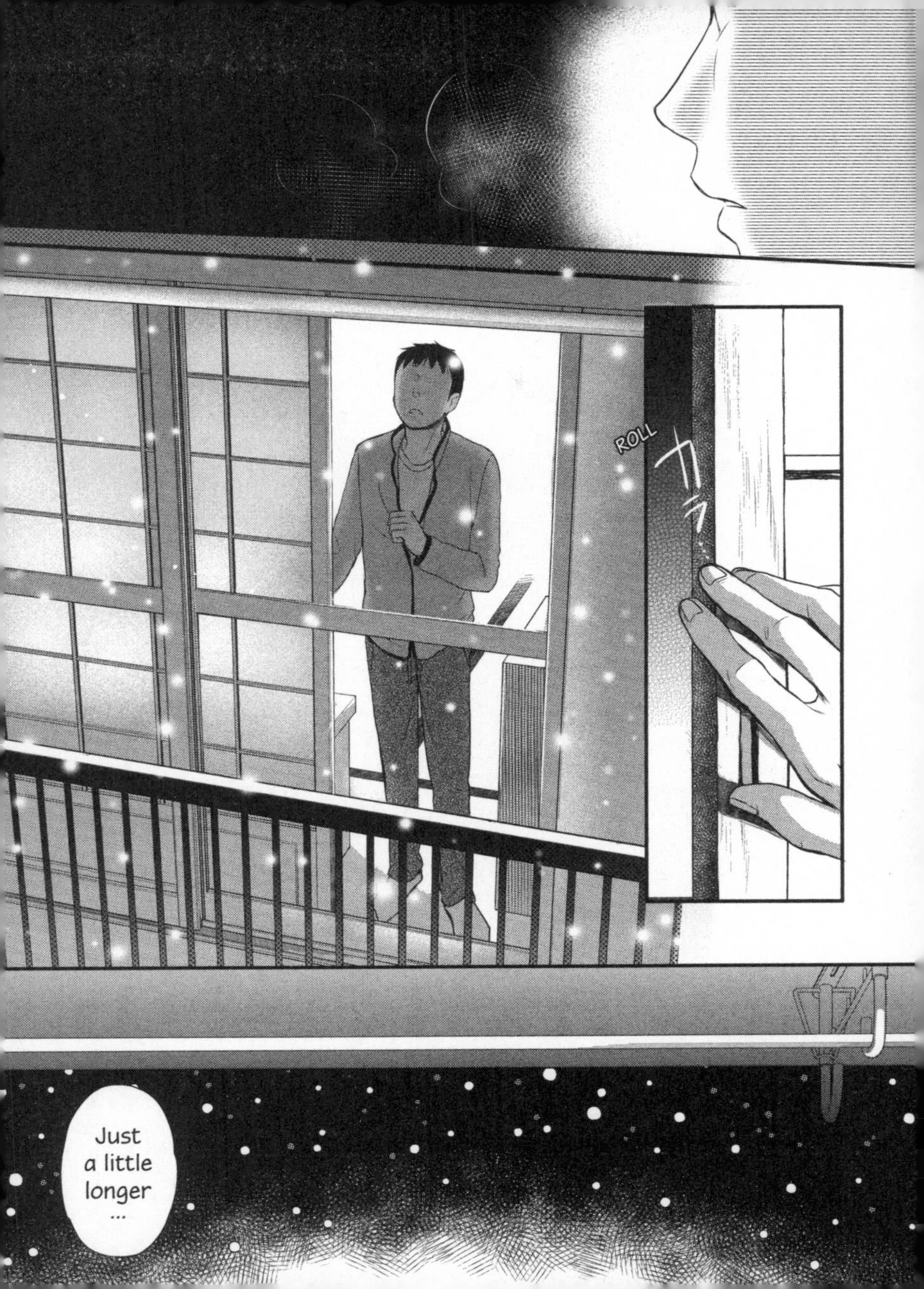
ROLL
Just a little longer ...

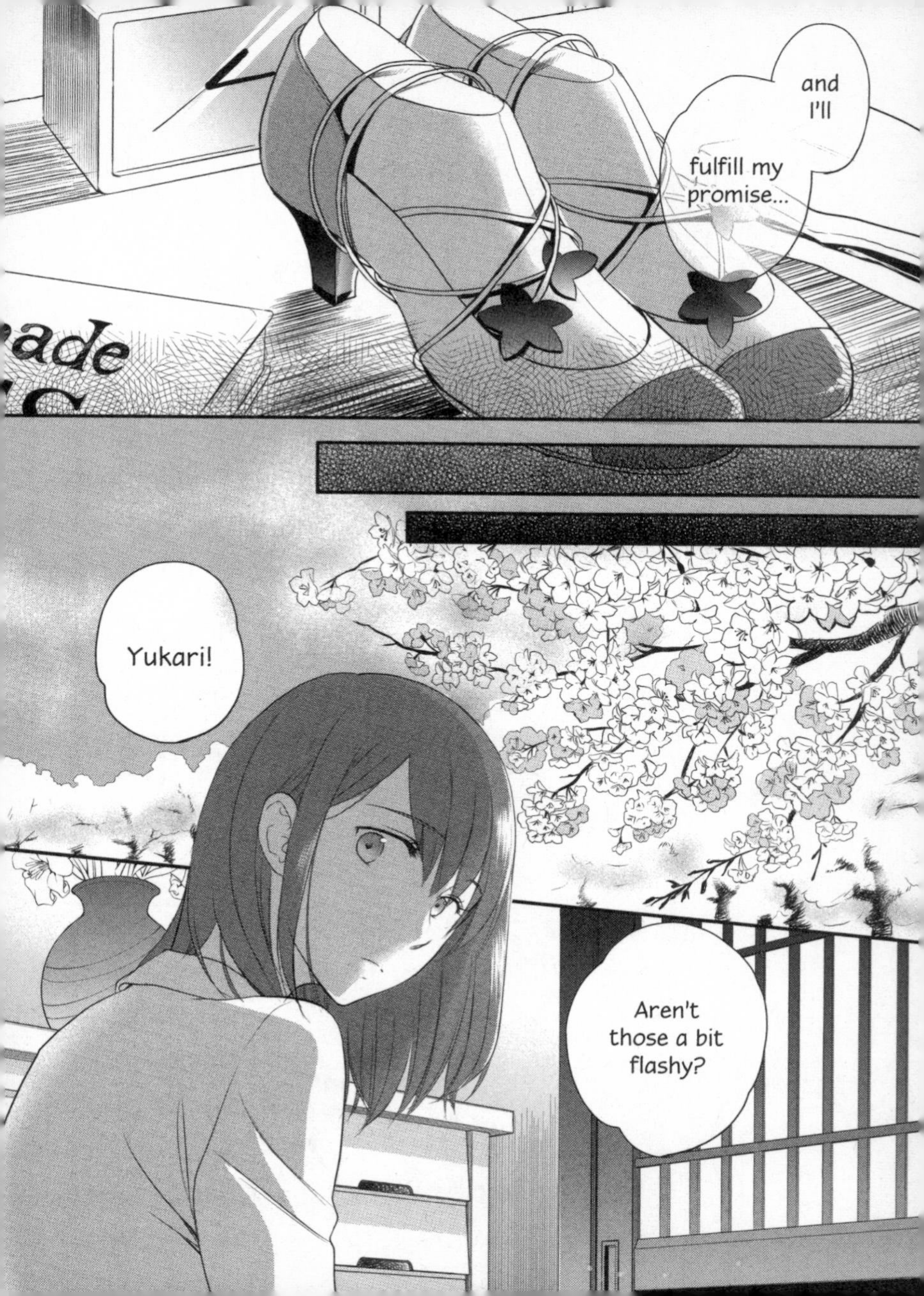
and I'll fulfill my promise...
Yukari!
Aren't those a bit flashy?

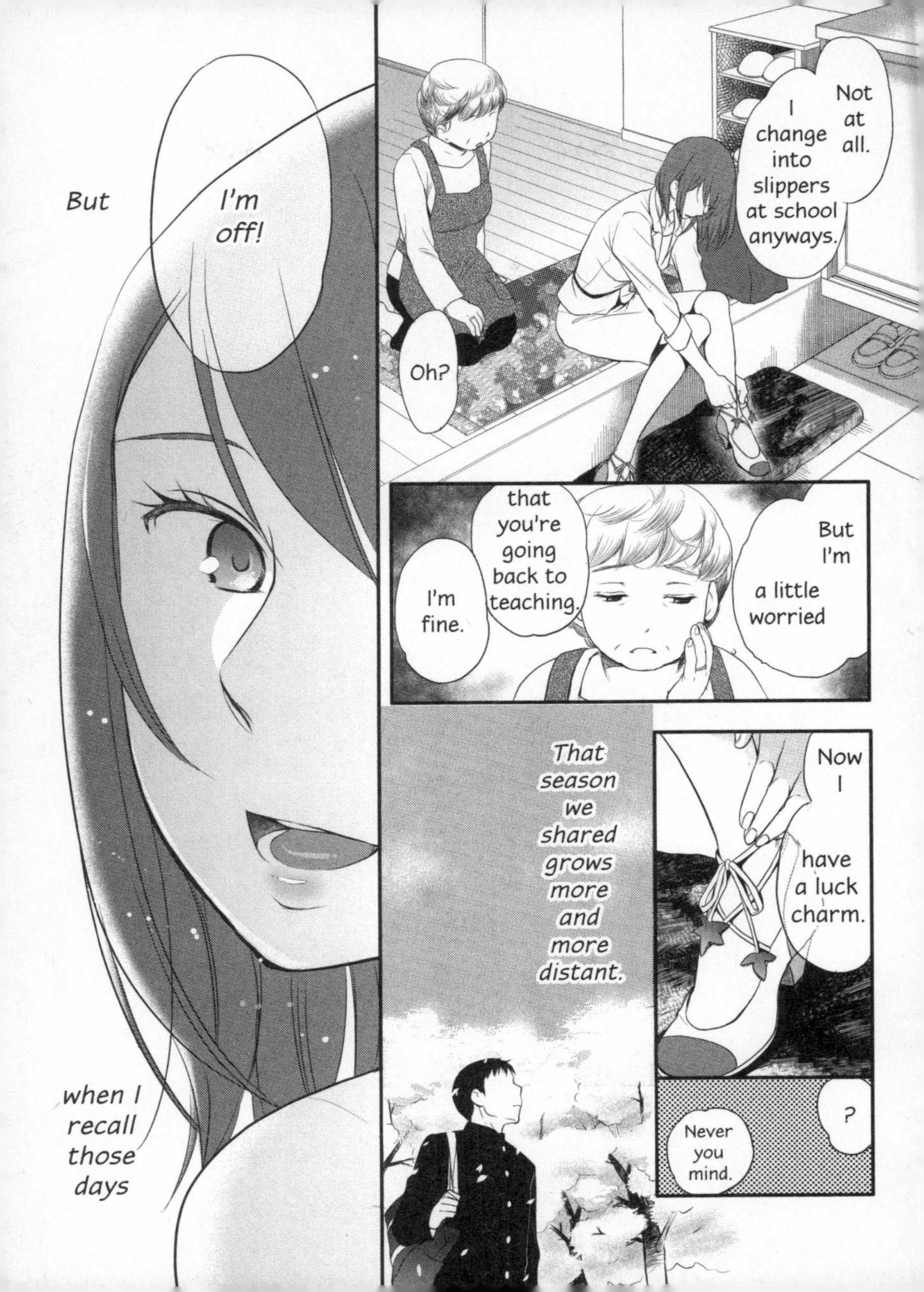
Not at all. I change into slippers at school anyways.
Oh?
But I'm a little worried
that you're going back to teaching.
I'm fine.
Now I have a luck charm.
?
Never you mind.
That season we shared grows more and more distant.
I'm off!
But
when I recall those days

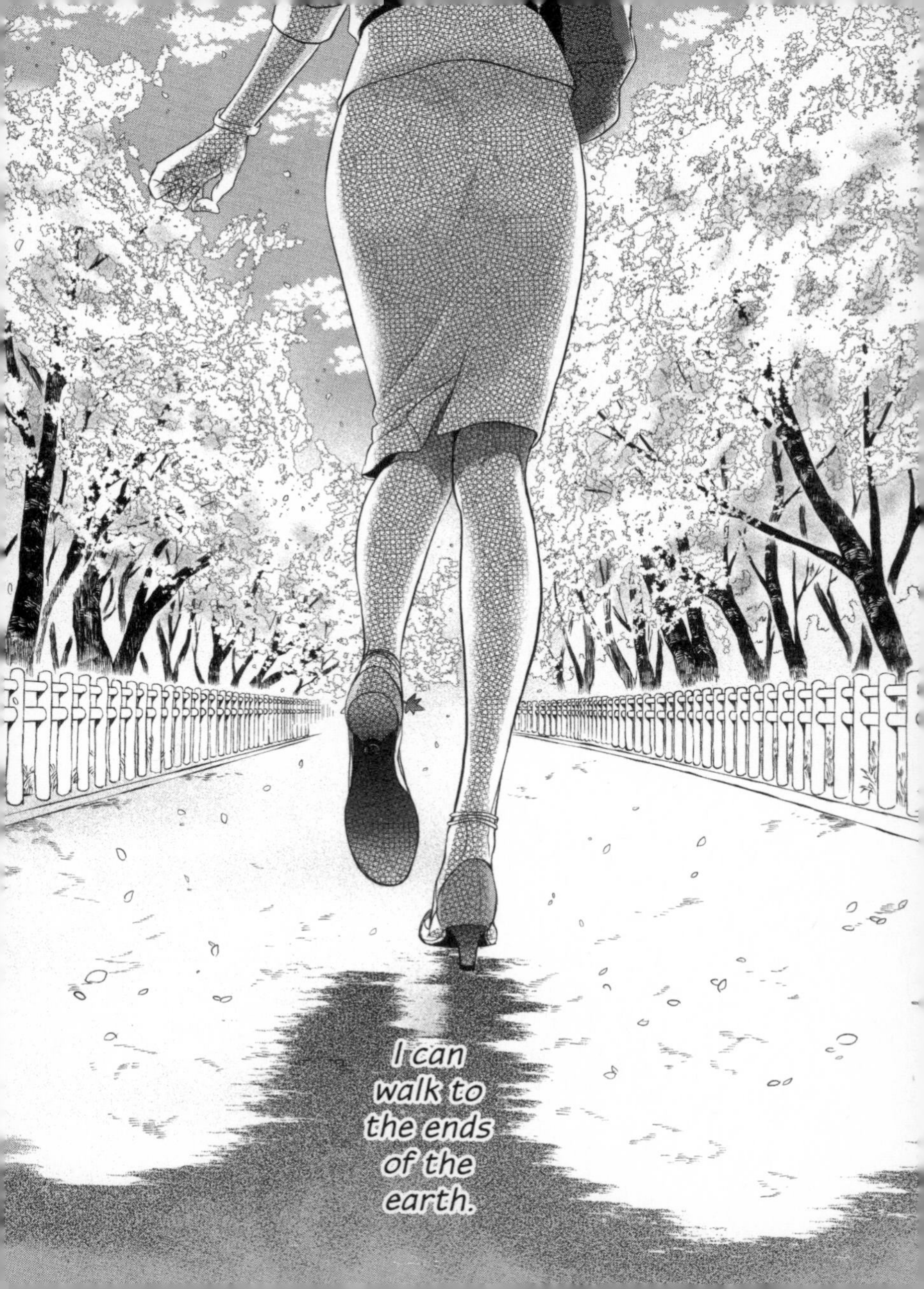
I can walk to the ends of the earth.

The Garden of Words

End

Teach me, Ms. Yukino

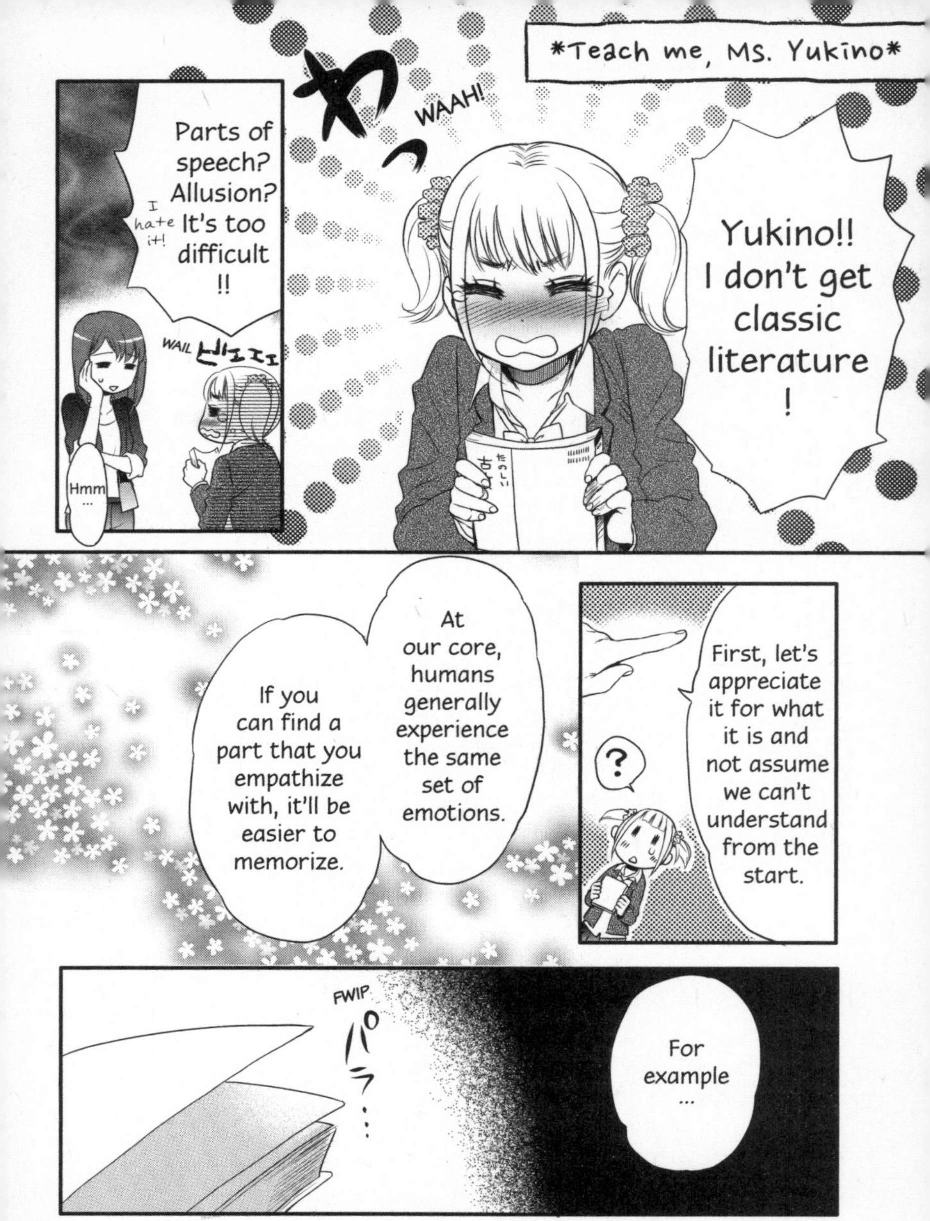
WAAH!
Yukino!! I don't get classic literature!
Parts of speech? Allusion? It's too difficult!!
I hate it!
WAIL
Hmm...
First, let's appreciate it for what it is and not assume we can't understand from the start.
?
At our core, humans generally experience the same set of emotions.
If you can find a part that you empathize with, it'll be easier to memorize.
For example...
FWIP

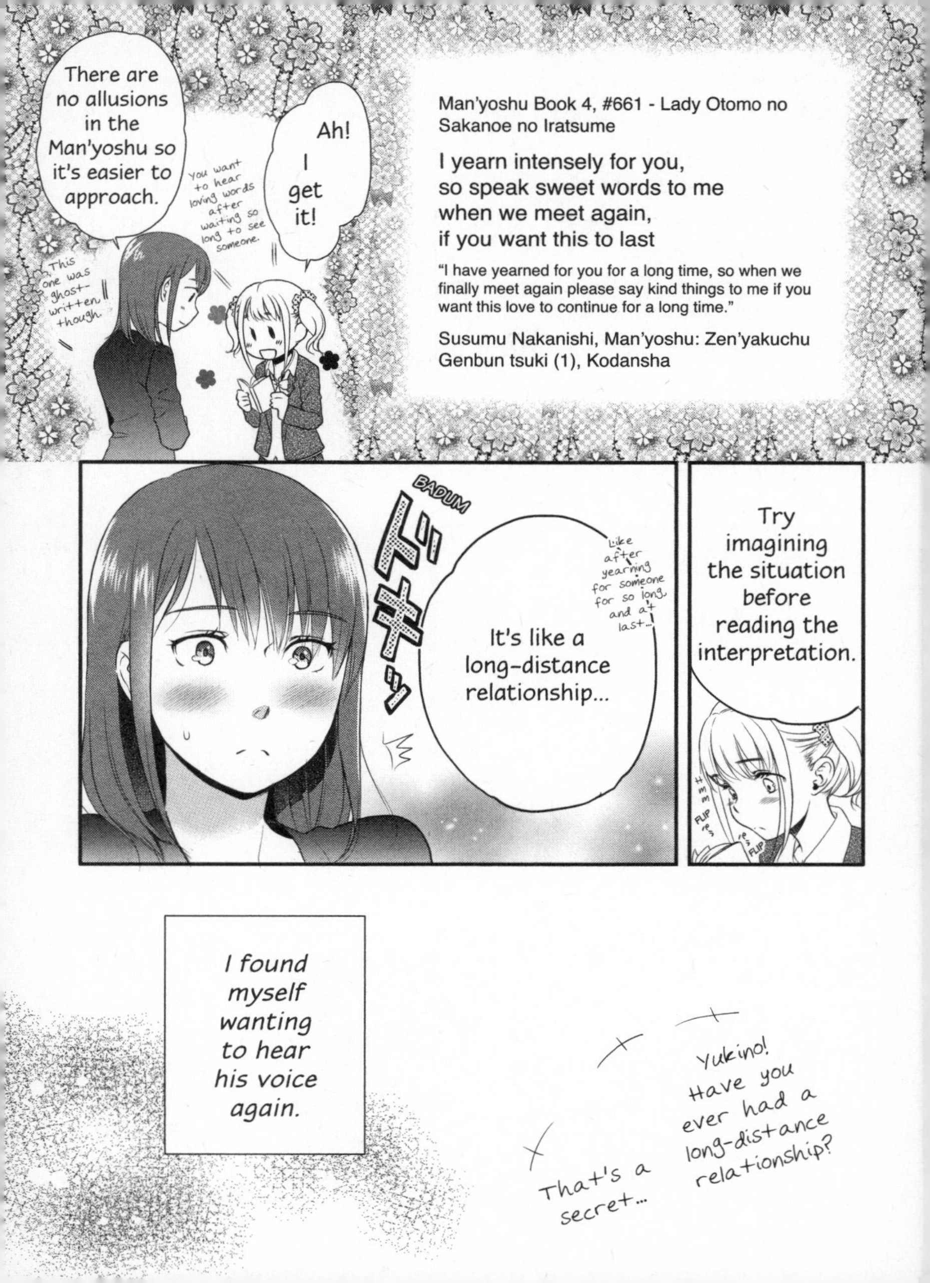
Man'yoshu Book 4, #661 - Lady Otomo no Sakanoe no Iratsume
I yearn intensely for you, so speak sweet words to me when we meet again, if you want this to last
"I have yearned for you for a long time, so when we finally meet again please say kind things to me if you want this love to continue for a long time."
Susumu Nakanishi, Man'yoshu: Zen'yakuchu Genbun tsuki (1), Kodansha
Ah! I get it!
You want to hear loving words after waiting so long to see someone.
There are no allusions in the Man'yoshu so it's easier to approach.
This one was ghost-written though.
Try imagining the situation before reading the interpretation.
Hmm
FLIP
FLIP
BADUM
Like after yearning for someone for so long, and at last...
It's like a long-distance relationship...
Yukino! Have you ever had a long-distance relationship?
That's a secret...
I found myself wanting to hear his voice again.

Afterword

Thank you for reading.
It was thanks to the help of various people that this omnibus edition was released.
I drew the artwork to the best of my abilities.

Special Thanks

Makoto Shinkai, Director
The team at CoMix Wave Films
Kawamura, managing editor

Art Assistants
Wataru Akizuki
Uta Isaki
Nozomi Isami
Hideyuki Ishikawa
Hano
Kagetora Hidari

My husband, my whole family, my friends the Dadamore Club— and to everyone who read this far.

Thank You Very Much.
Midori Motohashi

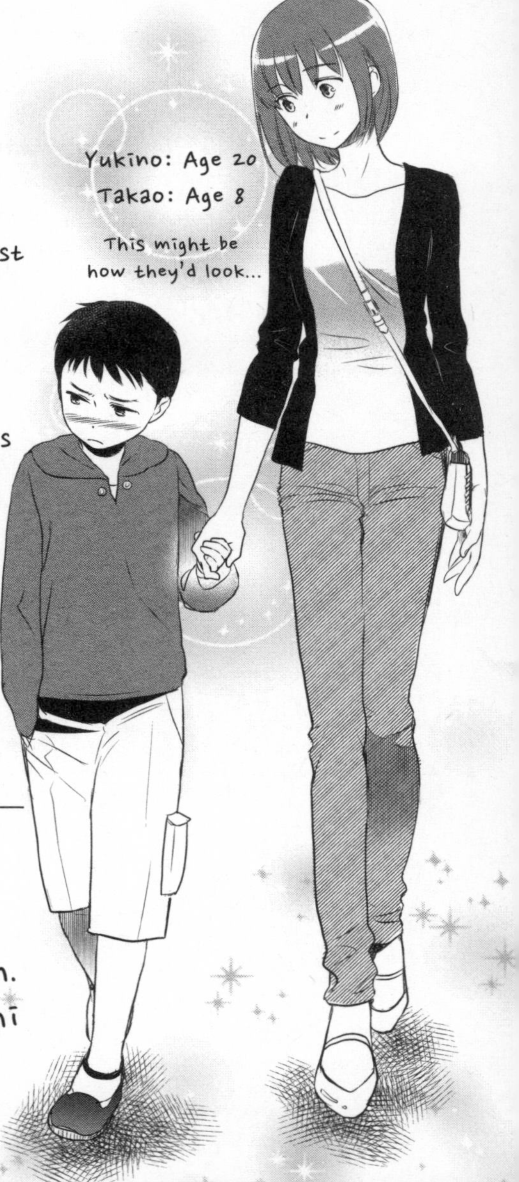

Yukino: Age 20
Takao: Age 8
This might be how they'd look...

The Garden of Words

A Vertical Comics Edition

Translation: Maya Rosewood
Production: Grace Lu
            Anthony Quintessenza

First published in Japan in 2013 by Kodansha, Ltd., Tokyo
Publication for this English edition arranged through Kodansha, Ltd., Tokyo
English language version produced by Vertical, Inc.

Translation provided by Vertical, Inc., 2014
Published by Vertical Comics, an imprint of Vertical, Inc., New York

Originally published in Japanese as *Kotonoha no Niwa* by Kodansha, Ltd., 2013
Kotonoha no Niwa first serialized in *Afternoon*, Kodansha, Ltd., 2013

This is a work of fiction.

ISBN: 978-1-939130-83-9

Manufactured in Canada

First Edition

Vertical, Inc.
451 Park Avenue South
7th Floor
New York, NY 10016
www.vertical-inc.com

WRONG WAY

Japanese books, including manga like this one,
are meant to be read from right to left.
So the front cover is actually the back cover, and vice versa.
To read this book, please flip it over
and start in the top right-hand corner.
Read the panels, and the bubbles in the panels,
from right to left,
then drop down to the next row and repeat.
It may make you dizzy at first,
but forcing your brain to do things backwards
makes you smarter in the long run.
We swear.